WALKING WITH THE

Women

OF THE

OLD
TESTAMENT

Heather Farrell deftly and generously bridges the gap between women of antiquity and the female reader of today. Her prose is warm and accessible and demonstrates a rich love for both the Old Testament women she brings out of obscurity and the modern-day audience that she writes for. As I read her words, I sense these women coming to life on the page before me, and I feel a renewed desire to allow their stories to mentor me, as Heather has.

—Amber Richardson, producer of *Splitting the Sky: Stories of Women Opening to God*

With a wealth of collected research and insights, Heather bring to life the powerful stories of women in the Old Testament. Through context and culture, she adds illuminating nuance to their personalities, experiences, and testimonies, Readers will discover anew the significant role of women in God's plan on both a personal and a collective level. The chapter of Eve changes the way I view my own covenants. I predict many readers will experience awe and finish the book determined to honor the compelling legacy of God's earliest daughters.

—Stephanie Dibb Sorenson, author of *Covenant Motherhood*, and adjunct professor at Brigham Young University

Walk with many of the women of the Old Testament through the pages of this book as Heather Farrell introduces you more intimately to each one. You'll gain personally relevant insights into their disparate, yet meaningful, lives. Accompany Mother Eve from the Paradisical Garden to the overwhelming challenges of the "lone and dreary world" we too must face. Eve's choices teach of women's glorious mission to be co-equal and crucial companions of men, enabling both to inherit Eternal Life. From Sarah's challenge to maintain belief in God's promises to Hagar's painfully gained testimony that "the God who sees her" truly does both see and hear her, we find application to our individual life journeys. The trials of Job's wife, the complicated rivalry of Leah and Rachel, Dinah's painful and unfair shame, Esther's wisdom and bravery, the pure faith of the "Little Maid," and so many more situations faced by women of ancient times all speak to us today and the similar joys and sorrows with which we deal. This is a book women can turn to often for inspiration to help meet those trials we now face, which mirror those of our sisters from long ago.

—Leslie Pearson Rees, author of *Ye Have Been Hid: Finding the Lost Tribes of Israel*

WALKING
WITH THE
Women
OF THE
OLD
TESTAMENT

· Written by ·
HEATHER FARRELL

· Art by ·
MANDY JANE WILLIAMS

CFI
AN IMPRINT OF CEDAR FORT, INC.
SPRINGVILLE, UTAH

ISBN 13: 978-1-4621-1944-8

Published by CFI, an imprint of Cedar Fort, Inc.
2373 W. 700 S., Springville, UT 84663
Distributed by Cedar Fort, Inc., www.cedarfort.com

LIBRARY OF CONGRESS CATALOGING-IN-PUBLICATION DATA

Farrell, Heather, author.
Walking with the women of the Old Testament / Heather Farrell and Mandy Williams.
pages cm
Includes bibliographical references and index.
Summary: Highlights many of the women in the Old Testament.
ISBN 978-1-4621-1944-8
LCCN: 2017032439

Cover design and interior layout/design by Shawnda T. Craig
Cover design © 2017 Cedar Fort, Inc.
Edited by Kaitlin Barwick

Printed in China
10 9 8 7 6 5 4 3 2 1

Printed on acid-free paper

For my mom.

—Heather

To those who lack courage:
May you feel warmth and strength from
our loving Heavenly Father and Mother.

—Mandy

I am grateful for the thousands of scholars, historians, priests and ordinary people who through the centuries have preserved the stories—especially those of the women—that we have in the Old Testament. It is remarkable, considering that many of these stories are thousands of years old, that we have them in our possession at all. It is truly a miracle, and one that we perhaps take for granted. So many have sacrificed so much so that we could have these stories, and I am incredibly grateful to have the stories—the ancient stories—that we have about women in the Old Testament.

I am also grateful for all the people who have helped me tackle the huge undertaking of writing about the Old Testament Women; for Annette Pimentel, who again, was the most helpful and honest editor a writer could have; for Mandy Williams, whose beautiful artwork really makes these women come alive, and for her countless hours with me on the phone and her patience and understanding; for Erika Decaster, whose list of female symbols in the scriptures was incredibly helpful and whose friendship and enthusiasm has been invaluable; for Linda Rees, for reading through my manuscript and giving me wonderful scholarly feedback, and for listening to me talk her ear off about the Old Testament; for Amber Richardson, Janeene Baagsgard, and Stephine Dibb Sorenson, who, on short notice, read through my manuscript and gave helpful feedback; and for the people at Cedar Fort who have put this amazing book together!

Mostly I am grateful for my husband, Jon, who for several months took time off from work (which he claims was not such a bad deal for him) so that I could finish this book on time. I am a lucky girl to have a such a good man in my life. I am also grateful for my children, who are my most enthusiastic fans.

And lastly, I am grateful for *you*, the person reading this book. All my work would simply be a waste without you. So, thank you.

—Heather

I would like to thank the many women who came together to help me with this project. I would like to thank my community, ward, and the kind people that live in the Grace Idaho Stake. Their support has been instrumental to me. I would like to thank each and every one of my beautiful models who were willing to prayerfully help convey these stories. I'm grateful for the unending support from my mom, Marlene Van Etten, and my mother-in-law Carol Williams. They encourage me in so many ways. I would especially like to thank my own beautiful little family, Kate, Case, Holland, Alice, and Brant, but most importantly, my husband, Bryan, for supporting me and upholding me throughout the chaos! In the words of Marjorie Pay Hinckley to her husband, "You have always given me wings to fly, and I have loved you for it."

I have learned many things as I have worked on this project. The time periods that took place during the Old Testament were melting pots of color and culture, where there were many variations of darker skin tones, but surprisingly, also lighter people with blond and red hair, like King David. I have felt overwhelmed many times as I worked on the daunting task of portraying biblical stories. I know that every detail cannot be historically accurate, but just like the artwork in the eras behind us, they catch our attention with a feeling, an essence, an emotion. I pray that some of those heart-felt feelings come through for you. I also hope that because of the illustrations you are able to remember the story, even if you see it in your own way. I have felt the Spirit helping me, and I know that we are deeply loved as daughters of God. More than anything, I wish for you to see God's hand in the lives of His servants, and in doing so, find your own identity as a precious daughter of God.

For a complete list of models, please go to mandyjanewilliamsart.com.

—*Mandy*

Table of Contents

Table of Contents ❖

Introduction

The first time I read the Old Testament, I was fourteen. I had just finished reading the Book of Mormon and the Doctrine and Covenants for the first time, and—beginning what has now been almost a twenty-year uninterrupted cycle—I had moved on to the Bible. For the next several years, I worked my way slowly through the Old Testament, painstakingly wading through its stories. I was determined to read every word. In order to make it through the long chapters of names, I kept a list of names that I liked and drew pictures of what I thought the people looked like. When I finally finished my read-through of the Old Testament, I thought, *I sure read a lot of pages, but I don't have a clue what any of it was about!*

Perhaps some of you can relate to that feeling. The Old Testament is a difficult book of scripture. It is long, repetitive, and hard to read. The customs and history are unusual and confusing to us, and the stories are often bizarre (Balaam's talking donkey, anyone?). On top of that, there is no clear spiritual theme or lesson to be learned from most of the stories. In the New Testament, the stories are given spiritual significance by the Gospel writers, and in the Book of Mormon, the prophet Mormon conveniently gives us explanations when stories and ideas are not clear. No such help is provided for us in the Old Testament. All we get are the stories, with very little commentary on what they mean.

While we might be tempted to view this as a weakness of the Old Testament, I think it is one of its great strengths. The meanings of the stories are left wide open. They are full of symbolism, and we are free to explore them like we would the treasures inside Ali Baba's cave, taking away from them our own individual pieces of wealth. All that is required is effort, patience, and the guidance of the Holy Ghost. The *Old Testament Student Manual* says, "One does not go to a great museum such as the Smithsonian Institution in Washington, D.C., and fully explore its treasure in an hour or two of leisurely browsing. Similarly, one does not exhaust the typology of the Old Testament in one quick reading of the book. A lifetime of exploration and pondering may be required before the Lord will fully reveal the extent to which He has filled the treasure house of symbolic teaching."[1]

I have now read the Old Testament a dozen times, and with every reading the stories have made more and more sense. In fact, the Spirit has chastised me, on more than one occasion, for spending more time in the Old Testament than I do any other book of scripture. I've wondered if I'm so interested in it because the Old Testament has, by far, the most women in it. (There are more than three hundred women!) Yet I know it is more than that. There is something powerful about these ancient stories. Something that resonates with the deepest and oldest part of my soul.

One of my favorite authors on women in the scriptures is Vanessa Ochs, whose words you find often in this book. I love an experience she shared in the introduction to her book *Sarah Laughed*. For most of her life, the women in the Bible held little interest for her. Then, at an extremely difficult time, she found herself drawn to the story of Tamar and Judah in the Old Testament. She wrote:

> It is there, at that crossroads, that I encountered Tamar and she entered my story. It's where she offered up an insight from her life as a gift to me that was right for that particular moment.

If you told me that something like this could happen to me, I'd have smirked. It's hard to explain what the experience is like, but it may be akin to what my Christian friends feel when they have a deep dilemma and they say, "I'll have to pray on it." The voice they hear isn't their own imagination but a wellspring of divine wisdom they believe comes from outside of them. I don't mean Tamar came flying through the trees or hung over my shoulder. I mean I had sat with her story long enough beforehand and had imagined it in great detail. I had engaged it so deeply that I could be present to what Tamar would teach me when the time was ripe for her to enter my life. And the time had come. . . .

Tamar came to me as a role model and spoke deeply to me when I stopped trying to enter into her story and started letting her into mine.[2]

The stories in the Old Testament are some of the oldest stories about women in the *world*. They are not just myths, not just bedtime stories. Though parts of them have been lost and pieces changed, the essence of what they teach us is real. When we discover what these women's stories mean, we begin to remember who we are. Learning our ancient roots can change everything about our future.

Here is my invitation to you: Invite these Old Testament women into your life. Sit with Hagar, travel with Rebekah, dance with Miriam, and weep with Jephthah's daughter. Stop worrying so much about the details and the history of the Old Testament, and instead let these women teach you. Take the time to study them and let them speak to you. They will tell you about their mistakes, their triumphs, their heartaches, their covenants, their wisdom, and their courage. If you let them, they will guide you into becoming the person God knows you can become. They are your ancient sisters.

Learning to See the Divine Feminine

Writing about the women in the Old Testament was tough. They are a diverse group of women from different places, cultures, and religions; their stories span nearly four thousand years of history. As I wrote about them, I struggled to find something that connected these women—a common thread that tied their stories together. They were just all so different!

Then one evening I was reading through the book *A Quiet Heart* by Patricia Holland. This quote struck me like a thunderbolt:

> I have heard it said by some that the reason women in the Church struggle somewhat to know themselves is that they don't have a divine female role model. . . .
>
> I have never questioned why our mother in heaven seems veiled to us, for I believe the Lord has his reasons for revealing as little as he has on that subject. . . . I believe we know more about our eternal nature than we think we do, and it is our sacred obligation to identify it and to teach it to our young sisters and daughters. In so doing, we can strengthen their faith and help them through the counterfeit confusions of these difficult latter days. . . .

The Lord has not placed us in this lone and dreary world without a blueprint for living. In Doctrine and Covenants 52:14 we read, "And again, I will give unto you a pattern in *all things, that ye may not be deceived*" (emphasis added). He certainly includes us as women in that promise. He has given us patterns in the Bible, the Book of Mormon, the Doctrine and Covenants, the Pearl of Great Price; and he has given us patterns in the temple ceremony.

> . . . We need to search, and we need always to look for deeper meaning. We should look for parallels and symbols. We should look for themes and motifs just as we would in a Bach or a Mozart composition, and we should look for patterns—repeated patterns—in the gospel.[1]

I realized that the one thing that connected all these women's stories together—their unifying thread—was they were all daughters of our Heavenly Mother. That each of them, in all their incredible diversity, were patterned after the great archetype of womanhood. The "original" woman. The woman from whom all of us, no matter when or where we have lived, are patterned.

More than that, though, I realized the stories of the women in the Old Testament are filled with female symbolism and patterns that teach us about who our Divine Mother is and what She is like. Like Sister Holland said, it is okay—and even our responsibility—to seek out these divine patterns and share them with others.

• Symbols and Archetypes •

The Old Testament is full of imagery that is female in nature. Many of these are obviously female: breasts, childbirth, mothers, the earth. Yet other things that are referred to as female are not as obvious: cities, trees, water, and wisdom. Whenever I come across anything that is described or personified as female, I mark it in my scriptures. Many of them are archetypes—a pattern of an original truth—which help us identify essential eternal ideas and themes. Here is a list of some of the female symbols I have discovered in my reading.[2]

• Symbols of Divine Womanhood in Scripture[3] •

Bodily Symbols	womb, breasts and nursing, navel, menstruation, virginity, birth (blood and water)
Symbols from Nature	evergreen trees (representing eternal life): palms, cypress, sycamore, pine fruit-bearing trees (representing life on earth): olive, oak, tamarisk, date, palm, almond, laurel, apple, etc. wood and oil from trees (especially ones mentioned above) water: the sea, pure waters, wells of water myrrh, flowers, the moon, circles, precious stones (especially ruby, crystal, and jasper)
Symbolic Animals	bees/beehive, doves, snakes mother animals: she bears, hens, cows, lionesses donkeys
Symbolic Foods	eggs, bread, milk, honey, fruit, fish
Symbolic Actions	veiling/coverings, sacred clothing, weaving/spinning dancing (especially circle dances), sexual love
Ideas/Things Personified as Female	wisdom (see especially Proverbs 1–9) charity, peace cities (especially Zion, Jerusalem, Babylon [corrupted]) ships, the earth, the Church

Roles (*Archetypes*)	mother, queen, sister, daughter, bride, harlot/whore (corrupted)
Tabernacle/ Temple Symbols	mercy seat (made of special wood), menorah (symbolic of a tree) Holy of Holies/sanctuary, ark of the covenant
Names	Elohim (plural form of "God," see page 9), El Shaddai[4] Asherah (corrupted), queen of heaven (corrupted), Great Mother (corrupted)

I find it fascinating that many of these more "female" symbols can also be applied to Jesus Christ. For example, bread and water are feminine symbols, having to do with creating and sustaining life, but Jesus called Himself the "living water" (John 4:10) and the "bread of life" (John 6:35), commanding us to eat of His body and blood that we might be "born again." He even compared Himself to a mother hen when He lamented to the Jews, "How often would I have gathered thy children together, as a hen doth gather her brood under her wings, and ye would not!" (Luke 13:34).

Writer Kathleen Shirts wrote how Christ's ability not just to understand and show compassion toward women but also to embody feminine qualities helps us to better understand our Divine Mother. She wrote:

Our concept of the divine Woman is itself ambiguous. . . .

We are tempted to fill the vacuum with images of a heavenly woman drawn from the earthly condition of women. We envision, perhaps, a nurturing figure devoted to innumerable spirit children but withdrawn from the wider realm of cosmic government. . . .

There have been attempts to fill out our idea of Heavenly Mother by borrowing from descriptions of goddesses in ancient cultures. . . . As appealing as we might find the concept of dynamic female deities, however, from the perspective of overall morality, the pagan goddesses are ultimately no better role models than are the pagan gods.

So how do we handle the absence of information about our Heavenly Mother, the divine being who could embody the spiritual identity of women? Perhaps it is easier to understand this absence when we realize that we lack a detailed description of our Heavenly Father as well. The Savior spoke of the Father at every turn, but when Philip asked to be shown the Father, Jesus replied that the Father was made manifest through the Son. "Have I been so long time with you, and yet hast thou not known me, Philip? he that hath seen me hath seen the Father; and how sayest thou then, Shew us the Father?" (John 14:9.)

When we ask about the Mother, might not the Lord give us a similar reply? "He that hath seen me hath seen the Mother." We think of the Godhead as united in purpose and similar in character. If we as Mormons are going to assert the existence of a female Deity, shouldn't we assume that her Son mirrors her perfection as well as that of the Father?"[5]

I believe as we better come to know and understand Christ, we simultaneously draw closer to both our Heavenly Father and our Heavenly Mother. They are a divine family, beautifully unified, and when we meet their Son, we also meet them.

• Our Divine Nature •

Once in a class at BYU, I asked a female professor why we didn't know very much about our Mother in Heaven. Her answer surprised and confused me: "When you come to embrace and understand your female body, you will know who She is." I have pondered on those words for a long time and have discovered that what she said is true.

Our female bodies are created after the image of our Mother in Heaven, and they are divine in their construct and purpose. If

Parley P. Pratt will forgive me, I will take a little liberty with something he said and "liken" it to women:

> An intelligent being, in the image of [Heavenly Mother], possesses every organ, attribute, sense, sympathy, affection, that is possessed by [Heavenly Mother herself].

> But these are possessed by [woman], in [her] rudimental state, in a subordinate sense of the word. Or, in other words, these attributes are in embryo, and are to be gradually developed. They resemble a bud, a germ, which gradually develops into bloom, and then, by progress, produces the mature fruit after its own kind.[6]

How incredible it is to think that our Heavenly Mother looks like us, that She possesses a uterus, ovaries, breasts, and everything else that makes us female. We are literally made in Her image. She is our Mother, and we are her daughters. That is an incredible relationship. Just as we inherit attributes and potential from our earthy mothers, we have also inherited the attributes of our Heavenly Mother. We have the potential to become like Her. Pratt explained that our divine nature is developed through the gift of the Holy Ghost, which "quickens all the intellectual faculties, increases, enlarges, expands, and purifies all the natural passions and affections; and adapts them, by the gift of wisdom, to their lawful use. It inspires, developes, cultivates and matures all the fine toned sympathies, joys, tastes, kindred feelings and affections of our nature. It inspires virtue, kindness, goodness, tenderness, gentleness and charity."[7]

As we come to know who we are, and as we come to love and accept our female bodies, we will find our Mother. She will speak to our hearts and guide our paths. Though we may at times feel, as poet Carol Lynn Pearson so beautifully put it, like daughters in a "motherless house,"[8] I hope that we will remember She is not forbidden, She is not hidden, and She has not abandoned us. She is in plain sight; we just need to know what we are looking for.

I have wondered if our relationship with our Heavenly Mother isn't all that different from the one I have with my babies. When they are infants, my babies were so dependent upon me for everything—milk, warmth, clothing, comfort—that for a long time it felt like we were extensions of each other. It was hard to distinguish where I ended and they began. As they grew, they began to "awaken" and discover who they were. They realized that they were an individual who could influence the world, make things change, and move independently. It was only then that I felt like they finally "saw" me—not as a warm, comforting feeling, but as a distinct person.

Perhaps in our relationship with Deity we are still all infants, not yet spiritually awake enough to distinguish where we end and She begins. "I have fed you with milk, and not with meat," Paul tells us, "for hitherto ye were not able to bear it, neither yet now are ye able" (1 Corinthians 3:2). Maybe as we progress in the gospel, as we better come to understand Her Son and shake off the dust and sin of this world, we will begin to see Her. Not just as a nice, warm feeling, but as a divine individual. I'd like to think I can hear our Heavenly Mother's voice in the scripture in Moses 6:63: "All things have their likeness, and all things are created and made to bear record of me, both things which are temporal, and things which are spiritual; things which are in the heavens above, and things which are on the earth, and things which are in the earth, and things which are under the earth, both above and beneath: all things bear record of me."

When we realize that everything—on the earth, in our bodies, and even within our relationships—are symbols that bear testimony of our Divine Father *and* our Divine Mother, the scriptures come alive in an incredibly feminine way. My hope is that as you study the Old Testament women, you will find archetypes and symbols that will open your eyes to Her and to our divine nature as women. The Old Testament, if you will take the time to search it and ponder on it, bears testimony of the greatest of *all* women in the scriptures—and finding Her is beautiful.

Eve

It is remarkable to think that the entire human family, with its diversity of languages, skin colors, and cultures, can be traced back to one unifying source—our mother Eve. Each of us, no matter where we live, what we look like, or what we believe, owe our existence on this earth to one woman, whose difficult choice opened the way into mortality. We are the children of Eve, and like any mother, her influence has shaped us—men and women—more than we realize. Author Carolyn Custis James wrote these insightful words:

> God cast the mold for all women when he created Eve. She embodies the secrets of his original blueprint for us. So we rightly turn to her to understand who we are [as women] and to discover God's purposes for us. We see and evaluate ourselves . . . through the definition we draw from her. Which makes Eve both powerful and dangerous. Mistakes with regard to our understanding of her are costly for everyone. Like the missile that launches only the slightest fraction off course, we will miss our ultimate target by light-years if we misinterpret Eve. Conversely, a better understanding of Eve as God created her promises much-needed direction and ensure we have a true target in our sights.[1]

When we understand Eve, we understand ourselves. Her journey is our journey; her choices are our choices. When we come to earth through the body of one of Eve's daughters, we walk the same path that she and Adam did. We often depict this path on the board in Sunday School with circles and arrows, and many of us could draw the plan of salvation with our eyes closed. Eve trailblazed this path, and we each are following in her footsteps.

• Eve's First Step: Premortal Life •

And God saw these souls that they were good, and he stood in the midst of them, and he said: These I will make my rulers; for he stood among those that were spirits, and he saw that they were good. . . .

And there stood one among them that was like unto God, and he said unto those who were with him: We will go down, for there is space there, and we will take of these materials, and we will make an earth whereon these may dwell;

And we will prove them herewith, to see if they will do all things whatsoever the Lord their God shall command them.

Abraham 3:23–25

Elder Bruce R. McConkie taught, "There is no language that can do credit to our glorious mother, Eve. . . . Eve—a daughter of God, one of the spirit offspring of the Almighty Elohim—was among the noble and great in the [premortal] existence. She ranked in spiritual stature, in faith and devotion, in conformity to eternal law with Michael."[2]

We know that Adam, whose premortal name was Michael, was "the spirit next in intelligence, power, dominion and righteousness to the great Jehovah himself."[3] It was he who chiefly assisted Jehovah in overseeing the creation of the earth. Elder McConkie also taught that Eve, along with "a host of mighty men and equally glorious women, comprised that group of 'the noble and great ones,' to whom the Lord Jesus said: 'We will go down, for there is space

there, and *we* will take of these materials, and *we* will make an earth whereon these may dwell' (Abraham 3:22–24; italics added)."[4]

It is inspiring to think about Eve and other valiant women assisting with the creation of the earth. While we do not know Eve's premortal name, we can surmise that she was one of the most powerful, intelligent, and righteous of all of God's spirit daughters. She was foreordained in the premortal world for her role as "the mother of all living" (Genesis 3:20). What a great honor to be the first mother, the gateway through which the entirety of God's children would come to earth. It was through her that God's entire plan—His plan of happiness—would begin.

• Eve's Second Step: Creation •

And God said, Let us make man in our image, after our likeness: and let them have dominion over the fish of the sea, and over the fowl of the air, and over the cattle, and over all the earth, and over every creeping thing that creepeth upon the earth.

So God created man in his own image, in the image of God created he him; male and female created he them.

Genesis 1:26–27

Scripture gives two accounts of Eve's creation. The first is on the sixth day of creation when God made man in "his own image . . . male and female created he them" (Genesis 1:27). The name of God used here is the Hebrew word *Elohim*. The *-im* ending in Hebrew is a plural ending (like adding an *-s* to the end of a word in English), so the name *Elohim* is plural. This makes sense considering Genesis 1:26 records that "God said, Let *us* make man in *our* image, after *our* likeness" (emphasis added). For Latter-day Saints, it is easy to see how this scripture refers to both our Heavenly Father and our Heavenly Mother, in whose image we are created. Early Apostle Erastus Snow said,

> Deity consists of man and woman. . . .
>
> How do you know? I only repeat what he says of himself; that he created man in the image of God, male and female created he them. . . .
>
> . . . There can be no God except he is composed of the man and woman united, and there is not in all the eternities that exist, nor ever will be, a God in any other way.[5]

Eve was first created in the image and likeness of her divine Mother, yet this creation was spiritual. God completed His Creation by physically creating all the things He had made spiritually before, including Adam and Eve. Adam was created first. The Creation account given in the book of Abraham states, "The Gods formed man from the dust of the ground, and took his spirit (that is, the man's spirit) and put it into him; and breathed into his nostrils the breath of life, and man became a living soul" (Abraham 5:7).

After Adam's creation the Lord placed him in the Garden of Eden to "dress it" and to "keep it." Author Diana Webb wrote, "The Hebrew word translated 'dress' is from the Hebrew word *avad*, which means 'to serve.' When this verb is made into a noun, it means 'service' or 'worship.' The word translated 'keep' is from the Hebrew *shamar*, which has the connotation of 'to guard' and 'to protect,' like the keep of a castle where the most precious treasures are safeguarded."[6]

In essence, the Garden of Eden was a temple, a place where Adam was to serve and worship God, freely converse with Him, and learn from Him. In the Genesis account of the Creation, God first created the beasts of the field and the fowls of the air. God then created Adam and presented the animals before him "to see what he would call them" (Genesis 2:19). I remember as a young girl thinking it was unfair that Adam got to name all the animals without Eve. Naming animals sounded fun to me! Yet it seems that Adam's naming of the animals was a specially designed learning experience. It must have been apparent to Adam after viewing and naming the vast variety of animals that he—among all of God's creations—was alone. Perhaps it was God's way of helping Adam be ready for Eve, to help him realize just how important she was and how he should treasure her. For nowhere else among the animals would Adam, as he now well knew, find a "help meet."[7]

• Eve as a Help Meet •

The common way in which the term "help meet" is interpreted is to mean that Eve, unlike the other beasts of the earth, was "appropriate for" or "worthy" of Adam. We think of her as his helper or companion on the earth. While this is certainly true, this interpretation does not do justice to what the Hebrew words really means.

The two Hebrew words that "help meet" is derived from are *ezer* and *kenegdo*. *Ezer*, which is commonly translated as "help," is a rich word with a much deeper meaning. In her book *Eve and the Choice Made in Eden*, Beverly Campbell explains, "According to biblical scholar David Freedman, . . . this word is a combination of two roots, one meaning 'to rescue,' 'to save,' and the other meaning, 'to be strong.' Just as the roots merged into one word, so did their meanings. At first *ezer* meant either 'to save' or 'to be strong,' but in time, said Freedman, *ezer* 'was always interpreted as "to help" a mixture of both nuances.'"[8]

Diana Webb, in her book *Forgotten Women of God*, also commented on the meaning of *ezer*. She wrote, "The noun *ezer* occurs twenty-one times in the Hebrew Bible. In eight of these instances the word means 'savior.' These examples are easy to identify because they are associated with other expressions of deliverance or saving. Elsewhere in the Bible, the root *ezer* means 'strength.'"[9] "The word is most frequently used to describe how God is an *ezer* to man."[10]

For example, the word *ebenezer* in 1 Samuel 7:12 is used to describe the power of God's deliverance. *Eben* means "rock," and *ezer* means "help" or "salvation." *Ebenezer*, therefore, means "rock of help" or "rock of salvation." When God used the word *ezer* to describe to Adam who Eve was, He was explaining that Eve was not intended to be just his helper and companion, but that she was also his savior, his deliverer.

In addition, the "meet" part of the term "help meet" is the Hebrew word *kenegdo*. It is hard to know exactly what the word *kenegdo* means because it only appears once in the entire Bible. Diana Webb explained, "*Neged*, a related word which means 'against,' was one of the first words I learned in Hebrew. I thought it was very strange that God would create a companion for Adam that was 'against' him! Later, I learned that *kenegdo* could also mean 'in front of' or 'opposite.' This still didn't help that much. Finally, I heard it explained as being 'exactly corresponding to,' like when you look at yourself in a mirror."[11]

Eve was not designed to be exactly like Adam. She was designed to be his mirror opposite, possessing the other half of the qualities, responsibilities, and attributes that he lacked. Just like Adam and Eve's sexual organs were physically mirror opposites (one being internal and the other external), so were their divine stewardships designed to be opposite but fit together perfectly to create life. Eve was Adam's complete spiritual equal, endowed with an essential saving power that was opposite of his.

I love how Beverly Campbell concluded her remarks about the term "help meet." She said, "Thus, it seems that through imprecise translation, our understanding of the powerful words used originally to describe Eve's role have been diminished. As a result, our understanding of Mother Eve has also been diminished. Suppose we had all, male and female alike, been taught to understand Genesis 2:18 as something like the following: 'It is not good that man should be alone. I will make him a companion of strength and power who has a saving power and is equal with him.'"[12]

• Adam's Rib •

After Adam's realization that there was no "help meet" for him, God caused a "deep sleep to fall upon Adam" (Genesis 2:21). During this sleep, God took one of Adam's ribs "and closed up the flesh instead thereof" (Genesis 2:21), and from that rib Eve was created. This process of creation is bizarrely mysterious and tells us very little about the actual method in which Eve was created. It leads us to suppose that this description is symbolic.[13]

The word translated as "rib" is the Hebrew word *tesla*, which means "side," as in the "side of a building." *Tesla* is used thirty-two times in the Bible, and the only place it is translated as "rib" is in the story of Adam and Eve. Elsewhere, *tesla* is translated as "chamber," "boards," and "beams." All referring to parts of a building, specifically parts of the tabernacle and ark of the covenant (see Exodus 26:26–27; Exodus 37:3, 5, 27; Ezekiel 41:5–11). Additionally, when the Lord "made" Eve from Adam's rib, the Hebrew word used is *banah*, which means "to build," as in "to build a house, or a family."[14]

Eve's creation is described in terms of creating a sacred building. Perhaps this is because Eve, and her daughters after her, would be—like the tabernacle and ark of the covenant—a place where sacred power would be housed.[15] Hugh Nibley touched on this when he wrote, "The word *rib* expresses ultimate in proximity, intimacy, and identity. . . . We are told not that the woman was made out of the rib or from the rib, but that she *was* the rib, a powerful metaphor."[16]

Eve's creation from Adam's rib also connotes unity. Elder Russell M. Nelson said, "I presume another bone could have been used, but the rib, coming as it does from the side, seems to denote partnership. The rib signifies neither dominion nor subservience, but a lateral relationship as partners, to work and to live, side by side."[17] It was Eve, presented in all her glory before him, that awakened Adam from his sleep (the Hebrew word means "trance") and helped him see more completely who he was. When Adam saw Eve for the first time, he exclaimed, "This I know now is bone of my bones, and flesh of my flesh. . . . Therefore shall a man leave his father and his mother, and shall cleave unto his wife; and they shall be one flesh" (Moses 3:23–24).

Inherent in Adam's words is the concept of marriage, that a man should leave his parents and covenant to his wife. The *Gospel Principles* manual teaches, "Adam and Eve were married by God [in the Garden of Eden] before there was any death in the world. They had an eternal marriage."[18] Eve, and his marriage to her, awakened Adam. I think this can still be true for men today. Marriage can often be the catalyst that helps a man awake and arise to his complete stature as a son of God.

• Eve's Third Step: The Fall •

And when the woman saw that the tree was good for food, and that it was pleasant to the eyes, and a tree to be desired to make one wise, she took of the fruit thereof, and did eat, and gave also unto her husband with her; and he did eat.

Genesis 3:6

In both the Genesis and Moses accounts, God's commandment to not eat of the tree of good and evil was given to Adam *before* Eve was created. In Moses 3:17, God told Adam, "Of the tree of knowledge of good and evil, thou shalt not eat of it, nevertheless, though mayest choose for thyself, for it is given unto thee." This differs from the Genesis account that simply says, "Thou shalt not eat of it" (Genesis 2:17). Elder John A. Widtsoe explained what this difference means:

> The eternal power of choice was respected by the Lord himself. . . . It really converts the command into a warning, as much as if to say, if you do this thing, you will bring upon yourself a certain punishment, but do it if you choose. . . . The Lord had warned Adam and Eve of the hard battle with earth conditions if they chose to eat of the tree of knowledge of good and evil. He would not subject his son and daughter to hardship and the death of their bodies unless it be of their own choice. They must choose for themselves. They chose wisely, in accord with the heavenly law of love for others.[19]

God had put Adam and Eve in a catch-22, a situation from which they could not escape because of contradictory rules. The first commandment that God gave, before Adam and Eve were even fully created, was that they should "be fruitful, and multiply, and replenish the earth" (Genesis 1:28). And yet we know from Eve's own words in Moses 5:11 that in the Garden of Eden they were unable to have children. The only way to have children was to eat of the tree of knowledge of good and evil and become mortal. Yet eating of the tree would go against another of God's commandments; they would die and be separated from God forever. Can you see the conundrum they were in?

I think that conundrum was exactly what God wanted to set up. Brigham Young taught, "It was necessary that sin should enter the into the world; no man could ever understand the principle of exaltation without its opposite. . . . How did Adam and Eve sin? Did they come out in direct opposition to God and to his government? No. But they transgressed a command of the Lord, and through that transgression sin came into the world."[20]

The story of Eve, in her choice to eat the forbidden fruit, has often been compared to the Greek story of Pandora, whose unrestrained curiosity led her to open Prometheus's forbidden box. In doing so, she let loose upon the earth all the terrible things it had never known before—hate, sickness, anger, violence, greed, and worry. Realizing what she had done, Pandora quickly shut the box, trapping inside the last of its contents—hope. Like Pandora, Eve has been blamed as the source of all human suffering. While we cannot fault her choice, we have to acknowledge this is partly true. It is because of Eve's choice that we live in a fallen and wicked world; a world in which we have wars, abuse, illness, hatred, poverty, and anger. Yet it is also because of Eve's choice that we have hope and personal agency to choose, to learn, to progress eternally, and to have children. Her choice was a two-edged sword; there was no way to bring good into the world without also bringing bad.

• Eve Was Beguiled •

It is possible that this conundrum of the tree of knowledge of good and evil might have especially fascinated Eve. As Beverly Campbell wrote, "Many Biblical scholars believe that a long period of time passed as Eve, along with Adam, evaluated and reevaluated the conflicting commandments that forced such a considered use of their power of agency. Could it have been one decade, one century, even more? Certainly there must have been impassioned pleading with God by Adam and Eve, jointly and separately, as to the right choice. Was God's promise to them any less than it is to us? 'Ask, and ye shall receive—knock, and it shall be opened unto you.' They, too, were surely learning line upon line."[21]

As "the mother of all living" (Genesis 3:20), Eve must have felt an important, perhaps even urgent, need to fulfill her foreordained mission. I can imagine all of us, as premortal spirits, up there watching her and urging her onward. We wanted her to partake—even though doing so would mean death, sin, and separation from God—because it was the only way for us to come to earth and progress. Eve must have felt the weight of that responsibility, and it is easy to imagine her wrestling with such a hard choice, perhaps for a long time.

According to Hebrew scholar Dr. Nehama Aschkenasy, Eve was not tricked or duped into partaking of the fruit by Satan as we often think. Aschkenasy claims that in Hebrew, the word that is translated as "beguiled" is a rare verb that "indicates an intense multilevel experience which evokes great emotional, psychological, and/or spiritual trauma."[22] It was the serpent's "beguiling" of Eve that was the catalyst that eventually helped Eve make her choice. We might say that Eve had the world's first "crisis of faith."

Satan's first interaction with Eve was to plant seeds of doubt when he asked, "Yea, hath God said, Ye shall not eat of every tree of the garden?" (Genesis 3:1). Eve responded by repeating what she knew: "We may eat of the fruit of the trees of the garden: But of the fruit of the tree which is in the midst of the garden, God hath said, Ye shall not eat of it, neither shall ye touch it, lest ye die" (Genesis 3:2–3). Satan then told Eve things she might not have known about the tree of knowledge, that "in the day ye eat thereof, then your eyes shall be opened, and ye shall be as gods, knowing good and evil" (Moses 4:11). Yet along with that piece of truth he also gave her a lie, telling her that if she ate of the tree she would "not surely die" (verse 10). Though he is the "father of all lies" (verse 4), Satan is rarely (if ever) a straight-out liar. He usually works with half-truths.

In addition to telling her a half-truth, Satan also presented himself as something (or someone) he was not. Though the meaning of the symbol has been corrupted, anciently the snake (because it shed its skin and was "reborn") was a symbol of resurrection and eternal life. Remember how Moses held up a snake on his staff to heal the Israelites? He used the symbol of a serpent because it was representative of Jesus Christ. Satan was attempting to deceive Eve into thinking he had power and authority from God.

Yet I don't think that Eve was completely taken in by Satan's ruse. She seemed to know, right from the start, that things weren't quite right. What Satan's beguiling did do was make her question what she knew and send her on a soul-searching journey. She was faced with conflicting ideas, and she had to search and ponder until the correct pathway became clear. In the end, we know that Eve ate of the tree of knowledge because she "saw that the tree was good," it "became pleasant to the eyes," and she "desired [it] to make her wise" (Moses 4:12). I love that the fruit was "pleasant to the eyes" or, as the phrase could be interpreted in Hebrew, "the longing's of one's heart."[23] Perhaps the fruit tasted good, and Eve ate it because she was hungry—ravenously hungry—for the spiritual knowledge it could give her.

• Getting Adam to Partake •

After eating of the fruit, Eve faced the task of getting Adam to eat of it too. I once made a big decision (as in, I rented a house) without the consent of my husband, knowing that he was opposed to it. It was a disaster. I can only imagine what Eve must have felt having to approach Adam with her choice, knowing how he felt about it. She knew that if she could not get him to understand, if she could not get him to see things as she did, that everything would be lost. Satan would have won.

Hugh Nibley explained,

> The perfect and beautiful union of Adam and Eve excited the envy and jealousy of the Evil One, who made it his prime objective to break it up. . . .
>
> His first step (or wedge) had been to get one of them to make an important decision without consulting the other. He approached Adam in the absence of Eve with a proposition to make him wise, and being turned down he sought out the woman to find her alone and thus undermine her resistance more easily. . . .
>
> After Eve had eaten the fruit and Satan had won his round, the two were now drastically separated, for they were of different natures."[24]

It is interesting to think that maybe the real problem with Eve eating the fruit was that she did it without Adam. That perhaps she "jumped the gun," so to speak, and made a big choice—a huge choice—without the support of her husband. Later the Lord instructs Eve to "hearken" to Adam. I don't think this was intended as a punishment. Rather, I think it was God's way of reminding Eve that in this world she and Adam were to walk side by side, with neither the man nor the woman running the show.

In fact, sometimes when I think of the great spiritual distance that must have separated Adam and Eve, I am convinced that there is nothing that a man and a woman cannot work out, if they both stay close to God. Satan's intent from the beginning had been to pull Adam and Eve apart, and while he may have come dangerously close, Adam and Eve were able to work it out—something that must have taken forgiveness, understanding, humility, and spiritual insight on both sides.

• Eve's Fourth Step: The Atonement •

Unto Adam also and to his wife did the Lord God make coats of skins, and clothed them.

Genesis 3:21

We often forget that Eve ate of the forbidden fruit with no knowledge of the promise of a redeemer. For that, if nothing else, she should be lauded for her courage to make such a self-sacrificing leap into mortality. We can only imagine the joy that she must have felt when she learned about the Atonement and realized that while she might die physically, she would not die spiritually. There would be a way back to God, provided through the sacrifice of Jesus Christ.

After their Fall, Adam and Eve's spiritual eyes were opened, and they began to see the difference between right and wrong more clearly. They also saw that they were naked. I am sure that this referred to their physical state, but I think it also referred to their spiritual status as well. We know from the scriptures that those with spiritual power, such as the Levites in the tabernacle, were clothed in sacred clothing. In fact, the need to clothe ourselves is one of the main things that makes us different from animals. We have no scales, feathers, or fur with which to cover our nakedness (see Genesis 9:23 and Exodus 28:42). We are born helpless and vulnerable and need to be covered. The clothing we wear is a sort of armor or protection for us, and like the armor worn by knights or warriors, it can be symbol of power. The Apostle Paul even called sacred clothing the "amour of God" (Ephesians 6:11), clothing that is made spiritually powerful by the faith, covenants, and righteousness of the one wearing it.

Adam and Eve made their own attempt at a covering, using the leaves of a fig tree to sew themselves aprons. An apron would not have covered much more than their reproductive parts, a sign that Adam and Eve understood that those were powerful—sacred—parts of their bodies. With their limited knowledge, they did the best they could to cover themselves. Later, after explaining to them the plan of salvation and the role of Jesus Christ, God would clothe Adam and Eve in "coats of skins" (Genesis 3:21). A coat (also called a garment or a tunic) made out of skins is a powerful symbol because

such clothing requires the death of the animal out of whom the coat is made. By clothing Adam and Eve in animal skin, rather than leaves or another material, God was symbolizing that they were "covered" by the Atonement of Jesus Christ—the great and last sacrifice.

As Latter-day Saints we associate these coats of skins with the clothing of the temple. It is incredible to realize that Eve, the first woman, was clothed with the robes of the priesthood. This information changes how we look at the rest of the stories of women in the scriptures; from the beginning, God endowed his daughters with priesthood power. I love how Beverly Campbell explained this:

> Imagine, the royal robes of the holy priesthood, crafted by the hand of God, placed on his chosen Adam and Eve that they might be properly protected throughout their sojourns here on earth. What a grand expression of infinite love!
>
> The world pauses to watch the investiture ceremonies of kings and queens, popes, and Supreme Court justices. Yet these worldly ceremonies pale beside that glorious event. . . .
>
> The significance of this investiture should not be overlooked. It should be recalled to our minds, for the Lord offers that same divine protection today to each man and woman who enters the temple to claim the blessings of the endowment.[25]

• Eve's Curse? •

After God found Adam and Eve hiding, He asked them why they were hiding. Even though we may be tempted to think they were embarrassed, there is no apparent shame in Adam and Eve's reply. Adam simply stated that he ate because Eve had eaten; he was following God's commandment to stay with her and have a family. He ended with a statement of responsibility, not blaming Eve but claiming, "I did eat" (Genesis 3:12). God then turned to Eve and asked, "What is this that thou hast done?" (Genesis 3:13). Eve replied that the serpent had beguiled her, but, like Adam, she took responsibility for her choice, saying, "I did eat" (Genesis 3:13).

God then cursed the serpent and promised that there would be "enmity between thee and the woman, and between thy seed and her seed; and he shall bruise thy head, and thou shalt bruise his heel" (Moses 4:21). This promise foreshadowed Jesus Christ, who would be the seed of a woman, and His triumph over Satan. I think it also tells us that Satan has it in for women; he hates them. Not only did Eve outwit his attempt to destroy God's work, but there is only one way to come to earth and one way to progress. That is through the blood and sacrifice of a daughter of Eve. Satan and his followers will never have bodies created by women, so they are damned (stopped in their progression).

The next part of God's conversation with Adam and Eve might be deemed "the talk," in which God explained to Adam and Eve the "birds and the bees" of what would happen to their bodies in a fallen world. To Eve he explained that He would "greatly multiply thy sorrow and thy conception" (Genesis 3:16). The Hebrew word for "multiply" is *rabah*, meaning "to become great," and is the same word that is used when God told Adam and Eve to "multiply, and replenish" (Genesis 1:28). The Hebrew word interpreted as "sorrow" here means "toil" and is the same word God used for Adam when He told him "in sorrow" he would eat of the ground (Genesis 3:17). God was telling Eve that He would multiply her—that she would have a great posterity—and that it would occur through conception. Just as Adam would have to work hard to bring forth food from the earth to sustain life, Eve would also have to work hard to create life and nurture a family.

This would have been nothing but good news to Eve, whose desire to have a family was what motivated her to leave the garden in the first place. She must have felt akin to a woman who, despairing that she would ever have children, was being told she would be the mother of a large family. She may have felt elation that, finally, she would be able to fulfill her foreordained role. Yet I also suspect that she probably did not comprehend the amount of "toil" that such an endeavor would require!

God then told Eve, "In sorrow thou shalt bring forth children" (Genesis 3:16). The word *sorrow* used here is a different word in Hebrew than the one used previously. Instead of meaning "toil," it means "pain, travail, hurt," and refers to creation. Though we only get one sentence of the conversation, I think this must have been the time when God explained to Eve what "bring[ing] forth children" entailed. In each of my pregnancies, I have thought about Eve and what being the first woman to be pregnant and give birth must have been like. I'm glad to think that God (or Heavenly Mother) gave her a heads-up as to what was coming.

God next told Eve that her desire would "be to [her] husband" (Genesis 3:16). Again, I believe God was explaining to Adam and Eve the details of the process of sex and conception. It also was a promise to Eve that she would not have to shoulder the enormous burden of bringing children into this world by herself. Her love for Adam, and his love for her, would be a powerful force that would bind them together. Desire, physical and spiritual, would ensure that she would not undertake this journey alone but that they would do it as a family.

Along with God's promise to Eve about desire came the statement that Adam "shall rule over thee" (Genesis 3:16). Unfortunately, there is no nice clarification of the words *rule over* in Hebrew. It means just what it sounds like, "to rule, have dominion, reign." This verse of scripture, perhaps more than any other, has been the cause of great suffering to women throughout history. Men have used it to justify unrighteous domination and control over women. Yet I am certain that was not God's intent.

Its interesting to think that perhaps God's instruction that Adam should have a leadership responsibility was intended to "level the playing field" and make Adam and Eve's responsibilities more equal. Eve had just been given the enormous task of creating and nurturing the entire human race. Eve, as the matriarch of the human family, wielded significant power, power that if not held in check might completely overpower the patriarchal power held by Adam. Hugh Nibley explained, "Why do we lay more emphasis on the patriarchal order than the matriarchy in our world today? That is unavoidable if we would maintain a balance between the two, for the matriarchal succession enjoys the great natural advantage that, where it prevails, renders the other all but helpless."[26]

Though we are not accustomed to thinking of it as powerful, the matriarchal creative power given to women is the most powerful use of God's power on earth. It is the most "godlike" power granted to anyone. Elder Jeffrey R. Holland said:

> Human life—that is the greatest of God's powers, the most mysterious and magnificent chemistry of it all—and you and I have been given it, but under the most serious and sacred of restrictions. You and I who can make neither mountain nor moonlight, not one raindrop nor a single rose—yet we have this greater gift in an absolutely unlimited way. . . .
>
> Surely God's trust in us to respect this future-forming gift is awesomely staggering. We who may not be able to repair a bicycle nor assemble an average jigsaw puzzle—yet with all our weaknesses and imperfections, we carry this procreative power that makes us very much like God in at least one grand and majestic way.[27]

If Eve, as the matriarch, was given the responsibility to create human life, what was left for Adam to do, besides a little farming and donating sperm? As things stood at this point, Eve had nearly the complete responsibility for humanity on her shoulders. God needed to even things out. He needed to give Adam a stewardship, just as he had Eve.

Hugh Nibley explained, "There is no patriarchy or matriarchy in the Garden; the two supervise each other. Adam is given no arbitrary power; Eve is to heed him only insofar as he obeys the Father—and who decides that? She must keep check on him as much as he does on her. It is, if you will, a system of checks and balances in which each party is as distinct and independent in its sphere as are the departments of the government under the Constitution—and just as dependent on each other."[28]

Adam's stewardship was to lead—not to control or rule over with an iron fist but to guide and direct the human race in their journey back to God. Adam would be the first patriarch of the earth, the first to hold the priesthood keys and administer the ordinances that would unlock the path back to our Father in Heaven. Joseph Smith taught, "The Priesthood is an everlasting principle, and existed with God from eternity. . . . Christ is the Great High Priest; Adam next."[29] "The priesthood was first given to Adam. . . . He obtained it in the Creation, before the world was formed."[30] Under that priesthood, God would expect Adam, and all men, to lead based on the guidelines of "the principles of righteousness" described in Doctrine and Covenants 121—persuasion, longsuffering, gentleness, meekness, love unfeigned, kindness, and pure knowledge (see verses 41–42). Eve and her daughters were not to be domineered or directed, but cherished and protected.

Here is the main thing to remember—don't get hung up by prepositions. The entirety of God's plan for his daughters is *not* determined by one small word. Whether the instruction is to rule *with*, *over*, *to*, or *unto*, don't let everything else you know about God's love and plan for His daughters go out the window because of a preposition. God wasn't setting up Eve as a second-class citizen. He gave her some incredible blessings and outlined the way in which men and women were to work together to create, nurture, and lead the family of the earth.

• Eve's Fifth Step: Mortal Life •

And it came to pass that after I, the Lord God, had driven them out, that Adam began to till the earth, and to have dominion over all the beasts of the field, and to eat his bread by the sweat of his brow, as I the Lord had commanded him. And Eve, also, his wife, did labor with him.

Moses 5:1

After their conversation in the garden, God "drove out" Adam and Eve from the Garden of Eden and placed cherubim and a flaming sword to guard the tree of life. Adam and Eve were being given, as Alma the Younger explained, "a probationary time, a time to repent and serve God. For behold, if Adam had put forth his hand immediately, and partaken of the tree of life, he would have lived forever, according to the word of God, having no space for repentance" (Alma 42:4–5).

Adam and Eve were fallen, but it was not God's intent that they should remain so. He wanted them to return to Him, to come back and partake of the tree of life. In their new world, Adam and Eve were to work to help each other and their children walk the path back to God. Kathleen Slaugh Bahr and Chari A. Loveless wrote,

> When they exercised their agency and partook of the fruit, Adam and Eve left their peaceful, labor-free existence and began one of hard work. They were each given a specific area of responsibility, yet they helped each other in their labors. Adam brought forth the fruit of the earth, and Eve worked along with him. Eve bore children, and Adam

joined her in teaching them. They were not given a choice about these two lifetime labors; these were commandments. . . .

. . . According to the New Testament, the work of bearing and rearing children was . . . intended as a blessing. Writes the Apostle Paul, "[Eve] *shall be saved* in childbearing, if they continue in faith and charity and holiness with sobriety." Significantly, Joseph Smith corrected the verse to read, "*They* shall be saved in childbearing," indicating that more than sparing of Eve's physical life was at issue here. *Both Adam and Eve would be privileged to return to their Heavenly Father through the labor of bringing forth and nurturing their offspring.*[31]

This partnership between Adam and Eve is evident in Moses 5 when Eve "did labor with" Adam and they taught their children to till the land and to live in a family (see Moses 5:1–3). We also see Adam and Eve approaching the Lord in prayer together, giving us the first example of family prayer. During their prayer, God spoke to both, instructing them that they should offer "the firstlings of their flocks, for an offering to unto the Lord" (Moses 5:5).

Adam and Eve were obedient to this commandment. After "many days" of offering these sacrifices, an angel came to Adam and asked him, "Why dost thou offer sacrifices unto the Lord?" (Moses 5:6). Adam responded, "I know not, save the Lord commanded me" (Moses 5:6). The angel, seeing Adam's obedience, explained to him that the sacrifices he offered were in "a similitude of the sacrifice of the Only Begotten of the Father" (Moses 5:7). After this explanation, "the Holy Ghost fell upon Adam," and he gained knowledge that it would be through "the Only Begotten of the Father" that he, and all mankind, would be redeemed (Moses 5:9).

After this manifestation of the spirit, Adam "was filled, and began to prophesy" and said, "Blessed be the name of God, for because of my transgression my eyes are opened, and in this life I shall have joy, and again in the flesh I shall see God" (Moses 5:10). Eve also rejoiced and said, "Were it not for our transgression we never should have had seed, and never should have known good and evil, and the joy of our redemption, and the eternal life which God giveth unto all the obedient" (Moses 5:11). Eve had learned, as Lehi would later say, "There is opposition in all things. If not so, . . . righteousness could not be brought to pass, neither wickedness, neither holiness nor misery, neither good nor bad. . . . Wherefore, it must needs have been created for a thing of naught" (2 Nephi 2:11–12).

It seems that up until this point, Adam and Eve had been practicing their religion without understanding why. It was only as they *did* the everyday things the Lord had told them to, that they were finally able—with the assistance of the Holy Ghost—to completely understand the importance of the choice they had made in the garden. There is a great lesson to be learned here. Like Adam and Eve, we have each fallen and have forgotten who we are and the choices we made before we came to earth. God has given us commandments not to control us but to help us remember, to help us find in our daily religious practices the meaning and purpose behind our existence on this earth. It is only as we are obedient to the light and knowledge that we already have that the Lord is able to give us more.

After their great "aha" moment, Adam and Eve "blessed the name of God" and became the world's first missionaries by making the things they had learned "known unto their sons and their daughters" (Moses 5:12). Yet despite their valiant missionary efforts in their home, not all their children believed. Satan was still among them, and he worked hard to deceive Adam and Eve's children, convincing some to "believe it not" (Moses 5:13). Adam and Eve's response was "[to cease] not to call upon God" (Moses 5:16), a powerful reminder that sometimes all we can do is pray for loved ones who are struggling.

Despite Eve's prayers, her son Cain refused to "hearken." He boasted, "Who is the Lord that I should know him?" (Moses 5:16). Cain "loved Satan more than God" (Moses 5:18) and entered into false covenants with him, luring away others of Adam and Eve's children—including their daughters—into sin. Cain even went so far as to kill his brother Abel, who was the birthright son. This caused Adam and Eve incredible grief. Moses 5:27 tells us that they "mourned before the Lord, because of Cain and his brethren."

The last we hear about Eve is in Moses 6:2 at the birth of her son Seth, who was in Adam's "own likeness, after his own image" (Moses 6:10) and was a righteous man. He brought joy to his parents because "he rebelled not, but offered an acceptable sacrifice, like unto his brother Abel" (Moses 6:3). It was Seth who replaced Abel as Adam's heir, inheriting from him the priesthood and the responsibility of overseeing the covenants.

• Eve's Sixth Step: Exaltation •

Among the great and mighty ones who were assembled in this vast congregation of the righteous were Father Adam, the Ancient of Days and father of all,

And our glorious Mother Eve, with many of her faithful daughters who had lived through the ages and worshiped the true and living God.

D&C 138:38–39

We know that Adam lived to be 930 years old and saw eight generations of his posterity (see Genesis 5:5). We don't know how long Eve lived, but it is beautiful to think about her living to see her eighth-generation grandsons and granddaughters.[32] If I could speak to my eighth-generation grandmother, she would my ancestress who came over on the Mayflower in 1620! Eve would have had plenty of opportunities to teach and guide future generations, to do the important work of grandmothering!

The beautiful thing about Eve's story is that we see her come full circle: from her existence in the premortal world as a "great and noble spirit" assisting with the creation of the world, to her difficult choice in the Garden of Eden, to her fall and struggle in mortality, to her return to the Father to sit on a throne beside her Adam in a state of exaltation. In President Joseph F. Smith's great vision of the spirit world, he saw "the great and mighty ones" among whom was "our glorious Mother Eve, with many of her faithful daughters who had lived through the ages and worshiped the true and living God" (D&C 138:38–39). In another vision given to Joseph Smith and several other men, it was recorded that "the heavens gradually opened, and they saw a golden throne, on a circular foundation, something like a light house, and on the throne were two aged personages, having white hair, and clothed in white garments. They were the

two most beautiful and perfect specimens of mankind he ever saw. Joseph said, 'They are our first parents, Adam and Eve.' Adam was a large, broad-shouldered man, and Eve as a woman, was as large in proportion."[33]

I love the image of Eve being a large, beautiful woman sitting with Adam on a single throne. If ever there was an image that should put our minds to rest about the perceived lesser role of women in God's plan, it should be this—the image of Eve, not a shrinking violet or an insignificant wallflower compared to Adam, but a large woman of equal stature. What better symbol of unity and parity could we hope for than Eve sitting, not on a throne beside or below her husband, but on a shared throne. Don't get hung up on details or prepositions, because this Latter-day revelation makes it clear that Adam and Eve reign *together*.

> "They are our first parents, Adam and Eve."

• The Matriarchal Order •

The patriarchal order of the priesthood is easily evident in the Old Testament. It began with Adam, who received the priesthood from God and then passed it down to his son Seth. Seth then passed the priesthood down to his son. We call it the "patriarchal" order because priesthood is, ideally, passed down from father to son. Moses 6:5–8 explains that Adam and his sons kept a "book of remembrance" in which sacred writings were preserved and "a genealogy was kept of the children of God." One of the purposes of this genealogical record was to track the priesthood lineage as it was passed down from father to son. As a church, we still do this, and today when men are ordained to the priesthood, they are given their line of authority, showing the lineage through which that power came to them.

This patriarchal order is important because it is the priesthood, held by men, that has the power to perform the ordinances—sacrament, baptism, endowment, sealings—that God's children need to be "reborn" into His kingdom. In a similar way, though much less recognized, there is also a matriarchal order at work in God's plan.[34]

There is no other way to create human life—life which differs from the animals and birds by its potential to become like God—than to pass through the body of a woman. You can't sneak in the back door to mortality. If you want to come to earth, get a body, and have a shot at exaltation, then you must accept the sacrifice of a mother—a woman who will risk her life, shed her blood, and pass on to you life-activating cells to bring you into the world. There is no other way.

I loved how author and scientist Bryan Sykes explained his own feelings about this connection to the women in his past:

> I am on a stage. Before me, in the dim light, all the people who have ever lived are lined up, rank upon rank, stretching far into the distance. . . . I have in my hand the end of a thread which connects me to my ancestral mother way at the back. I pull on the thread and one woman's face in every generation, feeling the tug, looks up at me. Their faces stand out from the crowd, and they are illuminated by a strange light. These are my ancestors. I recognize my grandmother in the front row, but in the generations behind her the faces are unfamiliar to me. . . . These are all my mothers who passed this precious messenger [mitochondrial DNA] from one to another through a thousand births, a thousand screams, a thousand embraces of a thousand new-born babies. The thread becomes an umbilical cord.[35]

The matriarchal order is the way—the lineage—through which all of God's children have entered, and will enter, mortality. It connects us all in an unbroken line back to our Mother Eve.

God's goal is not to have a dominant matriarchy or a patriarchy, but rather to see those two powers harnessed together for the ultimate purpose of exalting all His children. Just like a child is born into the world through the blood and water shed by its mother, all those who wish to enter the Kingdom of God must be "reborn," as Christ told Nicodemus (see John 3:1–21), through the blood and sacrifice of Jesus Christ. Priesthood ordinances, administered by the fathers, is the method through which this rebirth process happens, creating an unbroken sealing link all the way back to Adam.

The unity of the patriarchal and the matriarchal order can be seen no more clearly, or beautifully, than in the family history work we do in the temple. We spend our time pouring over records, tracing the matriarchal order—the physical, birth connections of our family—only then to turn around and create a patriarchal order—the spiritual, priesthood connection to God. Author Beverly Campbell said, "What insight this fundamental connection gives us of the gathering into families in the hereafter and therefore of the importance of genealogy and temple work. How marvelous is the plan of God and His wonderful scales of justice as He places recognition of the linkage of humankind through the mother and the lineage of the priesthood through the father."[36]

God's plan is beautiful, one in which men and women work together to forge a matriarchal *and* a patriarchal order—endlessly sealing all of God's children together for eternity.

Adah and *Zillah*

And Lamech said unto his wives, Adah and Zillah: Hear my voice, ye wives of Lamech, hearken unto my speech; for I have slain a man to my wounding, and a young man to my hurt. . . .

For Lamech having entered into a covenant with Satan, after the manner of Cain, wherein he became Master Mahan, master of that great secret which was administered unto Cain by Satan; and Irad, the son of Enoch, having known their secret, began to reveal it unto the sons of Adam.

Moses 5:47, 49

In the seventh generation after Adam, two very different groups of people were living on the earth. The first were the descendants of Seth and were living in an order set up by God. Their leader was the prophet Enoch, and they had built the city of Zion, which would later be taken up to heaven for its righteousness. The other group were the descendants of Cain who were living in what we might call the world, Babylon, or even anti-Zion. They were involved in secret combinations.

Among these descendants of Cain was a man named Lamech and his two wives, Adah and Zillah. Genesis 4 tells us that Adah gave birth to two sons, one named Jabal, who was "the father of such as dwell in tents, and of such as have cattle," and the other named Jubal, who was "the father of all such as handle the harp and organ" (Genesis 4:20–21). Zillah also had two children, a son named Tubal-cain who was "an instructor of every artificer in brass and iron" and a daughter named Naamah (Genesis 4:22). The name *Naamah* can be translated in Hebrew to mean "to sing," and so it is thought that from her came the tradition of vocal music.[1]

This is all we know about Lamech and his wives from the Genesis account, but the Pearl of Great Price gives us deeper insight into their story. In Moses 5 we learn that Lamech had, like Cain before him, "entered into a covenant with Satan" (Moses 5:49) and was acting as "Master Mahan," the officiator of secret combinations. Lamech boasted to his wives that he killed a man who had "hurt" or offended him. The man's name was Irad, and he had revealed some of the secret oaths to "the sons of Adam" (verse 49). As result of Irad's betrayal, Lamech was obligated to kill him, not to get gain like Cain had killed Abel, but rather "for the oath's sake" (verse 50).

Lamech, however, in boasting to his wives about what he had done, broke the oath of secrecy. Among the followers of Cain, Lamech became "despised, and cast out, and came not among the sons of men" (verse 54), because he was afraid of being killed. Moses 5:53 tells us that until Adah and Zillah learned them, these secret combinations were not "among the daughters of men." Adah and Zillah became the first women to enter this covenant with Satan because Lamech "had spoken the secret unto his wives" (verse 53).

After learning these secret combinations, Adah and Zillah "declared these things abroad" (verse 53) not caring that doing so put Lamech in danger. It was after their support of these secrets that "the works of darkness began to prevail among all the sons of men" (verse 55). It is interesting that these wicked ideas didn't become popular or widespread until the women got behind them. Just as women have a great potential to build righteous civilizations, they also have an equally influential role in building wicked ones.

So what was this great secret? Cain tells us himself in Moses 5:31: "Truly I am Mahan, the master of this great secret, *that I may murder and get gain*" (emphasis added).

Compare this goal, to murder to get gain, with God's goal, which is "to bring to pass the immortality and eternal life of man" (Moses 1:39). God's purpose, in all things, is to perpetuate life, both physical and spiritual. He is the great life-giver, and His delight is in His children. Satan, on the other hand, is impotent, both physically and spiritually. He lacks a physical body and will never father any children. He has also chosen the path of spiritual death. Satan is diametrically opposed to the creation of life. While God offers us a rebirth into eternal, celestial life—a life without end—all Satan can offer is death and everlasting darkness.

Satan's promise to Cain and Lamech was that they could destroy life to gain money. Hugh Nibley explained, "Cain was free to enter a formal agreement with Satan, by which he would receive instruction in the techniques of achieving power and gain: 'Truly I am Mahan, the master of this great secret [The language is that of ancient colleges or guilds where the secret is the mystery of the trade or profession; in this case, his secret is how to convert life into property], that I may murder and get gain.'"[2]

When Cain killed Abel, he "gloried in that which he had done, saying: I am free; surely the flocks of my brother falleth into my hands" (Moses 5:33). In Satan's world, freedom and power are gained by having money. Satan has no priesthood power. Unlike God, who has the powers of creation and life, Satan's power comes through manipulating and exploiting the earth and her inhabitants

> *"I am free; surely the flocks of my brother falleth into my hands."*

for riches and influence. He has set himself up as a false god, one whose power is accessed through avenues of wealth and money.

When I was in college, I had a powerful visual experience that illustrated the dichotomy between these two kingdoms. I was in New York City with a school group during the week of Easter. On Good Friday, a group of us found ourselves near the famous St. Patrick's Cathedral and decided to attend Mass. The service was in Latin, and because I couldn't understand what was going on, I spent most of the time looking at the beautiful stained glass images of Christ placed all over the church. Even though it was a gloomy day, the windows were still lit up, and I had a feeling of deep reverence and peace. When the service was over, I left my pew, took one last look at the stained glass window above the altar, and turned around to face the back doors of the church, which had been thrown open. I nearly jumped back because looming outside the door was a dark, enormous statue of the Greek god Atlas.

The statue was across the street outside the Rockefeller Center, but the huge statue was perfectly framed between the cathedral doors. It felt like it was ominously lurking over the faithful churchgoers. As I made my way out of the church, I had the depressing feeling that I was leaving a place of sanctuary and entering the domain of that dark and foreboding false god. I have never felt so clearly the divide between what is God's domain—one in which light and life reign supreme—and that of Satan, in which money is the supreme power.

The Book of Mormon prophet Mormon taught that these secret combinations—this anti-Zion, anti-life, and anti-Christ mentality—are "had among all people" and that it was this mindset that caused the destruction of the Jaredites and the Nephites (Ether 8:20). Mormon also gave a warning, specific to our day, that "whatsoever nation shall uphold such secret combinations, to get power and gain, until they shall spread over the nation, behold, they shall be destroyed. . . . Wherefore, O ye Gentiles, it is wisdom in God that these things should be shown unto you, that thereby ye may repent of your sins, and suffer not that these murderous combinations shall get above you, which are built up to get power and gain—and the work, yea, even the work of destruction come upon you" (verses 22–23).

It is important for us to study these ancient stories because though the world has changed over the last several centuries, Satan's plans have not. He still works among us in much the same way he did in the days of Lamech, promising that power is to be gained through money and the destruction of life. Yet just as Enoch's city of Zion flourished alongside these secret combinations, we too can work to build Zion in our hearts, our homes, and our churches. While Satan's kingdom is based on scarcity and competition, Zion is based on principles of abundance, where "the earth is full, and there is enough and to spare" (D&C 104:17) and one has "milk and honey, without money and without price" (2 Nephi 26:25). In God's kingdom, the things of most value are those that cannot be bought with money.

• Matriarchy and Patriarchy •

Tension between women (the matriarchy) and men (the patriarchy) is a theme that runs the full length of the Old Testament. From the beginning, when he tried to separate Adam and Eve, Satan's great design has been to put animosity between men and women. Beverley Campbell wrote,

> Throughout the whole garden story we find that a consistent element in Satan's attempts to thwart the designs of God is his desire to disrupt the eternal, vital and delicate balance of male-female relationships.
>
> If he (Satan) can make men and women see one another, not as empowering partners, but as individuals who are of unequal worth or competitors, seeking gifts the other has, he can cause great pain and anguish. He can distort the concept of deity, spiritual powers, and the priesthood and thereby distort our response to each other.[3]

For all of earth's history, Satan has worked hard to create animosity and tension between men and women. This is because he knows that when men and women are unified—truly one—they have incredible power. Together, they have power to create life, peace, happiness, and prosperity for all of God's children. Hugh Nibley said:

> Thinking back, what was Satan's express purpose in inaugurating a rule of blood and horror, power and gain on this earth? It was to reach that wall of enmity that protected "the seed of the woman" from his direct attack. Only the covenants of Adam and Abraham and the church of God can overcome it. Though nothing is to be gained by men and women in fighting for the whip handle, that disgraceful tussle will continue until God cuts it short in righteousness.
>
> So one must choose between patriarchy and matriarchy until the Zion of God is truly established upon the earth. It is that old Devil's dilemma, . . . his means of decoying us away from our true dedication to the celestial order established in the beginning.[4]

As you read the Old Testament, you will see evidence of times when men and women—the patriarchy and the matriarchy—are unified and cooperative. Such stories include Abraham and Sarah, who equally made covenants to God; Elisheba and Aaron, who together ate of the sacrifices of the tabernacle; Hannah and Elkanah, who honored each other's vows; and Adam and Eve, who worked together to teach their children. These stories illustrate the balance between male and female, with neither the matriarchy or the patriarchy domineering or controlling.

Yet most the stories in the Old Testament do not display this level of harmony and cooperation between men and women. As Doctrine and Covenants 121:39 teaches us, this is because "it is the nature and disposition of almost all men [and women], as soon as they get a little authority, as they suppose, they will immediately begin to exercise unrighteous dominion." Satan is still hard at work among Adam and Eve's children, and *both* the matriarchy and the patriarchy are easily corrupted by power. Nibley said, "According to the oldest mythologies, all the troubles of the race are but a perennial feud between the matriarchy and patriarchy; between men and women seeking power and gain at each other's expense."[5] The Old Testament stories are layered with symbolism and remnants of ancient mythology. As you read them, it will be helpful to identify some of the symbols that represent a righteous matriarchy and patriarchy and those that represent a corrupted or "fallen world" matriarchy and patriarchy.

A righteous patriarchy—in mythology "the sky father"—has a primary energy of being expansive, penetrating, and providing. The righteous patriarchy is connected and provides, through rain, sun, and air, the necessities that the earth needs to flourish. Symbols of a righteous patriarchy are stable (rocks, mountains, and cornerstones). Its actions are things that tend and cultivate (shepherding, sowing, planting seeds, and husbandry of animals and plants). The patriarchy corrupts when it becomes disconnected, violent, and nomadic; it results in violence, domination, abuse, and abandonment. Nibley explained that the hero in a corrupted patriarchy "is the wandering Odysseus or knight errant, . . . the pirate, condottiere, the free enterpriser—not the farmer tied to wife and soil, but the hunter, and solider out for adventure, glory, and loot. . . . Its gods are sky gods with the raging sun at their head. Its depredations are not by decay but by fire and sword. As predatory and greedy as the matriarchy, it cumulates its wealth not by unquestioned immemorial custom but by sacred and self-serving laws."[6]

A righteous matriarchy—in mythology the "earth mother"—has a primary energy that is rooted, home-centered, agricultural, cyclical, and receptive. A righteous matriarchy is symbolized by things that are life giving (eggs, trees, water) and things that are reliable and organized (beehives, the moon, seasons). Like fruit rotting on a vine, the matriarchy corrupts by decay and neglect; it results in a society that is licentious, permissive, unethical, and immoral. Nibley explained, "The classic image is that of the great, rich, corrupt, age-old, and oppressive city Babylon, queen of the world, metropolis, fashion center, the super mall, the scarlet woman, the whore of all the earth, whose merchants and bankers are the oppressors of all people. Though the matriarchy makes for softness and decay, beneath the gentle or beguiling or glittering exterior is the fierce toughness, cunning, and ambition of Miss Piggy, Becky Sharp or Scarlett O'Hara."[7]

Throughout the Old Testament, you will see righteous and unrighteous patriarchies and matriarchies spar back and forth with one another. One of the best examples of this is in the story of Jezebel and Elijah, in which a corrupted matriarchy (embodied by Jezebel) goes head to head with a righteous patriarchy (embodied in Elijah).[8] When the matriarchy gets out of control, the patriarchy rises to reign it back in. We see other examples of this corrupted matriarchy in the stories of Maachah and the queen mothers of Judah versus the prophets, Gomer versus Hosea, and the women who baked bread for the queen of heaven versus Jeremiah.

Yet similarly when, like in the book of Judges, a corrupt patriarchy runs rampant, we have women like Deborah who rise to restore the matriarchy and bring balance. We have other such examples of a righteous matriarchy stepping up against a corrupt patriarchy in the stories of Tamar and Judah, Ruth and Boaz, Abigail and David, and Huldah and Josiah. The women in Moses's life—Jochebed, Puah, Shiphrah, and Miriam—are also examples of a righteous matriarchy rising to protect life and helping to restore a righteous, and more balanced, patriarchy.

As you study the women in the Old Testament, you might consider making your own list of examples of righteous matriarchies and patriarchies you find, as well as examples of times in which the matriarchy or the patriarchy is corrupted. The conflict between patriarchy and matriarchy is still alive and well in our modern world. These tensions permeate our homes, marriages, politics, and even our churches. Learning to identify examples of corrupt matriarchies or corrupt patriarchies in the scriptures helps us better identify similar institutions and mindsets in our lives. We must remember that this not how the relationship between our Heavenly Parents is. They are beautifully unified—something They desire for all Their sons and daughters.

Noah's Wife

And God spake unto Noah, saying,

Go forth of the ark, thou, and thy wife, and thy sons, and thy sons' wives with thee.

Bring forth with thee every living thing that is with thee, of all flesh, both of fowl, and of cattle, and of every creeping thing that creepeth upon the earth; that they may breed abundantly in the earth, and be fruitful, and multiply upon the earth.

And Noah went forth, and his sons, and his wife, and his sons' wives with him.

Genesis 8:15–18

Nine generations after Adam and Eve's creation, the world had become "corrupt before God" (Genesis 6:11) and was filled with violence. It was so wicked that the Lord "repented . . . that he had made man on the earth" (verse 6) and vowed to "destroy [them] from the face of the earth; both man, and beast and the creeping thing, and the fowls of the air" (verse 7). Amidst all this wickedness lived a very remarkable woman, the wife of Noah. We can assume that she, like her husband, remained faithful and found "grace in the eyes of the Lord" (verse 8).

There are many traditions and stories about Noah's wife, and she is called by many different names, but we still know very little about her, which is astonishing considering her part in the story.[1] She, like Eve, was a mother of the human race. It was through her and her daughters-in-law that all the nations of the earth were born after the flood.

Noah and his wife were a second Adam and Eve, though perhaps more correctly we might say they were the *antithesis* of Adam and Eve. While Adam and Eve went from the garden, a world of innocence and purity, to a world of corruption and sin, Noah and his wife went from a world of corruption and sin to a world washed clean, one of innocence and purity. They, and the entire world, got a second chance. This is a theme we can all relate to. As children, we are all like Adam and Eve, innocent and pure. As we grow, we became like Noah and his wife, corrupted by the sin around us. Like the earth, we needed baptism, an immersion that washed away our sin and mistakes. We all need the second chance the gospel gives us.

While Noah and his wife's escape was a very literal one—rising above everything on the face of the earth—ours is often more spiritual in nature. One of the places I find transcendence is the temple. Like the ark, the temple has been divinely designed as a place of safety and peace amidst a world filled with violence and wickedness. In the temple, we are reminded of who we are and what we have been sent here to do. Like the ark, the covenants we make in the temple carry us through the fallen world and give us a glimpse of the clean and pure one we will enter someday.

In the temple, we are sealed together as a couple—two by two—just as the animals (and humans) entered the ark two by two. Actually, if you read closely, only the animals that were unclean were taken on to the ark in twos. The fowls and the clean beasts were taken in groups of seven—seven females and seven males. Yet even in here we still see that the animals all came on in pairs, each having a corresponding mate, or as the Genesis account states, "the male and his female" (Genesis 7:2). Demographically, having one male and seven female animals would have achieved about the same number of new babies, so I think we can assume that God's instructions to have seven females and seven males was not just about population.

This is significant because one of the main reasons that God wanted to destroy the earth was that it had become completely corrupt, especially sexually. Even the "sons of God" were abusing their privileges and taking "of all which they chose" among the "daughters of men" (Genesis 6:2). There is a scholarly tradition that explains these "sons of God" as being heavenly beings—sometimes called "the watchers" or the Nephilim—who came to earth to teach and restore righteousness but who were tempted and seduced by the beautiful women on the earth. The offspring of these "sons of God" were said to be the fathers of the "giants" spoken of elsewhere in the Bible.

The book of Moses, part of Joseph Smith's translation of the Bible, gives us a different perspective, explaining that when Noah and his son "hearkened unto the Lord, and gave heed . . . they were called the sons of God" (Moses 8:13). Hugh Nibley explained the following:

> It is the Joseph Smith Enoch which gives the most convincing solution: the beings who fell were not angels but men who had become sons of God. From the beginning, it tells us, mortal men could qualify as "sons of God," beginning with Adam. "Behold, thou [Adam] art one in me, a son of God; and thus may *all* become my sons." (Moses 6:68; italics added.) How? By believing and entering the covenant. "Our father Adam taught these things, and many have believed, and become the sons of God." (Moses 7:1.) Thus when "Noah and his sons hearkened unto the Lord, and gave heed . . . they were called the sons of God." (Moses 8:13.) In short, the sons of God are those who accept and live by the law of God. When "the sons of men" (as Enoch calls them) broke their covenant, they still insisted on that exalted title: "Behold, we are the sons of God; have we not taken unto ourselves the daughters of men?" (Moses 8:21), even as "the sons of men," reversing the order, married the daughters of those "called the sons of God," thereby forfeiting their title, "for," said God to Noah, "they will not hearken to my voice." (Moses 8:15.) The situation was, then, that the sons of God, or their daughters who had been initiated into a spiritual order, departed from it and broke their vows, mingling with those who observed only a carnal law.[2]

In the book of Moses, we read that Lord also told Noah that "the daughter of [his] sons" who had broken their covenants and married "sons of men" had "sold themselves" (Moses 8:15). This is even

• Egyptus •

Thanks to Joseph Smith's translation of the Abraham papyri, we know the name of one of the four women who boarded the ark with Noah—Egyptus. Egyptus was the wife of Ham, Noah's youngest son, and it was her daughter (also named Egyptus) who discovered the land of Egypt when it was "under water" (Abraham 1:24). Egyptus, the daughter of Ham, and her sons settled the land of Egypt. The first Pharaoh was the oldest son of Egyptus, a righteous man who sought "earnestly to imitate that order established by the fathers in the first generations, . . . even in the reign of Adam, and also of Noah, . . . who blessed him with the blessings of the earth, and with the blessings of wisdom, but cursed him as pertaining to the Priesthood" (verse 26).

Ham and his posterity had been "cursed" by Noah after an incident where Ham "saw the nakedness of his father" (Genesis 9:22) while Noah was drunk. Shem and Japheth took Noah's garment and covered their father with it, and did not see his nakedness. For this, Noah blessed his older sons and cursed his younger. This is a strange story, and there is much we do not understand. Yet, it is likely that this event had something to do with temple ordinances and sacred clothing. Ham apparently did something wicked by seeing "the nakedness" of Noah, which caused him and his posterity to lose the right to hold the priesthood.

All we know about the other two women on board the ark comes from what we know of their husband and sons. Japheth, who was Noah's eldest son, was blessed by his father that "God shall enlarge Japheth, and he shall dwell in the tents of Shem; and Canaan [referring to Ham] shall be his servant" (Genesis 9:27). His descendants are described as "gentiles," the first time that word is used in the scriptures (see Genesis 10:2–5). Shem was not the oldest son of Noah, but he was the birthright son. Doctrine and Covenants 138:41 calls him "the great high priest," meaning that he held the Melchizedek priesthood. It was through Shem's posterity that Jesus Christ was born.

sadder when we realize that later, when the flood came, Noah and his wife would have had to leave these daughters behind.

For forty days and nights, Noah and his family—and all those animals—were sealed inside the ark. That must have been a dark time for them, not just because the ark was probably dimly lit but because of what was going on outside. Can you imagine what it would feel like to experience the destruction of the entire world? Noah's family trusted in God, but I don't think that means they wouldn't have been nervous as they listened to the water accumulate outside their door. I am sure they wondered if the nails they had put in were strong enough and if the ark would stand up against the storm.

It did. God kept his promise and "remembered Noah, and every living thing . . . and God made a wind to pass over the earth, and the waters assuaged. . . . The rain from heaven was restrained; and the waters returned from off the earth" (Genesis 8:1–3). It took more than a year for the water to completely subside. That's a long time to be in a boat with lots of animals! Yet at the end of forty days, Noah opened the window and sent out a raven, followed by a dove. The raven "went forth to and fro, until the waters were dried up" (verse 7), but the dove "found no rest for the sole of her foot" (verse 9) she returned to Noah on the ark. I have always loved it that the dove was a girl.

Noah waited seven more days and then sent the dove out again. This time she returned to him in the evening with an olive leaf in her mouth. From that "Noah knew that the waters were abated from off the earth" (verse 11). This image of a dove with an olive leaf in her mouth has been adopted as a worldwide symbol of peace. I have often wondered why. An insight came to me one evening as I was studying Doctrine and Covenants 88, which is a revelation designated by Joseph Smith as the "'olive leaf' . . . plucked from the Tree of Paradise, the Lord's message of peace to us" (D&C 88, section heading). Section 88 is full of glimpses of things beyond this life—the governing of the world by the light of Christ, the power of the celestial glory, of a time when God will be comprehended by man, "unveil[ing] his face unto you" (verse 68), the hastening of God's work, and the signs and upheavals of the Second Coming. That evening I wrote in the margins of my scriptures, "This section is an olive leaf because it gives us a glimpse of what is beyond us. Just like the dove did for Noah, it gives us hope and faith in the life ahead of us."

The dove's return with an olive leaf in her mouth was a testament to Noah that there was something beyond what he could see. The olive leaf was the promise that even though the world looked completely hopeless, there was something beautiful just beyond the horizon. Later, under the Mosaic law, doves would become a sacrificial animal used to make atonement and to purify—they were a symbol of Jesus Christ. I think this is one of the reasons the dove and olive leaf are still our most recognizable symbol of peace; they remind us that there is always hope and that God gives us a peace that "passeth all understanding" (Philippians 4:7).

The last that we hear of Noah's wife is after the waters subside and she, along with Noah, her sons, and daughters-in-law, "went forth" from the ark (Genesis 8:18). In this new world, the first thing they did was to build an altar and offer a sacrifice to God. In response, God covenanted with Noah and his sons, promising that he would establish his covenant—His everlasting covenant—with them and their posterity. As part of this covenant, God promised Noah that He would never destroy the world again by water. The "token" of this covenant was the rainbow that God put in the sky.

The Joseph Smith Translation illuminates the nature of this covenant and token. God told Noah, "This is mine everlasting covenant, that when thy posterity shall embrace the truth, and look upwards, then shall Zion look downward, and all the heavens shall shake with gladness, and the earth shall tremble with joy; and the general assembly of the church of the firstborn shall come down out of heaven, and possess the earth, and shall have place until the end come. And this is mine everlasting covenant, which I made with thy father Enoch" (Joseph Smith Translation, Genesis 9:22–23 [in Genesis 9:16, footnote *a*]).

Wow, what a promise! The rainbow is the token of the promise that God has made to establish Zion again on the earth. Not only does that mean that there will be a righteous city upon the earth but also that Enoch's holy city and all those who belong to the Savior's church will come down from heaven and dwell together. I don't know about you, but that gets me excited. It helps me remember that no matter how wicked the world gets, there is nothing that can stop God's promised Zion from being built.

> "And all the heavens shall shake with gladness."

Job's Wife

Then said his wife unto him, Dost thou still retain thine integrity? curse God, and die.

But he said unto her, Thou speakest as one of the foolish women speaketh. What? shall we receive good at the hand of God, and shall we not receive evil? In all this did not Job sin with his lips.

Job 2:9–10

Job's wife is famous for her bad attitude. When her husband, a man of wealth and prestige, became destitute and severely ill, she responded to the trial by urging him to curse God and then kill himself—not exactly a model of long-suffering and womanly support. In fact, St. Augustine wrote about her as the "Devil's Accomplice." John Calvin called her "an instrument of Satan" and a "Diabolical Fury," and she has been held up in many more sermons as the epitome of the faithless wife.[1] Perhaps this caricature is true, but I think that there is another (more forgiving) way to look at her story as well.

The first chapter of Job tells us the story of a day "when the sons of God came to present themselves before the Lord, and Satan came also among them" (Job 1:6). It is interesting that the *only* Joseph Smith Translation correction for the entire book of Job is to change this verse from the "sons" of God to the "children" of God.[2] This is a subtle but significant change because it invites women into the picture. In fact, these verses almost seem like they could be a glimpse into the premortal world, a time when God's entire family were gathered together to council.[3]

During this council God described Job as "a perfect and an upright man, one that feareth God, and escheweth evil" (Job 1:8). Yet Satan challenged God, saying that Job was only righteous because "thou made a hedge about him" and had blessed him (verse 10). "Put forth thine hand now," Satan challenged, "and touch all that he hath, and he will curse thee to thy face" (verse 11). God, appearing to have all confidence in Job, then allowed all types of misfortune to befall him. His vast herd of oxen and asses were raided, a fire destroyed his sheep flock and killed his servants, his camels were stolen, and most tragically a great wind tore down the house where all his sons and daughters were gathered and killed them all. Yet even with all these misfortunes, Job retained his integrity and refused to curse God.

Seeing Job's integrity in the face of trials, Satan again challenged God, saying that it wasn't enough just to take away Job's physical wealth. If God gave Job trials of the body, he would then "curse thee to thy face" (Job 2:5). God agreed to allow Job to be tested with a physical trial, and Job soon broke out with "sore boils from the sole of his foot unto his crown" (verse 7). At this point, it was not Job who broke down and cursed God but rather his wife. It is important to remember that she, too, had just lost her home, her livelihood, and all ten of her children. Seeing Job sitting in ashes, scraping his sores with a broken piece of pottery, seems to have been too much

for her. She lamented to her husband, "Dost thou still retain thine integrity? curse God, and die" (verse 9).

Many commentators make Job's wife out to be the devil's advocate, who slyly tried to get Job to give in and make Satan the winner of his debate with God. Yet I wonder if we might give her the benefit of the doubt and assume she was simply having a crisis of faith. In fact, I think that many of us can relate to Job's wife. How often, when faced with a situation or a person that we cannot change, do we find ourselves wishing that it (or they) would disappear? I have a friend who, after struggling with a very difficult divorce for years, confided to me that she felt guilty for sometimes wishing that her ex-husband would die. She couldn't foresee any way for her situation to improve unless the person whom she perceived as the root of the problem was out of the picture.

Perhaps Job's wife was in a similar situation. Not only had she suffered great personal loss, but she was now also the sole care provider for a husband suffering from poverty, extreme illness, and depression. It is easy to see how she could feel trapped and full of despair. Thus, her faith in God wavered. In the movie adaptation of *Anne of Green Gables*, the character Marilla Cuthbert tells Anne, "To despair is to turn your back on God."[4] I think those are wise words. When we have faith in God and trust that He oversees our lives, it hard to despair. It is only when we turn away from Him that we feel the power of darkness and begin to lose hope. It seems that, perhaps for a time, Job's wife began to despair; she lost her focus on God and lost hope.

An apocryphal book, *The Testament of Job*, supports this interpretation and gives us more insight into her. We learn that Job's wife's name was Sitis and that before Job's downfall she was a great lady who was often generous to the poor. When her husband became destitute and sick, she became a slave to provide for herself and her husband. She even sold her hair (the ultimate act of disgrace) to buy bread to eat. After this deep degradation, the account says that "Satan followed her along the road, walking stealthily, and leading her heart astray."[5] When she came to where Job was sitting, her resolve finally broke and she cried, "Job, Job, How long will you sit on the dung heap outside the city thinking, 'Only a little longer!' and awaiting the hope of your salvation? . . . Your memorial has been wiped away from the earth—my sons and my daughters of my womb for whom I toiled with hardship in vain. And here you sit in worm-infested rottenness, passing night in the open air. And I for my part am a wretch immersed in labor by day and in pain by night, just so I might provide a loaf of bread and bring it to you."[6] Then in words similar to her lament in the Bible she exclaimed, "In the weakness of my heart, my bones are crushed. Rise, take the loaves, be satisfied. And then speak some word against the Lord and die."[7]

These were the words of a woman who had been pushed to her breaking point, emotionally and spiritually. The words "my bones are crushed" are heavy words, ones that paint a picture of a woman who was deeply weary and did not have the strength to continue. She was hopeless. Death, for her and her husband, seemed like her only option for escape.

In response to her lament, Job responded compassionately. He told her, "Thou speakest as one of the foolish women speaketh. What? shall we receive good at the hand of God, and shall we not receive evil?" (Job 2:10). I love how writer Daniel Darling imagined this scene:

> I imagine Job lifts his blistered hand and strokes her hair. At first, his words read like a harsh rebuke: "You speak as one of the foolish women would speak. Shall we receive good from God, and shall we not receive evil?"
>
> Yet, if you listen to Job, you almost hear admiration. "You speak as one of the foolish women." He didn't say his wife was foolish. He didn't even say her words were foolish. He said, "She sounds *like* one of the foolish women."
>
> In other words, "You don't sound like yourself." You might read these words like this: Sweetheart, that's not you talking. *This doesn't sound like the woman of God I know and married. That is not you talking, my wife. Let's remember God's promises. Let's remember his goodness.*[8]

I wonder how much of Job's wife's unhappiness was due to a feeling that things were not as they should be, that her life was not just unfair but that it had been ruined. I was once in a testimony meeting where a man defined coveting in a way I'd never thought of before. He said that coveting is not trusting that what God has given us is enough. He suggested that we must be willing to accept the good that God gives us along with the bad, trusting that *all* of it is a blessing (even if it doesn't feel like it).

Job's wife certainly had her share of trials. It must have been hard for her to understand why. Why did all those horrible things have to happen to her? Why did she and Job have to suffer so much, when others did not? Why? Why? Why? I can't answer those questions for Job's wife, any more than I can answer them for myself or anyone else. The truth is that sometimes we don't know why the Lord lets us suffer. Elder Russel M. Ballard taught the following about trusting the Lord:

> Trust that the Lord knows what He is doing with you and that He can accomplish it for your eternal good even though you cannot understand how He can possibly do it. We are like infants in our understanding of eternal matters and their impact on us here in mortality. Yet at times we act as if we knew it all. When you pass through trials for His purposes, as you trust Him, exercise faith in Him, He will help you. That support will generally come step by step, a portion at a time. While you are passing through each phase, the pain and difficulty that comes from being enlarged will continue. If all matters were immediately resolved at your first petition, you could not grow.[9]

Fortunately, Job's story ended well. After his sufferings and trials had run their course, God blessed Job with "twice as much as he had before" (Job 42:10). His friends and family returned to support him, and he was blessed with great wealth. Best of all, he was blessed with more children, seven sons and three daughters, so that "the Lord blessed the latter end of Job more than his beginning" (verse 12). We don't know if Job's wife was still living at this point of the story, but I feel like it doesn't matter. Job's good fortune was also her good fortune. Just like her husband, she endured trials that would crack the noblest of souls. She may have faltered, but I'd like to think that, like Job, she was refined by her trials.

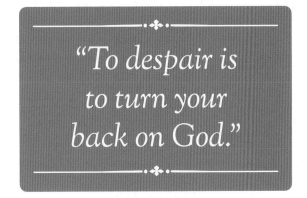

"To despair is to turn your back on God."

Jemima, Kezia, and Keren-happuch

were the three daughters born to Job after his tribulation. Unlike his previous daughters, whose behavior often worried Job, these daughters only gave Job cause to rejoice.[10] In fact, Job 42:15 tells us that, "in all the land there were no women found so fair as the daughters of Job." These young women must have been something else!

Job's daughters are also interesting because Job "gave them inheritance among their brethren" (verse 15). There are other stories in the Bible in which daughters inherit from their fathers, but it appears that was only customary if a man had no sons. It would have been unusual for daughters to be made heirs along *with* their brothers, though author James Baker mentions several instances when such an event did occur anciently: "The Code of Lipit-Ishtar permitted daughters who became priestesses to be full heirs with their brothers. A priestess served in the temple and did not receive a marital dowry. Such women thus could inherit land. Since such a daughter/priestess would never have children, their brothers became their heirs. The Code of Hammurabi permitted a soldier to deed any land he owned that he had not received as a gift from the king for military service to his wife or daughter. The Code of Hammurabi also contained a provision permitting inheritance rights for a priestess and added that a father could give his priestess daughter full power to bequeath her inheritance to whomever she wished."[11]

It is important to note that the book of Job is the oldest book in the Bible—perhaps the oldest book in the world—and is thought to have been written in the time of the early patriarchs. Anciently, receiving an inheritance was more than just a financial exchange; it often brought with it spiritual expectations and responsibilities.[12] It is likely that there was spiritual significance connected with Job's daughters' inheritance.

I wouldn't be surprised if, like the ancient texts suggests, the reason Job's daughters inherited from their father was that they were priestesses, although not priestesses to a pagan goddess like the Code of Hammurabi was referring to. Instead, I imagine them as priestesses in the sense that women endowed in the temple are priestesses today.[13] Today when women go to the temple, they receive their own spiritual inheritance, which, as it says in Doctrine and Covenants 38:32, is "power from on high."

In the temple, this spiritual inheritance is given to both men and women—to God's sons and daughters. I feel like something similar was happening in the case of Job's daughters. By including his daughters among his heirs, Job indicated that he saw them as deserving as their brothers and that he knew they could shoulder the spiritual responsibilities of inheritance.

> *"In all the land there were no women found so fair as the daughters of Job."*

Sarah

And God said unto Abraham, As for Sarai thy wife, thou shalt not call her name Sarai, but Sarah shall her name be.

And I will bless her, and give thee a son also of her: yea, I will bless her, and she shall be a mother of nations; kings of people shall be of her.

Genesis 17:15–16

We know more about Sarah than any other woman in the scriptures. We just get snapshots of other women, but we have nine chapters (plus more in the Pearl of Great Price) about Sarah and her life with Abraham. We get to follow her throughout her life, meeting her as a new bride in Genesis 11 and saying goodbye to her as the matriarch of a great nation in Genesis 23. Her life, like many of our lives, can be traced by the places she lived. She and Abraham moved many times, and each move brought with it its own adventure and lesson.

Sarah, who before her name was changed was called Sarai, was married to Abraham in the land of Ur. Genesis 11 explains that a man named Terah (a descendent of Noah's son Shem) had three sons: Abraham, Nahor, and Haran. Haran had three children, a son named Lot and two daughters named Milcah and Iscah. When their brother Haran died, Nahor married Milcah and Abraham married Sarai (see Abraham's Family Tree on page 283). Later we learn from Abraham that Sarai was his half-sister (see Genesis 20:12).

After the death of his son, Terah left Ur to go to the land of Canaan, where he settled in Haran with Abram, Sarai, and his grandson Lot. The book of Abraham in the Pearl of Great Price gives us insight into why Terah made this move. After recounting his miraculous deliverance from the altar of the Egyptian priest where he was to be offered as a human sacrifice by his father, Abraham tells us how a famine hit the land of Ur and his father was "sorely tormented" (Abraham 1:30) by it and repented of his past behavior. In Abraham 2:1, we even learn that it was because of this famine that Haran, Abraham's brother, had died.

We know very little about Sarah's life in Haran, but Jewish tradition remembers it as time of great prosperity. It is said that Abraham's tent had doors that opened on every side—north, south, east, and west—so that he could welcome travelers into his home from every direction. Abraham and Sarah became legendary for their hospitality. One scholar explained the part that Sarah was thought to have played in their home:

> And Sarah, his wife, was sharing in the charitable work of her aged husband. Indefatigably she worked day and night. During the day she assisted her husband and waited upon the travellers, offering them food and drink; and during the night she worked assiduously and industriously, weaving, with her own hands, garments to cover the naked. . . . Her candle never went out at night, from Saturday to Saturday.

> And the more Abraham and his wife Sarah worked and labored for the benefit and in the interests of the poor and needy, the miserable, afflicted and suffering, the greater grew their fame, and the Lord blessed their work, and they became a blessing."[1]

This is only a legend, but we do know from Genesis that when Abraham and Sarah were eventually commanded to leave Haran, they left with great wealth and "the souls they had gotten in Haran" (Genesis 12:5). The footnote clarifies that the word *gotten* means "made, or converted" (in Genesis 12:5, footnote d). In the Pearl of Great Price, Abraham says they left with "the souls we had won" (Abraham 2:15). Even though Abraham and Sarah were not able to have children, they became the "father" and "mother" to a great posterity of converts.

I have often thought about Abraham and Sarah's example of missionary work. They make it look so easy! What I have learned from their story is that sometimes the best way to do missionary work is to simply to have a generous heart. My husband is a great example to me of someone with a generous and charitable heart. He is always the person who stops on the side of the road when someone needs help, or the one offering service to those in need. It has been a testimony builder to me to see how sometimes (not always) these acts of service lead to opportunities for him to share his testimony or to build someone's faith. When we live our lives with charity and open our hearts and homes to others, we will find ways to share the light of the gospel with others.

Despite the success he and Sarah were having with converts in Haran, Abraham tells us that his father "turned again unto his idolatry" (Abraham 2:5). While praying to know what to do about this problem, Abraham and Lot received direction from the Lord to "Get thee out of thy country, and from thy kindred, and from thy father's house, unto a land that I will shew thee" (Genesis 12:1). Those must not have been easy words for Abram and Lot to hear.

They had built up great wealth and prestige in Haran, which must have been hard to leave behind. It was also where their father was. Did God want them to leave their father behind?

The answer was yes. "For I have purposed to take thee away out of Haran," the Lord told Abraham, "and to make of thee a minster to bear my name in a strange land which I will give unto thy seed after thee for an everlasting possession, when they hearken to my voice" (Abraham 2:6). Though she is not mentioned, we must remember that Sarah was involved in all of these decisions as well. Her choice was between staying where she was safe and comfortable or stepping out into the unknown, having no idea where life would take her.

It is interesting to me that the scriptures are full of stories about people whom God moved from place to place—Lehi and Sariah, the Jaredites, Moses and the children of Israel, and even Brigham Young and the early Latter-day Saints. These people were willing to "dwell in a tent," so to speak. They were willing to forgo security and stability to go where the Lord directed them. Even though tents may be pitched for long periods of time, tents (unlike houses) are not permanent structures and can be taken down to move where the Lord commands.

No matter what God's plan for us is, part of being a disciple of Christ is being willing to "dwell in a tent." That doesn't mean we need to go live in the wilderness, or even move from our houses, but we need be willing to go and do whatever God commands. Instead of having our hearts tied to our houses, our riches, and our desire for comfort, we should be willing to place our future in the Lord's hand and follow where He leads. Sometimes, like Abraham

and Sarah, this means leaving things and people behind, but it also means that our promise land lies ahead.

Abraham and Sarah were led to the plain of Mamre, where they built an altar at Beth-el and, as Abraham wrote, "called on the Lord devoutly, because we had already come into the land of this idolatrous nation" (Abraham 2:18). Even though this land was already inhabited, God promised Abraham that this land would be given to him and his children as their inheritance. Yet, the famine was still "very grievous" (verse 21), so Abraham and Sarah went to Egypt where food and water were more plentiful.

On the way to Egypt, Abraham told Sarai that she should tell the Egyptians that she was his sister and not his wife. We learn the reason for this in the Pearl of Great Price: "The Lord said unto me," wrote Abraham, "Behold, Sarai, thy wife, is a very fair woman to look upon; Therefore it shall come to pass, when the Egyptians shall see her . . . they will kill you, but will save her alive" (Abraham 2:22–23). The Dead Sea Scrolls also recorded that Abraham had a dream that alerted him of this impending catastrophe.[2]

When Abraham and Sarah arrived in Egypt, it was just as they had feared. The Egyptians saw that she was "very fair," and the pharaoh took her into his harem. In return, Pharaoh paid Abraham very well for his "sister," giving him sheep, oxen, asses, menservants and maidservants, asses, and camels. While we don't know how Sarah felt about this abduction, the Dead Sea Scrolls record Abraham's feelings:

> And I, Abram, wept aloud that night, I and my nephew Lot, because Sarai had been taken from me by force. I prayed that night and

I begged and implored, and I said in my sorrow while my tears ran down: 'Blessed art Thou, O Most High God, Lord of all the worlds. . . . I cry now before thee . . . because of my wife who has been taken from me by force. Judge him for me that I may see Thy mighty hand raised against him and against all his household, and that he may not be able to defile my wife this night (separating her) from me, and that they may know Thee, my Lord, that Thou art Lord of all the kings of the earth.' And I wept and was sorrowful.³

Not only does this record give us insight into to the deep love that Abraham had for Sarah, but it also helps us appreciate the miracle that happened next. Genesis 12:17 tells us that "the Lord plagued Pharaoh and his house with great plagues because of Sarai Abram's wife." We don't know what sort of plague this was, though the Dead Sea Scrolls tell us that it made Pharaoh "unable to approach her, and although he was with her for two years, he knew her not."⁴ Some commentators have speculated that perhaps these plagues were sexually transmitted diseases that made it physically impossible for Pharaoh to be intimate with Sarah.

According to the Dead Sea Scrolls, Pharaoh sent for all the wise men of Egypt to try to heal him without success. Finally, he called in Abraham, who explained to him that it was Sarai—his wife—who was the cause of the plague. The scrolls record what Abraham did next: "So I [Abraham] prayed . . . and I laid my hands on his [head]; and the scourge departed from him and the evil [sprit] was expelled [from him] and he lived."⁵ Pharaoh then commanded Abraham and Sarah to leave Egypt, taking with them the great wealth they had gained there.

Sarah's deliverance from Pharaoh's bed is just as miraculous as Abraham's deliverance from the altar of the Egyptian priest (which, interestingly, was shaped like a bed). Just like Abraham, Sarah underwent her own trial of faith, a period of time when she had to rely on the power of God to keep her safe. Just as Abraham's trial helped him come to know and understand God, we can assume that Sarah's trial and her miraculous deliverance helped increase her faith in Jehovah, the one true God.

After leaving Egypt, Sarah, Abraham, and Lot traveled back to the plain of Mamre, where they had been before they left for Egypt. Abraham and Lot soon discovered that between them they had too many animals and people to live in the same spot. Lot chose to take the more prosperous northern land, close to Sodom, while Abraham took the less fertile land to the south. In this land, Abraham and Sarah would live for most of their remaining years. It was also here that Abraham and Sarah were promised that they would be blessed with posterity; that Sarah would give Abraham her maidservant Hagar (see page 50) as a wife; that Ishmael, Hagar's son, would be born; and that Abraham and Sarah would be given the everlasting covenant (see chart on page 46).

When they received the Abrahamic covenant, Sarah was ninety years old and Abraham was ninety-nine. Sarah had been waiting her whole life for a baby that now, it seemed, would never come to her. I wonder how she interpreted God's promise that she would be the "mother of nations" (Genesis 17:16). Perhaps she imagined, as I think we are inclined to do when promises are slow in coming, that the promise was more symbolic than literal. Perhaps she felt she had already become a "mother of nations" through the people to

• Promises of the Everlasting Covenant[3] •

The Abrahamic Covenant	Abraham	Sarah
Genesis 17 outlines the Abrahamic covenant, which promises eternal posterity and increase. While we call it the "Abrahamic" covenant, it is important to notice that the covenant was also made with Sarah. A covenant dealing with endless posterity must include a woman. In fact, when you look at what God promised Abraham and what he promised Sarah, you find that their blessings are remarkably similar.	Name changed from Abram to Abraham (Genesis 17:5)	Name changed from Sarai to Sarah (Genesis 17:15)
	Promised that he would be exceedingly fruitful (Genesis 17:6)	Blessed and promised that she would bear a son (Genesis 17:16)
	Promised he would "make nations" of him (Genesis 17:6)	Promised she would be a "mother of nations" (Genesis 17:16)
	Promised that "kings shall come out" of him (Genesis 17:6)	Promised that "kings of people shall be of her" (Genesis 17:16)
	Told it would be an everlasting covenant with his posterity (Genesis 17:7)	Told the covenant would be with her posterity (Genesis 17:19)
	Told his posterity would be given the land of Canaan (Genesis 17:8)	
	Instructed that every male child must be circumcised (Genesis 17:10–14)	

God gave Abraham and Sarah the everlasting covenant (Genesis 17:7) and promised eternal increase. Today couples who are sealed in the temple are taking part in the new and everlasting covenant (see D&C 132). This is the same covenant that God gave to Abraham and Sarah. Just like in Abraham and Sarah's time, the covenant is between a man, a woman, and God. The promises of Abraham, Isaac, and Jacob are also the promises of Sarah, Rebekah, and Rachel.

whom she had taught the gospel. Author Vanessa Ochs wrote the following about Sarah's "mothering":

> Sarah discovered other opportunities to be maternal and matriarchal. She got on with her life, finding alternative ways to express herself, to give love and find fulfillment. The ancient legends (which cannot bear to think of Sarah the Matriarch languishing or being despondent) say she became a teacher and a spiritual guide, teaching women about God and God's covenant. She was a hostess extraordinaire, whose capacious tent was a place where travelers on their journeys could feel temporarily at home and could become refreshed and emboldened to continue on their own paths. The legends of the Midrash insist that Sarah was graced with an abundant spiritual presence; a cloud of divine presence was always with her.[6]

Perhaps in her heart of hearts Sarah still hoped for a child, but we might also speculate that she and Abraham had come to peace with their life.

When three messengers (the JST calls them "angels which were holy men" [in Genesis 18:22, footnote *a*]) came to Abraham's tent, he welcomed them warmly, calling them "brethren" (in Genesis 18:3, footnote *a*). After Abraham fed them and made them comfortable, the three men asked Abraham where Sarah his wife was. He told them that she was in her tent where, as it was customary (as it still is in some countries) for women to eat separately when there was company. Ochs wrote, "Women who wanted to hear news of the outside world and still respect their culture's rules of gender separation had to keep their ears open."[7]

It appears that this was just what the three holy men wanted to hear because their message was for Sarah and not for Abraham.

They told her that "according to the time of life" (Genesis 18:10) she would have a son. On hearing this message, Sarah "laugh[ed]" (Genesis 18:13). The Hebrew word is *tsachaq,* and it means "mocking," often used in reference to things sexual in nature. Perhaps Sarah laughed for joy at the news, but that isn't what the text seems to suggest. Genesis 18:12 says that Sarah "laughed within herself, saying, After I am waxed old shall I have pleasure, my lord being old also?" It seems that Sarah had stopped menstruating and that she doubted Abraham's ability as a ninety-nine-year-old man to sire a child.

I also wonder if her laugh was one of irony. Perhaps she felt like a friend of mine did when the baby she had seen in a dream when she was a young mother was born to her years after she had felt she was done having children. She had teenagers when her little girl was finally born. Initially, instead of feeling joy about, it she thought, "Really, God? Why now? Why not ten years ago when I was waiting for her?" I wonder if Sarah had similar feelings; she had a dream fulfilled, just not when she expected. Sometimes we hold on to dreams, other times we let them go, and sometimes things happen when we least expect them to and they turn our lives upside down. Ochs wrote about how each of us can learn from Sarah:

> We can ask her to help us pursue our dreams wisely, with the appropriate doggedness, and to know when they might be better laid to rest for a while, or even forever. We ask her to assure us that if we relinquish a dream, it is not a betrayal. We ask her to help us to notice when the closing of one door signals the opening of another. She can give us the strength to laugh when our good dreams come true at inappropriate or just curious times. While Sarah joins us in appreciating the irony of a dream belatedly fulfilled, we ask her to keep us from

being too cynical or bitter to accept good tidings that come our way and celebrate them for what they can mean to us now, even when they come clumsily out of season. . . .

You might offer this blessing: May I be blessed, as our mother Sarah was, to receive dreams that come true in their own season.[8]

Before Sarah's son (whose name Isaac means "laughter") was born, she and Abraham would make another move. This time, they went to Kadesh and sojourned in land ruled over by Abimelech, the king of Gerar. Just as they had in Egypt, Sarah pretended to be Abraham's sister, and again she was forcibly taken into the household of Abimelech. You'd think they would have learned from what happened last time! This time, though, God intervened quickly on Sarah's behalf and told Abimelech in a dream that he had taken Abraham's wife and that if he didn't give her back, his household would be destroyed. Abimelech asked Abraham why he had said that Sarah was his sister. Abraham explained that he had feared for his life and that Sarah had agreed to the situation. Abimelech then restored Sarah to Abraham and gave her a thousand pieces of silver as a recompense for what had happened to her. Then, as he had for Pharaoh, Abraham prayed for Abimelech and healed him and his entire household because the "Lord had fast closed up all the wombs of the house of Abimelech, because of Sarah Abraham's wife" (Genesis 20:18).

We don't know why Sarah had to once again undergo such a trial, but after this experience she and Abraham stayed in the land near Abimelech and were on (mostly) friendly terms with him. In fact, perhaps one reason for Sarah's experience was to convert Abimelech and his household to the gospel. Later, Abimelech acknowledged that "God [was] with" Abraham in all that he did and made Abraham swear "by God" that he would be honest with him and his sons (Genesis 21:22–23). His use of the word "God," without any qualification that he was referring to "Abraham's God," may suggest that Abimelech had also taken God—Jehovah—as his own.

After this experience in Gerar, Sarah finally conceived and gave birth the to the child of the promise—Isaac. Then, in the only time we hear Sarah's voice in her entire story, she exclaimed, "God hath made me to laugh, so that all that hear will laugh with me. . . . Who would have said unto Abraham, that Sarah should have given children suck? For I have born him a son in his old age" (Genesis 21:6–7). When Isaac was weaned, probably around the age three or four, Abraham threw a celebration for him, during which Sarah ordered Hagar and Ishmael to leave. After this event, we hear nothing else about Sarah—not even during the near sacrifice of Isaac on Mount Moriah—until her death at the age of one hundred and twenty-seven.

The Bible takes an entire chapter to describe Abraham's purchase of Sarah's burying place, which tells us that something important was happening in this transaction. Abraham had been promised the entire land of Canaan for his posterity, but at the time of Sarah's death, he didn't own any land at all. In searching for a place to bury Sarah, he approached the sons of Heth who owned the land. They acknowledged Abraham as "a mighty prince among [them]" (Genesis 23:6). (Sarah, as her name suggests, had truly become a princess!) Abraham asked the sons of Heth if they would sell him a piece of land to "bury [his] dead out of [his] sight" (Genesis 23:4).

Selling land was unusual in the ancient world. It was usually obtained through inheritance or by conquering it. The fact that Abraham was able to buy a portion of land, in what was to become his posterity's promised land, was miraculous. Sarah, the matriarch of the Abrahamic covenant, was the first to be laid to rest in the promised land—the homeland of the Jews.

• Milcah •

Milcah was Sarah's sister-in-law, the daughter of Abraham's brother Haran, who died. She had a brother named Lot and a sister named Iscah. She married Abraham's other brother Nahor—her uncle—about the same time that Sarah married Abraham (Genesis 11:29). When Abraham, Sarah, Lot, and Terah left Ur to go to Haran, Nahor and Milcah were not with them. This means that either they remained behind in Ur or that they had already moved to Haran before Abraham. Either way, we know that Nahor and Milcah eventually settled in Haran, where Milcah gave birth to eight sons. We also know that Nahor had a concubine named Reumah who bore him four sons (see Genesis 22:24).

When Abraham, Sarah, and Lot were commanded by the Lord to leave Haran and travel into Canaan (see Genesis 12), Milcah and Nahor remained behind. In fact, while Abraham and Sarah moved all over the place, Milcah and Nahor stayed in the same spot. This became important later when Abraham needed to find a good wife for his son Isaac. He knew exactly where his brother and his posterity were and could send his servant to Haran to find a wife for Isaac. The servant traveled to Haran and found Rebekah, the daughter of Milcah's youngest son, Bethuel.

Sometimes our lives are more like that of Milcah, who, unlike Sarah, was commanded to stay where she was. I have no doubt that Milcah's life was just as guided by the Spirit as Sarah's, but her instructions were to stay, not to go. That is sometimes the harder choice.

Recently several of our close friends in our ward moved away. As I was thinking about how sad I was that they couldn't stay in our ward forever, an interesting thought came to me. I thought about the parable of the olive trees in Jacob 5 and how the master in that vineyard was busy either grafting parts of trees together or "dunging about" the trees with fertilizer. I realized that sometimes we are "grafted" into a place; bound and permanently fixed. When we are grafted into a ward or a community, we truly become a part of it, and our presence there not only strengthens it but changes the very nature of the tree. Other times, though, the Lord uses us as "dung," and our mission in that ward or area is to fertilize and revitalize the tree. Unlike grafting, fertilizer is not permanent and must be reapplied with a new supply every so often. I realized that my friends who were leaving to be grafted into a new home had been like fertilizer for our ward, giving us much needed support, energy, and spiritual nourishment.

We need to remember that whether we are being grafted in or being used to "dung about," whether we are a Sarah who moved her whole life or a Milcah who stayed in the same spot, our lives can be guided by the Lord. We can trust that He has positioned us exactly where He needs us to be.

Hagar

Now Sarai Abram's wife bare him no children: and she had an handmaid, an Egyptian, whose name was Hagar.

And Sarai said unto Abram, Behold now, the Lord hath restrained me from bearing: I pray thee, go in unto my maid; it may be that I may obtain children by her. And Abram hearkened to the voice of Sarai.

Genesis 16:1–2

Hagar is sometimes seen as the black sheep of Abraham's family, the outsider whose son Ishmael just caused trouble for the chosen son, Isaac. Yet nothing can be further from the truth. Hagar not only spoke with God twice, something that few people in the scriptures (male or female) can claim, but she, like her counterpart Sarah, was also blessed with a noble posterity. She is held in high esteem by Muslims, who believe that the prophet Muhammad was a direct descendant of her son Ishmael.

Hagar was an Egyptian and the maidservant of Sarah, the wife of Abraham. We don't know how Hagar came to be owned by Sarah, but it is a good guess to assume that she was among the "menservants and maidservants" (Genesis 12:16) that Abraham and Sarah received from Pharaoh during their stay in Egypt. According to Jewish tradition, Hagar was one of Pharaoh's daughters who loved Sarah and believed in her God and chose to become her servant rather than stay in her father's house and worship the Egyptian gods.

In Genesis 15, God promised Abram that even though Sarah had not yet born a child, he would be blessed with a son to inherit his property. Despite this promise, Sarah was still unable to have children. She described herself as being "restrained" from bearing (Genesis 16:2). In Genesis 18:11, she told the messengers (who again promised her a child) that she had ceased to be "after the manner of women," meaning that she had gone through menopause. Perhaps she held onto the hope that she would have a child, until she finally saw her monthly cycle cease.

When Sarai realized that there was no physical way for her to have a child, she told Abraham to take Hagar as his second wife, "that [she] may obtain children by her" (Genesis 16:2). In ancient times, it was an accepted practice for a woman who was unable to have children to gain children through one of her servants by "giving" the servant to her husband. The children born to the servant from this union would not be considered hers but would legally belong to her mistress. Think of it as the ancient form of surrogacy.[1]

We don't know how much say Hagar had in the arrangement, but we know that as a servant she had few rights over anything in her life, including her body. Sarai had the right to force Hagar to obey her, but it seems unlikely that was the case in this situation. The Book of Jasher, an apocryphal text, gives us insight into the relationship between Hagar and Sarai: "For Hagar learned all the ways of Sarai as Sarai taught her, she was not in any way deficient in following her good ways."[2] We might suppose that Sarai even selected Hagar to bear children for her because she loved her and because of Hagar's good character. I think most women in Sarai's position would naturally choose a good friend or someone they trusted to carry their child, certainly not an enemy or a rival.

Hagar became pregnant not long after her marriage to Abram. This pregnancy changed the relationship between Sarai and Hagar. Genesis 16:5 tells us, "Once she [Hagar] saw that she had conceived, her mistress was despised in her eyes." Again, we don't understand all that took place between Hagar and Sarai, but the Book of Jasher records the following:

> When Hagar saw that she had conceived she rejoiced greatly, and her mistress was despised in her eyes, and she said within herself, This can only be that I am better before God than Sarai my mistress, for all the days that my mistress has been with my lord, she did not conceive, but me the Lord has caused in so short a time to conceive by him.

> And when Sarai saw that Hagar had conceived by Abram, Sarai was jealous of her handmaid, and Sarai said within herself, This is surely nothing else but that she must be better than I am.[3]

This change in Hagar made things difficult between her and Sarai, and after appealing to Abram for help, Sarai "dealt hardly with her" (Genesis 16:6). The words "dealt hardly with" are translated from the Hebrew word *anah*, which means "to humble" or "to afflict."[5] The word isn't used to describe physical afflictions but rather ones of the soul. I don't think it means that Sarai beat Hagar or physically hurt her. I think it means that she humbled her—afflicted her soul—perhaps by treating Hagar unkindly or simply by reminding Hagar that she was still a slave and her child would be Sarai's.

While we can only speculate about circumstances, I think we can deduce that Hagar felt her situation was desperate. To escape the situation, Hagar ran away. She had traveled quite a distance when she came to a "fountain of water in the wilderness," where she was met by the angel of the Lord (Genesis 16:7). The angel addressed her as "Hagar, Sarai's maid" (verse 8), a gentle reminder that even though she had a name and identity of her own, she was still obligated to serve Sarai. He also told her that she should "return to [her] mistress and submit [herself] under her hands" (verse 9). The word translated as "submit" is the Hebrew word *anah*, the same word that was used to describe Sarai's treatment of Hagar. God was telling her to go back to Sarai and Abram and to humble herself to her situation. He didn't say, "Go back and I'll make everything better." He simply told her to go back and to be humble, trusting that He had a plan for her and for her child.

God then gave Hagar a deeply personal revelation about the child she was carrying, including his gender, his name, his future mission in life, and a glimpse of the great nation that would spring from him. In her book *Forgotten Women of God*, Diana Webb wrote this about Hagar:

> Since there are so few annunciation scenes in the scripture, and since each is so significant, we can see what a great honor God pays to Hagar in Genesis 16. He has been especially mindful of her afflictions, and he tells her so. Hagar is a different woman from the one who has fled into the wilderness. She now knows that a power higher than herself notices her and that knowledge transforms her. She is now free in a way that returning to slavery can never eradicate. She is important to God, and that gives her a new sense of self-worth. . . . Hagar has learned that God has a plan for her. . . . She will tell her story to Abram and Sarai and teach them things about God that they need to know: That God does indeed hear the cries of the suffering, the downcast, and the abandoned; that every human soul has dignity and worth. Hagar's new knowledge is empowering. If God is with her, she can survive anything."[5]

After this revelation, Hagar did something that no one else in the scriptures ever does. While others, such as Jacob and Abraham, named the place where they saw God, Hagar gave God a name. She called Him "Thou God seest me" (Genesis 16:13), or more plainly, "the God that sees me." God is called by many names in the scriptures, but out of them all Hagar's is my personal favorite. It reminds me, like it did her, that no matter where I am or what is happening to me, God can literally see me. The Creator of the universe—a being of unfathomable power and glory—sees and cares about me. In some of the hardest moments of my life, I have found myself calling out in prayer to "the God that sees me."

Not only did Hagar name God but she also named the well where she had her visit Beer-lahai-roi, which means "the well of him who liveth and seeth me" (Genesis 16:14).[6] I think the image of a well, especially a deep well of fresh water in the desert, is appropriate for God. He is the source of all life, all understanding, and all peace. Yet so often when we are struggling we, like Hagar, are blindly focused on our problems and are unaware of the depth of the blessings in front of us.

In fact, if you read Hagar's story closely, you will see that God promised her, just like He did Abraham and Sarah in the Abrahamic covenant, that He would, "multiply [her] seed exceedingly, that it shall not be numbered for multitude" (Genesis 16:10). The

Bible later tells us that Ishmael had twelve sons who were "twelve princes according to their nations" (Genesis 25:16),[7] just like Sarah's son Isaac, whose grandsons would later become the twelve tribes of Israel. In fact, Muslims believe that the Arab nations trace their lineage back to Ishmael.

The Lord had blessed Hagar, but she couldn't see it. God knew that Hagar needed a little eternal perspective. Getting a glimpse of the bigger picture and gaining a testimony that God heard her cries and that He could *literally* see her changed everything for Hagar. With that knowledge, she could return to Abram and Sarai and give birth to her son, Ishmael, whose name so appropriately, means "God hears" (see Genesis 16:11).

The second time we meet Hagar, her situation is much different. After returning to Sarah, she spent two decades in Abraham's household, supposedly at peace with her situation. She would have watched as her son Ishmael grew into a young man, beloved by his father. She also would have been witness to the miraculous events surrounding the birth of Isaac, who was born when Ishmael was about fourteen years old.[8]

Several years after Isaac's birth, Sarah became concerned that Ishmael, who would have been around seventeen or eighteen years old at this point, was "mocking" (Genesis 21:9).[9] The text doesn't say that he was mocking *Isaac*, just that he was mocking.[10] The Hebrew word used here for mocking is *tsachaq*, which means to "laugh outright in merriment or scorn." It is the same word that is used when Sarah "laughed" when the sacred messengers tell them they will have a child, but it also used elsewhere in the Bible to describe situations of irreverent (and sexually suggestive) revelry.[11]

It may have been that Ishmael's "mocking" was not so much making fun of Isaac but that he was showing a general scorn or disregard for sacred things. It is interesting that Hagar was told when she was pregnant with Ishmael that he would be "a wild man" (Genesis 16:12). In Hebrew, this means "wild ass," indicating that he would be freedom loving and perhaps as stubborn as the wild donkeys who dwelt in the desert. This prophecy certainly referred to Ishmael's future in which he, and later his people, would live as nomads in the desert. Yet, it may have also been indicative of his personality—freedom loving and stubborn—which may have made living in Abraham's household difficult.

Because of Ishmael's "mocking," Sarah told Abraham that she thought he should send Ishmael and Hagar away, "for the son of this bondwoman shall not be heir with my son, even with Isaac" (Genesis 21:10). It sounds like, even after all this time, there was still debate over who would be Abraham's heir. Technically, Ishmael was Abraham's firstborn son who traditionally received the birthright and a double portion of his father's inheritance. Yet in what is often the case in the Bible, the birthright did not necessarily have to go to the oldest son.[12] It was the patriarch's prerogative to entrust the birthright to the son he felt was most deserving of it. It sounds like Sarah, who knew that Isaac was intended to be the recipient of the covenant made to *her* and Abraham, was concerned that Abraham might give the birthright to Ishmael, for whom it was not intended and who it appears would not have taken it seriously.

In response to Sarah's concerns, Abraham was "very griev[ed] . . . because of his son" (Genesis 21:11) and approached the Lord about what he should do. God told Abraham not to worry and to "hearken" unto the voice of Sarah. He gave Abraham a confirmation of what Sarah already knew that "in Isaac shall thy seed be called" (verse 12). Even so, Abraham was reluctant to send Ishmael and Hagar away because he loved them. God assured him that He would take care of them and that from "the son of the bondwoman will I make a nation, because he is thy seed" (verse 13). The "God who sees me" had been mindful of Hagar's situation thus far, and he was not going to leave her alone now. Abraham's treatment of Hagar and Ishmael seems harsh, especially since the offense appears to be minor. Muslims, who believe Ishmael was the covenant son instead of Isaac, teach that God commanded Abraham to leave Hagar and Ishmael in the desert to test their obedience to His commandments.[13] If such an explanation is true, it wouldn't be the first time God had sent a chosen person—or people—into the wilderness to refine and test them.

After wandering in the desert, Hagar and Ishmael eventually ran out of water and were unable to find a well. Even though the Bible text calls him a "child," Ishmael would have been a teenager. He became dehydrated and sick. Hagar, unable to do anything for him, "cast the child under one of the shrubs" and went away "as it were a bowshot" from him so that she did not have to see him die (Genesis 21:15–16). Her situation looked desperate and bleak. She had lost everything—her home, her husband, her security. Now she was losing her son. This time not only could she not *see* the well, but she didn't even think there *was* a well. She did what most of us would do and "lift[ed] up her voice, and wept" (verse 16).

As she wept, the angel of the Lord called to her out of heaven and told her, "Fear not; for God hath heard the voice of the lad where he is. Arise, lift up the lad, and hold him in thine hand; for I will make him a great nation" (Genesis 21:17–18). Then "God opened her eyes, and she saw a well of water" (verse 19). How surprised she must have been to realize that water, the very thing she needed most, had been right below her the whole time. She simply couldn't see it.

After seeing the well of water, she was able to fill her bottle and give her son something to drink. Ishmael recovered, and he and his mother dwelt in the wilderness of Paran, which today is eastern Saudi Arabia. When it was time to marry, his mother chose an Egyptian wife for him, and he dwelt in the desert. He became an archer, and even though he was not the covenant son, "God was with the lad" (Genesis 21:20). When Abraham died many years later, Ishmael and Isaac buried their father together, an indication that there was no lingering animosity between them (see Genesis 25:9).

Hagar, whose life was never easy, is a testament that we each have a "God who sees me." A God who knows who we are, who we have been, and who we are destined to become. He sees the big picture of our life and is often in the details of it, guiding and directing in ways we cannot see. I think this is most true at the times life doesn't go as we hoped. Those are the times that God leads us down new and often rocky and dry paths. Like Hagar, taking a new path can make us feel alone and confused, but we can trust that God has a well of water prepared for us. Just because we can't see the well doesn't mean it isn't there. We just need to allow God to open our eyes and show us where to drink.

• Polygamy •

The story of Sarah and Hagar raises some interesting questions about polygamy. In fact, polygamy is something that many of the Bible's main characters (Abraham, Jacob, David, and Solomon) practiced. From a Latter-day Saint perspective, the topic is even more interesting because Joseph Smith was told by God that he would "restore all things" (D&C 132:45) pertaining to the priesthood, which included the principle of plural marriage. This gives us insight that polygamy, as practiced by the early patriarchs and prophets, was not just a cultural practice but rather a spiritual one.

The topic of polygamy can be hard for us to understand. Before God explained the law of plural marriage to Joseph Smith, he told him to "prepare thy heart to receive and obey the instructions which I am about to give unto you" (D&C 132:3), knowing that what he was about to teach Joseph would be difficult for him to comprehend and to follow. I know that coming to understand God's laws on marriage—including plural marriage—can increase our testimony rather than weaken it.

One of the best places to start the discussion of plural marriage is in the Book of Mormon where the prophet Jacob taught the Nephites that God's commandment for them was, "There shall not be any man among you have save it be one wife; and concubines he shall have none" (Jacob 2:27). Many of the Nephite men had been taking multiple wives because they sought "to excuse themselves in committing whoredoms" (verse 23). They justified their actions because David and Solomon had also taken many wives and concubines. Jacob explained to them that what David and Solomon had done had been "abominable" (verse 24) in God's eyes because, while God had approved of some of their marriages, they both took other wives who were not permitted by God to gratify their lust.[14]

Jacob explained to the Nephites that polygamy was only permissible when it was given as a commandment, through God's chosen prophet. "For if I will, saith the Lord of Hosts, raise up seed unto me, I will command my people" (Jacob 2:30). Otherwise, God's law was monogamy. That is a pattern that still is true today. Polygamy is only allowed when God reveals it to His prophet and commands His people to live it; otherwise the law is always one man, one woman.

The story of Hagar and Sarah also helps us better understand God's laws about plural marriage. Doctrine and Covenants 132:34 illuminates their story by telling us that "God commanded Abraham, and Sarah gave Hagar to Abraham to wife. And why did she do it? Because this was the law; and from Hagar sprang many people. This, therefore was fulfilling, among other things, the promises." This verse tells us several important things. First it tells us that Hagar became Abraham's wife, not simply because Sarah wanted children as the Genesis account states, but because God had commanded Abraham to practice plural marriage.

Second, this verse tells us that Abraham taught Sarah this commandment and that she followed it, and even suggested to Abraham that he choose Hagar because she thought (at the time) that it would be a good match. I think this is an important distinction because it makes it clear that Abraham wasn't lusting after Hagar but that Sarah arranged the marriage herself. Later, when the situation became difficult for all three of them, Sarah blamed Abraham, telling him, "My wrong be upon thee" (Genesis 16:5), or in other words, "You are responsible for the wrong I am suffering." After venting her feelings, she calmed down and ended her remarks with, "The Lord judge between me and thee" (verse 5), which today might sound like, "God judge who is wrong, me or you." These words may indicate that Sarah recognized the choice to bring Hagar into their family had not just been Abraham's but was her responsibility as well.

The third thing that Doctrine and Covenants 132:34 makes clear is that polygamy is part of God's law of marriage. This doesn't mean that everyone is to practice it, but I think the scriptures make it clear that plural marriage, as it relates to sealing ordinances and the Abrahamic covenant, does have a place in God's plan. Fourth, we learn that "from Hagar sprang many people" (D&C 132:34) and that one of the purposes of polygamy was, as Jacob taught in the Book or Mormon, to "raise up seed" (Jacob 2:30) unto God.

Last, this scripture tells us that Hagar's marriage to Abraham was "fulfilling, among other things, the promises" (D&C 132:34). That phrase, "the promises," is used elsewhere in scripture and appears to refer to temple covenants and the sealing power. For example, Doctrine and Covenants 2:2–3 restates the famous scripture about the return of Elijah: "He shall plant in the hearts of the children *the promises* made to the fathers, and the hearts of the children shall turn

to their fathers. If it were not so, the whole earth would be utterly wasted at his coming" (emphasis added). These promises are also mentioned again in Doctrine and Covenants 132:63, where God explains that one of the purposes of plural marriage was "to fulfil the promise which was given by my Father before the foundation of the world."

It is interesting to remember that a synonym for the word *promise* is *covenant*. We often explain the concept of a covenant as a "two-way promise." If you promise God that you will (fill in the blank), then He will promise you that He will (fill in the blank). Covenants can be formal, such as baptism and the temple ordinances, but they can also be intensely personal, such as the ones we make in our prayers and in our intimate relationships with God. If you go back and reread those verses about "the promises" but instead substitute in the word *covenants,* I think it illuminates their meaning. Though we may not always understand how, I think God wants us to understand that plural marriage is a way in which He honors and fulfills His promises—His covenants—with *all* His children.

I like to think that Sarah, when she chose to give Hagar to Abraham, understood the eternal nature of what she was doing. Though it wasn't easy for either of them, Sarah and Hagar created the house of Israel and the house of Ishmael—two nations of promise—through whom the Lord would perform His work.

Lot's Wife

Then the Lord rained upon Sodom and upon Gomorrah brimstone and fire from the Lord out of heaven. . . .

But his wife looked back from behind him, and she became a pillar of salt.

Genesis 19:24, 26

The story of Lot and his wife is told in Genesis 19. The Joseph Smith Translation makes extensive changes to this story, giving us added insight and clarification. The first thing the Joseph Smith Translation clarifies is that Lot was not sitting at the "gate of Sodom" (Genesis 19:1) but rather "in the door of his house in the city of Sodom" when not two, but three, angels were sent to find him (in Genesis 19:1, footnote *a*). This is an interesting detail because it tells us that Lot was living in a house within Sodom itself.[1]

In Sunday School when we share the story of Lot, we tend of focus on the fact that when Lot and Abraham separated after their time in Egypt, Lot chose the northern, more prosperous land and "pitched his tent toward Sodom" (Genesis 13:12). The lesson then usually follows that we must watch what we set our hearts on, or figuratively "pitch our tents" toward, because, like Lot, we might find ourselves not sitting on the outside but eventually *inside* the sinful city itself.

Yet the Apostle Peter gives us a much different picture of Lot. He says that God "delivered Lot, vexed with the filthy conversation of the wicked" and describes Lot as a "righteous man dwelling among them [the people of Sodom], in seeing and hearing, vexed his righteous soul from day to day with their unlawful deeds" (2 Peter 2:7–8). Peter's account makes it sound like God had sent Lot, a righteous man, to Sodom to warn or teach them.

In Luke 17:32, Jesus also admonished the Pharisees to "remember Lot's wife," but his meaning was unclear. Was he holding her up as a good example or a bad example? Peter would have known better than any of us what Jesus meant, and his words about Lot let us view him and his family differently. Perhaps they were not a rotten bunch like some have portrayed them, but rather a righteous family living in a wicked city, trying their best to make good choices. This is a theme many modern-day readers can certainly relate to.

When the men of Sodom learned that there were three holy men in Lot's house, they surrounded the house and demanded that Lot "bring them out unto us, that we may know them" (Genesis 19:5). The footnote to this verse explains that the word *know* used here is "a euphemism in place of a sexual word" (in Genesis 19:5, footnote *a*). If you use your imagination, I am sure you can think of what crude word the men would have used today to describe what they planned to do. There is a reason that we use the word *sodomy* to describe perverted sexuality today.

In Genesis 19:8, we read that Lot tried to pawn his daughters off on these wicked men instead of letting them defile his guests. Thankfully, the Joseph Smith Translation removes this part of the story and clarifies that when Lot refused to let the men of Sodom have his guests, they threatened to take his daughters instead. According to the Joseph Smith Translation of Genesis 19:8, Lot pled for his daughters' safety and would not let the men into his house, even when they tried to break down the door (Joseph Smith Translation, Genesis 19:13, [in Genesis 19:8, footnote *a*]).

After the Sodomites left, the three holy men told Lot to take himself, his wife, his daughters, and his sons-in-law and leave the city immediately. Right away, Lot went and spoke to his sons-in-law and his married daughters and told them that they needed to leave that very night because God was going to destroy the city. Yet Lot's sons-in-law would not listen to him. They thought "he seemed as one that mocked" (Genesis 19:14).

Lot and his wife were now faced with a difficult choice. The holy men were telling them that they had to leave, quickly, but doing so meant leaving their married daughters, sons-in-law, and perhaps grandchildren behind in the city. It is no wonder that scriptures tell us that Lot and his wife "lingered" (verse 16) in the city. I doubt that their hesitation had much to do with leaving behind their home or possessions but rather leaving behind their children. Wouldn't each of us, if we knew that the lives of our loved ones were in immediate danger, stay if we thought we could convince them they were in danger?

Eventually, because the Lord was "merciful unto him," the three holy men "laid hold" upon Lot's hand and the hands of his wife and two unmarried daughters and "set [them] without the city" (Genesis 19:16). They instructed Lot and his family to "escape for thy life;

look not behind thee, neither stay thou in all the plain; escape to the mountain, lest thou be consumed" (Genesis 19:17). Sodom was known for its "slimepits," which means "bitumen pits" (in Genesis 14:10, footnote *a*). According to the International Standard Bible Encyclopedia, "Bitumen is a hydrocarbon allied to petroleum and natural gas. It is a lustrous black solid, breaking with a conchoidal fracture, burning with a yellow flame, and melting when ignited. It is probably derived from natural gas and petroleum by a process of oxidation and evaporation. . . . It is found in small lumps and larger masses in the cretaceous limestone on the west side of the Dead Sea, and there is reason to believe that considerable quantities of it rise to the surface of the Dead Sea during earthquakes."[2]

Some scholars speculate that there was a huge earthquake in Sodom that liquefied and ignited these bitumen pits, thus creating a huge, fiery landslide that sunk Sodom into the ground. If this happened, then the instructions the holy men gave Lot makes sense. Their instruction to "look not behind you" wasn't a warning that looking back would result in some magical punishment from God. As any runner or swimmer will tell you, even the slight turn of your head to view where your opponent is or what is behind you can slow you down significantly. It may have been that these holy men were telling Lot's family that they had waited too long in the city and now it was time to run for their lives. They didn't even have time to look over their shoulders.

Lot, realizing perhaps that he was old and not as limber as he once had been, told the holy men that he didn't think he could make it to the mountain. He asked their permission to flee to a nearby city called Zoar, where he thought he would be safe. The holy men accepted Lot's new plan and told Lot they would hold back the destruction of Sodom until he and his family had safely reached the city (see Genesis 19:18–23). Yet, it appears that Lot's wife never made it. Genesis 19:26 tells us that when Lot fled, "his wife looked back from behind him, and she became a pillar of salt." The phrase "behind him" tells us that Lot's wife was not with him. She had either lingered longer behind, she was slower than him, or she had purposely turned back to Sodom.

I wonder how many of us can truly fault her. Behind her, in Sodom, were her daughters, their husbands, and her grandchildren. How many of us, even running for our lives, would be able to forget that and not, even just in our hearts, look back? Elder Holland, in his beautiful talk "Remember Lot's Wife," says that Lot's wife reminds us that *"faith is always pointed toward the future. Faith always has to do with blessings and truths and events that will yet be efficacious in our lives. So a more theological way to talk about Lot's wife is to say that she did not have faith. She doubted the Lord's ability to give her something better than she already had. Apparently she thought—fatally, as it turned out—that nothing that lay ahead could possibly be as good as those moments she was leaving behind."[3]

I agree with Elder Holland that, even in times of great trial, we must always have our hearts filled with faith to the future. Yet I think we also must remember that Lot's wife was thinking about her children. How could she leave them behind to be destroyed? I imagine her, like a mother dashing into a burning building to save her baby, turning back to Sodom, not longing for its comforts but trying to save her children.

The consequence for her look back was that she "became a pillar of salt" (Genesis 19:26). The Hebrew word for "pillar" is *nětsiyb*, and it means "something stationary, as in a military post, a statue." It is most often translated in the Old Testament as the word *garrison*, indicating someone who is positioned as a guard or sentinel. Also, we know that salt is a symbolic substance in the scriptures and was often used in making covenants. If we think about Lot's wife becoming a "sentinel of salt," that changes our understanding of her story in an incredible way. Michelle Stone provided some intriguing insight into this symbol:

> A pillar of salt—what an amazing symbol! Seen in this symbolic light it becomes one of the greatest and most powerful compliments God could give us. It speaks of incredible power to save. If we become a pillar of salt, we have joined the Savior in his work in a remarkable way. Our greatest exemplar, the one we strive above all to emulate, willingly gave His life to save others. He was not concerned about his own comfort, safety, or even salvation. He could have easily saved himself, but he looked outward, rather than inward. His heart was so drawn out in love toward His fellow man, that he did not count the personal cost, but rather gave everything in an effort to save. What then of His commandment to "love one another as I have loved you?" (John 13:34) Does that not compel us to also have our hearts so drawn out in love that we are willing to give anything and everything, even our lives if necessary, to save others? This seems to be one of the many parallels between motherhood and the role of the Savior, for that is where this kind of love most naturally occurs. His beautiful self-prophetic statement, "Greater love hath no man than this, that a man lay down his life for his friends," (John 15:13) rings out in invitation to each of us. The truth of this beautiful validation is not diminished if

we read it, "greater love hath no woman than this, that a mother lay down her life for her children."[4]

It is also interesting to think that if Sodom was destroyed unexpectedly by some sort of explosion or fiery earthquake, something similar to what happened in the Roman city of Pompeii might have occurred. People were "frozen" in place by the ash, becoming statues. If Lot's wife had been caught out on the plain during the destruction of Sodom, rather than within the safety of the city, it is possible she may have literally become a volcanic statue. Sodom was very close to the Dead Sea, and things there often become covered with salt. She, or something very like her, may have *literally* been preserved for people to see for years afterward—a powerful monument to a mother's love.

I see another powerful lesson in her story. As much as we may wish to, we cannot "save" people from their sins or the consequences of their choices. As I have served in the Relief Society, I have seen how easy it is, when faced with people's problems, to want to jump in and try to save them. A post someone shared on my blog entitled "'Relief' Society vs. 'Fix-it' Society" changed my whole perspective. The author wrote:

> Only Christ has the power to fix.
>
> We are directed to give *relief*, not to fix. The work of fixing is the work of the Atonement. We can't fix situations and we can't fix people. For example, when someone loses a loved one, we can't bring them back to life; when someone loses their job, we can't get it back for them.
>
> We understand that we can't fix those situations. . . .

Why does a child feel better when he cuts his finger and Mom soothes, cleanses, applies antiseptic, and a bandage, and then kisses their owie? The child feels better because someone 1) understood his pain/need [and] 2) offered the help that was possible.

That is what Relief is:

–understanding someone, their needs and their pain
–offering acceptance and love
–offering the help that is possible

When someone breaks their arm, a doctor can't fix it. Instead the doctor understands there is pain and offers relief. He provides alignment and support. But the work of healing happens on the inside.

Sometimes surgery is needed. But I am not a surgeon—Christ is the great physician. . . .

We are not capable of fixing anyone. And it is not our responsibility.[5]

I think this tendency to want to "fix" people becomes even more pronounced when the people are members of our family. Our love for them compels us to help. Yet, like Lot's wife, sometimes there is nothing we can do. As much as it hurts, we must allow people to feel the natural consequences for their sins and choices. Even if it means seeing them struggle or hit "rock bottom." All we can do for people is to love them and point them toward the source of true healing—Jesus Christ.

I don't know if any of us would have acted differently if we had been in the shoes of Lot's wife. I hope that as we think of her—not as a disobedient villain but as a loving mother—her story can rise in our estimation and that we will see her as a symbol of the type of love our Savior has for us. I love these words by Michelle Stone about Lot's wife:

Her voice seems to cry out and mingle with the Savior's, "What use to save myself when the precious ones I love will be destroyed? I will not selfishly abandon them! Even if it requires the sacrifice of my own life, I will never turn my back! I will never stop loving, stop reaching out, or stop striving for their salvation." What a powerful message for all of us, but especially for mothers! True, Christ said, "He that loveth father or mother more than me is not worthy of me: and he that loveth son or daughter more than me is not worthy of me" (Matt 10:37). But Lot's wife did not choose her children over Christ, she chose them over her own self preservation. She did not follow them into sin—she reached out in an infinitely loving attempt to save them from the sin of their society. She is a type of Christ, and that is why he wants us to remember her. She does not judge and turn away, she loves and turns back, and by so doing gives us permission to do the same.[6]

> "*Greater love hath no woman than this, that a mother lay down her life for her children.*"

Lot's Daughters

After their narrow escape from Sodom, Lot's daughters did something bizarre. They got their father drunk and then both slept with him. Their justification for this was, "Our father has become old, and there is not a man on the earth to come in unto us to live with us after the manner of all that live on the earth" (Joseph Smith Translation, Genesis 19:37). It seems that, after having just witnessed the complete destruction of Sodom, they feared that the entire world had been destroyed. As far as they knew, their father might have been the last man on the earth. Their desire was to "preserve the seed of our father" (Genesis 19:32), which makes sense, seeing that their mother and the rest of their family had all just been destroyed.

The Joseph Smith Translation clarifies that in these two daughters "did wickedly" (Joseph Smith Translation, Genesis 19:39 [in Genesis 19:35, footnote *a*]) and that they did these things without their father's awareness (He must have been very drunk!). Both the daughters became pregnant by their father. The firstborn daughter gave birth to a son named Moab, and the younger daughter gave birth to son named Ben-ammi. Moab became the father of the Moabites, and Ben-ammi became the father of the Ammonites, two peoples who feature in the Old Testament as enemies to the house of Israel.

Rebekah

And they called Rebekah, and said unto her, Wilt thou go with this man? And she said, I will go. . . .

And they blessed Rebekah, and said unto her, Thou art our sister, be thou the mother of thousands of millions, and let thy seed possess the gate of those which hate them.

And Rebekah arose, and her damsels, and they rode upon the camels, and followed the man: and the servant took Rebekah, and went his way.

Genesis 24:58, 60–61

President Julie B. Beck stated that Rebekah was "one of the most pivotal and important people in the history of mankind."[1] This, President Beck went on to explain, is because "without a Rebekah who knew who she was, the house of Israel would not have been brought forth. Without a Rebekah who knew her responsibilities in the house of Israel, that house would not have come to pass. Without a Rebekah who knew how to receive revelation, the house of Israel would not have been brought forth. Without a Rebekah who understood the blessings of the priesthood, the house of Israel would not have been brought forth."[2]

Rebekah was a pivotal character in the preservation and construction of the house of Israel and a guardian of the Abrahamic covenant, a covenant that blesses the lives of all of God's children.

• I Will Go •

After Sarah's death, Abraham sent his servant to find a wife for his son Isaac from among the posterity of Abraham's brother Nahor and to bring her back to Abraham's tent. The servant was apprehensive about this request and asked Abraham, "[What if] the woman will not be willing to follow me unto this land"? (Genesis 24:5). Abraham was adamant and explained to the servant that the Lord had commanded him. There was a woman, somewhere among Abraham's kindred, who God had prepared to be a wife for Isaac.

With faith that he would find this special woman—and convince her to leave her family forever, travel hundreds of miles through the desert, and marry an unknown man—the servant set off with a caravan of ten camels. When he arrived at the city of Nahor, where he supposed Abraham's brother resided, he rested by a well outside of the city. It was evening, the time when the women of the city went out to draw water, and Abraham's servant, not having any idea how he was to find "the one," asked God for a sign (Genesis 24:12–14).[3]

"Behold, I stand here by the well of water," the servant prayed. "Let it come to pass, that the damsel to whom I shall say, Let down thy pitcher, I pray thee, that I may drink; and she shall say, Drink, and I will give thy camels drink also: Let the same be she that thou hast appointed for thy servant Isaac" (Genesis 24:13–14). This was no small sign that the servant was asking for. He had a caravan of ten camels who had been traveling a long distance. When thirsty, camels can drink up to thirty-five gallons of water. If a woman were to give the camels just a small drink, say ten gallons each, that would have been a total of one hundred gallons of water she'd have to pull up from the well!

Immediately after the servant finished his prayer, Rebekah came to the well. Though the servant did not know it yet, Rebekah was the daughter of Bethuel, who was the son of Micah, the wife of Abraham's brother. She was very beautiful, and the Joseph Smith Translation tells us that she was "a virgin, very fair to look upon, such as the servant of Abraham had not seen, neither had any man known the like unto her" (Joseph Smith Translation, Genesis 24:16). As Rebekah approached the well, Abraham's servant ran to meet her and asked her, "Let me, I pray thee, drink a little water of thy pitcher" (Genesis 24:17). She graciously offered him a drink, and when he was finished she told him she would "draw water for thy camels also, until they have done drinking" (verse 19).

> ———— •✦• ————
>
> Abraham's servant wasn't basing his decision on who should be Isaac's wife based on frivolous qualities such as being beautiful, well-dressed, or rich. He was looking for a girl who was Christlike and had inner strength (and some good muscles). A girl who would go above and beyond and show charity to a stranger. How great would it be if all young adults, when seeking a spouse, had this type of mindset? How might we each construct our own "camel test" to determine the inner goodness and spirit of a potential partner?
>
> ———— •✦• ————

I love it that she doesn't ask him if she can water his camels for him; she just does it. I've wondered if watering camels was something she often did for travelers or if it was an impulsive offer (that perhaps after hauling her ninetieth bucket of water, she may have repented of). Either way, it is apparent that Rebekah was heeding the promptings of the Holy Ghost and was at the right place, doing the right thing at the right time. She'd simply had a generous thought and acted on it.

President Bonnie D. Parkinson shared this story, which reminds me of Rebekah:

My daughter-in-law's mother, Susan, was a wonderful seamstress. President Kimball lived in their ward. One Sunday, Susan noticed that he had a new suit. Her father had recently returned from a trip to New York and had brought her some exquisite silk fabric. Susan thought that fabric would make a handsome tie to go with President Kimball's new suit. So on Monday she made the tie. She wrapped it in tissue paper and walked up the block to President Kimball's home.

On her way to the front door, she suddenly stopped and thought, "Who am I to make a tie for the prophet? He probably has plenty of them." Deciding she had made a mistake, she turned to leave.

Just then Sister Kimball opened the front door and said, "Oh, Susan!"

Stumbling all over herself, Susan said, "I saw President Kimball in his new suit on Sunday. Dad just brought me some silk from New York . . . and so I made him a tie."

Before Susan could continue, Sister Kimball stopped her, took hold of her shoulders, and said: "Susan, never suppress a generous thought."[4]

I have those words, "Never suppress a generous thought," displayed in my home. They remind me that all good things come from God and that when we have generous or charitable thoughts, we shouldn't ignore them or rationalize them away. Like Rebekah offering to water ten thirsty camels, we never know when our display of kindness will be the answer to someone else's prayer.

As Rebekah watered his camels (which probably took her a while), Abraham's servant "held his peace" (Genesis 24:21), wondering if this could be the girl God had chosen for Isaac. She had fulfilled his sign by watering the camels, but he had been commanded to take a woman from among Abraham's relatives. The servant still didn't know what this young woman's lineage was. When Rebekah finished watering the camels, the servant gave her a golden earring and two gold bracelets. There was only one "earring" because it was most likely a nose ring! It would have been worn like a cuff on the side of the nose and was very stylish—and in no way forbidden—in Rebekah's time.[5]

The servant then asked Rebekah two probing questions. First, he asked, "Whose daughter art thou?" (Genesis 24:23). He was hoping that she was related to Abraham's brother Nahor and thus be "the one" he had been sent to find. Second, he asked, "Is there room in thy father's house for us to lodge in?" (verse 23). This was a sly way of finding out whether she lived in her "father's house" or her "husband's house." When Abraham's servant heard her response, which was that she was Abraham's niece and that there was room in her "father's house," he bowed his head and began to praise God, thanking Him for leading him to the woman destined to be Isaac's wife.

She was excited by the evening's events and ran back to tell her family. When Rebekah's brother, Laban, saw the jewelry and heard Rebekah's story, he went to meet the servant at the well and invited him into their home. Though they prepared a nice meal for him, the servant would not eat until he had told them what his errand was. He told Laban and Bethuel[6] of the task that Abraham had given him and how Rebekah had been the answer to his prayer. After hearing the story, Laban and Bethuel were convinced that "the thing proceedeth from the Lord" (Genesis 24:50) and readily agreed to Rebekah's marriage with Isaac.

The servant provided the family with a generous bride-price consisting of "jewels of silver, and jewels of gold, and raiment" given specifically to Rebekah, and other precious things given to Laban and Rebekah's mother (Genesis 24:53). The servant ate and talked with them all night and in the morning prepared to return to his master, Abraham. This alarmed Rebekah's family, who had assumed they would have time to prepare the things Rebekah would need before her departure. They asked that he wait at least ten days, but Abraham's servant insisted that he would leave that very day. This abrupt change of plans seems to have made Rebekah's family reconsider the arrangement, but they decided to ask Rebekah's opinion. When the situation was explained to her, Rebekah replied with three simple words: "I will go" (Genesis 24:58).

Those of us who grew up singing the Primary refrain of "I will go; I will do the thing the Lord commands"[7] will recognize Rebekah's words being echoed by Nephi generations later, when he too was asked to do a difficult task. These words not only demonstrate faith and obedience to God but also preparedness. Rebekah was ready to go the moment she was called upon. I'd like to think that the Lord had been preparing Rebekah and that she had been preparing herself to be ready for this moment.

Before Rebekah left her family, presumably never to see them again, her brother gave her a blessing. In it, he blessed her that she would be the "mother of thousands of millions" and that her seed would "possess the gate of those which hate them," which means they would conquer the cities of their enemies (Genesis 24:60). Rebekah must have been awed by this blessing. Not only did it promise her that her posterity would conquer and become a great nation, but that she would be the mother of "thousands of millions." Today we would call that a billion, but in Rebekah's time this would have been an inconceivable number. Though her family did not have much time to prepare her a dowry, they sent her off with something much more important—her patriarchal blessing.

After this blessing, Rebekah went with Abraham's servant, just one day after meeting him at the well. She traveled on the back of a camel for many miles until they reached Lahai-roi, where they saw Isaac meditating in the field. Genesis 24:64 tells us that when Rebekah saw Isaac "she lighted off the camel." In Hebrew, this can mean she "fell" off her camel! Perhaps she lost her balance or was distracted by Isaac's handsomeness. Or maybe she was just the type of girl who falls off camels (I think I'd be one of those too). Rebekah's ungraceful entrance didn't seem to bother Isaac at all. He loved her right from the start. He took her "into his mother Sarah's tent" and "she became his wife; and he loved her" (verse 67). This is such a beautiful love story.

• "Why Am I Thus?" •

The next we hear about Rebekah is twenty years later when, after struggling with infertility, Isaac "entreated the Lord for his wife" (Genesis 25:21). After this prayer, Rebekah, who was probably close to forty years old, became pregnant. It seems she had a very hard pregnancy because "the children struggled together within her"

• Deborah, Rebekah's Nurse •

When the word *nurse* is used in the scriptures, it usually refers to a woman who breastfed a child other than her own. In today's lingo, we would call them a "wet nurse." Often a nurse was employed to breastfeed a baby whose mother had died or who was too ill to sustain them. In the ancient world, there was no such thing as formula, so a child's only hope at a healthy life was if another woman took the baby to her breast and fed it, often for several years.

Apparently, something must have happened that necessitated a wet nurse for the baby Rebekah. We know that Rebekah's mother was living at the time Rebekah was married, so we can only speculate on why Deborah was chosen to nurse her. Was her mother ill sometime after her birth? Was her mother unwilling or unable to breastfeed? Did Deborah have her own baby that she nursed alongside Rebekah? Had Deborah lost her own child and so had an extra supply of milk?

No matter the circumstances, it is evident that Deborah and Rebekah shared a unique bond. Not only did Deborah go with Rebekah when she was married into Isaac's house (see Genesis 24:59), but the book of Genesis specifically mentions her death and gives the place of her burial (see Genesis 35:8). Normally, death announcements in the Bible are reserved for the great patriarchs and their wives. She must have been a great influence in Rebekah's life and a great woman to be so remembered.

(verse 22). We don't know what this means but Josephus, an ancient Jewish historian, records that "her belly was greatly burdened."[8] Other Jewish traditions say that she was in great pain and she couldn't find another woman who had been through something similar. This concern, confusion, and perhaps anguish over what was happening in her body led her to the Lord for guidance. Genesis 25:22 says that she "went to inquire of the Lord" and cried unto Him, "If it be so, why am I thus?" When faced with an unsolvable situation, Rebekah sought guidance from the Lord.

In reply to her prayer, the Lord gave her an incredible revelation. He told her, "Two nations are in thy womb, and two manner of people shall be separated from thy bowels; and the one people shall be stronger than the other people; and the elder shall serve the younger" (Genesis 25:23). In other words, she was carrying twins who would be born safely and live to fulfill their adult missions in life. That is the news every pregnant woman wants to hear! More troubling, God told her that her twins would "struggle" with each other and that the older twin would serve the younger. We see later how this information becomes crucial to understanding why she assisted her youngest son, Jacob, in securing the birthright from his father instead of letting it go to his older brother, Esau. Rebekah was not a manipulative mother who favored one son over another. She was acting on revelation God gave her before her sons were even born.

Like Rebekah, we can inquire of God and receive personal revelation about our bodies, our children, and our future. Julie B. Beck stated:

The ability to qualify for, receive, and act on personal revelation is the single most important skill that can be acquired in this life. . . .

Revelation can come hour by hour and moment by moment, as we do the right things. . . . Being in the right places allows us to receive guidance. It requires a conscious effort to diminish distractions, but having the Spirit of revelation makes it possible to prevail over opposition and persist in faith through difficult days and essential routine tasks. Personal revelation gives us the understanding of what to do every day to increase faith and personal righteousness, strengthen families and homes, and seek those who need our help. Because personal revelation is a constantly renewable source of strength, it is possible to feel bathed in help even during turbulent times.[9]

Things went just as the Lord had promised Rebekah they would, and she gave birth to twin boys, Esau and Jacob. Esau, who "came out red, all over like an hairy garment" (Genesis 25:25) became a hunter who married outside of the covenant and was a "grief of mind unto Isaac and to Rebekah" (Genesis 26:35). Jacob, on the other hand, was a "plain man" (Genesis 25:27), meaning he was "whole; complete; having moral integrity."

• A Lioness at the Gate: Jacob's Blessing •

Perhaps the most confusing and troubling part of Rebekah's story is her interference with the transfer of the birthright. We know that Esau had sold his birthright—his right to inherit the priesthood and the Abrahamic covenant—to Jacob because he did not value it (Genesis 25:29–34). Taking the wild and irreverent behavior of Esau into consideration, it seems obvious that Jacob would be the better son to inherit his father's birthright. Yet the scriptures tell us that Isaac favored Esau "because he did eat of his venison" (Genesis 25:28) and still intended to give Esau the birthright before he died.

When Rebekah heard this, she realized that Isaac was about to make a great mistake. She knew the type of women Esau had married, and she knew that they were not the type of women who would teach her grandchildren to follow God. She knew she could not entrust Esau, or his wives, to carry on the Abrahamic covenant—they were not worthy. God had given the revelation about who the birthright son was supposed to be to Rebekah, not Isaac. Isaac, it seems, was not aware of this, or refused to acknowledge it. So what was Rebekah supposed to do?

She made a bold choice and told Jacob to get two goats so that she could prepare a "savory meat" for his father that "he may bless thee before his death" (Genesis 27:9–10). Jacob was apprehensive about this, knowing that his father would be able to tell him apart from Esau. Rebekah didn't seem to be worried about this; she was confident in her plan and told Jacob she would take total responsibility for it. She simply told him, "Obey my voice" (Genesis 27:13).

Author Diana Webb gave some incredible insight into the meaning and significance of the blessing that Rebekah prepared Jacob to receive:

> Rebekah, knowing that this blessing will "before the Lord" (Genesis 27:7), is aware of the formality of this covenant blessing. (Many times in the Old Testament, "before the Lord" refers to a male Israelite appearing at the temple for certain holy day celebrations.) For this reason, she carefully clothes him in the sacred vestments of the birthright son. Since Rebekah has alerted us to the ritual nature of

this blessing, we can widen our view of the seemingly simple dialogue between Isaac and Jacob.

> Rebekah prepares the savory delicacies just as she knows Isaac likes them. She drapes the skins of the two kid-goats across Jacob's hands and neck. Isaac will not be able to "see" his son Esau, but Jacob will "feel" like Esau. Her beloved husband's eyes have become dim, but Rebekah will help him "see" clearly in bestowing the blessing upon the proper son. She will be his eyes. She is acting as a guardian of the covenant and is in control of the destiny of the house of Israel.[10]

Jacob then went to Isaac's tent, having been prepared for the encounter by his mother, and sought Isaac's blessing. Diana Webb continued:

> Jacob gives the name of his firstborn brother to his patriarch father in order to legitimize the blessing. That name is a key word that he knows his father will be listening for. In all probability, this was one of the instructions from Rebekah when she twice enjoined Jacob to "obey my voice." . . .

> Rebekah has anticipated the signs of recognition that Isaac would be looking for in her son. Isaac must test the birthright son to make sure he is not there unworthily. Rebekah has prepared Jacob's hands so that he will pass the test of recognition put forth by Isaac. . . .

> Following the ritual meal, Isaac entreats his son to come close and kiss him. While in this mutual embrace, he is satisfied that the tokens of recognition have been met. All his doubts seem to disperse, and Isaac blesses Jacob with the coveted patriarchal blessing.[11]

There are two possibilities we can consider. One is that Isaac, being senile and confused, could no longer tell his sons apart—not even by their voice—and that he was completely in the dark throughout the whole blessing. The other possibility is that Isaac, upon hearing Jacob's voice and hearing him give all the signs of recognition, had a change of heart and realized, as Rebekah had, that Jacob was the correct son to receive the birthright. Either situation is possible, but I think based on Isaac's reaction later, when he refuses to revoke the blessing he gave Jacob (something he could have done), we see that he was aware of and took responsibility for what he had done.

After Jacob received the blessing, Rebekah began to fear for his life. Esau was extremely angry about what had happened and vowed to kill Jacob. Rebekah went to Jacob and warned him to steer clear of his brother. Again, she told him to "obey my voice" (Genesis 27:43) and to go to her brother Laban in Haran and stay there until it was safe to come home. "I will send, and fetch thee from thence," Rebekah promised. "Why should I be deprived also of you both in one day?" (verse 45). She knew that if she didn't do something soon she would lose both of her sons.

Rebekah, though, was not completely honest with Jacob. She had an ulterior motive. Like Abraham had before her, Rebekah knew that to protect the covenant, Jacob needed to marry a woman who would share a similar faith. She was willing to let her son go, perhaps never seeing him again, if it meant that the sacred covenant would continue.

Rebekah told Isaac that she was "weary of [her] life" because of the women Esau had married and that "if Jacob take a wife of these daughters of Heth ... what good shall my life do me?" (Genesis 27:46). She had spent her whole life following God and preparing her sons to bear the priesthood and honor the covenants. If neither of them did, she felt her life would be a failure. Isaac talked to Jacob and told him to go to Laban's house and to find a wife—an instruction that would excite most young men.

After Jacob's departure, we hear nothing more of Rebekah. As far as we know, she never saw Jacob again. Yet through her son and the righteous women he would marry, her mission to guard and perpetuate the Abrahamic covenant was fulfilled. The Joseph Smith Translation for Rebekah's blessing, the one in which she was promised to be the "mother of thousands of millions" was changed by Joseph Smith to read, "Be thou *blessed* of thousands of millions" (Joseph Smith Translation, Genesis 24:65; emphasis added). Though we may not always realize it, all—thousands of millions—of us are eternally indebted to Rebekah for her wisdom and her ability to discern what was most important.

Her mission is now *our* mission. Sister Beck said:

> The lesson for me in all the hours and months of studying Rebekah and her family is that each of us in our day is as important to our generation and to our time as Rebekah was in her time. We each are pivotal in our families, and the success of the house of Israel is now dependent on millions of Rebekah's who understand what their place and mission is on the earth. Each of us is a daughter of heavenly parents, and as part of the house of Israel, we come from royal blood. When we choose our mission, we have power and influence in that royal house and in the Lord's work. He is depending on us.[12]

Like Rebekah, let's be prepared so that when God calls upon us, when He needs us to shape the future of the world, we will be ready to go.

• Keturah •

After Sarah's death, Abraham married a woman named Keturah, who bore him six sons. Genesis 25 tells us that this marriage occurred after Isaac's marriage to Rebekah and that Keturah gave birth to all six of her children *before* Rebekah could get pregnant for the first time. There is no mention of animosity between Rebekah and Keturah, but I can only imagine that watching Keturah bear children to her father-in-law, when she so desperately wanted a child of her own, must have been difficult for Rebekah.

Other than her name and the names of her sons, we know little else about Keturah. Before Abraham died, he specified Isaac as the heir of all his property and recipient of the birthright, and entrusted him with the Abrahamic covenant. Yet Abraham gave Keturah's six sons gifts and sent them away into the "east country" (Genesis 25:6). Keturah's son Midian would later become the father of the Midianites, a powerful nomadic group from whom Jethro, the father-in-law of Moses, would be born. The Old Testament calls Jethro "the priest of Midian," and the Doctrine and Covenants clarifies by telling us that Jethro held the Melchizedek Priesthood. It was from Jethro that Moses received the Melchizedek Priesthood and was schooled in the ways of the gospel (D&C 84:6–7). Jethro's priesthood suggests that even though Keturah's sons were not Abraham's heirs, they too received blessings of priesthood authority from their father.

Leah *and* Rachel

And Laban had two daughters: the name of the elder was Leah, and the name of the younger was Rachel.

Leah was tender eyed; but Rachel was beautiful and well favoured.

Genesis 29:16–17

My intent when I first began to write about Rachel and Leah was to give them each their own chapter. Their story is always told together, and they rarely get individual attention. Yet as I began writing, I realized that the stories of these two sisters are so intertwined that it is impossible to do justice to one story without simultaneously telling the other. In Rachel and Leah, we find joy, envy, cooperation, longsuffering, sacrifice—the agony and ecstasy that comes from sharing your life with a sister.

When Jacob fled from his brother, Esau, he traveled to Haran to find his mother's brother Laban. When Jacob arrived, he inquired for directions at a well where several shepherds were waiting with their flocks for the stone cover to be removed. They told Jacob that Laban lived nearby and that his daughter Rachel was just arriving at the well with her father's sheep, "for she kept them" (Genesis 29:9). Anciently, it was customary for the youngest capable child in the family to shepherd the sheep.[1] Watching sheep was a boring, easy job, and so it was often entrusted to young children. My husband's great-grandfather and his brother were sent out to watch their family's sheep for a week at a time at the ages of eight and five! We don't know how old Rachel was at this point, but we can guess that she was young.

From the first moment Jacob saw Rachel, he was smitten. The Genesis account doesn't tell us much about their encounter at the well, except that Jacob (perhaps fueled by a desire to impress Rachel) removed the stone cover from the well single-handedly and that when he met Rachel he kissed her and "lifted up his voice, and wept" (Genesis 29:10–11). Diana Webb wrote, "The Talmud fills in the void in the Genesis text. It informs us that when Jacob sees Rachel and kisses her, he immediately asks for her hand in marriage and she consents."[2]

Jacob appears to have taken his father's instructions that he was to seek a wife from among Laban's family seriously. I also wonder how much of the situation just seemed serendipitous to him. Most likely he had grown up hearing stories about his mother's betrothal experience. Perhaps he and Rachel felt that their meeting at the well, the very same well where his mother met Abraham's servant, was no coincidence but rather a sign that they were destined to be together. After this meeting, Rachel, as her aunt Rebekah had, ran back to her family to tell them who she had met at the well. Again, as he had with his sister Rebekah, Laban ran out to meet Jacob at the well and invited him into his house.

Jacob stayed with Laban and was introduced to his oldest daughter, Leah. The only description given of Leah is that she was "tender-eyed" (Genesis 29:17). This might just mean that she had memorable eyes, very "delicate "or "soft." Some translators claim that the best way to describe her was having "cow eyes," or what we might call doe-eyed. Yet, several other translations of the Bible render this phrase as "Leah had weak eyes," meaning that she had poor eyesight or another problem with her eyes.[3] All my life I have had very poor eyesight. If I take my contacts out I am legally blind and can only see a blur of colors. I have often thought about what life for someone like me would have been like in Bible times. If Leah was "tender-eyed" like I am, even the most basic things a woman did, such as cooking, sewing, or taking care of children, would have been difficult.

Contrastingly, Rachel was "beautiful" and "well favoured" (Genesis 29:17). It seems clear from how they are introduced to us that Leah, even if she had striking eyes, couldn't measure up to Rachel when it came to appearance. Jacob seemed to think so too, because when Laban asked him what he should pay him for the work he was doing, Jacob replied that all he wanted was Rachel. "I will serve thee seven years," Jacob told Laban, "for Rachel thy younger daughter" (Genesis 29:18). Jacob was penniless and had no money with which to offer a bride-price for Rachel. Instead he would work for her hand in marriage. Seven years of free work was a very generous bride-price. Perhaps this was the amount of time needed until Rachel would be old enough to marry, or perhaps Jacob felt that was what she was worth. Either way, the seven years "seemed unto him but a few days, for the love he had" for Rachel (verse 20).

When Jacob's seven years were over, Leah was still unmarried. Laban decided to trick Jacob by giving him Leah as a bride instead of the promised Rachel. Some Jewish traditions claim that Leah had been the intended bride of Esau, but since he had been unworthy she had been left without a bridegroom. Other traditions propose that Laban, seeing how greatly he had prospered with Jacob's help, wanted to find a way to snare him into working for him another seven years. Some traditions even claim that Rachel knew of the deception and helped her sister learn the secret signals that she and Jacob had made so that they would know each other in the dark. No matter what the truth, it was a strange situation.

To celebrate Jacob's wedding, Laban held a great feast. Jacob would not have seen his bride until she was brought, usually veiled, to his tent and presented to him as his wife. The tent was dark, and when Jacob woke in the morning, after having spent a wedding night with his bride, he was shocked to discover that it was Leah and not Rachel. Can you imagine what Leah must have felt when she saw her new husband's reaction? How it must have hurt to know that the man she loved, and was now married to, didn't love her back? How must Rachel have felt knowing that the man she loved had spent the night with her sister? Ouch.

When Jacob realized the deception, he confronted Laban and demanded to know why he had been deceived. "Did I not serve with thee for Rachel?" cried Jacob. "Wherefore then hast thou beguiled me?" (Genesis 29:25). Laban explained that in "our country," stressing the fact that Jacob was a stranger, it was not customary to marry the younger daughter before the firstborn was married. It seems strange that, if this was true, Jacob hadn't been aware of it before. Yet Laban promised Jacob that if he would "fulfill her week" (meaning finish out the seven-day wedding feast) and retain Leah as his wife that he would give Jacob Rachel as well—for another seven years of service. This deal seemed to appease Jacob, and he agreed to keep Leah as his wife and serve seven years for her, just as he had Rachel.

It is easy to see how these events could create, from the start, a polarized and turbulent family arrangement for Jacob, Leah, and Rachel. Yet some scholars suggest that the Hebrew text suggests that their marriages did not start out on the wrong foot. Webb explained:

> Most scholars translate the Hebrew of Genesis 29:30 as "And [Jacob] loved Rachel more than Leah." Although there are different translations most interpretations contain the idea that Jacob loved Rachel

over Leah. Translators are perplexed over the Hebrew word *gam* (which means "also") that appears after the words "he loved." The Hassidic rabbi Levi Yitzhak renders the verse as: "*He loved Rachel also [ie. even more] because of Leah. . . .*" It is clear that while Jacob's purpose in working for Laban was to marry Rachel, Jacob in fact, wed Leah. And it was Rachel [by her silence] who was responsible for this. Now Jacob's love was twofold; he loved her for herself, but he loved her *also*, even more, because she brought him so pious a wife as Leah.[4]

Leah got her honeymoon week, the only week in her life when she had Jacob all to herself. When that week was over, Jacob married Rachel. Yet Genesis 29:31 tells us that "when the Lord saw that Leah was hated, he opened her womb: but Rachel was barren." The word *hate* is a strong one, especially when talking about the feelings of a husband toward his wife. I doubt that Jacob *hated* Leah, in that he felt anger or repulsion toward her. Perhaps she was neglected, always coming in last in Jacob's affection and attention. I think any woman who knows the pain of having "lost" her husband to another woman, pornography, or even a consuming job or hobby can relate to Leah.

God gave Leah and Rachel equally hard trials. We often focus on Rachel's trial of barrenness but tend to forget Leah's pain. Just as Rachel longed desperately for a child, Leah longed for her husband's love and attention. It seems ironic, doesn't it? Rachel, who had Jacob's love in abundance, longed for children, while Leah, who had children in abundance, longed for Jacob's love. I had to smile when I read something Sister Holland wrote: "I have only three children and have wept that I could not have eight. (Some of you have eight and weep that you can't have three.) And I know

some of you without any have wept too."[5] I think we need to avoid the temptation to label one type of trial as harder than the other. God calibrates the circumstances of our lives to be unique, and we are given the type of experiences we personally need. This insight by Sara Picard is important:

> When I look to the scriptures, I don't find examples of women being solely cast as mothers. Most scripture stories about women exemplify a characteristic or trait that I am actively working on developing in my life. . . .
>
> I think one of the worst things that happens is the false contention created by the comparison of women. Working full-time is hard. I'm lonely. I hate feeling the full responsibility of adult life set squarely on my shoulders. However! From what I hear, it's also difficult waking up in the middle of the night to feed babies or take care of sick kids. Or feeling like no one appreciates what you do. Or putting your body through the ringer to bring life into the world.
>
> Why do we compare? One isn't better than the other. Any and all feelings of contention are not coming from God. . . . When the Savior is at the center of our lives, and we live according to our faith, we are all on the same team.
>
> Our goal is to become like Christ. The women that I have read about in scripture and associated with in my life are some of the most Christ-like people I have ever met.
>
> What is uniquely characteristic of all these women is their faith. Faith being evidenced by things hoped for but not seen. Faith that through Christ, things can and will be made right.[6]

With every child that Leah bore, she had hope that it would soften Jacob's feelings toward her. When she gave birth to Jacob's firstborn son, she seemed hopeful that he would change things. She named her son Reuben (a name that means "look, a son") and said, "Now therefore my husband will love me" (Genesis 29:32). Yet it seems that having a son did little to improve Leah and Jacob's relationship, even though being the mother of the firstborn son would have greatly elevated her position in the household.

When her second son was born, Leah named him Simeon (whose name means "hearing") and said, "Because the Lord hath heard I was hated, he hath therefore given me this son also" (Genesis 29:33). Leah appears to have been very open and outspoken about being unhappy and feeling neglected in her marriage. When Leah gave birth to Jacob's third son, Levi, she maintained hope that because of her children Jacob would love her. The name Levi means "pledged" or "joined." When Levi was born Leah said, "Now this time will my husband be joined unto me, because I have born him three sons" (Genesis 29:34). She appears to have found great worth in her sons and might even have felt that since it was she, and not Rachel, who had given birth to Jacob's children—sons who would inherit the Abrahamic covenant—that God loved her more than Rachel.

Yet by the time her fourth son was born, her attitude had changed. When Judah, whose name means "praise," was born, she made no comments about deserving or demanding Jacob's love. Instead she said, "Now will I praise the Lord" (Genesis 29:35). Perhaps by this time in her life Leah had come to accept her situation, and instead of pining away for what she didn't have—her husband's love—she realized what she did have—four beautiful children—and praised

the Lord for that blessing. I find it significant that Leah seems to have found this peace with the birth of Judah, the son through whom Jesus Christ would be born. It's a beautiful reminder that we, like I hope Leah did, can find solace to our deepest wounds and joy in our trials when we invite Jesus Christ into our lives.

After Judah's birth, Leah "left bearing," meaning she did not get pregnant again (Genesis 29:35). It is at this point that Rachel began to despair. Genesis 30:1 tells us that she "envied her sister" and that she exclaimed to Jacob, "Give me children, or else I die." The anguish of a woman bereft of children is a uniquely feminine pain. It rocks the very core meaning and value of a woman's soul. One of my friends who struggles with infertility told me that she can relate to Rachel's pain, feeling anguish that that her female body is unable to do what it was designed by God to do—give life. In response to Rachel's demand, Jacob replied rather harshly, asking her, "Am I in God's stead, who hath withheld from thee the fruit of the womb?" (Genesis 30:2). Who am I, Jacob wanted to know, to be able to give you only what God can?

After this outcry, Rachel gave her handmaiden Bilhah to Jacob, like Sarah gave Hagar to Abraham so that she "shall bear upon my knees, that I may also have children by her" (Genesis 30:3). Rachel named the children that Bilhah bore, and she called the first son Dan (whose name means "judged, or vindicated"). Rachel said, "God hath judged me, and hath also heard my voice" (Genesis 30:6). The second son Bilhah bore Rachel named Naphtali (meaning "the wrestlings of God") and stated, "With great wrestlings have I wrestled with my sister" (Genesis 30:8). We don't know if this means that she and Leah had openly argued and been contentious about bearing children, or if Rachel had just struggled in her heart, feeling envy and anger toward her sister. We might suppose that now, with two adoptive sons of her own, some of the pain in Rachel's heart had been appeased.

Leah also gave Jacob her servant Zilpah as a wife. Zilpah had two sons, whom Leah named Gad (whose name means "good fortune") and Asher (whose name means "happy"). If we can use the names of her sons as an indication of her mental state, we might conclude that this was a happy and joyful time for Leah, despite that fact that her relationship with Jacob did not appear to be any better than it had before. Perhaps she had found joy and fulfillment in her children, relishing the role of mother and matriarch.

Sometime after these births, Leah's son Reuben found some mandrakes, which were the ancient equivalent of fertility drugs. Both Leah and Rachel wanted these mandrakes, and in this, the only conversation we have between them, the tensions that existed in their relationship are evident. "Give me, I pray thee," Rachel demanded, "of thy son's mandrakes" (Genesis 30:14). "Is it a small matter that thou hast taken my husband?" Leah responded back. "Wouldest thou take away my son's mandrakes also?" (verse 15). Rachel, desperate for the mandrakes, made a deal with Leah. She told Leah, Jacob "shall lie with thee to night for thy son's mandrakes" (verse 15).

This remark gives us a glimpse into the intimate dynamics of Jacob's household. Jacob, it appears, was not sleeping or living with Leah. Instead, his affection and time were still dominated by Rachel. Rachel, since she was Jacob's first betrothed wife, was "*the*

chief wife"; the woman in charge of the household. While giving birth to Jacob's first son improved Leah's household status, she was just "*a* chief wife." Rachel called the shots, even when it came to who could and could not sleep with Jacob. So Leah jumped at the chance to have a night with her husband.

That evening, she met Jacob as he came in from the field and told him (rather unromantically, in my opinion), "Thou must come in unto me; for surely I have hired thee with my son's mandrakes" (Genesis 30:16). Jacob made no recorded objection to this and went to her that night. Apparently not needing the assistance of the mandrakes, Leah conceived and again bore Jacob a son. This son she named Issachar, which means "recompense," explaining that she felt he was a blessing to her because she had "given my maiden to my husband" (Genesis 30:18). That comment gives us an interesting insight into why Leah gave Jacob Zilpah as a wife. It wasn't just about keeping up with her sister but instead seems to have been something Leah felt God had wanted her to do and was now blessing her for doing.

After this, Leah bore her sixth son, whom she named Zebulun, meaning "exalted abode." Here, her old longing resurfaces, and we hear her claim, "Now will my husband dwell with me, because I have born him six sons" (Genesis 30:20). Finally, Leah gave birth to her last child—and only daughter—Dinah (see page 81). It wasn't until Leah was completely done bearing children that "God remembered Rachel" (verse 22) and she gave birth to her first child—Joseph. Rachel also makes a prophetic statement after Joseph's birth that "the Lord shall add to me another son" (verse 24). This proves to be right, and we can only wonder how she knew that.

• Family Council •

After Joseph's birth, Jacob felt the urgent need to leave Laban's household and return to his homeland, even though that might mean facing his brother's wrath. Jacob's desire to leave may have been prompted by the fact that, with the birth of Joseph, he now had an heir to whom he would pass down the Abrahamic covenant. He may have felt a desire to return to the land that had been promised him. He also probably considered that, because he was becoming significantly richer than his father-in-law, Laban's "countenance [was] not towards him as before" (Genesis 31:2).

Yet before he made such a big decision, Jacob did something that our Church leaders have been urging us to do—he held a family council. Even though he was the patriarch of the family, he didn't decide without consulting his wives. He called Rachel and Leah to meet him in the field where he kept his flocks and explained to them that he had been visited by an angel in a dream who told him to "return unto the land of thy fathers, and to thy kindred; and I will be with thee" (Genesis 31:3). He also explained that he had concerns about their father.

Jacob is such a good model here of what a family council should look like. He wasn't *telling* his wives what he was going to do, or what he thought should be done. He simply explained the situation to them and *asked* them to give their thoughts about what the family should do. He seems genuinely interested in their response and seems to indicate to them that he will respect their ideas. In response, Rachel and Leah were quick to give their opinions. "Is there yet any portion or inheritance for us in our father's house?" they

asked. "Are we not counted of him strangers? For he hath sold us, and hath quite devoured also our money" (Genesis 31:14–15). They were speaking about their dowries, which it seems their father had spent rather than saving for them.

Rachel and Leah felt that it would be better for them, and their children, if they were to take everything that was theirs and go. With a final stamp of approval, they told Jacob, "Whatsoever God hath said unto thee, do" (Genesis 31:16). Knowing that Laban would oppose them, Jacob and his family "stole away unawares to Laban" (Genesis 31:20). This would probably have been the first time Leah and Rachel had traveled far away from the place they had been born. Like their mother-in-law, Rebekah, who made a similar trek, they showed courage and faith in departing from their home forever.

As they traveled closer to Canaan, Jacob began to have some big doubts about whether it was safe for him to meet Esau. Many years had passed since Esau had vowed to kill him, but Jacob still held the birthright and Esau did not. Jacob didn't know how Esau felt about that and was worried he and his family would be met with violence. As he prayed to know what to do, the Lord revealed a plan to Jacob; he was to give Esau a present. Jacob instructed his servants to take large groups of goats, sheep, camels, bulls, asses, and horses ahead of his caravan. Each group of herders was to space themselves apart so that they would arrive in Canaan at different times. He also told them that if they were asked whom all this wealth belonged to, they were to respond, "They be thy servant Jacob's; it is a present sent unto my Lord Esau" (Genesis 32:18).

He then divided his wives into three groups, like you might in a military campaign. As Tikva Frymer-Kensky explains, "When Jacob believes that danger threatens in his meeting with Esau, he arranges his family so that the maids and their children are placed first, then Leah and her children, and last and most protected, Rachel and Joseph. . . . Despite all her children, Leah is still second best."[7]

Jacob had nothing to fear. Whether his gift softened Esau's heart or his brother had long ago forgiven him, we don't know. But when Esau saw Jacob, he "ran to meet him, and embraced him, and fell on his neck, and kissed him: and they wept" (Genesis 33:4). After this emotional meeting, each of the wives and their children came forward, in their respective order, and bowed to Esau. Esau welcomed them graciously, and they dwelt in a land near to him in Canaan.

It was here that two tragedies struck Jacob's family. First Leah's daughter Dinah was raped (see page 81), and Rachel died while giving birth to her second child, a boy they named Benjamin. Rachel's death is especially tragic. She went into labor while Jacob's family was on the road, moving from Beth-el to Ephrath. Her labor was very difficult, and it seems that at one point she feared that she would not be able to deliver her baby. Yet the midwife who was attending her had faith in her and told Rachel, "Fear not, thou shalt have this son also"(Genesis 35:17). After delivering the baby, Rachel began to die. Genesis 35:18 says that "as her soul was in departing" she named her son Ben-oni, meaning "son of my sorrow." Jacob, perhaps not wanting his son to go through life with such a sad name, changed it to Benjamin, which means "son of the right hand." It is sadly ironic that Rachel, who before exclaimed "give me children, or else I die," would actually die giving birth to the very children she so desperately wanted. Perhaps that is one of the most powerful things about motherhood; a woman is willing to give her own life so that someone else might live.

It appears they did not have time or resources to move Rachel's body, so she was buried "in the way to Ephrath" (Genesis 35:19) where one day the town of Bethlehem would be built. Jacob marked her grave with a pillar of rocks. Hundreds of years later, the tribe of Benjamin would inherit the land upon which Rachel's body was buried. It would also be in Bethlehem, the final resting place of Rachel, where Jesus Christ would be born.

After Rachel's death, we hear nothing more about Leah, except where she was buried. In Genesis 49:31, we learn that when Jacob died, his sons buried him in the cave of Machpelah, where Abraham, Sarah, Isaac, Rebekah, and Leah were buried. It is sweet to me to think about Leah, who all her life longed for her husband to lie beside her, was buried next to him for eternity. Her presence in that tomb makes her a matriarch of the Abrahamic covenant. In fact, Leah gave birth to half of the twelve tribes of Israel—Reuben, Simeon, Levi, Judah, Issachar, and Zebulon. She, out of all the matriarchs, was the only one blessed with fertility, and it was mainly from her that the house of Israel was built.

It seems to have bothered Jacob, even years after Leah's death, that Rachel had not been able to be buried in Abraham's cave as well (see Genesis 48:7). She too was a matriarch of the covenant, and it would be her son, Joseph, who would inherit the birthright and the priesthood from his father. While Jacob's other sons were often wild and violent, Joseph was obedient, pious, and worthy at a young age to receive the "coat of many colours" (Genesis 37:23) and inherit the Abrahamic covenant from his father. Even though Rachel died when Joseph was young, we might suppose that her early teaching and the love she had for him were powerful guiding forces in his life.

As we look back over the story of Rachel and Leah, I hope we will not focus on their struggles but rather on their triumphs. Like all of us, these two sisters felt envy, anger, and heartache. Yet they also displayed incredible courage, faith, and trust in God's plan for them and for their family. Together, Rachel and Leah (and their handmaidens Bilhah and Zilpah) built the foundation of the house of Israel. It is through their efforts, both physical and spiritual, that all of God's children can claim an inheritance in Abraham's family and become heirs of the greatest blessings that God has for His children.

• Rachel and the Teraphim •

One of the strangest stories in the Bible is Rachel's theft of her father's teraphim. In Genesis 31:19, we read that when Jacob, Leah, and Rachel stole away secretly from Laban's house that Rachel stole her father's "images." The Hebrew word is *teraphim* and refers to household gods, usually in human form, that were common among the Canaanites, Phoenicians, and other peoples of this time. We know that the teraphim Rachel had were relatively small, because they were portable and fit in her saddlebag. Yet Michal, the wife of David, hid teraphim under the blankets to trick her father into thinking David was sleeping while he escaped out the window (see 1 Samuel 19:13). Those teraphim must have been considerably larger. Archeological evidence suggests that teraphim, unlike other idols that were carved or "graven," were made from clay or poured from molds. Archeologist have found evidence of many such small clay figures—often in the shape of female goddesses—and believe that these images were widely used in goddess worship in most societies, including that of the Israelites, during Bible times.[8]

We don't know why Rachel stole her father's teraphim. Josephus explained that Rachel took the images, which were "sacred paternal images"[9] worshiped by Laban and his forefathers, because she feared that they would be overtaken by her father and that she would be able to use them as a bargaining tool.[10] Josephus makes it clear that Rachel had been taught by Jacob to "despise such worship of those gods" and that she took them not for herself but as precaution against her father. I have also wondered if maybe Rachel took them just so that her father couldn't worship them anymore. Sort of like a granddaughter who knows her grandpa shouldn't be smoking and so steals his cigarettes and hides them. Perhaps Rachel felt that if she stole the teraphim, her father would stop his worship of false gods.

We don't know what Rachel did with the teraphim after her successful concealment of them. But after Jacob and his family had to relocate due to the violence resulting from Dinah's rape, God instructed Jacob to "put away the strange gods that are among you, and be clean, and change your garments" (Genesis 35:2). Jacob then took the teraphim, as well as "all their earrings which were in their ears" (verse 4) and buried them under an oak tree.

Dinah

And Dinah the daughter of Leah, which she bare unto Jacob, went out to see the daughters of the land.

And when Shechem the son of Hamor the Hivite, prince of the country, saw her, he took her, and lay with her, and defiled her.

Genesis 34:1–2

The most stunning thing about Dinah's story is her absolute silence; we do not hear a single word from her. Not only was she the victim of a rape, but her brothers, in their anger about what had happened to her, murdered an entire city of men. Her story is terrible. Yet perhaps, like the organization who helps women tell their stories about sexual abuse, as we study and learn about Dinah we can "Break the Silence," and hear her voice talk to us from the pages of the Old Testament.

Dinah was the only daughter born to Jacob and Leah. She had eleven older brothers! When Jacob and his family returned to his homeland, they settled near a Canaanite city called Shechem. Her story begins when we read that Dinah "went out to see the daughters of the land" (Genesis 34:1). Josephus explained that there was a festival in Shechem, and Dinah went to go see the finery of the women, perhaps referring to fabric and other things women might have sold.[1] We are not told if she went unaccompanied or if she went with other women or family members.

While she was in the city, the prince, also named Shechem, saw her and "he took her, and lay with her, and defiled her" (Genesis 34:2). Many times it is Dinah who gets blamed for what happened to her. Some readers claim that she was bold and unwise to leave her home and venture into the marketplace where Shechem could see her. People have even suggested that perhaps Dinah's behavior in Shechem was inappropriate and that she attracted, or even welcomed, the attentions of Shechem. I feel that such an argument is unkind to Dinah and to all women who have experienced sexual attacks. Even if Dinah had tried to attract Shechem's attention, she did not deserve to be treated the way she was.

In the *Old Testament Student Manual*, we learn, "The Hebrew word that is translated 'took' in the phrase 'he took her' can mean 'to take away, sometimes with violence and force; to take possession, to capture, to seize upon.'"[2] It is clear in the Hebrew text that Shechem kidnapped and forcibly raped Dinah. Even though later we read that Shechem's "soul clave unto Dinah" (verse 3) and that he loved her, that doesn't make his actions okay. Regardless of how *he* felt after what he had done, he had still forced Dinah and kept her captive in his home.

It is interesting that the story of Dinah being forcibly taken by the prince of a foreign city is similar to what happened to her great-grandmother Sarah (and her grandmother Rebekah, see Genesis 26) when she was forcibly taken from Abraham by the Pharaoh. Yet unlike Sarah and Rebekah, the Lord did not protect Dinah from harm. She was raped and hurt by the man who abducted her. I have often wondered why. Why did God not protect Dinah? I don't think I have an answer for that question. Yet I appreciate the insight given by Leslie G. Nelson, herself a survivor of sexual abuse, who wrote:

> Next to shame, I think the most painful thing for me was the feeling of abandonment. When I felt the Lord had left me and I had done nothing wrong—the feeling I described as the Jaws of Hell consumed me. . . .
>
> As I thought, pondered and wrestled with these ideas, a realization came to me. . . .
>
> Even Christ who was perfect could not escape suffering. Because of His suffering, He knows how to help us, and through *our pain* we can become more like Him. . . .
>
> I do not mean to say that God "gave us" sexual abuse or rape to help us grow. Certainly He did not give these horrors to anyone. They are a result of other people's sins and their free agency to choose. God allows it, as He allowed his own Son to suffer, and He can use this trauma to help us be better, stronger and more like Him. If we allow our pain to crush us and defeat us, Satan has won a victory. But if we hold on, if we drink our personal bitter cup, and overcome (as Christ accepted His Gethsemane,) then we become more like Him, and that is absolutely a victory for Him and for us.[3]

The rest of Dinah's story is dominated by her brothers Simeon and Levi. After Dinah's rape, Shechem's father, Hamor, went to Jacob and asked if he would marry Dinah to his son. He offered Jacob as much a bride-price for her as he wished. Hamor's real intention was not just to secure Dinah but to negotiate a trade agreement with Jacob, where they would dwell together (and thus share in Jacob's wealth) by marrying their daughters to one another's sons. In response to Hamor's request, Simeon and Levi told him that they could only marry their daughters to men who were circumcised and that if all the men in Shechem would be circumcised they would consent to such a marriage arrangement. They told Hamor, "We will become one people" (Genesis 34:16).

Perhaps Simeon and Levi had been bluffing. Maybe, not knowing a better diplomatic way to handle the situation, they supposed that the men of Shechem would be scared off by the prospect of circumcision and just give Dinah back to them. Their bluff failed and all the men of Shechem (thinking how rich they might come by marrying into Jacob's family) agreed to be circumcised. At this point, Simeon and Levi were in a real pickle. They had made a mockery out of God's sacred token and had allowed people who were unworthy to become circumcised. There was no way that they could honor their promise with the men of Shechem. So Simeon and Levi resorted to violence, and on the day when all the men of Shechem were "sore" from having been circumcised, they went into the city and killed all the men, seized their animals and wealth, took the women and children captive, and then "took Dinah out of Shechem's house, and went out" (Genesis 34:25–26).

To Dinah this may have been a heroic rescue, but I doubt she was happy to see the bloodshed and pain that her rescue cost. Jacob was especially troubled by what Levi and Simeon had done and years later, when giving them their patriarchal blessing, stated, "Instruments of cruelty are in their habitations. . . . Cursed be their anger, for it was fierce; and their wrath, for it was cruel" (Genesis 49:5, 7). While Shechem erred in his behavior toward Dinah, Simeon and Levi in their anger had done much worse. After this event, Jacob and his family were forced to move.

That is where Dinah's story ends. The abrupt way she disappears from the text, while her brothers remain prominent for another fourteen chapters, leaves me wondering what happened to her. More than anything, I wonder if she ever regained the courage to venture out again, like she had on the day when she was kidnapped. She had been brave that day, setting off into a new place to meet new people and make friends. Vanessa Ochs wrote:

> If Dina's story had not ended violently with abuse and revenge, we'd have been better able to see the positive gesture that is Dina's hallmark, her stepping out. That gesture, her legacy to us, is her willingness to move beyond the familiar relationships in safe, cozy settings and forge new bonds on unfamiliar turf. Dina had gumption. . . .
>
> . . . We must meet people who are different from us, people who might not like us at first, people who rattle us and leave us unbalanced. . . .
>
> It is too risky, Dina teaches, for us to remain in our own tents. The global implications are obvious. We need to journey across our thresholds toward one another—with or without roadmaps—and there, at the crossroads where we happen to meet, we might break bread.[4]

At times, each of us have been like Dinah, bravely venturing out to see a new place and meet new people. Each of us also have experienced the pain that comes when such ventures end badly, not necessarily in sexual assault but in unkindness, embarrassment, ridicule, and judgment. It can be hard to "put ourselves out there" and trust others. It is much easier to stay in our tents. Yet I hope that we can be like Dinah stepping out, risking the unknown, and taking chances. Yes, bad things may happen to us, but if we never leave our tent, we will never know what we are capable of or what beauty is in the world. Don't let the possibilities of what could go wrong keep you from seeing what could go right. God can use all our experiences—good and bad—to help us be better, stronger, and more like Him. Don't be afraid to step out.

Tamar

It was told Judah, saying, Tamar thy daughter in law hath played the harlot; and also, behold, she is with child by whoredom. And Judah said, Bring her forth, and let her be burnt.

When she was brought forth, she sent to her father in law, saying, By the man, whose these are, am I with child: and she said, Discern, I pray thee, whose are these, the signet, and bracelets, and staff.

And Judah acknowledged them, and said, She hath been more righteous than I; because that I gave her not to Shelah my son. And he knew her again no more.

Genesis 38:24–26

Tamar is one of the most misunderstood women in the scriptures. Her story is, admittedly, very confusing. It is full of customs and choices that seem bizarre and even downright wrong to modern readers. Yet I think that when we better understand the cultural context of Tamar's story, we see that she was a brave woman who made good choices when faced with challenging circumstances. Tamar's choices ultimately allowed for ancient promises to be fulfilled.

Tamar married Er, the son of Judah. Er was the oldest of Judah's sons, his other two being Onan and Shelah. Eventually, the Lord slew Er because he "was wicked in the sight of the Lord" (Genesis 38:7). Er's death made Tamar a widow, which meant a drop in her social status and the loss of the security and prosperity she had expected when she married a firstborn son. On top of that, Tamar and Er hadn't had any children.

According to the custom of Levirate marriage (see sidebar) Judah arranged for his next son, Onan, to provide Tamar with a child. Yet as Genesis 38:9 says, "Onan knew that the seed should not be his." If Tamar remained childless, all Er's inheritance as the firstborn son—a double portion—would go to Onan. So, when he was with Tamar, he "spilled [his seed] on the ground, lest that he should give seed to his brother" (Genesis 38:9). Onan was willing, and perhaps more than happy, to use Tamar for his sexual pleasure, but when it came to creating life with her—life that might make his financial situation harder—he was unwilling. We can only imagine the difficult place that Tamar found herself in: being used to gratify the lust of a man who was unwilling to allow for the life that might be created.

We don't know how long Onan treated her like this, but it may have been a long time. Eventually, the Lord heard Tamar because Genesis 38:10 says, "That the thing which [Onan] did displeased the Lord: wherefore he slew him also." The "also" in this verse is interesting because it references the fact that the Lord also slew Tamar's first husband, Er, for wickedness. We don't know what type of wickedness Er was doing, but, if like his brother, he was also using his sexual power inappropriately, it just makes your heart ache for poor Tamar.

At this point, Tamar had reason to expect that because Judah's only remaining son, Shelah, had not yet reached puberty that Judah would do his duty as her father-in-law and raise up seed to his deceased son. Yet instead of doing what he should, Judah told Tamar to go back to her father's house and remain a widow until Shelah was grown. Judah freely admitted that he wanted her to leave because he was afraid that Shelah might "die also, as his brethren did" (Genesis 38:11). Tamar didn't have a good track history with men, and it made Judah wary.

Being sent back to her father's home, without releasing her from her marriage contract, made Tamar's situation even more difficult. As a childless widow, she was not free to remarry, and she would have had no social standing, no economic security, and no future.

• Levirate Marriage •

Anciently, many cultures had a practice, which later became known as Levirate marriage, in which if a man died without any children it was the responsibility of one of his brothers to marry his widow and conceive a child with her.[6] It didn't matter if he was already married because the child she conceived would not legally be his but would belong to the deceased brother, continue his deceased brother's name, and inherit the deceased brother's property. This custom was for the benefit of the widowed woman, and it was her right to demand it from her brothers-in-law. They could refuse her, but doing so was viewed as selfish and often resulted in public humiliation. If all the brothers refused the widow's demand, or if there were no brothers-in-law, then it was the duty of her father-in-law to provide her with a child.[7] Later, under the Mosaic law, the Lord would forbid sexual interactions between daughters-in-law and fathers-in-law, but at the time of Tamar's story there was no such provision (see Leviticus 18).

Despite this disgrace, Tamar put on her widow garments, went back to her father's house, and waited. Yet when Shelah was grown, he was married to someone else. It became obvious that Judah never had any intention of fulfilling his promise to Tamar.

Tamar made a hard but ultimately history-changing decision. After all those years of waiting, she probably felt her biological clock ticking and she knew what she needed to do. The only problem was that none of the men in her life were willing to do their part. They were interested in having sex with her but not in fulfilling their responsibilities to her or to her unborn children. Tamar was in the same situation that many righteous women find themselves in today: they are willing to have children, but their men are unwilling to make the financial, social, physical, or emotional sacrifices required to bring those spirits to the earth.

Tamar decided that passive waiting and praying was no longer enough and decided to act. She heard that Judah's wife had died and that he had gone to Timnath to shear his sheep. She cast off her widow clothing, veiled her face, and dressed like a prostitute. As Diana Webb explained:

> Cult prostitutes were common in the ancient Near East. They were women who offered their "services" to would-be-takers and donated their earnings to the temple. Genesis uses two different words to refer to Tamar on the road to Timnah. The word for harlot as we understand it today is *zonah*. This word is used first, and later the word *kedeshah* is used, which means "consecrated woman" and refers to a female associated with cult worship. Tamar probably knows that Judah is likely to visit a cult prostitute at shearing time. Apparently, he has adopted this custom in order ensure and increase in his herds during his sojourn in Adullam. Tamar knows Judah well enough to

now that the plan she has concocted will be successful. She presses Judah to do what he *should* have done by engineering events that will lead to his fulfilling the law.[5]

When Judah saw Tamar veiled as a prostitute, he didn't recognize her and arranged to pay her a kid from his flock for her services. Tamar, being wise, required a pledge from Judah that he would pay his promise to her; she asked for his signet, bracelets, and staff. Obviously, this was a common expectation, and Judah readily agreed. "And he gave it her, and came in unto her, and she conceived by him" (Genesis 38:18).

Judah then went on his way. Tamar laid aside her prostitute clothing and returned home to her father's house to again wait. In the meantime, Judah tried to find the harlot to pay his debt and recover his pledge, but no one seemed to know who he was talking about. When he was unable to find the harlot, he made a public declaration that he had tried to pay his debt but was unable.

Three months later, word reached Judah that his daughter-in-law Tamar was pregnant. Enraged by her lack of virtue (remember that she was still considered to be a married woman), he ordered her to be brought before him and burnt. Yet when she was brought to him she held out the signet, bracelet, and staff that Judah had given her and declared, "By the man, whose these are, am I with child" (Genesis 38:25). Judah immediately recognized them as the pledge that he had given the harlot. He understood what Tamar had done and why she had done it.

Surprisingly, instead of being angry with Tamar, Judah was humbled. He knew that he had treated Tamar unfairly and that he had not done his duty to her as he should have. Her resorting to trickery to force him to live up to his responsibilities pricked him to his soul and opened his spiritual eyes. It is important to remember that in his father's blessing Jacob blessed Judah that the promised Savior would be born through his lineage (see Genesis 49:10). At this point in his life Judah was not living with his brethren. He had married outside of the covenant and was not living by the principles his father taught him. Yet Tamar's actions awakened something in him and he freely admitted that "she hath been more righteous than I" (Genesis 38:26).

After that Judah "knew her again no more" (Genesis 38:26), and several months later Tamar gave birth to twin boys named Pharez and Zarah. Through the lineage of Pharez, the firstborn grandson of the house of Judah, came the promised Messiah, Jesus Christ. In Christ's lineage given in Matthew chapter 1, Tamar is listed among the prominent women of Christ's genealogy. Tamar was an instrument in God's hand to ensure that his promise to Judah that the Savior would be born through his lineage would be fulfilled. Tamar is the mother of the Jewish people.

The story of Tamar is an important one. Not only is it an example of a strong woman who takes the initiative to do what is right, but her story teaches important lessons about the consequences that result when we begin began to separate the act of sex from the creation of life. All the men in Tamar's story were willing to have sex with her, but none of them were willing to take responsibility for her wellbeing or for the new life that might possibly come from that union. Tamar was treated as a sexual object, where her greatest value was in being attractive and sexually available.

It seems Judah had bought into this mindset. He had been taught truth and promised great things by his father, Jacob, but he had chosen to live a secular life, among a secular people, and had adopted their attitudes toward sex and procreation. He'd been blinded by fear, worldly ideas, and selfishness to what was most important. It took Tamar, a woman whose heart was "turned" to her unborn children to wake him up to his responsibilities and to see things clearly.

Judah's declaration that "she [Tamar] hath been more righteous than I" (Genesis 38:26) was a changing point for him, and the Judah we read about in the rest of Genesis was a different man. Not only did he rejoin his family and reclaim his blessings, but when his brother Joseph (whom earlier he helped sell into slavery) threatened to imprison his younger brother Benjamin, it was Judah who stepped forward and offered to take the place of his brother (see Genesis 44:18–34). It is evident that his heart had been changed and was now in the right place.

I think that, like Tamar, righteous women can have a strong impact on the men in their lives, helping them to keep their hearts soft and open to life. This doesn't mean I think that women should trick their husbands into having children like Tamar did. Hers was an extreme case, and I am sure she only acted after having received spiritual confirmation of the course she was to pursue. Yet I think that what Tamar's story does teach us is that a heart open to life is a powerful force for good in the world and that when we open our hearts toward heaven we bless generations. Furthermore, her story teaches us that God can change hearts and that when it comes to the creation of life God can work miracles.

He certainly did for Tamar.

Potiphar's Wife

And it came to pass after these things, that his master's wife cast her eyes upon Joseph; and she said, Lie with me.

But he refused, and said unto his master's wife, Behold, my master wotteth not what is with me in the house, and he hath committed all that he hath to my hand;

There is none greater in this house than I; neither hath he kept back any thing from me but thee, because thou art his wife: how then can I do this great wickedness, and sin against God?

And it came to pass, as she spake to Joseph day by day, that he hearkened not unto her, to lie by her, or to be with her.

Genesis 39:7–10

For a long time, most of what I knew about Potiphar's wife came from Andrew Lloyd Webber's musical *Joseph and the Amazing Technicolor Dreamcoat* and the narrator's unendearing song about her.[1]

It had never dawned on me that there might be something to learn from the story of a woman who was vilified as a sexually promiscuous "man-eater." Then one day for my scripture study, I randomly opened to Genesis 39. As I read the story of Potiphar's wife, I saw her story with new eyes.

Genesis 39 is almost always taught from Joseph's perspective and is used as an example of how to flee from sexual sin. I think that this is an important aspect of the story, and I agree that Joseph should be upheld as a worthy example. Yet what I saw that day as I studied the scriptures was not the promiscuous sexual predator that Potiphar's wife is often made out to be. Instead, I saw a bored, lonely rich woman whose life was not everything she had dreamed it would be. Perhaps her marriage with Potiphar was unhappy, perhaps she lacked intellectual stimulation, perhaps she was far from home and family, or perhaps she felt unwanted or undervalued. It has also been speculated that Potiphar was a eunuch, and she may have lacked intimacy and the possibility for children.[2]

There are hundreds of reasons she could have begun, perhaps even unknowingly, to "cast her eyes" (Genesis 39:7) around in search of something else. It just so happened that her eyes fell upon Joseph—young, handsome, talented, honest, smart, loyal, and blessed by the Lord. She may have compared him to Potiphar and seen in Joseph all the things she felt her marriage and life were lacking. Joseph would have been a hard man to resist.

Of course there are many different ways to interpret Bible stories, but I think that a close study of the story of Potiphar's wife makes it apparent that her passion for Joseph was built over time. I don't think she saw Joseph and then a few days later chased him around trying to get him into bed with her. The story suggests that she and Joseph knew each other well and that she allowed an emotional intimacy to build between them—way before she ever asked Joseph to sleep with her.

Consider the way Joseph rejected her initial invitation. The first time she offered herself to him, Joseph did not run away or dismiss her rudely. Instead he spoke kindly to her and explained in great depth (by Bible standards) why he could not be with her. He told her, "Behold, my master wotteth not what is with me in the house, and he hath committed all that he hath to my hand; There is none greater in this house than I; neither hath he kept back anything from me but thee, because thou art his wife." (Genesis 39:8–9).

These aren't the words of someone who is trying to escape the advances of a "man-eater," but rather his manner indicates that he cares about her feelings and wants to treat them with respect. His words sound to me like he is speaking to a friend. In fact, his final phrase to her indicates that she knows him well enough to understand his heart and his moral beliefs. He tells her, "How then can I do this great wickedness, and sin against God?" (Genesis 39:9).

She didn't accept this answer. Maybe she was convinced that Joseph cared for her and that if she tried hard enough she could make him choose her over his God. Or maybe she was used to getting what she wanted. She didn't take "no" for an answer. Genesis 39:10 tells us that she continued speaking to Joseph "day by day, [but] that he hearkened not unto her, to lie by her, or to be with her."

Because they lived in the same household, Joseph was unable to completely avoid her. One day, when all the other men servants were out of the house, she cornered Joseph and begged him to sleep with her. She was probably not physically strong enough to force him into intimacy, and so she clung to his clothes. This time Joseph, knowing he had been trapped, fled and left his clothes in her hands.

After this rejection, she was angry and tried to hurt Joseph. She kept his garment and called in the other men servants and, perhaps playing off of already existing jealousy among the servants, told them how her husband "hath brought in an Hebrew unto us to mock us" (Genesis 39:14) and claimed that Joseph made sexual advances to her. Later, she told the same story to Potiphar, and the relative meekness of Joseph's punishment (only imprisonment when he should have had him killed) indicates that Potiphar may not have totally believed her story.

The story of Potiphar's wife is a sad example of what happens when a husband or wife allows themselves to "cast their eyes" around. Sexual sin rarely happens quickly. It is often something that is built slowly and steadily over time. It usually begins with people becoming emotionally intimate first. In a 2009 *Ensign* article, Kenneth W. Matheson explained how infidelity occurs:

> Fidelity includes refraining from physical contact—but that is not all. Fidelity also means complete commitment, trust, and respect between husband and wife. . . .

> Physical infidelity is only one of the many temptations Satan uses to break up families and marriages. Emotional infidelity, which occurs when emotions and thoughts are focused on someone other than a spouse, is an insidious threat that can weaken the trust between a couple and shatter peace of mind.

> Emotional infidelity doesn't usually happen suddenly; rather, it occurs gradually—often imperceptibly at first. This is one reason why those involved often feel innocent of any wrongdoing.[3]

Being unfaithful to your spouse starts with your thoughts. It begins when you start comparing your spouse to someone else. It escalates when you start rationalizing the time you are spending with someone else and climaxes when you start investing the energy that should go into fixing your marriage into creating a new relationship with someone other than your spouse.

The story of Potiphar's wife is just as applicable in our modern world as it was in ancient times. In fact, I think that the opportunity for married people to "cast their eyes" about is even greater now than it has ever been. Not only do we have multiple opportunities to interact closely with men and women in work, school, and church settings, but we also have the expanded world of the Internet. "Casting your eyes" about can start with seemingly small interactions, such as reconnecting with an old friend or boyfriend on Facebook, confiding your ideas and dreams with a friend rather than your spouse, or saving up your thoughts to tell to a coworker who seems to understand you much better.

I can't help but feel sorry for Potiphar's wife. She had numerous occasions to stop and walk away from the mess she had created, but she didn't. She let her appetites and desires rule her spirit, and it resulted in tragedy—for Joseph, for her, and for Potiphar. I think we can all from her mistake and choose to be fiercely loyal to our spouse—heart, mind, and body.

Asenath

And unto Joseph were born two sons before the years of famine came,
which Asenath the daughter of Poti-pherah priest of On bare unto him.

Genesis 41:50

Asenath is the forgotten matriarch. We often talk about the faith of Sarah, the strength of Rebekah, the patience of Rachel, and the fecundity of Leah and acknowledge their important role in establishing the house of Israel. Yet somehow Asenath is always forgotten. Perhaps it is because we know so little about her, or perhaps it is because she doesn't fit the stereotypical "matriarch" mold and makes us uncomfortable.

Asenath was the wife of Joseph, who was sold into Egypt. After Joseph had successfully interpreted the Pharaoh's dream, he was rewarded by becoming the ruler over Egypt, sort of like a prime minister does today. Joseph's name was changed to Zaphnath-paaneah, and Pharaoh gave him Asenath, the daughter of Poti-pherah, the priest of On, as his wife.

After marrying Asenath, Joseph "went throughout all the land of Egypt" (Genesis 41:46), overseeing the effort to save food in the storehouses for the seven years of famine that would follow the seven years of plenty. During those seven years of plenty, Asenath gave birth to two sons whom Joseph named Manassah and Ephraim (see Genesis 41:50–52). Manassah, whose name means "forgetting," was the firstborn son, while Ephraim, whose name means "fruitful," was the younger brother. Ephraim, the younger brother, was chosen as the heir of the Abrahamic covenant.

One of the big questions about Asenath is why, after all the painstaking work God went through to ensure that Isaac and Jacob married women among their own people, did he allow Joseph, the birthright son of the Abrahamic covenant, to marry an Egyptian woman? Yet not just *any* Egyptian woman but an Egyptian woman who was also the daughter of a pagan priest. Scholars even think that Asenath's name in Egyptian means "she who belongs to Neith (the goddess)." It is likely that she had been taught from her youth to worship and sacrifice to the Egyptian gods. She wasn't exactly the type of woman you'd think God would entrust His covenant to, and certainly not the type of woman one would imagine to become a matriarch of the house of Abraham. Yet she was.

In fact, many Latter-day Saints who have received their patriarchal blessings know they are from the lineage of Ephraim, which means Asenath is their matriarch. She is their link—their branch—in the family of Abraham. So how do we explain Asenath?

An apocryphal book called *Joseph and Asenath* details the story of Asenath's conversion to the God of Abraham. The book is thought to have been originally written in Greek and to be a Jewish work composed sometime between 1 BC and 2 AD to explain why Joseph would have married a woman outside of the covenant, let alone the daughter of a pagan priest.[1]

The story says that while Joseph was collecting grain, he went to the Egyptian city of On and visited Asenath's father, the priest there. Asenath, who was watching from the window, saw Joseph, and immediately fell in love with him. Her father invited her down to meet him and Joseph talked to her, blessed her, and treated her kindly. But he dismissed her as a prospective wife because she was an idol worshiper. After their meeting, Asenath returned to her room, where she was so overcome that she removed all her finery, threw it out the window, and clothed herself in sackcloth and ashes. She did not eat for seven days or nights.

On the eighth day Asenath prayed to God to forgive her for her mistakes and being deceived by the gods of Egypt. When she finished her prayer, she saw the morning star rise and began to rejoice, saying, "The Lord God has indeed heard me, for this star is a messenger and herald of the light of the great day." Then a light appeared, and an angel called her by name and told her, "Take heart, Aseneth, for lo, the Lord has heard the words of your confession. . . . From to-day you will be made new, and refashioned, and given new life. . . . You shall no more be called Aseneth, but 'City of Refuge' shall be your name; for many nations shall take refuge in you, and under your wings shall many peoples find shelter, and within your walls those who give their allegiance to God in penitence will find security."

The angel told her to put on her wedding clothes and prepare a feast (followed by a miracle with a honeycomb and bees) and that he would go get Joseph for her to marry. When Joseph arrived, he saw the change in Asenath and knew she had been converted to the one true God. They were married soon after.

While much of the apocryphal *Joseph and Asenath* narrative seems a bit too fantastic to be completely authentic, I think that the overarching message of the book is true—that Asenath underwent a powerful conversion to the gospel and the true and living God. I think that the fruits of her life—as evidenced through her two sons—indicate that she understood what it meant to make and honor covenants, and taught her children to do the same.

I wouldn't be surprised if she did, like the Joseph and Asenath narrative suggests, receive a visit from a heavenly being and receive divine instruction from heaven. God had a lot riding on Asenath. It was through her and Joseph's lineage that the Abrahamic covenant had to be passed on for God to keep his promise to Abraham. God needed a woman who would teach her children and prepare them to receive and honor the blessings and responsibilities of His covenant. He couldn't just leave things to chance.

Several times in the scriptures, we read how when God needs to get someone to shape up, He provides them with sudden, unexpected, and miraculous conversions, such as those of Paul and Alma the Younger. It is beautiful to think of Asenath as being a female recipient of such a miraculous conversion. Just like Paul or Alma the Younger she turned her life around and became a strong, holy woman of God; a powerful force for truth that has echoed down through the ages to all of her posterity.

Finally, it is significant to me that one of the missions given to the tribe of Ephraim is to carry the message of the Restoration of the gospel to the world and to lead the gathering of the ten scattered tribes. The children of Ephraim are to seek out those who are wandering in darkness and bring them to a knowledge of Jesus Christ and help receive their covenants (see Deuteronomy 33:13–17; D&C 64:36, 133:26–34).[2] How fitting it is, then, that the mother of that tribe would be a convert herself.

The *Women* Who Delivered *Moses:* Jochebed, Puah, Shiphrah, and Pharaoh's Daughter

The story of Moses is filled with incredible women. Moses owed his existence to women who made deeply personal choices that allowed God to raise up a deliverer to restore the children of Israel to the light, power, and glory promised them by their Father Abraham. These women "delivered the deliverer."

• Jochebed •

Jochebed was Moses's mother. She was of priestly lineage, and Numbers 26:59 tells us that she was "the daughter of Levi, whom her mother bare to Levi in Egypt." It is unclear here if this means she was the actual daughter of Levi, the son of Jacob, or if she was the daughter of one of his decedents who was also named Levi.[1] Either way, it is significant that she was from the lineage whose family would later bear the Aaronic, also called the Levitical, Priesthood.

Jochebed married Amram, who was a Levite (he also happened to be her nephew; see Exodus 6:20). They lived in Egypt when the Hebrews were in bondage. The book of Exodus paints a grim picture of what life was like for the Hebrews in Egypt. The pharaoh was concerned at how quickly the Hebrews were having children and feared that they would soon outnumber the Egyptians. His first attempt at diminishing the Hebrew population was to enslave them and force them into hard physical work. Yet not even extreme poverty and slavery could dissuade the Hebrews from having more children. Pharaoh then ordered that all the male children of the Hebrews be thrown into the river.

If ever a couple had a valid reason for avoiding pregnancy, it was Jochebed and Amram. In fact, the apocryphal book of Jasher states that when Pharaoh made his horrible decree, many of the Hebrew men sent their wives away so that they would not get pregnant. Amram, the book of Jasher says, sent Jochebed away for three years. Yet Moses's sister, Miriam, changed that. Jasher stated, "At that time the spirit of God was upon Miriam the daughter of Amram the sister of Aaron, and she went forth and prophesied about the house, saying, Behold a son will be born unto us from my father and mother this time, and he will save Israel from the hands of Egypt. And when Amram heard the words of his daughter, he went and took his wife back to the house, after he had driven her away at the time when Pharaoh ordered every male child of the house of Jacob to be thrown into the water."[2]

After Miriam's prophecy, Jochebed and Amram had the faith to reunite and conceive another child, even though they knew there was a strong possibility their child would be killed. I am sure that Jochebed, as she and Amram followed the revelation they had received, wondered how things would work out. Having a baby probably did not seem like the logical or safe thing to do. Yet she had faith and chose life even amidst violence, poverty, and uncertainty. Her courageous choice would pave the way for God to restore and deliver His chosen people.

> *These women "delivered the deliverer."*

• Puah and Shiphrah •

The book of Exodus tells us that when Pharaoh saw that his population control measures were not working, he told two of the midwives, Puah and Shiphrah, "When you do the office of a midwife to the Hebrew women, and see them upon the stools; if it be a son, then ye shall kill him: but if it be a daughter, then she shall live" (Exodus 1:16).

Exodus doesn't make it clear if Puah and Shiphrah were Egyptian or if they were Hebrew. The text simply tells us that they were "the Hebrew midwives," which may have meant they were the midwives that attended the Hebrews, or they were Hebrews themselves.

According to Josephus, to make sure that the children really were killed, Pharaoh employed Egyptian midwives to watch over the labors of the Hebrew women. He wrote, "For those were the women who were enjoined to do the office of midwives to them; and by reason of their relation to the king would not transgress his commands. He enjoined also, That if any parents should disobey him, and venture to save their male children alive, they and their families should be destroyed."[3]

It makes sense to me that Pharaoh would not have trusted Hebrew midwives to destroy their own children, and would have instead put Egyptian women in charge. Yet the names Puah and Shiphrah are both Hebrew names, so their nationality is unclear.[4]

Regardless, these two women showed incredible integrity. Against what must have been immense political and social pressure to follow Pharaoh's orders, Puah and Shiphrah (and probably many other midwives) refused to destroy life. The Hebrew women continued to bear children, and the midwives continued to deliver them and saved all the children they could, regardless of their gender.

When Pharaoh called them back and asked why there were still so many male babies running around, they told him, "Because the Hebrew women are not as the Egyptian women; for they are lively, and are delivered ere the midwives come in unto them" (Exodus 1:19). This was a thinly veiled excuse, and it must have taken some

real moral courage to stand up to Pharaoh and the culture of the time. They remind me of the many modern women who, against the tide of popular culture, take a stand for the lives of children—born and unborn.

The book of Jasher tells how Pharaoh would send his men out every day to look for male babies. If they found any, they would throw them in the river. It also says that many of the Egyptian women would walk through the Hebrew homes with their crying children so that if other children were hiding they would also start crying. If the Egyptian women heard a child, they would find the soldiers and send them to the house.[5]

Something of that nature happened to Jochebed, because after three months, she "could no longer hide [Moses]" (Exodus 2:3). Some Jewish writings suggest that Jochebed hid Moses for so long by making a dugout under the floor of the house and covering it with blankets.[6] It wrings my heart to think about the anguish and worry that Jochebed must have gone through those three months as she desperately tried to save her baby's life. Yet it appears that even as she tried to hide him, she had also prepared for a circumstance in which she would have to let him go. I love these words by author Vanessa Ochs about Jochebed's strength to let her baby go:

"Let my people go" is the famous refrain from the Exodus story, spoken by Moses to Pharaoh over and over until Pharaoh finally relents. From Moses's mother, Yocheved, we can learn about a different, although related, kind of letting go.

Yocheved teaches us that as much as we are loath to let a child go, we must nonetheless find safe and wise ways to launch our children into the world if they are to survive and flourish as independent, skillful, and competent people. . . .

Had Yocheved not let her son go at the right time and in the right place and with all the right precautions in place, Moses would surely not have survived infancy. He would not have grown into a man whose own life experiences, growing up in the house of Pharaoh, prepared him to lead his people out of a place of constriction and oppression and into openness and freedom.[7]

Many situations force mothers to make the difficult decision to let their children go. Yet just like Jochebed, I think we can prepare ourselves and our children for those moments by following the instructions we get from the Spirit. Jochebed built a small ark in which to place Moses and carefully lined it with pitch so it wouldn't leak. She did all that was within her power, and then she turned the rest over to God. She went to the Nile River and carefully laid the ark among the reeds along the riverbank. She instructed Miriam to stay with it and watch over it. Visual depictions of Moses always show him careening down rapids in his cradle, yet I don't think Jochebed was that careless. I think it is more likely that Jochebed placed the ark somewhere she knew it might be found by a compassionate Egyptian woman, which is exactly what happened.

"Let my people go."

• Pharaoh's Daughter •

Several different stories explain why Pharaoh's daughter (Jewish tradition gives her name as Batya or Bathia) went down to the river to bathe. According to Jewish tradition, she went to the river because she had a dream that instructed her to bathe there. Another account claims that she had a skin condition that was irritated by the hot baths in the palace.[8] The Book of Jasher describes a "terrible heat in the land of Egypt, which burned up the flesh of man like the sun in his circuit, and it greatly oppressed the Egyptians."[9] Something compelled the princess to bathe in the river, rather than privately, where she found the ark that Jochebed had left in the reeds. When she opened it, "she saw the child: and, behold, the babe wept. And she had compassion on him, and said, This is one of the Hebrews' children" (Exodus 2:6).

I love that phrase "and she had compassion on him." Here was a woman who, as far as we know, had no children of her own but who had a "mother heart." Her father had commanded that all Hebrew boys should be killed, yet despite the consequences that might come, Pharaoh's daughter didn't hesitate. She saved Moses's life by claiming him as her own son. Her heart was open to life, and it motivated her to love and care for a child that wasn't her own. Author Diana Webb compared Pharaoh's daughter's lifting Moses out of the Nile to the act of giving birth: "She [Pharaoh's daughter] delivers him from waters that could have caused him to lose his life at any moment. Without her intervention, the fate of the Hebrew baby boy would have been, in all probability, tragic. Batya's act of recovering Jochebed's basket 'is as vital . . . as [his mother's] act of giving the baby life. Both acts gave life to Moses.'"[10]

I have watched women make the same choice that Pharaoh's daughter did as they open their hearts and their homes to children who need safety, love, and the best chance at a future. Sometimes it is as big as adopting a child or organizing international aid for suffering children. Other times it is as simple as loving the struggling child in their neighborhood or taking the wayward teenager under their arm. Like Pharaoh's daughter, these women give life to children through their love and guidance.

The Bible account states that after the baby was found, Miriam, Moses's sister, approached Pharaoh's daughter and asked her if she should find a woman from among the Hebrews to nurse him (Exodus 2:8–9). It is unclear why Miriam would have been familiar or bold enough with the princess to offer such a suggestion. The Book of Jasher suggests that after finding the child, Pharaoh's daughter tried to find a nurse for the baby among the Egyptian women, but baby Moses wouldn't nurse from any of them. Eventually Miriam, who had been watching from afar, approached Pharaoh's daughter and told her that she knew a nurse among the Hebrew women who could nurse the child. Pharaoh's daughter, who probably suspected Miriam knew who the baby's mother was, told her to bring this woman to her. Of course, Miriam returned with Jochebed, and she stayed with her baby and nursed him until he was old enough to be weaned. What a tender mercy that must have been for Jochebed, who thought she would never see him again.

When I think of the relationship between Pharaoh's daughter and Jochebed, I am reminded of the women I know who have adopted children but still have strong connections with their children's birth mothers. These birth mothers are often major figures in their children's lives, reaffirming to the children their roots and their heritage. Just like Pharaoh's daughter and Jochebed, both mothers are important and both have a shaping and defining influence on their children's lives. Motherhood is not limited by biology, and Pharaoh's daughter is a powerful example of that truth.

The life of Moses is a remarkable example of how God works through individuals to bless entire nations. E. T. Sullivan wrote, "When God wants a great work done in the world or a great wrong righted, he goes about it in a very unusual way. He doesn't stir up his earthquakes or send forth his thunderbolts. Instead, he has a helpless baby born, perhaps in a simple home out of some obscure mother. And then God puts the idea into the mother's heart, and she puts it into the baby's mind. And then God waits. The greatest forces in the world are not the earthquakes and the thunderbolts. The greatest forces in the world are babies."[11]

Moses was one such baby. Many individuals made personal sacrifices to nurture and protect him as a baby: Miriam, who felt of his divine mission before he was even born; his father, who had faith to bring another child into his family even under dire circumstances; Jochebed, who was willing to carry and bear a child knowing that he would probably die; Puah and Shiphrah, who risked their lives to stand up for the sanctity of life; and Pharaoh's daughter, whose mother heart prompted her to feel love and compassion for a child that was not her own. Even when they were surrounded by death and darkness, they chose life and love, and it made all the difference.

• What does it mean for a woman to be "unclean"? •

One of the most bothersome words in the Old Testament is the word *unclean*, especially when it relates to menstruation, childbirth, sexual intimacy, and women's bodies. For example, in Leviticus 15:19–20, it says,

> And if a woman have an issue, and her issue in her flesh be blood, she shall be put apart seven days: and whosoever toucheth her shall be unclean until the even.

> And every thing that she lieth upon in her separation shall be unclean: every thing also that she sitteth upon shall be unclean.

These scriptures go on for thirteen more verses explaining all the ways women can be unclean during menstruation. Leviticus 12 explains that a woman was unclean after childbirth, and that she was doubly unclean after giving birth to a girl. It seems like the Bible is filled with examples of how a woman's body, especially the blood she sheds, is unclean. This disturbed me. How could God consider something so good as the creation of human life dirty or sinful?

He doesn't.

The first thing to understand is that the Hebrew word that is translated as "unclean" in the KJV is the word *tuma*, and it does not mean "dirty" or "contaminated." The word *tuma* is a complex word that can't be directly translated into English. The simplest explanation is that it is the "energy of death" that fills the world. It comes from the word *tamai* which means "spiritually impure," as in being separated from the presence of God. In fact, according to Jewish teachings, *tuma* is what Adam and Eve brought into the world when they took

of the fruit of the tree of knowledge of good and evil. *Tuma* is the loss of spiritual power that comes from being distanced from God and being able to die, both physically and spiritually.

A dead body is the highest form of uncleanliness (*tuma*) because a living person, organized in the image of God, has the greatest spiritual potential of all God's creations. When a person dies, their spiritual potential departs and creates a "spiritual vacuum," an absence of the divine power which animated it. The empty shell of a body is then considered *tuma*. Without Jesus Christ's Atonement and Resurrection, that body would be forever separated from God, forever *tuma*.

In a similar way, a woman when she is pregnant is filled with potential life and the spiritual power of creation. Yet when her child is born, that spiritual power departs and she becomes *tuma*. In addition, by bringing a new person into the world, she has also brought more death, because each child who lives must also, one day, die. In a sense each one of us "fell" on the day we were born, leaving the presence of God where we were pure and sinless. When we were born we became subject to the "natural man" and gained the ability to sin, thus distancing us further from God. Perhaps this is also the reason that a woman who gave birth to a girl was considered twice as "unclean" (see Leviticus 12) because each girl born means more life which brings with it death, sin, and separation from God—more *tuma*.

A man was also considered to be *tuma* after sexual intercourse because of the loss of potential life contained in each the sperm he spilled. In a similar way a woman was considered unclean after menstruation because each egg that she shed had the potential to become a new human life. Each egg inside a woman is filled with divine power, the power to activate and create human life. While the egg remains inside of her, its spiritual potential is high. Yet once the egg passes through her body that spiritual potential leaves, putting her in a state of *tuma*.

To become clean (ritually pure) from *tuma*, you had to bathe in a ceremonial bath called a *mikvah*. The *mikvah* served no hygienic purpose because before someone bathed in it they had to wash themselves completely from head to toe. In many ways, it was much like baptism; immersing yourself completely under the water to become spiritually clean and reconciled with God. I loved how this Jewish woman explained her understanding of *tuma* and the *mikvah*. She wrote:

> In the words of Rabbi Aryeh Kaplan, ". . . water represents the womb of Creation. When a person immerses in the *mikvah*, he is placing himself in the state of the world yet unborn, subjecting himself totally to G-d's creative power." In this context, it is easy to understand why immersion in a *mikvah* removes *tuma*. After the contact with death, we submerge ourselves in the substance from which life emerged.[1]

Christ fulfilled the law of Moses and enabled us to become clean from our sins, and from our *tuma*. Each week we take the sacrament we are becoming clean-- re-born-- in much the same way that the *mikvah* made ancient Jews clean from their fallen state, their state of *tuma*. It is beautiful symbolism and was designed to turn the children of Israel's hearts towards their need for a Savior, the One who saves us from our continual state of *tuma*.

These laws also had other lessons to teach. The same Jewish woman I quote above also wrote,

> The menstrual Laws, like all the Laws of Judaism, imbue us with a constant consciousness of the miracles which comprise our daily existence. We certainly do not view the menstruation cycle as disgusting, or even as routine and ordinary. Rather, these Laws enable us to recognize the awesome potential of life as it regenerates itself within our very own bodies.[2]

When we come to understand—truly understand—the incredible power that we house within our bodies it changes the way we feel about ourselves. Think, how incredible it is that every woman who is born into the world has hundreds of thousands of eggs laying wait in her body. At puberty, her power to transform those eggs into another human being becomes activated. From that point on every month, for the next thirty or forty years, she will shed her blood as a constant tribute to the continuation of life. Even if none of those eggs ever become a living human person, her body is a powerhouse of life, creating and sacrificing each month with continual hope. That isn't "dirty" or "unclean" in any way, just plain miraculous.

Zipporah

And it came to pass by the way in the inn, that the Lord met [Moses], and sought to kill him.

Then Zipporah took a sharp stone, and cut off the foreskin of her son, and cast it at his feet, and said, Surely a bloody husband art thou to me.

So he let him go: then she said, A bloody husband thou art, because of the circumcision.

Exodus 4:24–26

Zipporah was the wife of Moses. After Moses killed an Egyptian, he fled into the desert and rested near a well in the land of Midian. There he met the seven daughters of the "priest of Midian" (named Jethro¹), who were drawing water for their father's flocks. They were being harassed by other shepherds who would not let them near the well. Moses championed the young women and "stood up and helped them, and watered their flock" (Exodus 2:17).

Then, in a scene very reminiscent of the matriarchs Rebekah and Rachel, the seven girls went back to their father and told them about the man they had met at the well. When Jethro learned they had left him at the well, he told them to go back and "call him, that he may eat bread" (Exodus 2:20). Moses was content to stay with Jethro and lived with him for forty years, eventually marrying Zipporah and having two sons with her—Gershom and Eliezer.

Author James R. Baker suggests that Moses's marriage to Zipporah was an unusual one, one called a "metronymic marriage." Baker explained:

> In a metronymic marriage the husband joined his wife's family, and the children took the name of the mother or her father. Other indications a marriage was metronymic were the absence of a bride-price, dowry, or contract; the wife remaining in her father's house; a stipulation that the father's inheritance passed to the daughter's children; the use of kinship terms between father-in-law and son-in-law such as "father" and "son"; the husband seeking permission of the father-in-law for decisions; and similar acts of deference to the father-in-law.[2]

Baker points to several indications in Moses's story that indicate that this may have been the arrangement Moses was in with Zipporah's father:

> The scriptures do not mention a bride-price or dowry, the absence of which is one evidence of metronymic marriage. Second, "Moses kept the flock of Jethro his father in law, the priest of Midian" (Exodus 3:1), not under contract like Jacob, for it is never raised as an issue. Moses became a member of Jethro's household. A third indication that this was a metronymic marriage is that when God commanded Moses to go to Egypt and free Israel from bondage, Moses asked Jethro's permission (Ex 4:18)....
>
> After Moses had delivered Israel from bondage, Jethro brought Zipporah and their sons to Moses in the desert (Ex 18:1–5). It appears that Jethro terminated Moses' obligation to him as his metronymic father-in-law. Jethro returned to Midian (vs.27), and there is no record that they ever saw each other again. By relinquishing whatever rights he had, Jethro was released from the responsibility for supporting Zipporah and her two children in the harsh desert of Midian.[3]

The only other story we have of Zipporah is in Exodus 4 when she, Moses, and their two sons traveled to Egypt to confront Pharaoh. When they stopped for the night at an inn, the Lord appeared to Moses and was angry, "and [God's] hand was about to fall upon [Moses] to kill him" (Joseph Smith Translation, Exodus 4:24 [in the Bible appendix]). God was angry because Moses had not circumcised his son. We don't know for sure which son Moses had neglected to circumcise, or why he had not yet performed this ritual, which was usually done by the time the baby was eight days old.[4] For some reason, Moses had been hesitant or neglectful of this important practice.

It is interesting how many parallels exist between Moses and the Prophet Joseph Smith, both of whom were called by God to bring back, or "restore" God's covenant relationship with his people. Moses's experience with circumcision reminds me of an experience Joseph Smith had when he was hesitant to practice the commandment of plural marriage. An essay on LDS.org describes an experience Joseph Smith had similar to Moses's experience:

> When God commands a difficult task, He sometimes sends additional messengers to encourage His people to obey. Consistent with this pattern, Joseph told associates that an angel appeared to him three times between 1834 and 1842 and commanded him to proceed with plural marriage when he hesitated to move forward. During the third and final appearance, the angel came with a drawn sword, threatening Joseph with destruction unless he went forward and obeyed the commandment fully.[5]

Like Moses, Joseph Smith had been threatened with death if he would not obey God's commandment. This was a crucial moment for both prophets because if they refused to obey, then God would remove them from their role.

In Moses's case, it was Zipporah who saved him. Seeing that Moses was crippled with fear and unable to act, she boldly took a sharp stone and circumcised her son. The Joseph Smith Translation clarifies that when she was finished she threw "the stone," not the foreskin, at Moses's feet and told him, "Thou art a bloody husband to me" (Joseph Smith Translation, Exodus 4:25 [in Bible appendix]). In Hebrew, this phrase means a "bridegroom of blood," and we don't really know what it means. Footnote *b* to this scripture states that "there is some covenant significance in this." Beyond this we don't know what Zipporah meant.

Because we don't completely understand this story, we should focus on Zipporah's initiative. Circumcision was usually done by a child's father, and it was a "token" of the Abrahamic covenant. Zipporah circumcising her son would have been like a woman baptizing her child or giving him a baby blessing. Thus, it is surprising that God accepted the ordinance and "spared Moses and let him go, because Zipporah, his wife, circumcised the child" (Joseph Smith Translation, Exodus 4:26 [in Bible appendix]). Instead of being angry at Zipporah, God seems to acknowledge that she had done the right thing,

The Joseph Smith Translation gives us more insight into this story, telling us that after Zipporah performed the circumcision that "Moses was ashamed, and hid his face from the Lord, and said, I have sinned before the Lord" (Joseph Smith Translation, Exodus 4:26 [in Bible appendix]). It is clear from this addition that Moses realized that he had made a mistake and that Zipporah had stepped in and done what he should have done.[6]

This brings up interesting questions. Can a woman perform an ordinance? What if a husband is unwilling or unworthy to do it? Could she, like Zipporah step in? One thing I have learned from the scriptures is that for every rule or commandment God gives, there is always an exception. Yet just because there is one exception in the scriptures, that doesn't mean the exception applies to everyone. For example, the Spirit directed Nephi to kill Laban, but we don't have permission to go around cutting off people's heads. I think Zipporah, put in a very serious situation, probably acted as the Spirit directed. She stood in for her husband, and the Lord accepted her offering and blessed her and Moses for it.

I think that Zipporah teaches us that even though women aren't authorized to perform ordinances such as baptisms or baby blessings, we can act with spiritual power. When God, through the Holy Ghost, offers us opportunities to act with His power, we need to accept those opportunities. A friend told me how one day when she was home by herself caring for her newborn daughter, she received a powerful prompting to give her daughter a blessing. She held the little girl in her arms and said the words that the Spirit poured into her mind. It was a beautiful blessing—a *mother's* blessing—and she felt that everything she had said in it had been guided by the Spirit. This blessing didn't replace the baby blessing that her husband performed later for their daughter. She had simply followed the Spirit and accepted the opportunity that had been given to her.

In a similar way, women whose husbands, such as Moses, are hesitant to perform the roles a father should assume in the home—such as presiding at family home evening and overseeing family prayer and scripture study—shouldn't hesitate to step in. I think the Lord rejoices when He sees mothers leading their children in prayer, family scripture study, and family home evening. For example, a new convert in our ward has three little children and little support from her husband. I have been so impressed as I have watched her, with her blossoming understanding of the gospel, put forth the effort to hold family home evening and prayers with her little family. In her own simple way, she reminds me of Zipporah—stepping up to do what needs to done and leading her family with strength.

Zipporah's example, of stepping in and performing the circumcision when Moses wouldn't, humbled Moses and changed him. He was a different man after the incident at the inn. Never again did he falter or doubt. He became stalwart in his obedience to God and became God's great lawgiver, restoring to the Israelites the priesthood and the ordinances of the gospel. I'd like to think that was because Zipporah's example inspired him to grow into the type of man and prophet that God and the Israelite nation needed him to be.

• Circumcision •

When God covenanted with Abraham that he would be the father of many nations (see Genesis 17), he also gave him the token—a mark—by which this covenant would be passed on to his descendants. "This is my covenant, which ye shall keep, between me and you and thy seed after thee," God told Abraham. "Every man child among you shall be circumcised. And ye shall circumcise the flesh of your foreskin; and *it shall be a token of the covenant* betwixt me and you" (Genesis 17:10–11; emphasis added).

Circumcision was the sign that one had entered a covenant relationship with God, that one was part of the "everlasting covenant" and heir to all the blessings of Abraham. In fact, in the time of Moses a Jewish man who was not circumcised was considered "cut off" from the house of Israel and was not permitted to eat of the Passover. The token of circumcision was also connected with the giving of a name. Abraham got his new name at the time he made the covenant and underwent circumcision. In the New Testament, we also know that John the Baptist wasn't given a name until his circumcision, which happened at eight days old (see Luke 1:59). Christ also was given his name at the time He was circumcised (see Luke 2:21).

Circumcision was a unique offering because unlike other sacrifices that required the life of an animal, the Abrahamic covenant required a blood sacrifice from the person covenanting. The removal of the foreskin is a painful, bloody process that leaves a man forever changed and marked. The word *circumcision* means "around" (circum-) and "cutting" (-cision), and it is a round mark made on a man's body to remind him of the covenant he had made with a God; a covenant that represents his submission to God and a promise to use his procreative power righteously.

I like how Rochel Holzkenner explained the spiritual significance of circumcision (called here *brit*):

> Circumcision is not an intellectual or glamorous act. It's probably as gory as you get. Yet G–d describes this act of commitment as one of great importance. . . . More than other commandments, circumcision creates an irrevocable bond between G–d and His people. . . .

> . . . Our bond of nationhood and communion with G–d isn't expressed in a mantra or a meditation, but in a cutting of flesh. The *brit* is the only conduit for this covenant, a sublime and irreversible connection to G–d. . . .

> Circumcision is a tangible reminder to all men that they are the masters of their bodies, that they are in control of their sexual urges. Cutting back the foreskin represents tapering the self-centered nature of lust. It's not only about me, but about another person's dignity and desires. It's not all about the pleasure that I want, but about the pleasure that G–d wants me to have.[7]

Women like Sarah were also included in the Abrahamic covenant but were not required to be circumcised. Yet it is interesting that soon after Abraham circumcised himself, Sarah began to menstruate again. Abraham's blood offering thus coincided with Sarah's blood offering, both her monthly blood and the blood she shed at childbirth. For Sarah, as it was for Abraham, God's "covenant shall be in your flesh" (Genesis 17:13).

Today in the LDS Church, we still believe in Abraham's covenant and call it the "new and everlasting covenant." The covenant is "new" partly because it no longer involves circumcision. In the Book of Mormon, we read that Jesus Christ was promised to be the "great and last sacrifice" and that through him there would be "a stop to the shedding of blood" (Alma 34:13), including animal sacrifices and circumcision. In the New Testament, Paul taught that Jesus "was a minister of the circumcision for the truth of God, to confirm the promises made unto the fathers" (Romans 15:8) and that "circumcision is nothing, and uncircumcision is nothing, but the keeping of the commandments of God" (1 Corinthians 7:19). The Book of Mormon prophet Mormon compared circumcision to infant baptism, saying that neither were needed because of Jesus Christ.[8] Through Jesus Christ, and His great sacrifice, the promises of the Abrahamic covenant are sure.

Today, God requires the higher law. Instead of circumcising our children, we should "circumcise therefore the foreskin of [our] heart[s]" (Deuteronomy 10:16). The removal of the covering of our hearts is perhaps a harder and more painful process than that of physical circumcision. It requires that we submit our will to God, that we master our passions and demonstrate obedience, that we are willing to open ourselves completely to God. Just as in Abraham and Sarah's day, partaking of God's covenant requires a deeply personal sacrifice of *ourselves*.

Miriam

And they said, Hath the Lord indeed spoken only by Moses? Hath he not spoken also by us? And the Lord heard it. . . .

And the cloud departed from off the tabernacle; and, behold, Miriam became leprous, white as snow: and Aaron looked upon Miriam, and, behold, she was leprous.

And Aaron said unto Moses, Alas, my lord, I beseech thee, lay not the sin upon us, wherein we have done foolishly, and wherein we have sinned.

Let her not be as one dead, of whom the flesh is half consumed when he cometh out of his mother's womb.

Numbers 12:2, 10–12

Miriam, the older sister of Moses, was blessed with spiritual gifts, specifically the gift of prophecy. In fact, Miriam's gift was so powerful that she was known as "the prophetess." She had the ability to speak with power and with authority. Numbers 12 tells the story of how Miriam and Aaron publicly criticized Moses for his marriage to an Ethiopian woman. Miriam spoke boldly against Moses, saying, "Hath the Lord indeed spoken only by Moses? Hath he not spoken also by us?" (Numbers 12:2).

Miriam's question wasn't wrong—it was a good question about the way in which God was operating His kingdom on the earth. Later, we see that her process of questioning opened an important dialogue with God about the prophet's role and responsibilities. It was because of her question that the Lord could give the children of Israel more understanding about how the priesthood and God's kingdom operate. Her question wasn't the problem. The problem was that Miriam had, at her core, what I have heard called "spiritual ego." I love this explanation:

> What is spiritual ego? . . .
>
> . . . It is that part of self that feels it has accomplished something very special and it causes us to feel superior in relation to others because we believe we have attained something that sets us apart from the masses.
>
> If we find ourselves at any point along the path of spiritual awareness and expanding consciousness, feeling that we've arrived, conquered or accomplished something really spiritually superior, or special, and that this accomplishment puts us above others in any way, we can rest assured, we've activated the spiritual ego.[1]

When we have spiritual ego, we have an over-inflated sense of our own spiritual ability and understanding. We begin to think that we are somehow unique, that God has told us or given us something that others don't have. When we have spiritual ego, we don't ask questions sincerely desiring an answer or direction. Instead, we ask a question, already thinking that we know what the answer should be. The problem is that when the answer comes and it isn't what we were expecting, it can be hard to humble ourselves and accept counsel. As a result, it is usually spiritual ego that causes people to apostatize or leave the Church.

Brigham Young taught the following about spiritual ego:

> Whenever there is a disposition manifested in any of the members of this Church to question the right of the President of the whole Church to direct in all things, you see manifested evidences of apostasy—of a spirit which, if encouraged, will lead to a separation from the Church and to final destruction. . . .
>
> When a man begins to find fault, inquiring in regard to this, that, and the other, saying, "Does this or that look as though the Lord dictated it?" you may know that that person has more or less of the spirit of apostasy. . . .
>
> Many imbibe [conceive] the idea that they are capable of leading out in teaching principles that never have been taught. They are not aware that the moment they give way to this hallucination the Devil has power over them to lead them onto unholy ground. . . .
>
> [Such a person] will make false prophecies, yet he will do it by the spirit of prophecy; he will feel that he is a prophet and can prophesy, but he does it by another spirit and power than that which was given him of the Lord. He uses the gift as much as you and I use ours.[2]

Can you see Miriam in what Brigham Young was saying? Whether she realized it or not, she had a bad case of spiritual ego, the type of pride that, if it goes unchecked, results in apostasy.

Compare this to Moses whom it says in Numbers 12:3 "was very meek, above all the men which were upon the face of the earth." Moses, who was the prophet of the Lord, was devoid of all spiritual ego. He was humble, contrite, and teachable. He had seen a vision of all of God's creations and knew "that man is nothing"

(Moses 1:10). He understood, he *saw*, and as a result he was meek and humble. His attitude was the opposite of Miriam's and Aaron's.

Because of their pride, God called Aaron and Miriam to the tabernacle. He explained to them the difference between possessing the spiritual gift of prophecy—which both Aaron and Miriam had—and the calling of *the* prophet—which only Moses had: "If there be a prophet [one who has the gift of prophecy] among you, I the Lord will make myself known unto him in a vision, and will speak unto him in a dream" (Numbers 12:6).

Both Aaron and Miriam could relate to this. Perhaps they had seen the Lord in a dream or had strong spiritual promptings that had led them to believe that they had more authority and understanding than they did. Then the Lord clarified that Moses was not this type of prophet; he was *the* prophet who had been called and chosen by God to lead his people and that "with him will I speak mouth to mouth, even apparently, and not in dark speeches; and the similitude of the Lord shall he behold" (Numbers 12:8).

With these words, the Lord was clarifying how His priesthood power worked and who held the right to receive revelation for the Church. He was making clear that it was not Miriam or Aaron who held these keys and this power. This was an important clarification and one that Miriam's questions helped bring about.

• Leprosy and Living Death •

After speaking with the Lord in the tabernacle, Miriam was struck with leprosy. It is interesting to me that Miriam, not Aaron, ended up with leprosy. At first this seems supremely unfair. Even Aaron admitted, "*We* have done foolishly, and wherein *we* have sinned" (Numbers 12:11; emphasis added). If they were both at fault, if they both asked the question, then why was only Miriam cursed with leprosy?

The text in Numbers 12:1 gives us some clues. First, in Hebrew the verb that is translated as "spake against" is in the feminine tense, indicating that Miriam was the main speaker. Second, Miriam's name is listed before Aaron's in the story, suggesting that, while Aaron certainly was involved, it may have been primarily Miriam who instigated and led the opposition to Moses.

The curse of leprosy is a significant consequence for Miriam's actions. The law of Moses consisted of many physical rules. While they often had health benefits, they were primarily designed to bear witness of the need for Jesus Christ. Leprosy was no exception, and Miriam's bout with leprosy was designed to be a physical symbol of her spiritual ailment.

Leprosy in the Bible included a wide variety of skin ailments. Among them was what we know as leprosy today, a highly contagious bacterial disease that results in nerve damage, especially in the skin, eyes, and respiratory tract. Because of this nerve damage, many people with leprosy are unable to feel pain and often lose parts of their hands, feet, and other extremities due to repeated injuries. It is also possible for the infection to lie dormant for five to twenty years before symptoms begin to manifest. In Bible times, leprosy was thought to be a curse from God because no one knew how it was contracted, it spread from person to person, and there was no cure for it. Even today, though scientists can treat and cure leprosy, they are still unsure about how it is spread.

Understanding the nature of leprosy makes it easy to see why ancient people were terrified of the disease and often required lepers to live outside of cities and limited their contact with others. In fact, in the Old Testament, the law of Moses gives a detailed set of rules concerning how leprosy should be dealt with among the children of Israel. Leviticus 13:45–46 instructs that a leper's "clothes shall be rent, and his head bare, and he shall put a covering upon his upper lip [cover his mouth] and shall cry, Unclean, Unclean. . . . [And] he shall dwell alone; without the camp shall his habitation be." There were also complex rules for determining if a person, a piece of clothing, and even a house were infected with leprosy (see Leviticus 13–14).

The Bible speaks of people being "cleansed" from leprosy and not "healed" (see Matthew 8:3; Mark 1:42; Leviticus 14:7). This is because among the Israelites someone having leprosy was considered "unclean," *tuma* in Hebrew. Being *tuma* did not mean you were physically dirty or repulsive, but rather the word indicated a loss of spiritual power. For example, having contact with a dead body made someone *tuma* because they had touched something that had lost its innate spiritual power. Having leprosy made someone *tuma* because there was no cure for it, and in the eyes of the camp, the person was a good as dead.

Miriam was cursed with leprosy—living death—because her spiritual ego had caused her to fight against God. Her outward condition of leprosy was a sign of the inward condition of her soul. She had "spiritual leprosy," the eating away of the spirit that comes through apostasy and sin. Just like physical leprosy kills nerves and destroys the ability to feel, spiritual leprosy destroys the soul's power and

results in a decrease of the ability to feel or to perceive the promptings of the Spirit. Brigham Young taught, "Let a man or woman who has received much of the power of God, visions and revelations, turn away from the holy commandments of the Lord, and it seems that their senses are taken from them, their understanding and judgment in righteousness are taken away, they go into darkness, and become like a blind person who gropes by the wall."[3] (See Isaiah 59:9–10; Deuteronomy 28:29.)

Just like physical leprosy, spiritual leprosy can spread through close contact. It doesn't take much to spread germs of discontent, anger, fear, doubt, and sin. And just like physical leprosy, those germs may lay dormant for years until a person realizes they have been infected. The ancient Israelites dealt with leprosy by closely monitoring people for the disease, going through complicated procedures to diagnosis it, and separating the person from the rest of the camp when a case was confirmed.

Today, excommunication and disfellowship are our tools for coping with outbreaks of "spiritual leprosy" among our congregations. Like the Israelites of old, we closely examine people for the signs of spiritual leprosy and go through complex procedures to diagnose the disease. We also do everything within our power to help cure or help the infected person. Yet, when there is a real case of "leprosy"—apostasy—it is imperative for the health of everyone to separate that person from the rest of the group. The key thing to remember, though, is that this separation is not done out of anger, hatred, or even fear.

When Moses and Aaron found out that Miriam had leprosy, they mourned and begged God on her behalf, saying, "Let her not be as one dead, of whom the flesh is half consumed when he cometh out of his mother's womb. . . . Heal her now, O God" (Numbers 12:12–13). Even after their pleading, the Lord told them that Miriam *must* be taken without the camp for seven days. The Lord reminded them that she was sick with leprosy—both physically *and* spiritually—and that the only way for her to get better was to go through the processes that He had set up to "cleanse" those who had been eaten away at. God reminded them that if she wasn't separated—if she wasn't excommunicated—she would never heal and go through the process to become whole.

In what must have been a tragically sad procession, Miriam was taken without the camp and left for seven days, "and the people journeyed not till Miriam was brought in again" (Numbers 12:15). They didn't give up hope in Miriam! They had faith that she would be healed of her leprosy—both spiritually and physically—and that she would return to them. They shut her out of their community, but they didn't walk away from her. This is a powerful reminder to me that we should never give up or walk away from those who have been excommunicated or disfellowshipped or who have left the Church voluntarily. We may still need to be smart—distancing ourselves emotionally or intellectually from them so that we don't also get infected—but we don't need to give up on them.

I also love the line in Numbers 12:15 that says, "Miriam was *brought in again*" (emphasis added). She had been deceived, preached things that were not true, challenged the priesthood authority of the prophet, been full of spiritual ego and pride, had lost her spiritual power, and been shut out of the presence of God and her people. It would have been easy for her to succumb to her anger and her

pride and forsake her covenants, her God, and her people. But she didn't—*Miriam came back.*

She is an incredible example of a woman who, having experienced the pain of spiritual leprosy, humbled herself, accepted guidance from the Lord, and went through the process that God had outlined for becoming clean—whole—and full of God's power again. She reminds us that spiritual leprosy has a cure. It is the Atonement of Jesus Christ.

After she returned to the camp, the only other mention we have of Miriam is that she died in a place called Kedesh and that the children of Israel buried her there (see Numbers 20:1). We don't know if after Miriam's return to the camp she regained her position of leadership among the children of Israel, but I'd like to think she did. God teaches us that, "Behold, [she] who has repented of [her] sins, the same is forgiven, and I, the Lord, remember them no more" (D&C 58:42). Even today, people who come back after excommunication have their records washed clean, with no mention of excommunication on them. Perhaps the same was true for Miriam. Regardless, what we do know is after she came back, she traveled with her people and dwelt with them again until the day of her death.

Miriam's story has been important for me as I've thought about the people I know who have fallen away from the Church. My heart aches for them as I see the spiritual leprosy eat away at their souls. Yet like the children of Israel, I am not going to walk away and leave them behind. I am going to wait; filling my heart with prayers and living with hope and anticipation for that day when—just like Miriam did—they come back and claim their spiritual power, *again.*

• The Ancient "Relief Society" of the Old Testament •

After the children of Israel miraculously passed through the Red Sea on dry ground, Miriam took a timbrel and led the women of Israel in a song and dance, singing, "Sing ye to the Lord, for he hath triumphed gloriously; the horse and his rider hath he thrown into the sea" (Exodus 15:20–21). Tradition has it that Miriam was the leader of the Israelite women, while Moses and Aaron were the leaders of the men. In fact, Miriam's leadership position among the congregation was so solid that the prophet Micah, in reminding his people about their deliverance from Egypt, listed Moses, Aaron, *and* Miriam as Israel's leaders. He wrote: "For I brought thee up out of the land of Egypt, and redeemed thee out of the house of servants; and I sent before thee Moses, Aaron, and Miriam" (Micah 6:4).

Miriam's inclusion in this list is fascinating to me. We can easily understand the leadership roles of Moses and Aaron—Moses was *the* prophet and Aaron was his counselor, spokesman, and the high priest of the tabernacle. Miriam's role is a bit more ambiguous. Her leadership of the women during the song suggests that she had a position specific to women. In addition, her confrontation with Moses about the right to receive prophecy and her title as a "prophetess" indicates that she was accustomed to receiving revelation and direction from the Lord.

We know, through the Prophet Joseph Smith, that God's priesthood organization for women (the Relief Society) is an ancient organization that has existed in past dispensations.[4] President Lorenzo Snow, in speaking to a group of Relief Society sisters, said, "You have *ever* been found at the side of the Priesthood, ready to strengthen their hands and to do your part in helping to advance the interests of the kingdom of God."[5] It is interesting to think that some form of ancient organization for women, led by women, may have existed anciently in the time of Moses and that Miriam may have overseen it.

Moses and his siblings were Levites, the tribe given the responsibility to hold the priesthood and administer the ordinances of the tabernacle. Perhaps God was organizing His Church and priesthood authority through them. We might make a chart that looks like this:

Moses—Melchizedek Priesthood Authority

Aaron—Aaronic Priesthood Authority

Miriam—Relief Society/Sisterhood/Priestess Authority

It seems that God's Church and the organization of his priesthood are *never* complete until the women are also organized.

Moses's Ethiopian Wife

Not long after Moses led the children of Israel and set up the tabernacle in the wilderness, we read that he married an Ethiopian woman and that this marriage upset his siblings, Miriam and Aaron. Who this Ethiopian woman was and why her marriage to Moses was so controversial is largely a mystery. One of the largest obstacles in understanding this Ethiopian woman's story is the fact that Moses was already married to Zipporah.

There are four scenarios I can think of that might explain this Ethiopian woman. First, Moses could have married her before Zipporah. According to Josephus, Moses married an Ethiopian woman while he was leading the Egyptian military in Ethiopia. She married Moses as a political alliance to save her people. We don't know what happened to her, but it could be possible that when Moses returned to Egypt, she rejoined him and went with him into the wilderness. Other explanations are that Zipporah had died and he was remarrying; that Zipporah was of actually of Ethiopian descent, making them the same person; or that that Moses had multiple wives.

Doctrine and Covenants seems to support the last possibility. In section 132, where the Lord explained plural marriage to Joseph Smith, the Lord listed former prophets whom he commanded to live the law of plural marriage: "David also received many wives and concubines, and also Solomon and *Moses* my servants" (D&C 132:38; emphasis added). It is possible that this Ethiopian woman may have been one of Moses's plural wives. In that case, Miriam's opposition to Moses's marriage may have been theological rather than personal, disagreeing with him on plural marriage.

Elisheba and the Daughters of Aaron

And Aaron took him Elisheba, daughter of Amminadab, sister of Naashon,
to wife; and she bare him Nadab, and Abihu, Eleazar, and Ithamar.

Exodus 6:23

Elisheba, whose name in Greek is "Elisabeth," was the wife of Aaron, the older brother and spokesman of Moses. She was from the tribe of Judah, and her brother Nashon was the "prince of the children of Judah," meaning he was the chief of the tribe (1 Chronicles 2:10). By marrying Aaron, Elisheba united the tribe of Judah (the line of the Savior) and the tribe of Levi (the line of the priesthood). This would later be significant when her husband and four sons—named Nadab, Abihu, Eleazar, and Ithamar—were set apart to hold the Levitical, or what we today call the Aaronic, priesthood.[1]

During their first year in the wilderness, the children of Israel were commanded to build a tabernacle—a holy house—for the Lord. After the tabernacle was built, Moses brought his sons to the door of the tabernacle and washed them. Then he anointed them with a holy oil and dressed them in sacred clothing (see Exodus 29). These special garments were made of "fine twined linen" and included a coat, a girdle (a belt), and a bonnet (a hat). Aaron, as the high priest, wore the same clothing but had several additional pieces.[2]

After being clothed, Moses then instructed them to lay their hands upon a bullock and two rams, which symbolically became substitutes for their sins. The priests were then required to kill the sacrifices and burn them on the altar. Afterward, Moses took blood from the sacrifice and daubed some on each priest "upon the tip of their right ear, and upon the thumbs of their right hands, and upon the great toes of their right feet . . . and sprinkled the blood upon the altar round about" (Leviticus 8:24). After this setting apart, Aaron and his sons were considered endowed with priesthood power.

The Levites' main responsibility was to oversee the sacrifices that were brought to the tabernacle. There were several different types of sacrifices (see Offerings Chart on page 120) and six important steps involved with each sacrifice:

1. The presentation of the sacrifice at the door of the tabernacle *by the person* wishing to offer the sacrifice. (Leviticus 1:3)

2. The laying on of hands *by the person* offering the sacrifice. This was done to dedicate the animal to God and to make it a representative and a substitute for the person offering it. (Leviticus 1:4)

3. The slaughtering of the animal. This was done *by the person* offering the sacrifice and was done on the north side of the altar.[3] (Leviticus 1:5)

4. The pouring out or sprinkling of the blood. After the animal was killed, *the priest* collected the blood and applied in different places. (Leviticus 1:11)

5. The burning of the sacrifice on the altar *by the priest*. (Leviticus 1:7–9)

6. The sacrificial meal (only for peace offerings). After the fat was burnt off and the priestly portions taken out, the rest of the animal was eaten *by the one who offered the sacrifice*, his family, and poor Levites in the tabernacle. (Leviticus 6:14–18)

While only Levite men served as priests, it is important to note that most of the process of offering a sacrifice was done by the *individual* presenting it. There is evidence that both men and women could offer sacrifices at the tabernacle and that women may have even been able to kill the sacrifice themselves.[4] The process of offering a sacrifice would have been a deeply personal, hands-on experience for the person offering it. The priest oversaw the procedure but did relatively little of the actual sacrificing.

Elisheba and the other Levite women would also have been involved of the eating of some of the sacrifices, which was an important and symbolic part of the process. When a sin offering was given, the best pieces were completely burnt on the altar, and the remaining portions were eaten by the priest and only his sons in a holy place. If the sacrifice was a burnt offering, which was offered by the priests every morning and evening, then all the animal (except for its skin which was kept by the priest) was completely burnt on the altar. In the case of a peace offering, the fat was burnt on the altar. According to the Bible Dictionary, "The wave breast (the portion of the priests generally) and the heave thigh (the portion of the officiating priest) were eaten by their sons and *their daughters* in a clean place. The rest was given back to the sacrifiers for them with their families and the Levites to eat" (Bible Dictionary, "Sacrifice"; emphasis added).

Though we no longer practice this type of worship, it is easy for modern-day Church members, who weekly partake of the sacrament, to understand the symbolism inherent in eating a holy and dedicated meal. It is interesting that it was only the priest and his sons—who were representing Jesus Christ—who could eat the sacrifice when it was given to make atonement for a sin. Yet when the sacrifice was given as a peace offering, one that symbolized unity with God, Levite women were *required* to eat of it along with the men. The instructions the Lord gave them made it clear that the act of eating the offered sacrifice was symbolic of the covenant relationship God had with both men and women. He said, "And this is thine; the heave offering of their gift, with all the wave offerings of the children of Israel: I have given them unto thee, and to thy sons *and to thy daughters with thee*, by a statute for ever: every one that is clean in thy house shall eat of it. . . . It is a covenant of salt for ever before the Lord unto thee and to thy seed with thee" (Numbers 18:11, 19; emphasis added).

The term "covenant of salt" is a meaningful phrase. Salt, like water and bread, is essential to life. In ancient times, it was valued highly and was even sometimes used as currency.[5] In the New Testament, the temple in Jerusalem had an entire chamber dedicated to storing salt because, just like in Old Testament times, all the sacrifices burnt on the altar were required to be salted so that they would have a "sweet savour unto the Lord" (Numbers 29:2).

Everything in the Mosaic law was designed to teach the children of Israel about Jesus Christ. It is easy for us to understand how a blood sacrifice, in the form of an animal, was symbolic of Christ's Atonement, but it may be harder for us to understand the symbolism of salt as part of the covenant. It is interesting that the Latin word for "salt" is *sal* and is the root of the word *salvation*, which means "to save the soul." One of the qualities of salt is that it saves, or preserves, things. Its unique chemical makeup works a transformation on meat, vegetables, or other substances it encounters, making them impenetrable to harmful bacteria or germs.[6] The salt literally "saves" the meat from going bad and having to be thrown away. By using salt as a part of His covenant, God was promising the children of Israel that He, through His son, would save and preserve them forever.

Understanding these two parts of the covenant, the blood and the salt, has deepened my understanding of Christ's Atonement. For years, I sat in sacrament meeting, patiently waiting for the bread and water, racking my brain for all the ways in which I had sinned or fell short that week and trying to hurriedly repent for them. It was an exercise that usually left me feeling discouraged and drained. Every week I resolved to do better, and every week I found myself reciting the same list of faults.

Then I heard Elder Bednar give his talk about the "enabling power of the Atonement," which he described as being the power that "strengthens us to do and be good and to serve beyond our own individual desire and natural capacity."[7] After that talk, I began to look at the sacrament differently. Instead of listing the ways in which I had fallen short, I began instead to list the ways in which I had seen God's hand in my life. The first Sunday I began, I was amazed at how easily I found things to be grateful for. I thought about how I'd had patience that week with a child I normally wasn't patient with. I thought of the unexpected visit from someone I'd felt estranged from and how that had healed my heart. I thought of how that week I'd had the right words come into my mind at just the right time and of a prompting I'd followed that allowed me to be an answer to someone else's prayer.

This enabling power is the "salt" part of the covenant; God's promise that when we uphold our promise to Him, He will strengthen us and preserve us from the things in the world that try to break us down and tear us apart. Shifting my thinking toward gratitude instead of guilt completely changed my sacrament experience. Instead of feeling discouraged that I was just going to keep messing up, I felt empowered and excited. I saw the power of the Atonement already at work in my life, protecting, preserving, and changing my very nature.

It is beautiful to think about Elisheba and her daughters making covenants with the Lord and partaking of holy emblems designed to purify and preserve them. These were covenant women, women who participated in the sacrificial process and had a seat alongside their husbands, sons, and brothers in the work of the tabernacle. In addition to teaching us about the power of the Atonement, their story also has much to teach us about women's relationship to the temple and to the priesthood.

In Doctrine and Covenants 84:20, God makes it clear that it is through the ordinances of the priesthood—baptism, endowment, and sealing—that "the power of godliness is manifest." The power of godliness is God's power, and God's power is priesthood power. There is no other type of power; it all comes from the same source. Every priesthood ordinance we participate in gives us additional spiritual power.

For example, the Savior stated that those who are baptized have the power to "cast out devils," "speak with new tongues," "take up serpents," "drink any deadly thing" without it hurting them, and "lay hands on the sick [so] they shall recover" (Mark 16:17–18).

The temple also outlines other incredible power, which is granted equally to both men and women through the ordinances they obtain there. This power of godliness comes to us through the men who administer the ordinances, to both God's sons and His daughters. He doesn't give us power to simply have it and hold it. He gives us power to use it.

As I've studied the story of Elisheba and the daughters of Aaron, I've been struck with the simple thought that God wants His daughters not only to participate in the covenant work of His holy houses but to use the power those covenants give them to bless others.

Using this power requires obedience, sacrifice, and making covenants with our Father in Heaven. I'd like to imagine that as Elisheba and her daughters sat down in the tabernacle to eat the sacrificial meal, they knew this too. That they had learned that keeping and honoring covenants brings power—the power of godliness—into our lives and the lives of our posterity.

> *The Atonement "strengthens us to do and be good and to serve beyond our own individual desire and natural capacity."*

• Type of Offerings Chart •

Type of Offering	Purpose of the Sacrifice	What It Is Symbolic Of	Type of Acceptable Animals	Part of Animal Sacrificed	What Was Done with the Blood	Other Requirements
Sin or Trespass (Leviticus 4–7)	To make restitution for a sin or to become clean after having become ritually unclean Trespass: A trespass (also called a "guilt") offering was specifically for sins that could be considered robbery, either to God, the king, or to another person.	Christ's Atonement	Sin: *Young Bullock* (for priests) *He-Goat* (for the people collectively, or to atone for one who was "prince" of the congregation") *She-Goat or She-Lamb* (for common person) *Two Turtle Doves or Pigeons* (for purification from uncleanliness or for the poor) *1/10 Ephah of Flour* (for those unable to afford doves or pigeons) Trespass: *always a Ram* (except in the case of Nazarites and Lepers when it would be a lamb)	The best parts of the flesh, including the fat. The remaining meat was eaten by the priest and his sons in a holy place.	Was smeared on the horns of the altar where the burnt offering was made. In the case of the high priest, or for the people collectively, it was sprinkled on the veil seven times and put upon the horns of the altar of incense.	Trespass: In addition to an animal sacrifice, it also required monetary compensation to the party transgressed against (see Leviticus 5:15–16).

Type of Offering	Purpose of the Sacrifice	What It Is Symbolic Of	Type of Acceptable Animals	Part of Animal Sacrificed	What Was Done with the Blood	Other Requirements
Burnt (Leviticus 1)	Was made every morning and evening by the priests to represent Israel's continual reliance on and submission to God	Sanctification	*Male Bullocks, Rams, and He-Goats without blemish* *Turtle Doves and Pigeons (for the poor)*	Completely burnt on the altar, except for the skin which was kept by the priest.	Sprinkled on the altar of burnt offerings	Required a Minchah, also called the "meal" offering. It was composed of unleavened bread and wine, which were offered with salt, oil, and incense. Leaven and honey could not be included in it (see Leviticus 2).
Peace (Leviticus 3)	Made by one who was at peace with God, but who desired to express gratitude or seek for greater joy and understanding	Fellowship with the Lord	*Oxen, Sheep, He-Goats and She-Goats without blemish*	Only the fat of the animal was burnt. The "wave breast" and the "heave thigh" were eaten by the priests and their sons and daughters in a clean place. The rest was eaten in a special meal by the one offering the sacrifice.	Sprinkled on the altar of burnt offerings	Also required a Minchah, or non-bloody sacrifice. Part of it was placed on the altar and the other part was eaten by the priests in a holy place. (see Leviticus 6:14–18, 23)

The *Wise-Hearted Women*

And they came, every one whose heart stirred him up, and every one whom his spirit made willing, and they brought the Lord's offering to the work of the tabernacle of the congregation, and for all his service, and for the holy garments. . . .

And all the women that were wise hearted did spin with their hands, and brought that which they had spun, both of blue, and of purple, and of scarlet, and of fine linen.

And all the women whose heart stirred them up in wisdom spun goats' hair.

Exodus 35:21, 25–26

During the construction of the tabernacle, the Lord commanded Moses to call for "all that are wise hearted, whom I have filled with the spirit of wisdom" (Exodus 28:3), that they should make the holy garments required for Aaron and his sons. God also called for "every wise hearted among you" (Exodus 35:10) to donate materials for the tabernacle; from the cloth required to build the outside walls, to the candlesticks and altar required on the inside. He also invited all those who were "wise hearted" to use their talents to construct the tabernacle and make it beautiful.

The footnotes explain that *wise hearted* means "talented or skilled" (Exodus 35:10, footnote *a*). The Lord also defines the term by saying that the wise hearted were "those whom I have filled with the spirit of wisdom" (Exodus 28:3). Excepting the master craftsmen, there were no assignments given in the building of the tabernacle. Instead, "they came, every one whose heart stirred him up, and every one whom his spirit made willing" (Exodus 35:21). In fact, the people were so generous with their donations of gold, silver, grass, fine linen, skins, wood, and oil that Moses had to send out a proclamation instructing them to stop brining things because "the stuff they had was sufficient for all the work to make it, and too much" (Exodus 36:7).

Among those who brought donations for the temple were many "women that were wise hearted," who spun the blue, purple, and scarlet linen for the veil of the temple and the priestly garments (Exodus 35:25; see also Exodus 26:31). They also spun the goat's hair that was used to construct the strong outer walls of the tabernacle (see Exodus 35:26 and 26:1) and hammered gold into fine threads to be used in weaving of Aaron's garments (see Exodus 39:3). It seems that while spinning was mainly a woman's occupation, weaving and embroidery were done by both men and women.[8] The account in Exodus 35 makes it clear that the construction of the tabernacle and the making of the priestly clothes was a joint effort between men and women, with each contributing his or her own abilities and resources.

Sometimes we may feel that we don't have any special talent, skill, or resource to contribute to God's work. When I was in college I struggled to understand the scripture, given in both the Doctrine and Covenants and the New Testament, which states, "For many are called, but few are chosen" (Matthew 22:14; see also D&C 121:34). More than anything, I wanted to be one of "the chosen." I felt much like an eager school child standing hopefully in line waiting to get picked for a game of kickball. I was devastated to think that, as much as I tried, I might not ever be good enough. I worried that God would never "choose" me. Then one day as I was agonizing, yet again, with feelings of self-doubt, I felt my heart fill with light, and I heard the Spirit tell me, "Heather, if you want to be chosen, then you are. It isn't God who does the choosing. It is you who chooses Him." That thought leapt through my body like lightning, and even years after, I can still feel the joy it brought to my heart.

I realized that God's "chosen" and "elect" are not a special class of people, predetermined by birth or destiny. Doctrine and Covenants 29:7 teaches that they are those that "hear my voice and harden not their hearts." Much like the wise-hearted women of Exodus, it is our willingness and our own desire to serve that qualifies us for God's work. Elder Dallin H. Oaks taught, "Desires dictate our priorities, priorities shape our choices, and choices determine our actions. The desires we act on determine our changing, our achieving, and our becoming."[9] Who we are and what we do in this life is often determined by our desires and choices.

God has already called each one of us to his work. It is simply up to us to "choose" ourselves to use the talents and skills he has given us to do that work. If, like the wise-hearted women, you feel your "heart stirred" to do a certain work or to follow a certain path, then know that you have already been called and chosen—just get to work.

• Women Assembled at the Door of the Tabernacle of the Congregation •

These women are mentioned in Exodus 38:8 when they donated their "lookingglasses" to be melted down to construct the brass laver used for washing in the tabernacle. They are again spoken of in 1 Samuel 2:22 when Eli lamented that his sons, who were priests in the tabernacle, were misusing their power and "lay with the women that assembled at the door of the tabernacle of the congregation."[10] Their presence at the door of the tabernacle, and not beyond, seems to suggest that women were not allowed past the gate into the actual courtyard of the tabernacle. Hannah's story in 1 Samuel also seems to suggest this. When she went to the tabernacle to make her vow, she was near the spot where Eli, the high priest, sat "by a post [gate] of the temple" (1 Samuel 1:9).[11] This separation of women would also be in keeping with what we know of the temple practices in New Testament times.[12]

The most interesting thing about these women who were assembled before the door is that the word that is translated as "assembled" is the Hebrew word *tsaba'*, which means "to mass (an army or servants), assemble, fight, perform, muster, serve (at a sacred tent)."[13] It is the same word used when God commanded Moses to instruct the Levite men to "wait upon" the priestly service of the tabernacle. The use of this word might indicate that these women were not just assembled at the door of the tabernacle waiting idly, but that they were engaged in formal service in the Lord's house.[14] While we don't know exactly what type of service these women performed in the tabernacle, I think it valuable to know that women, though not ordained to the priesthood, were given the opportunity and privilege of serving in God's house, something that is still true for women today.

Daughters of Zelophehad: Mahlah, Noah, Hoglah, Milcah, Tirzah

Then came the daughters of Zelophehad . . . Mahlah, Noah, and Hoglah, and Milcah, and Tirzah.

And they stood before Moses, and before Eleazar the priest, and before the princes and all the congregation, by the door of the tabernacle of the congregation, saying, . . .

Why should the name of our father be done away from among his family, because he hath no son? Give unto us therefore a possession among the brethren of our father.

And Moses brought their cause before the Lord.

And the Lord spake unto Moses, saying,

The daughters of Zelophehad speak right: thou shalt surely give them a possession of an inheritance among their father's brethren; and thou shalt cause the inheritance of their father to pass unto them.

Numbers 27:1–7

In Jane Austen's classic story *Pride and Prejudice*, inheritance law imperils the five Bennett sisters—Jane, Elizabeth, Mary, Kitty, and Lydia. Their father's estate is entailed, meaning that because he had only daughters and no sons, his estate would go to a distant male cousin when he died. So, the daughters needed to find men to marry who had financial resources to provide for them. As modern readers, we can see how this inheritance law sets up the plot, but it also rankles. Why shouldn't the daughters have as much right to inheritance as a son?

The right to inherit is an important legal right, and we know that unfair laws about it bothered women in ancient times too. The Old Testament tells the story of another set of five sisters, the daughters of Zelophehad—Mahlah, Noah, Hoglah, Milcah, and Tirzah—who, like the Bennett sisters, faced disinheritance. But instead of solving their problem by catching the nearest well-to-do gentlemen, they took their grievance to Moses and questioned the status quo of male inheritance.

Their story began during Israel's sojourn in the wilderness when Moses was commanded to "take the sum of all the congregation of the children of Israel, from twenty years old and upward" (Numbers 26:2). The purpose of this was to determine how many men there were that could go to war, as well as help them divide up inheritances in the promised land when they obtained it. During the numbering, it was noted that Zelophehad, one of the heirs of the tribe of Manasseh, had no sons but five daughters, Mahlah, Noah, Hoglah, Milcah, and Tirzah (Numbers 26:33).

Zelophehad, who was a direct descendant of Manasseh, the son of Joseph, followed Moses out of Egypt but died in the wilderness before reaching the promised land.[1] After their father's death, these five young women approached Moses, Eleazar the high priest, the tribal leaders, and the whole congregation of Israel to petition on their father's behalf. Because they had no brothers, and daughters were not allowed to inherit from their fathers, they were afraid that their father's name and their family's inheritance would be lost forever. They asked, "Why should the name of our father be done away from among his family, because he hath no son?" (Numbers 27:4). They may have been especially concerned because as an oldest son, Zelophehad would have been entitled to a double portion of the inheritance.

I can relate to this because on my father's side—my Thomas side—I have only five boy cousins. Of those five boys only *one* of them, my brother, was born to a Thomas son. This means that out of all my grandparents' posterity, he is the only one, under traditional American naming traditions, who will carry on the Thomas name. When my brother had a little boy, my grandmother got weepy and impressed upon my brother what an important role he had in keeping the Thomas name and legacy going.

I imagine that the feelings of the daughters of Zelophehad were similar to those of my grandmother, except magnified. The societal structure of the Bible was tribal, and the needs and wants of the individual were not as important as those of the family. It was hard for these daughters to accept the thought that their father's name, and the inheritance of land that was due to their family, would be lost forever simply because they were girls. This injustice prompted them to request from Moses that he "give unto us therefore a possession among the brethren of our father" (Numbers 27:4).

In making their petition, they told Moses that their father had not been among the company of Korah but that he had "died in his own sins" (Numbers 27:3). In Numbers 16, we learn that earlier Korah, a Levite, felt that Moses and Aaron had taken too much upon themselves or as he told Moses, "Wherefore then lift ye up yourselves above the congregation of the Lord" (Numbers 16:3). Korah felt that it was unfair that only some of the Levite men held the priesthood. He was upset that some of the Levite families had not been allowed the priesthood but were instead given the responsibility of taking care of the tabernacle (transporting, repairing, assembling it, and so on). Feeling slighted, Korah rallied support and gathered "two hundred and fifty princes of the assembly, famous in the congregation, men of renown"" (Numbers 16:2) who approached Moses with the intent to force him to give them the priesthood.

Because of Korah's uprising, the Lord caused the earth to open and swallow the men who had rebelled as well as their tents, their wives, and their children. When the children of Israel murmured against Moses and Aaron saying, "Ye have killed the people of the Lord" (Numbers 16:41), they were afflicted with a plague that killed 14,700 people. By citing this story, perhaps the daughters of Zelophehad were making it clear that, while their father had not been a perfect man, he had not incited others to sin as did Korah, and that they were not asking for what Korah had.

In response to their request, Moses "brought their cause before the Lord" (Numbers 27:5). The Lord told Moses that "the daughters of Zelophehad speak right" (Numbers 27:6). I love that phrase, not only because it meant a victory for these brave young women but because it affirms something that many of us already know is true. It is okay—and even right—for women to speak up when they see unjust cultural practices in their church community. Just as these five sisters experienced, there may be times when we feel that something—or someone—in the Church is not fair or in harmony with gospel teachings. When that happens, the first thing we need to do is take it to the Lord, through the channels He has given us. This may mean that all we need to do is turn to the Lord in prayer to gain greater understanding or personal revelation about a doctrine or practice or how to handle a specific situation. Or it might mean that we, like the daughters of Zelophehad, need to speak to our priesthood leaders about our concerns.

The most important thing, though, is that no matter how large or small our concern, we approach it like the daughters of Zelophehad did. They didn't demand that there be change. They didn't agitate others together to support their cause, try to change it by degrees, or make it happen by a show of will or force. They simply brought their concern to the Lord, through the channels He had authorized, and humbly waited to hear what He had to say.

Priesthood leaders can also learn from this story. They, like Moses, need to take the concerns of women seriously; to treat their feelings and their ideas with respect and understanding. It would have been easy for Moses to have brushed these five young women aside and label them upstarts or complainers. Instead, he was humble. He listened to them and valued their idea enough to pray about it. In response, the Lord confirmed to him that what these young women had said was true, and instructed Moses that he should "surely give them a possession of an inheritance among their father's brethren" (Numbers 27:7). More than that, a new "statute of judgment" was created for *all* of Israel specifying that if any man died without a son, his inheritance would pass to his daughters, and if he had no daughters, then it would pass to his brethren (Numbers 27:8–11).

The story of the daughters of Zelophehad didn't end there. Sometime later, the chiefs of the tribe of Manasseh approached Moses with a concern about what would happen to these daughters' inheritances once they married and joined the tribe of their husband. Numbers 36:3 reads, "And if they be married to any of the sons of the other tribes of the children of Israel, then shall their inheritance be taken from the inheritance of our fathers, and shall be put to the inheritance of the tribe whereunto they are received: so shall it be taken from the lot of our inheritance."

Moses again took the problem to the Lord and came back with a solution. He told them that the daughters of Zelophehad should "marry to whom they think best," but that she should only marry someone from her own tribe "so shall not the inheritance of the children of Israel remove from tribe to tribe" (Numbers 36:6–7). He also commanded that any daughter who inherited from her father was also obligated to choose a husband from among her same tribe so that the inheritance would stay within the tribe.

Again, the daughters of Zelophehad displayed humility and concern for their family by obeying Moses's counsel. Each of the daughters chose to marry a cousin so that "their inheritance remained in the tribe of the family of their father" (Numbers 36:12). When the children of Israel finally took possession of the promised land, Joshua gathered the tribes to divide inheritances. The daughters of Zelophehad again approached Eleazar the high priest, Joshua, and the princes and reminded them that the Lord had commanded Moses to give them "an inheritance among our brethren" (Joshua 17:4).

Joshua honored the decision and accordingly gave each daughter a double portion of land as was due the heirs of a firstborn son. Their inheritance was "beside the land of Gilead and Bashan, which were on the other side Jordan; . . . and the rest of Manasseh's sons had the land of Gilead" (Joshua 17:5–6). If you look at map 3, "The Division of the 12 Tribes," in the Bible Maps section, you will notice that the tribe of Manasseh has two portions of land. The smaller of these, the portion on the left nearest the Mediterranean Sea, would have included the portion given to the daughters of Zelophehad. It was their courage to speak up against injustice and to petition the Lord through the proper channels that secured an inheritance for themselves and for all the descendants of Manasseh.

Rahab

[Rahab] brought them up to the roof of the house, and hid them with the stalks of flax, which she had laid in order upon the roof. . . .

And she said unto the men, I know that the Lord hath given you the land, and that your terror is fallen upon us, and that all the inhabitants of the land faint because of you. . . .

Now therefore, I pray you, swear unto me by the Lord, since I have shewed you kindness, that ye will also shew kindness unto my father's house, and give me a true token:

And that ye will save alive my father, and my mother, and my brethren, and my sisters, and all that they have, and deliver our lives from death.

And the men answered her, Our life for yours, if ye utter not this our business. And it shall be, when the Lord hath given us the land, that we will deal kindly and truly with thee.

Joshua 2:6, 9, 12–14

Rahab is an unlikely heroine. When Joshua sent spies into the land of Canaan to "view the land" (Joshua 2:1), they went first to the city of Jericho. When the spies arrived in Jericho, they found lodging in the house of a harlot named Rahab. Our first question might be, why would Israelites, even if they were spies, spend the night in the house of a prostitute? Such behavior goes against what we know these men believed. Author James R. Baker offers an explanation:

[Rahab's] Babylonian counterparts during the time of Hammurabi and a century and a half later under Ammisaduqa were translated as "ale-wives." Such women chose not to belong to traditional family units. These women owned their own public establishments, where they offered lodging, meals, alcoholic beverages, and sometimes themselves. They contracted metronymic marriage-like liaisons with their patrons and sometimes "married more than one patron—something called 'nair polyandry.'" Such a relationship safeguarded the woman's independence. The visiting patron had the privilege of the woman's bedroom, but all the property, including any that he might bring to the relationship and any children born of their union, belonged to her and could be inherited by her father's descendants. These women were not generally held in high esteem, for the Old Babylonian law dealt harshly with them.[1]

We can assume that the spies went to Rahab's not for any immoral reasons but rather because it was the ancient equivalent of a hotel. Not long after they arrived, their identities were known and report of Israelite spies entering the city had made its way to the king of Jericho. Apparently, these Israelites weren't very good spies—they got caught the minute they arrived!

The king sent a message to Rahab telling her to "bring forth the men that are come to thee . . . for they be come to search out all the country" (Joshua 2:3). Barker explained that anciently female innkeepers were subjected to strict royal regulation. He wrote, "Recognized as sources of information valuable to the king, the women were required to report and even arrest suspicious visitors. Section 109 [of the Code of Hammurabi] records, 'If outlaws have congregated in the establishment of a woman wine seller and she has not arrested those outlaws and did not take them to the palace, that wine seller shall be put to death.'"[2]

The king, perhaps assuming Rahab didn't know the nature of her guests, was informing her of her royal obligation to report them and have them arrested. If she didn't, her penalty may have been death.

In an act of true bravery, Rahab chose to hide the Israelite spies rather than turn them over to the king. She told the king that they had been at her house but that they had left and that she did not know where they had gone. She had hidden them on the roof of her house under piles of flax that had been laid out to dry. Flax is a long, stalky fiber that is used to make linen. To soften it, the stalks were soaked in water and then laid out to air dry. Hiding under such a soggy pile must not have been pleasant, perhaps one of the reasons that Rahab knew it would make a good hiding place.

The king sent men out to pursue the Israelite spies, whom he assumed were making their way back to their camp. After the king's men left, the city gate was shut, trapping the spies (still hiding under the flax) inside the city. But that night, before she went to bed, Rahab snuck up to roof and spoke with them. Her words must have surprised them. "I know that the Lord hath given you the land," Rahab announced to the spies, "for the Lord your God, he is God in heaven above, and in earth beneath" (Joshua 2:9, 11). Rahab was a believer! This unlikely "ale-wife" of Jericho had gained a testimony of the one and living God. How did that happen?

Rahab tells us herself: "For we have heard how the Lord dried up the water of the Red sea for you, when ye came out of Egypt" (Joshua 2:10) and that she had heard of their great victories against the Amorites, Sihon and Og, on the other side of the Jordan River. Simply from hearing of the miracles that followed them, Rahab had gained a testimony that that the God the Israelites followed was *the* God, a true God. She, like all the people of Canaan, was terrified of them. They seemed to be a holy army, led by a powerful god, divinely sanctioned to inherit the land of their forefathers. Even at the risk of her own life, Rahab was willing to protect them.

She told the Israelite spies that if they would "swear unto me by the Lord" and would spare her life and the lives of her father, mother, brothers, and sisters and "all that they have" (Joshua 2:12–13) that she would help them escape from the city. She also required that they give her a "true token" or a sign by which she might know their promise was in earnest. The spies readily agreed, acknowledging that their lives were in her hands. They gave her a piece of scarlet thread (probably thicker like yarn) to tie in the window of her house and instructed her that when they came to attack the city, she should gather her family into the house. They promised her that because she had shown them kindness, they would show her kindness and pass by her house when they destroyed the city.

In this act, we find symbolism of the Passover in which the firstborn children of the Jews in Egypt were saved when their parents painted their doorways with the blood of a lamb—symbolic of the blood of Jesus Christ. Even though she was not a Jew, Rahab was to have her own personal Passover. Not only would her faith in God and her willingness to risk her life for God's servants save her life, but it would also save the lives of her entire family.

After obtaining a promise from the Israelite spies that she would be safe when the Israelite army came, Rahab helped them escape out the window. Her house was "upon the town wall" (Joshua 2:15), meaning that it was built right up against the city wall. Archeologists have speculated that this area of town was a poorer one and was on the outskirts of town where it was more vulnerable to attack. The situation of her house made it easy for Rahab to throw a cord out the window and allow the spies to climb down the wall and escape.

With this brave action, Rahab became a hero to the Israelites, but to the people of Jericho, she was the ultimate traitor, the Benedict Arnold of her day. Not only did she harbor enemy spies, but she also gave the Israelites the information they were looking for. When the spies reported back to Joshua, they told him what Rahab had informed them of, that "the Lord hath delivered into our hands all the land; for even all the inhabitants of the country do faint because of us" (Joshua 2:24). This gave the Israelites confidence, and they began in earnest to prepare to take over the land of Canaan.

We don't know what Rahab did in the interval between helping the spies escape and when the Israelite army appeared outside the walls of Jericho. I'm inclined to think that she got busy with missionary work, gathering her family and explaining to them what was going to happen and the promise she had received of safety. While the city of Jericho prepared for a siege and "straightly shut up" its gates (Joshua 6:1), Rahab probably gathered in what was most precious to her—her family.

She, with a house built on the wall of the city, would have had a front seat view of the Israelites who for six days marched silently around the city of Jericho carrying the ark of the covenant. What a terrifying spectacle that would have been! It must have unnerved the people of Jericho to see the Israelites' silent display of confidence that their God would "go before them" and fight their battles. For Rahab, on the other hand, who had professed faith in God, such a scene must have been electrifying, a real testimony builder. These, she knew, were now *her* people.

On the seventh day, at Joshua's command, the priests blew their trumpets and the people shouted. "For the lord," Joshua told them, "hath given you the city" (Joshua 6:16). Their shouts produced a miracle because "the wall fell down flat" (Joshua 6:20). In Hebrew, this phrase connotes the idea that the wall collapsed, that it fell in on itself. Archeologists believe that it was the not the entire wall that collapsed but rather just one section of the wall. This hole allowed the Israelites to breach Jericho's fortifications and enter the city. This explanation makes sense, especially when we remember that Rahab's house was a built "upon the wall" but that it was still standing when the Israelites came into the city.

The Israelites "utterly destroyed all that was in the city, both man and woman, young and old, and ox, and sheep, and ass" when they came into Jericho (Joshua 6:21). The only thing left unscathed was Rahab and her household. Joshua commanded the two spies to "go into the harlot's house, and bring out thence the woman, and all that she hath, as ye sware unto her" (Joshua 6:22). They went and got Rahab and brought her to the camp of Israel where she and her family dwelled "even unto this day" (Joshua 6:25).

In the New Testament when Paul gave the Hebrews examples of great faith, he included in his list great figures such as Enoch, Abraham, Sarah, Moses, Jochebed, and Rahab saying, "By faith the harlot Rahab perished not with them that believed not, when she had received the spies with peace" (Hebrews 11:31). The prophet James too, upheld Rahab as a model of faith explaining, "By works a man is justified, and not by faith only. Likewise also was not Rahab the harlot justified by works, when she had received the messengers, and had sent them out another way? For as the body without the spirit is dead, so faith without works is dead also" (James 2:24–26).

Rahab gained her faith not just by believing but also by doing. The belief she had in God gave her courage to act, to risk her life, and become a traitor to her people. It was her faith that prompted her to tie the red thread in her window, trusting that the Israelites would be true to their word. It was her faith that helped her change her life around, to experience the saving and "passing over" grace of the Atonement, and to become a new person. Jewish legend remembers her as one of the four most beautiful (virtuous) women in history and claims that she married the prophet Joshua.[3] It is also widely believed that she is the "Rachab" Matthew lists in his genealogy of Jesus Christ (see Matthew 1:5). History remembers Rahab not for who she *was*—a harlot—but for who she *became*, a righteous woman of God. God loves the Rahabs of the world.

> "He is God in heaven above, and in earth beneath."

Achsah

And Caleb said, He that smiteth Kirjath-sepher, and taketh it, to him will I give Achsah my daughter to wife.

And Othniel the son of Kenaz, Caleb's younger brother, took it: and he gave him Achsah his daughter to wife.

And it came to pass, when she came to him, that she moved him to ask of her father a field: and she lighted from off her ass; and Caleb said unto her, What wilt thou?

And she said unto him, Give me a blessing: for thou hast given me a south land; give me also springs of water. And Caleb gave her the upper springs and the nether springs.

Judges 1:12–15

What type of qualities do you hope for in a future son-in-law? How might you go about finding a man you felt was good enough to marry your daughter? If you were Caleb, the leader of the tribe of Judah, you might challenge the young man to perform a seemingly impossible task with your daughter as the prize. That was how Achsah, Caleb's daughter, got her husband—and it turned out to be a pretty good match.

After the death of Joshua, much of Israel's promised land was still unconquered from the surrounding peoples. The Canaanites were one of the largest, and perhaps most powerful, groups the Israelites had to face. It seems that no one was eager to engage in conflict with them saying, "Who shall go up for us against the Canaanites first, to fight against them?" (Judges 1:1). The Lord told them, "Judah shall go up" because this land was destined to be their inheritance, and the Lord promised, "I have delivered the land into his hand" (Judges 1:2).

The tribe of Judah engaged the Canaanites and had great success, claiming lots of land, including the city that would later become Jerusalem. When they came to the Canaanite town of Kirjath-sepher, Caleb challenged his men by telling them, "He that smiteth Kirjath-sepher, and taketh it, to him will I give Achsah my daughter to wife" (Judges 1:12). As the "prince" of the tribe of Israel, Caleb could give his daughter a nice dowry, making her a desirable "catch" for any man. It is possible that Achsah was merely a trophy wife, a pawn used by her father to advance his military campaign.

However, I think we might view her story differently as well. I find it likely that Caleb, as the leader of his army, would have had a specific man (or perhaps several men) in mind when he issued his challenge. I don't think most men would offer their daughter willy-nilly like a king in a fairy tale. I think it much more likely that Caleb knew that character of his men and knew who was likely to succeed in his offer. Perhaps there was even a romantic story at work here, and Caleb knew that Achsah's hand as a reward would inspire one specific man, or two men who would fight especially hard to win her hand in marriage. Maybe Achsah was the fair lady inspiring her knight to victory.

Caleb's offer worked. His nephew, a man named Othniel, broke through the fortifications of Kirjath-sepher and conquered it. As promised, Caleb gave Achsah to Othniel as his wife. Othniel turned out to be a fantastic choice. He later delivered the Israelites from the Mesopotamians (see Judges 3:9) and became their judge, keeping peace for more than forty years.

Along with Othniel and Achsah's marriage, Caleb provided a large dowry that included land in the area newly conquered by the tribe of Judah. We don't know exactly what land he gave her, but she described it as a "southern land" (Judges 1:15). The southern part of the lands inherited by the tribe of Judah include the Negev desert, which is very rocky and arid. It was not a particularly desirable place to live, but it seems that this did not deter the new couple from planning on living there.

The account tells us that after Achsah and Othniel were married, Achsah "moved [Othniel] to ask of her father a field" (Judges 1:14). The word *moved* here means "persuaded,"[1] and the word *field* refers to a tract of land.[2] I've read sermons where Achsah has been described as the "pushy bride," a greedy woman who shows indiscretion in ordering her husband and her father around. Yet when we consider Achsah's position closely, I think we see a woman who was thinking ahead to what she and her posterity would need. She may have been "pushy" in her request, but I think that quality was exactly what was needed in this situation.

We see more evidence of Achsah's determined nature when we see that it was she, and not Othniel, who did the actual asking. We read that she traveled to her father riding an ass, which when she saw him she "lighted off" (Judges 1:14) of and met him respectfully. Caleb asked her, "What wilt thou?" (verse 14), or in other words, "What do you want?"

Achsah asked her father, "Give me a blessing" (Judges 1:15). The word *blessing* here is the same Hebrew word used when speaking about the father's blessings that Isaac gave Jacob or that Jacob gave his twelve sons. It implies giving someone the *source* of a blessing—like a covenant, a womb, or a pool of water—something from which future blessings will come to them and their posterity. Achsah wanted from her father such a blessing and told (not asked) him, "Thou hast given me a south land; give me also springs of water" (verse 15).

Achsah knew that if she and her posterity were to live in the desert of Negev that having water was essential. Having control of a spring would ensure that she and her children would be able to thrive in

their new, harsh home; without water they would struggle. She was acting as a matriarch for her posterity still unborn, securing them promised blessings of prosperity and life. Caleb appears to have seen the wisdom in her request and gave her more than she had asked for—"the upper springs, and the nether springs," or in other words, "the upper *and* the lower springs" (Judges 1:15).

Inherent in Caleb and Achsah's exchange is a pattern of our father-daughter relationship with our Heavenly Father. Just as Caleb wanted to bless Achsah, our Father in Heaven wants to give us gifts to bless us so that we don't just survive but that we thrive in our given environments. Christ is the "living water" in our lives, and it is by His grace that we thrive and bloom, even in the wilderness. As one scholar wrote, "[Achsah] asks for life itself—and receives it in double measure. Caleb gives not one spring but two. Unlike Caleb, perhaps, she knows that the two of them cannot live fruitfully on their own. They need that gift. And Caleb, asked, immediately recognizes this truth and blesses them with a gift that goes beyond the asking. Caleb's gift overflows."[3]

Like Caleb, our Heavenly Father wants to give us not just the basics of what we need, but blessings that overflow. If we are to claim these blessings, we must be a little bold like Achsah and be willing to ask Heavenly Father what we want. This doesn't mean we demand things from Him, but that like Achsah we approach Him respectfully coming down from our high horse and kneel humbly before Him. "For every one that asketh receiveth," taught Jesus, "and he that seeketh findeth; and to him that knocketh it shall be opened. . . . If ye then, being evil, know how to give good gifts unto your children, how much more shall your Father which is in heaven give good things to them that ask him?" (Matthew 7:8, 11).

In writing about the Negev desert, the land that Achsah inherited from her father, Isaiah wrote these prophetic words: "The desert shall rejoice, and blossom as the rose. It shall blossom abundantly, and rejoice even with joy and singing: . . . they shall see the glory of the Lord, and the excellency of our God" (Isaiah 35:1–2). He can make our things blossom, even in the barren and dry times of our life.

• Dowry and Bride-Price •

Anciently, marriage was viewed more like a business arrangement than it is today. There were contracts involved and two main monetary exchanges intended to protect and provide for the woman and any children she would have—the dowry and the bride-price. The dowry was given to a woman by her father (or her brothers if her father was dead) and was her inheritance. Women did not usually inherit land or money at the death of their father as sons did, though stories like the daughters of Zelophehad (see page 125) show us there were exceptions. Instead, women usually received their inheritance when they married, and their dowry could include land, money, servants, and any other valuable property. If a woman never married, then she would not receive an inheritance but could expect to be cared for by the double-portion estate left to her eldest brother.

In the case of Achsah, we see that the land of Negev was her dowry, given to her by her father at the time of her marriage. Pharaoh's daughter, the wife of Solomon, also received land—the city of Gezer—from her father when she married (see 1 Kings 9:16). A dowry was the woman's property, even after her marriage, and she often had economic control over it. We can see this in the way that Rachel and Leah directed their maidservants Bilhah and Zilpah, who were given to them by their father as part of their dowry (see Genesis 29:24, 29). Achsah's dowry was unique in that she asked for additional land, the springs, *after* her marriage. One scholar explained, "What is unusual about the gift of water is that a daughter asks for a gift that in effect is part of her brothers' inheritances and her father Caleb agrees. Thus, the story of Achsah demonstrates that a daughter's inheritance was limited to her dowry, but could also be procured under the guise of a gift. Whether the presence of this story indicates that such a practice commonly occurred in ancient Israel is uncertain."[4]

The other exchange often associated with marriages was the bride-price, which was paid by the groom to a bride's family to compensate them for the economic loss of their daughter. The paying of a bride-price showed that women were viewed as important assets to their families. The bride-price was often paid with money, but it appears it could also be satisfied through other ways as well. In Jacob's marriages to Rachel and Leah, we see that he worked fourteen years for their father. He paid a bride-price of seven years for each daughter (see Genesis 29). In the story of Achsah, it appears that Caleb set the bride-price for his daughter in the form of service—capturing the city of Kirjath-sepher. When Othniel took the city, he was fulfilling his debt to Caleb and was free to marry his daughter.

Deborah

And Deborah, a prophetess, the wife of Lapidoth, she judged Israel at that time.

And she dwelt under the palm tree of Deborah between Ramah and Beth-el in mount Ephraim: and the children of Israel came up to her for judgment.

And she sent and called Barak the son of Abinoam out of Kedesh-naphtali, and said unto him, Hath not the Lord God of Israel commanded, saying, Go and draw toward mount Tabor, and take with thee ten thousand men of the children of Naphtali and of the children of Zebulun? . . .

And Barak said unto her, If thou wilt go with me, then I will go: but if thou wilt not go with me, then I will not go.

Judges 4:4–6, 8

You probably know about Joan of Arc, who led the men of France to victory against the English and saved her country, but you may be less familiar with another female general who led men into battle and saved her nation—Deborah, the ancient judge, prophetess, and poet.

Deborah lived during a time when the children of Israel were struggling. The Israelites had settled near the cities of the Canaanites, who were a well-entrenched civilization with a strong religious practice of worshiping false gods. Judges 2 tells us that after the death of the prophet Joshua, the children of Israel "forsook the Lord God of their fathers, which brought them out of the land of Egypt, and followed other gods, of the gods of the people that were round about them. . . . They forsook the Lord, and served Baal and Ashtaroth" (Judges 2:12–13). As a result of their wickedness, they were continually attacked by their enemies, especially their neighbors the Canaanities. By Deborah's time, the Israelites had been sold into "the hand of Jabin, king of Cannan" (Judges 4:2) and were in captivity again.

Israel lacked both a king and a prophet figure, like Moses or Joshua, to lead them. Instead, they relied upon judges whose purpose was to settle disputes among Israel's people and to deliver "them out of the hand of those that spoiled them" (Judges 2:16). We don't know whether judges were selected by the Lord or by the people's choice, but verse 18 tells us that "when the Lord raised them up judges, then the Lord was with the Judge." Deborah was the first (and only) woman to hold the position of judge in Israel. We do not know how or why Deborah came to be Israel's judge, but we can be certain that the Lord was with her and approved of her position.

In addition to being a judge, Deborah was a "prophetess," meaning that she possessed the gift of prophecy (see Huldah on page 254). Herbert Lockyer, a famous scholar of biblical women, explained, "Deborah is one of several females in Scripture distinguished as being endowed with the prophetic gift, which means the ability to discern the mind and purpose of God and declare it to others."[1] She had the spiritual sensitivity to hear the Lord's voice and the courage and gift to explain it to others. Her prophetic gift is evident in the "Song of Deborah," recorded in Judges 5. This psalm, thought to be one of the oldest pieces of surviving poetry in the world, was sung by Deborah after her victory against the Canaanites. In it, she acknowledged the direction she received from God and the Lord's great mercy in delivering her people.

Deborah's home and seat of judgment was "under the palm tree of Deborah between Ramah and Beth-el" (Judges 4:5). Palm trees were symbols of peace and victory. Anciently, palm leaves were used to adorn the clothing or images of victors, and in the New Testament, Christ's disciples waved palm leaves to honor Him. Palms, because they are evergreens (they never lose their leaves) and fruit-bearing, were also associated with immortality and fertility. We don't know why Deborah chose to judge Israel from beneath a palm tree, but there is some interesting symbolism associated with it.

Central to Deborah's position as judge and prophetess is the title she gave herself, "a mother in Israel" (Judges 5:7). We know that Deborah was married to Lapidoth, but we have no evidence that she had children of her own.[2] Yet it appears that this phrase "mother in Israel" connotes a culturally understood, and accepted, position of female leadership. It is used only one another time in the Bible, in the story of the wise woman of Abel (see page 210) who, like Deborah, led her people spiritually and politically.

While we know much about the patriarchal leadership of Israel (it was the men, after all, who wrote the Bible), we know little about the matriarchal leadership. Deborah and the wise woman of Abel give us a glimpse into the important—and sometimes formal—role that the matriarchy played in the politics and everyday life of Israel. In fact, one of the most striking things about Deborah's story is the nonchalant way it is told; as if there is nothing surprising or unusual about a woman being a spiritual, political, and military leader.

We first meet Deborah when, after receiving revelation from God, she attempted to rally the children of Israel to go on the offensive against the Canaanites. She told them that the Lord had instructed them to "draw toward mount Tabor, and take with thee ten thousand men of the children of Naphtali and of the children of Zebulun" (Judges 4:6). Deborah was ready and raring to go, but her people were afraid—and with good reason. The Canaanites were one of the most advanced civilizations in the world at this time. Josephus wrote that Jabin, the king of the Canaanities, had an army of 300,000 footmen, 10,000 horses, and 3,000 chariots.[3] The Canaanite general, a man named Sisera, had 900 chariots—all made of iron—under his command. It was these iron chariots that scared the Israelites.

Though it may seem primitive to us, iron was a new invention, and opponents using iron weapons and iron chariots must have seemed super-human to the Israelites.[4] The iron chariots featured cutting-edge technology. Each carried three warriors, fully clad in armor. One warrior drove the chariot, one attacked with sword or lance, and the third shielded the others from counter-attack.[5] In contrast, the people of Israel were an emerging civilization and were armed simply with bows, arrows, slings, stones, and clubs. In her psalm, recorded in Judges 5, Deborah described how there was not a "shield or a spear seen among forty thousand in Israel" (verse 8). It would have been like facing armored tanks and machine guns with nothing but hunting rifles. Challenging the Canaanites must have seemed like suicide.

It took Deborah some time to convince the men of Israel to follow the instructions God had given her. The person most crucial to her success was a man named Barak, whom Deborah sent for. Deborah explained to him what God had in mind, that he was to take 10,000 men from the tribes of Naphtali and Zebulun and go to Mount Tabor. The mobilization of these forces would attract the attention of Sisera and his chariots, but they were to have no fear. Deborah told Barak the Lord promised that He would "deliver [Sisera] into thine hand" (Judges 4:7).

Barak, though he must have been nervous about such an endeavor, was willing but on one condition. He told Deborah, "If thou wilt go with me, then I will go; but if though wilt not go with me, then I will not go" (Judges 4:8). I think this is the real secret behind why Deborah and Barak were successful in defeating the Canaanites; Deborah (a woman) and Barak (a man) worked together to do the Lord's will. There is real power generated when men and women unite in a common cause. Deborah and Barak were united, working together and respecting one another's spiritual gifts. They both knew that they could not go forward with the Lord's plan until the other was on board.

Deborah and Barak teach us important things about leadership, especially within the Church. Imagine if in our wards and stakes men and women cooperated like Deborah and Barak did. The bishop, before moving forward with plans, would secure the support and insight of the Relief Society president. Conversely, the Relief Society president would consult with and rely upon the skills of the bishop, asking him, as Deborah did Barak, to rise to his true potential. We wouldn't hear comments about how "the women are more spiritual than the men" or that "the men can't be relied on to get anything done." Instead, we would have a spirit of cooperation in which the skills and spiritual insights of both men and women were respected.

Even on the most basic level of the Church, we would have marriages where husband and wife made decisions together; a cooperative paradigm rather than a competitive or domineering one. How powerful it would be if all men and women used Barak's words when dealing with each other: "If thou wilt go with me, then I will go, but if you won't, then I will not go (or make decisions) without you." Instead of the matriarchy and the patriarchy contending for power, they would be sharing it.

It didn't even seem to bother Barak that Deborah told him that the glory of the victory would not belong to him but rather "the Lord shall sell Sisera into the hand of a woman" (Judges 4:9). Barak must have assumed this meant that Deborah would get the glory for the victory, but that did not seem to change his feelings. He was humble enough to accept directions from the Lord in whatever form they came, and if Deborah was willing to stand with him against the Canaanites, then he was willing to attempt the impossible, modeling for us the incredible power that is possible when righteous men and women respect one another and partner fully in the Lord's work.

Following Deborah's instructions, Barak took his army to high ground, the top of Mount Tabor, where down in the valley of Jezreel they watched as Sisera's chariots assembled against them. Josephus records that the Israelites were "so affrighted at the multitude of those enemies, that they were resolved to march off, had not Deborah retained them, and commanded them to fight the enemy that very day, for that they should conquer them, and God would be their assistance."[6] The reality of their situation must have been terrifying.

With much faith and courage, the men followed Barak as they descended from their high ground on Mount Tabor to engage Sisera's chariots in the valley. Yet, as happens so often in the scriptures, God fought the Israelites' battle for them. The details are unclear, but it appears that after the Israelites went down from the mount a great rainstorm arose. Not only did the wind of this storm make it difficult for the Canaanites to see, but it caused the nearby Kishon river to overflow its banks, making the Canaanites' formidable chariots useless. In her psalm, Deborah sang how "the stars in their course fought against Sisera" and how "the river Kishon swept them away," causing the horses to break their hooves and forcing the Canaanites to engage the Israelites on foot.

The Canaanites were so "discomfited" (Judges 4:15) by this storm that even their general Sisera fled on foot from the Israelite forces. Unfortunately for him (but fortunately for the Israelites), he sought refuge in the tent of a Kenite woman named Jael, who instead of being the ally he thought, betrayed him by killing him with a tent peg. Sisera's death ended the conflict between the Canaanites and the Israelites, and after that "the hand of the children of Israel prospered and prevailed against Jabin the king of Canaan, until they had destroyed Jabin king of Cannan" (Judges 4:24).

Deborah and Barak, with the help of God, had done the impossible, the unthinkable. A small group of underdogs overthrew one of the largest and most powerful armies in the world. This situation is not unique in the Bible, or in history. God has often demonstrated that worldly power means nothing. When God stands beside an individual or a nation, they are certain of success, no matter how the odds are stacked against them.[7] I think what makes Deborah's story memorable is that the Lord chose to demonstrate His power through a woman. When Joan of Arc was asked why God would have chosen her, an obscure girl to save France, she replied simply,

"It pleased God thus to act through a simple maid."[8] I wonder if God had something similar in mind by calling Deborah, demonstrating to all of Israel that God works His "strange act" (Isaiah 28:21) through both men *and* women.

• Jael •

When the Canaanites realized that despite their military strength they had been defeated by the Israelites, their general, Sisera, fled on foot. He sought refuge at the tent of Jael, the wife of Heber the Kenite. The Kenites were a Midianite tribe who were skilled metal workers. While most of the Kenites were allied with the Israelites, Heber had "severed himself from the Kenites, and pitched his tent unto the plain of Zaanaim" (Judges 4:11), and made a peace pact with Jabin, the Canaanite king (see Judges 4:17). It is possible that he did this to work for the Canaanites by repairing their iron chariots and weapons.

Sisera fled to the Kenite tent, expecting that Jael would hide him from Barak. When he arrived, Jael, appearing to be the picture of hospitality, went out to meet him and invited him into her tent and hid him under a mantle, a thick rug. When He told her he was thirsty and requested water, she graciously brought him milk and "butter in a lordly dish" (Judges 5:25). Feeling confident of her hospitality, Sisera ordered her to "stand in the door of the tent, and it shall be, when any man doth come and inquire of thee, and say, Is there any man here? That thou shalt say, No" (Judges 4:20).

At her first opportunity, when Sisera was fast asleep in her tent, Jael "went softly unto him" and drove a tent nail into his head, killing him instantly (Judges 4:21). When Barak, who had been pursuing Sisera, arrived at Jael's tent, she showed him Sisera dead in her tent, the nail still in his head. Jael's actions may seem cruel, but they are also rich in symbolism. Camille Fronk Olsen wrote:

> A vivid symbolic image emerges from Jael's story. A nail or tent peg (*yathaid*) was a stake that measured as long as three feet. It was to be driven deep into the sandy terrain with a large mallet to anchor tents in place. . . . The mission of the Savior can be found within this imagery. Zechariah likened Jehovah to a *yathid* and cornerstone because He is the One who grounds and aligns us (Zech. 10:4; see also Ezra 9:8). Likewise, Isaiah testified that the Savior's mission included providing His children with a glorious throne in His Father's house, as a *yathid* that is fastened "in a sure place" (Isaiah 22:23). As Jael's tent peg brought a sure end to Sisera's life, so also Christ's mission of atonement certifies sure and certain blessings for eternity.[9]

Deborah acknowledged Jael as a heroine, singing in her psalm, "Blessed above women shall Jael the wife of Heber the Kenite be, blessed shall be above women in the tent" (Judges 5:24). She continued her praise by retelling Jael's heroics: "She put her hand to the nail, and her right hand to the workmen's hammer; and with the hammer she smote Sisera. . . . At her feet he bowed, he fell, he lay down; at her feet he bowed, he fell: where he bowed, there he fell down dead" (Judges 5:26–27). With courage and a willingness to raise her arm and act, Jael delivered Israel from oppression.

Jephthah's Daughter

And Jephthah vowed a vow unto the Lord, and said, If thou shalt without fail deliver the children of Ammon into mine hands,

Then it shall be, that whatsoever cometh forth of the doors of my house to meet me, when I return in peace from the children of Ammon, shall surely be the Lord's, and I will offer it up for a burnt offering. . . .

And Jephthah came to Mizpeh unto his house, and, behold, his daughter came out to meet him with timbrelsand with dances: and she was his only child; beside her he had neither son nor daughter.

And it came to pass, when he saw her, that he rent his clothes, and said, Alas, my daughter! thou hast brought me very low, and thou art one of them that trouble me: for I have opened my mouth unto the Lord, and I cannot go back.

Judges 11: 30-31, 34-35

When I told my husband the story of Jephthah's daughter, he stopped me mid-sentence and stated, "This story is so unlike how I want the scriptures to be." I smiled at his comment because I think it sums up how many of the stories about women in the Old Testament make us feel. There are powerful lessons to be learned from them, but there is also an inordinate amount of suffering and injustice in their stories. The story of Jephthah's daughter's is difficult, but it also teaches important lessons about the Atonement and Christ's love for us.

Jephthah, whose mother was a harlot, had been "thrust out" by his brothers when his father died (Judges 11:1–2). They told him that because he was the "son of a strange woman" (Judges 11:2), he would not be allowed to inherit with them. Jephthah fled from his brothers and took up company with "vain men" who "went out with him" (Judges 11:3). Basically, he was a robber with a gang. When the Ammonites began to attack Israel, Jephthah's brothers went to find to him, begging him and his gang to come and fight for them against the Ammonites. Seeing an opportunity, Jephthah told his brothers that he would go, but on one condition. If he defeated the Ammonites, they must make him their leader. The brothers were desperate and so they agreed.

When the battle with the Ammonites proved difficult, Jephthah "vowed a vow unto the Lord" (Judges 11:30) that if the Lord would give him victory that when he got home he would make a sacrifice to the Lord of "whatsoever cometh forth of the doors of my house to meet me" (Judges 11:31). Perhaps Jephthah expected that his dog, or another animal, might be the first one to run out to greet him when he got home. Or perhaps he expected it to be a servant or another less important member of his household. He certainly wasn't expecting it to be his daughter.

When Jephthah came home, triumphant as the leader of the Israelites, his daughter, his only child, was the first one to come out to meet him. It appears she had planned a grand reception for his homecoming, going out with "timbrels and with dances" (Judges 11:34). When Jephthah saw her he was devastated. "Alas, my daughter!" Jephthah cried as he rent his clothes. "Thou hast brought me very low" (Judges 11:35). He then told her about the vow he had

made and told her that since the Lord had made him victorious, he could not "go back" (Judges 11:35) on his promise.

His daughter's response was truly astounding. Instead of fighting against her father's vow, she respected it. "If thou hast opened thy mouth unto the Lord," she said, "do to me according to that which hath proceeded out of thy mouth" (Judges 11:36). She accepted her fate and that it was God's will. Her father had made a foolish vow. Even though human sacrifice was common among other idolatrous religions in this time, the law of Moses forbade it and had strict laws about what animals could be used for an acceptable sacrifice. Even so, she seemed to trust that everything was happening just as it should. If her life was the price required to free her people from the oppression of the Ammonites, then she was willing to pay it.

There is a powerful parallel between Jephthah's daughter and that of Isaac, whose father also promised to sacrifice him. Like Isaac, Jephthah's daughter was submissive and was willing to sacrifice her life to God. Yet unlike Isaac, there was no "ram in the thicket" (Genesis 22:13) for Jephthah's daughter. Her sacrifice was not symbolic; she sealed her testimony with her blood. She is a true Christ figure. Like Christ suffering for our mistakes and sins, Jephthah's daughter took her father's sin upon herself and atoned for it with her life.

Before her death, though, she made one request. "Let me alone two months," she asked her father, "that I may go up and down upon the mountains, and bewail my virginity, I and my fellows" (Judges 11:37). Apparently, by "alone" she just meant without male supervision because the word *fellows* means "beloved female companions."[1]

Her request was granted, and she and her companions went and "bewailed her virginity upon the mountains" (Judges 11:38), which might mean she was mourning the fact she would die before she was able to be married.

At times I wish women had written the Bible, because I would love to have known what they did up there on the mountain. Throughout the Old Testament when prophets wanted to speak to God, they went to the mountains. I wonder if this trek "up and down" upon the mountain, accompanied only by her closest friends, was something of a spiritual journey, a time for Jephthah's daughter to commune with God and come to know who she was.

I love the idea of these young women up in the mountains, away from the eyes of men, communing with God and finding support in one another. I think it is important, even today, for women to find ways to create such sisterhoods and carve out sacred types of gatherings. One of my friends has a beautiful tradition that she and her friends do at each seasonal solstice. She calls it "Soul-stice Sisters," and it is an example of such a sisterhood gathering. I asked her to describe what they do, and she wrote:

> For five years, three friends and I have met at the turn of each season in celebration. . . . There is a magic melding and meshing of talents and gifts to bring each celebration to life. We often trek boxes full of china, gold place settings, firefly lights, dressed in our ballet flats, lacy skirts and flower crowns into the summer woods where we set a feast of rosemary strawberry scones, and homemade cider sweetened for days with honey, cinnamon and oranges. In the winter, after lighting sparklers and writing our intentions for the next year in the frosty air, dressed in sequin skirts, boots and furry vests, we huddle around the kitchen table and fireplace for hot winter veggie soup, warm homemade bread, and bright red pomegranates. This is not a time of competition, comparison, or pride, but a true expression of creativity and connection. . . .
>
> The setting is magical, but the real magic happens in the moments around the candlelit table, or bonfire, when we witness for each other. We celebrate the dark parts (fears, worries, sadnesses) as well as the light parts (goals, dreams, creativity) equally. Each of us have known light and dark, yet each are able to sift through the grit and mine the flecks of gold from our experiences. We are "midwives" who help labor in the dark, to bring one another's dreams and stories to light. We don't hide, stuff, or mask our dark and pain and are there to whisper "me too" to those hard things or "not true" to those negative or false ideas we hold about ourselves. In this process we are nourished, and paradoxically lifted and grounded in this safe circle. We see more clearly our own divine identities and see how God sees us, which connects us easily, in turn, with God.
>
> Another translation for *atonement* is "reunion." In this space I feel that reunion, as I am nourished and enabled. As the candles dim and the bonfire quiets, we see the "beauty for ashes" this season has brought and feel strengthened for the upcoming season. What is born each season? Resiliency, confidence, connection, and perhaps most important, compassion. These are each virtues born of adversity. The light from the dark. We know we will meet again, as light outweighs dark, or dark outweighs light, or the light and dark are equally balanced, whatever the next season may bring.[2]

Though we have no idea what happened between Jephthah's daughter and her friends on the mountain, I'd like to think it was something like what my friend described happens in her gatherings—a time of deep reflection, atonement, and sisterhood. Though I do not envy Jephthah's daughter's circumstances, I do envy this experience. How different we might be if, like her, we took two months to mourn, prepare, find strength, and work on our relationship with God.

When Jephthah's daughter came down from the mountain, she "returned to her father, who did with her according to his vow" (Judges 11:39). The fact that she returned is impressive. I know I'd have been tempted to run away! We can only imagine that the actual sacrifice, at the hand of her father, must have been heart-rending. There was no angel or divine intervention on her behalf. Like the Savior, she went like a "lamb to the slaughter" (Isaiah 53:7) to fulfill her father's promise.

The last verse of Judges 11 tells us that after the death of Jephthah's daughter, "the daughters of Israel went yearly to lament the daughter of Jephthah the Gileadite four days in a year" (verse 40). What this young woman did was not quickly forgotten. Her sacrifice made a lasting impact on her nation. I love the idea of the young women of Israel reenacting Jephthah's daughter's sacred time on the mountain, communing with God in a sisterhood of grief and growth.

In that ritual, I see symbolism of the sacrament. The sacrament, like the tradition of the daughters of Israel remembering Jephthah's daughter, is a time to reflect on the sacrifice Jesus Christ made for us. Even though Christ's Atonement can seem abstract and mysterious to us, it is every bit as personal and intimate a sacrifice as Jephthah's daughter's sacrifice was for her father. Christ, innocent of any wrongdoing, willingly gave His life to atone for our foolish and selfish mistakes. Like Jephthah's daughter, He gave His life for us because He loves us, dearly. Such a sacrifice should not be forgotten or taken casually. It is important for us to always *remember*.

After his daughter's death, Jephthah judged Israel righteously for six years. This was impressive in an era when Israel's rulers were often wicked. It is likely that his daughter's example, her Christlike sacrifice on his behalf, humbled him and helped him make righteous choices for the rest of his life. Jephthah's daughter's example reminds us that unselfish love and sacrifice are powerful forces that have the potential to transform situations, people, and even cultures. This is the type of love our Savior has for us. His atoning love is a vote of confidence in our ability to change, to learn from our mistakes, and to become better. With His love anything is possible.

> Jephthah
> *"vowed a vow*
> *unto the Lord."*

Samson's Mother

And the angel of the Lord appeared unto the woman, and said unto her, Behold now, thou art barren, and bearest not: but thou shalt conceive, and bear a son.

Now therefore beware, I pray thee, and drink not wine nor strong drink, and eat not any unclean thing:

For, lo, thou shalt conceive, and bear a son; and no razor shall come on his head: for the child shall be a Nazarite unto God from the womb: and he shall begin to deliver Israel out of the hand of the Philistines.

Judges 13:3–5

Most Primary children can tell you the story of Samson, the long-haired Hercules who lost his strength and spiritual power because of a bad choice. Yet less well known, and perhaps even more remarkable than Samson's defeat, is the incredible story of his birth.

We don't know the name of Samson's mother, but we know she was married to a man named Manoah and that she struggled with infertility. Like all the "barren" women in the Bible, her childless situation wasn't permanent. In Judges 13:3, we read that one day an angel of the Lord appeared to her and promised her that she would bear a son. Along with this promise, he also told her that her son would be "a Nazarite unto God from the womb" (Judges 13:5).

A Nazarite was a man or a woman who had made a vow and was consecrated (dedicated) to God. The vow could be for their whole lives or for a limited amount of time. A person who made a Nazarite vow could not drink wine, vinegar, or any other strong drink; they couldn't eat grapes or anything that grew on a vine. They also could not cut their hair or touch a dead body or else their vow with God would be broken (see Numbers 6:1–9). For the entire time of their vow they were considered "holy unto the Lord" (Numbers 6:8).

Though it was probably an unusual practice, there are several examples in the scriptures of women who appear to have made Nazarite vows while they were pregnant. For example, Hannah the mother of Samuel promised, "I will give [Samuel] unto the Lord all the days of his life, and there shall no razor come upon his head" (1 Samuel 1:11). In Luke 1:15 the angel told Zacharias and Elisabeth that John, who would later become the Baptist, "shall drink neither wine nor strong drink; and shall be filled with the Holy Ghost, even from his mother's womb." It appears that these women's prenatal vows ensured that their children would be life-long Nazarites, consecrated to the Lord from the moment they were born.[1]

In her visit from the angel, Samson's mother was told that to ensure her son's divine mission, she would have to adhere to a higher level of spiritual commitment and bodily purity. She needed to avoid all the things that would cause her child to break his vow, even though he wasn't born yet. For the duration of her pregnancy she had to become a Nazarite as well. How different would our feelings be about pregnancy if we thought of a women being consecrated—set apart—during the time she was carrying a child? Perhaps it would transform pregnancy into a more spiritual experience.

After her visit with the angel, Samson's mother ran and told her husband, Manoah, about what she had learned. Instead of doubting her, Manoah believed her right away and even "entreated the Lord" that He would send the messenger back to them so that he could "teach us what we shall do unto the child that shall be born" (Judges 13:8). Notice that Manoah used plural pronouns in his prayer, indicating that even though Manoah was voicing the prayer, they were praying as a couple.

The answer to their prayer came quickly. The angel of God returned to speak with Samson's mother while she was alone in the field. I find it intriguing that even though it was Manoah who asked for another visit, the angel chose to appear *again* to just Samson's mother. It seems to follow a pattern in the scriptures where, with just a few exceptions, annunciation scenes (those in which an angel announces the coming of a child) are usually given to women.[2] I don't think this is coincidental. Elder M. Russell Ballard of the Quorum of the Twelve Apostles taught: "Men and women, though spiritually equal, are entrusted with different but equally significant roles. . . . Men are given stewardship over the sacred ordinances of the priesthood. To women, God gives stewardship over bestowing and nurturing mortal life, including providing physical bodies for God's spirit children and guiding those children toward a knowledge of gospel truths."[3]

Women are the gateways into this world, and the stewardship to bestow mortal life is given to them. Just like any person with a stewardship from the Lord, women can expect to receive special revelation about their children—born and unborn. Like Samson's mother, this revelation might just come to them and not their husband. Yet Samson's mother also exemplified the type of cooperation God wants between husbands and wives, because when she saw that the angel had returned she ran to get Manoah so that they could hear the message *together*.

When Manoah arrived, he asked the angel, "How shall we order the child, and how shall we do unto him?" (Judges 13:12). In response, the angel repeated his previous instructions. Basically, the angel told Manoah, "Just listen to your wife. I already told her what to do." After hearing the message, Manoah urged the angel to stay and eat with them, saying, "Let us detain thee, until we shall have made ready a kid for thee" (Judges 13:15). The angel told him that he would not eat but that they should make a burnt offering to the Lord. Apparently, up to this point Manoah had not realized that the man he'd been speaking to was an angel.

This is interesting because we know that, at the first visit of the angel, Manoah's wife had come back and described the person as "a man of God . . . and his countenance was like the countenance of an angel of God" (Judges 13:6). She also told Manoah that she didn't ask him who he was and that he didn't tell her, which contrasts with what Manoah did. In addition to inviting him to eat, Manoah also asked the angel his name so that they could honor him. In response, the angel told him that his name was "secret" (verse 18). The Hebrew word used here means "wonderful" or "incomprehensible."[4]

This "wonderful" nature became apparent to Manoah and his wife when, during their burnt offering to the Lord, the angel "ascended in the flame of the altar" to heaven (Judges 13:20). After seeing this miraculous event, Manoah and his wife did what most of us would do and "fell on their faces to the ground" (verse 20). It was only after this amazing event that Manoah finally understood that the man they had been speaking with was an angel of the Lord. This scared him, and he told his wife, "We shall surely die, because we have seen God" (verse 22). Yet his wife, who seemed to have understood the whole time whom they were speaking with, reassured him that if God was angry with them, He would not "have told us such things as these" (verse 23).

I think that one of the best lessons that the story of Samson's parents teaches us is that just like a woman can support her husband as the patriarch of the family, God also expects a man to support his wife's role as the matriarch, realizing that her calling also entitles her to specific and divine revelation. President James E. Faust taught, "Every father is to his family a patriarch and every mother a matriarch as coequals in their distinctive parental roles."[5] It almost seems like the whole long interaction with the angel was an attempt to help Manoah learn how to rely and listen to his wife. His wife had received revelation from God that was specific to her stewardship as a woman, and it was Manoah's responsibility as a husband to seek for his own spiritual confirmation of that revelation, which he did.

In their roles as matriarchs, women will, and should expect to, receive specific revelation about their families. Sometimes these revelations might come just to them and not their husbands. When this type of revelation occurs, they can follow the example of Samson's mother, who truly exemplified what it means to be a "help meet," encouraging and allowing her husband—the patriarchy—to receive a spiritual confirmation for himself.

Samson's Philistine Wife

Despite his parents' meticulous care to raise him as a Nazarite, one dedicated to God, Samson chose to marry outside of the covenant. Samson told his parents that he had seen a Philistine woman whom he desired for his wife. They responded like most devout parents would if their child made a rash decision to marry outside of their faith. "Is there never a woman among the daughter of thy brethren," his parents pleaded, "or among all my people, that thou goest to take a wife of the uncircumcised Philistines?" (Judges 14:3).

The scriptural account tells us that his parents responded this way because "they knew not that it [Samson's desire marry to the Philistine woman] was of the Lord" (Judges 14:4). The scriptures explain that God had arranged this marriage because He intended for Samson to be the means for delivering Israel out of Philistine control. Eventually, Samson's parents went with him and arranged his marriage with the Philistine woman. They supported his decision, even if they did not understand it or like it. Later we see that it was this marriage, which went badly (see Judges 14), that began Samson's lifelong conflict with the Philistines.

This tidbit is important because it reminds us that though we want our children to marry people of our faith, God can have a different plan for them. We need to trust that sometimes an unusual path might be "of God," even if we do not understand why. If we, or our children, find ourselves in a marriage situation like Samson, we need to remember to rely on the Spirit and make decisions based on the directions God gives us—even if it is not what we expect.

Delilah

[Samson] loved a woman in the valley of Sorek, whose name was Delilah.

And the lords of the Philistines came up unto her, and said unto her, Entice him, and see wherein his great strength lieth, and by what means we may prevail against him, that we may bind him to afflict him: and we will give thee every one of us eleven hundred pieces of silver.

And Delilah said to Samson, Tell me, I pray thee, wherein thy great strength lieth, and wherewith thou mightest be bound to afflict thee....

And when Delilah saw that he had told her all his heart, she sent and called for the lords of the Philistines, saying, Come up this once, for he hath shewed me all his heart. Then the lords of the Philistines came up unto her, and brought money in their hand.

Judges 16:4–6, 18

We know very little about Delilah except where she lived. We don't even know if she was a Philistine woman or an Israelite woman. People have speculated, perhaps because her story comes directly after Samson's stint with a harlot in Gaza (see Judges 16:1), that she was a harlot. Yet nowhere in her story are we told that, though her betrayal of Samson does smack of corruption and depravity. Delilah is an enigmatic, mysterious person whose motivations and character are hard to figure out.

The first we hear of her is when Samson went to the valley of Sorek and "loved a woman" named Delilah (Judges 16:4). While Samson's affections are clear, nowhere are we told if Delilah felt similarly. Only one verse after she is introduced, we see her make a deal with the Philistine lords, who had been unsuccessfully trying to catch Samson, to discover the source of his great strength. They told her that in return "we will give thee every one of us eleven hundred pieces of silver" (Judges 16:5). That was an incredible amount of money!

In 2 Samuel 18, we see that Joab offered ten shekels of silver to have Absalom, the king of Israel and Judah, killed. The man responded that even if he was paid 1,000 shekels of silver he wouldn't "put forth mine hand against the king's son" (2 Samuel 18:12). If ten shekels had been a good offer, 1,000 shekels was an exorbitant amount. This gives us an idea of just how much Delilah had been offered. Judas betrayed Jesus for merely thirty pieces of silver. Delilah's temptation was significantly greater.

Did she betray Samson just for money? Or could there possibly have been another reason? In Judges 14 we read the sad story of Samson's first wife, a Philistine woman. During their wedding feast Samson challenged his Philistine guests to answer a riddle, betting them "thirty sheets and thirty change of garments" (Judges 14:12) if they could figure it out. Clothing and material were valuable, and the Philistines, who could not figure out the riddle, threatened Samson's new wife: "Entice thy husband that he may declare unto us the riddle, lest we burn thee and thy father's house with fire" (verse 15). Talk about putting pressure on her!

Terrified of being killed, Samson's wife "wept before him" (Judges 14:16) and begged him to tell her the answer to the riddle. Samson refused, but his wife "lay sore upon him" (verse 17) for the seven days of their feast until Samson finally gave in and told her the answer. When Samson realized that his wife had betrayed him, he was angry and left. When he returned with a gift to make amends to his wife, he found that she had been married to someone else. Samson, in his anger, burned all the Philistines' cornfields, vineyards and olives trees to the ground. In retaliation, the Philistines took Samson's wife and "burnt her and her father with fire" (Judges 15:6).

These Philistines were not nice people. They hated Samson, whom they perceived as "public enemy number one," and were willing to resort to violence to get their way. The words the Philistine lords used when soliciting Delilah's help were like those said to Samson's first wife. They told Delilah, "*Entice him*, and see wherein his great strength lieth, and by what means we may prevail against him, that we may bind him to afflict him" (Judges 16:5; emphasis added). Could there, in addition to the money they offered, also have been a threat of violence hanging over Delilah's head? Perhaps such a threat would help us explain why she would betray someone who loved her.

Either way, Delilah seemed to believe, just like the Philistines, that Samson's strength lay in some sort of talisman or magic that she had to discover how to break. She asked Samson to tell her his secret, and perhaps because he didn't fully trust her, he told her that "if they bind me with seven green withs [ropes] that were never dried, then I will be weak, and be as another man" (Judges 16:7). Delilah told the Philistine lords, and they brought her the green ropes with which she bound Samson. Yet Samson easily broke through them.

Delilah angrily told Samson, "Thou has mocked me, and told me lies" (Judges 16:10), and tried to persuade Samson again to tell her his secret. This time Samson told her, "If they bind me fast with new ropes that never were occupied, then shall I be weak" (Judges 16:11). Delilah set up the trap, but again Samson escaped. The next time, Samson told her that he would become weak if "thou weavest the seven locks of my head with the web [of the loom]" (Judges 16:13). Once again, Delilah set up the trap and weaved Samson's hair in to the loom, but again Samson escaped. Pulling with his hair still attached to it, the entire beam came off the loom.

At this point in the story, we wonder why Samson didn't ditch Delilah. If a woman tied you up, wove your hair into a loom after you told her that was your only weakness, and kept letting the Philistines into your house, don't you think you'd get suspicious? Perhaps Delilah was much sneakier about these things than the Bible account gave her credit for. Perhaps she presented it all as a lover's game to Samson, one in which, because neither fully trusted the other, they tricked and manipulated each other. Either that or Samson was not the sharpest crayon in the box.

Finally, Delilah got serious and played her trump card. "How canst thou say, I love thee," Delilah told Samson, "when thine heart is not with me?" (Judges 16:15). She then "pressed him daily with her words" so much that Samson was "vexed unto death" (verse 16). I sometimes feel like that with my children who vex me "unto death" with their persistence for certain toys or privileges. I can only

imagine how hard it would be to be in an intimate relationship with someone who was using that love to manipulate and exploit you. It sounds like Delilah was being emotionally and verbally abusive to Samson.

Finally, this abuse was too much for Samson, and he told Delilah the truth. He explained to her that his power came because he was a Nazarite. Part of being a Nazarite was vowing not to cut his hair, and so he told Delilah, "If I be shaven, then my strength will go from me, and I shall become weak, and be like any other man" (verse 17). Realizing that this time Samson had been in earnest, Delilah sent for the Philistine lords. It appears they had given up on her because she had to convince them, saying "Come up this once, for he hath shewed me all his heart" (verse 18). They came with "money in their hand" (verse 18). Delilah was ready to sell Samson and his sacred secret for money.

This time Delilah made Samson "sleep upon her knees" (Judges 16:19) while she had someone else cut off his seven braids. Then the account says she "began to afflict him" (verse 19), which in Hebrew means she "humbled" him. We don't know what she did, but when he awoke, he discovered that "the Lord was departed from him" (verse 20). In this weakened state, the Philistines easily captured him and cut his eyes out. They took him to a stadium where he was to make "sport" (verse 25) for the wealthy Philistines. In one last herculean effort, Samson pulled on the pillars to which he was bound and brought the roof down upon the stadium, killing 3,000 men and women.

After her betrayal, Delilah abruptly disappears from the story. We have no idea what happened to her or how she felt about what she had done. The only possible clue we get is in Judges 17, the chapter directly after her story, that mentions a man named Micah who stole from his mother eleven hundred shekels of silver. This is the exact amount of money Delilah had received for her betrayal of Samson. That is an unusual sum and may suggest that Micah's mother was Delilah. When Micah returned the money to his mother, she stated, "I had wholly dedicated the silver unto the Lord" (Judges 17:3), specifying that she intended to use it to make a graven image.[1]

If this woman was indeed Delilah, it is telling that she had dedicated the money to the Lord, eventually using it to set up a form of worship similar to what went on in the tabernacle (see Judges 17–18). This action might suggest that she felt guilty or uneasy about the money she had gained. Perhaps like Judas, it wasn't until after the deed had been accomplished that she realized the full magnitude of what she had done. Like Judas, Delilah had been deceived and exchanged sacred knowledge for the enticement of money.

The story of Samson and Delilah is a cautionary tale. From Delilah, we learn how important it is to guard and keep sacred the hearts of the ones we love. Often in our marriage, friendships, and family relationships, we come to learn, better than anyone else, the weaknesses and flaws of another person. It can be tempting to use our knowledge for our own personal gain, to put someone down to make ourselves look better, or to sling mud at someone who has hurt us. When we give into that temptation, we are acting like Delilah did, betraying trust and destroying our intimate relationships. We have reason to suspect that Delilah later regretted what she did. Her story can help us remember to never give into temptation to uncover and divulge the secrets or weaknesses of a loved one. We may never be able to undo our actions.

> *"If I be shaven, then my strength will go from me, and I shall become weak, and be like any other man."*

The Concubine of Judges 19

But the men would not hearken to him: so the man took his concubine, and brought her forth unto them; and they knew her, and abused her all the night until the morning: and when the day began to spring, they let her go.

Then came the woman in the dawning of the day, and fell down at the door of the man's house where her lord was, till it was light.

And her lord rose up in the morning, and opened the doors of the house, and went out to go his way: and, behold, the woman his concubine was fallen down at the door of the house, and her hands were upon the threshold.

Judges 19:25–27

This story might just be one of the worst stories in the entire Bible; it is gruesome and cruel and raises the question, "Why?" Why was a story like this recorded? Why was it passed down through generations? Why did it even happen? I'm not sure if I can answer all those whys, but I hope that I can help shed some light on this terrible story.

This woman, whom I will simply call "the concubine," lived in Israel not long after the death of Samson. During this time, Israel was without a judge, and there was no one to unite and govern all the tribes. Instead, as it says in Judges 17:6, "Every man did that which was right in his own eyes." This meant that there was no law and no accountability, and a wicked patriarchy ran rampant. As you can imagine, women were some of the biggest causalities of this anarchy.

The concubine belonged to a Levite, a man of priestly lineage, who dwelt in Ephraim. The first information we get about her says that she "played the whore" (Judges 19:2) and left her husband to return to her parents' house in Beth-lehem-Judah. She was there for four months before her husband came looking for her "to speak friendly unto her and bring her again" (Judges 19:3). The word translated as "played the whore" in this chapter is the Hebrew word *zanah*. It means "harlot" but can also mean "to be angry, hateful" or to "feel repugnant against." Some scholars have suggested that this is a better translation because it seems strange, in a time when honor killings were normal, that the concubine would have been welcomed back by her family or been wanted back by the Levite if she had committed adultery. Josephus, an ancient Jewish historian,

seems to support this translation. In his version of this story, Josephus wrote the following:

> There was a Levite a man of a vulgar family, that belonged to the tribe of Ephraim, and dwelt therein: this man married a wife from Bethlehem, which is a place belonging to the tribe of Judah. Now he was very fond of his wife, and overcome with her beauty; but he was unhappy in this, that he did not meet with the like return of affection from her, for she was averse to him, which did more inflame his passion for her, so that they quarreled one with another perpetually; and at last the woman was so disgusted at these quarrels, that she left her husband, and went to her parents in the fourth month.[1]

After being separated for four months, the Levite showed up at the concubine's father's house to claim her. It says that her father "rejoiced to meet him" (Judges 19:3) and invited him to stay for three days, eating and drinking. On the fourth day, the Levite prepared to leave with his concubine, but the father convinced him to stay another night and "let thine heart be merry" (verse 6). On the fifth day, her father tried to convince the Levite to stay another night, but he insisted on leaving even though it was getting late in the day. That night the Levite and his concubine arrived in Gibeah, a city belonging to the tribe of Benjamin, and found shelter with an old man they met on the street.

While the old man and the Levite were "making their hearts merry" (verse 22), sons of Belial came to the door. The word *Belial* is a masculine noun meaning "worthless" or "wicked."[2] The sons of Belial demanded that the old man "bring forth the man that came into thine house, that we may know him" (verse 22). Josephus states that it wasn't the Levite they were sexually interested in but rather that "having seen the woman in the market-place, and admiring her beauty . . . they desired him to yield them up the strange woman. . . . They despised his righteous admonition, and laughed him to scorn. They also threatened to kill him if he became an obstacle to their inclinations."[3]

Trying to spare his guests, the old man offered them his daughter, a maiden. Yet, when the men refused her, the Levite gave them his concubine and they took her and "knew her, and abused her all the night until the morning" (Judges 19:25). When the sun began to rise, they finally let her go, and she crawled to the old man's doorstep where she died. By this time, it doesn't seem like this woman's story could get any worse, but it does. When her husband came to the door the next morning, he told her to get up. When he realized that she was dead, he took her body and laid in on the back of his donkey. Then, when he got home, he cut her up into twelve pieces and sent a piece of her body to each of the twelve tribes, to "all the coasts of Israel" (verse 29).

As I've studied the scriptures I've come to realize that many of the stories are not put in there as examples of what we should do, but rather as examples of things we *shouldn't* do. The story of the concubine in Judges 19 is a cautionary tale to warn us about what happens when an unrighteous patriarchy reigns unchecked. In fact, the reason that the Levite cut the concubine's body into pieces and sent one to each of the twelve tribes was exactly for that purpose, to warn and shock them. Later, in Judges 20 and 21, we see that the story of what had been done to the concubine so disgusted the Israelites that they launched a war against the men of Benjamin. They even refused to marry their daughters to the Benjaminites (see Judges 21) because they were so upset at what had happened.

As much as we would like to ignore it, the story of the concubine in Judges 19 is still being repeated every day, all over the world. There are women and children in slavery, within our own communities, who have as little say over what happens to their bodies as this concubine had. Like the plight of this concubine, many suffering women today are nearly "invisible" to us. I think sometimes, like the Israelites, we need something shocking to happen, such as having pieces of a woman's body show up on our doorstep, to get us motivated to "see" and help these women and children. If we ignore the suffering of the millions of women and children in the world who are in the same situation that this concubine was, we are on the same level as the people of Benjamin who sat idly by while this woman was tortured. The suffering women of the world need to be "seen," and they need to be helped.

Such a burden can be overwhelming. Yet the story of the concubine has helped me realize that one of the most important things we can do to help women is to raise righteous boys who will become righteous men. We can't focus on empowering our girls without out also focusing on our boys. We don't want to simply replace an overbearing patriarchy with an equally overbearing matriarchy. Instead, we want men and women who can work together, respect each other's divine gifts, and love one another like Christ loves us. In fact, I think that the most "feminist" act any one can do is to teach the gospel of Jesus Christ because nothing else has as much potential to do good in the lives of women all over the world.

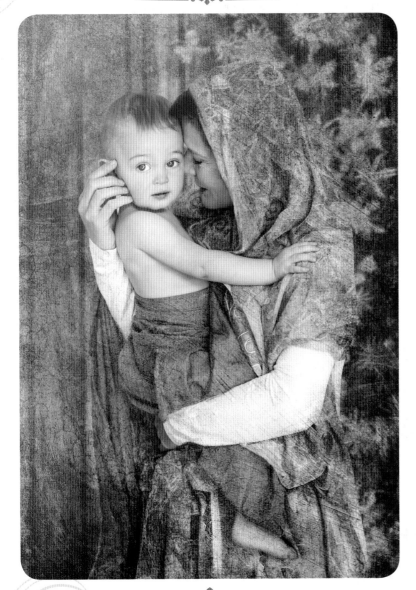

Naomi

So Boaz took Ruth, and she was his wife: and when he went in unto her, the Lord gave her conception, and she bare a son.

And the women said unto Naomi, Blessed be the Lord, which hath not left thee this day without a kinsman, that his name may be famous in Israel.

And he shall be unto thee a restorer of thy life, and a nourisher of thine old age: for thy daughter in law, which loveth thee, which is better to thee than seven sons, hath born him.

And Naomi took the child, and laid it in her bosom, and became nurse unto it.

Ruth 4:13–16

Nothing in Naomi's life seems to have gone like she planned. Due to famine, she and her husband, Elimelech, were compelled to leave their homeland of Judah and travel to Moab. While in Moab, Elimelech died, leaving Naomi alone in a strange country to raise her two sons, Mahlon and Chilion. Her sons eventually married Moabite women, Ruth and Orpah, who proved to be a great blessing in Naomi's life. Yet after ten years of marriage, neither of her daughters-in-law had been able to have children, something I am sure was hard on the whole family. To make it even worse, both Mahlon and Chilion died, and all three women were left widows.

This last tragedy seems to have finally broken Naomi's heart. She decided to return home to Bethlehem to live with her extended family. She begged her Moabite daughters-in-law to return home to their "mother's house" (Ruth 1:8). The phrase "mother's house" is unusual and is only used three other times in the Bible.[1] The phrase is always used in connection with marital arrangements, suggesting that perhaps ancient mothers played an important part in arranging their daughters' marriages. According to scholar Carol Meyers, the phrase also gives us a glimpse into the importance of a woman's domestic sphere:

> The Ruth passage and all the other text using "mother's house" are women's texts—either they speak in the female voice or they tell a woman's story. For that reason, "mother's house" can be regarded as the term used for the household when women are referring to their family and its abode. Furthermore, because women in the agrarian household of ancient Israel controlled many of the domestic activities, the term may be accurate in designating internal household dynamics; the term "father's house" may be more appropriate in referring to the household in its relation to supra-household interactions.[2]

Naomi hoped that, by sending Ruth and Orpah each back to her "mother's house," they would have a good chance at remarrying and having children. She knew that going with her, a penniless widow, to Bethlehem would not present them with many opportunities for the future. Yet Ruth and Orpah both resisted Naomi's instruction, insisting that they would "return with thee unto thy people" (Ruth 1:10). Again Naomi told them to go home to their mothers. "Are there any more sons in my womb, that they may be your husbands?" she asked. "Turn again, my daughters, go your way; for I am too old to have an husband" (Ruth 1:11–12).

Naomi felt that her life had been cursed. After all, hadn't all the men in her life died? She felt that if Ruth and Orpah stayed with her, they would share her same misfortune. She told them, "It grieveth me for your sakes that the hand of the Lord is gone out against me" (Ruth 1:13). After this discussion, Orpah decided to return home to her family, but Ruth insisted on accompanying Naomi, pledging, "Whither thou goest, I will go. . . . Thy people shall be my people, and thy God my God" (verse 16). Perhaps both gratefully and regretfully, Naomi returned to Bethlehem with Ruth in tow.

When they arrived, the whole city came out to greet them, asking in excitement and disbelief, "Is this Naomi?" (Ruth 1:19). Much had happened to Naomi since she had left her family in Bethlehem. I imagine that she didn't resemble, or even feel like, the same woman who had left years before. Naomi even told them that they should no longer call her Naomi, which means "pleasant or delightful," but that instead that they should call her Mara, which means "bitter." She explained, "For the Almighty hath dealt very bitterly with me. I went out full, and the Lord hath brought me home again empty; why then call ye me Naomi, seeing the Lord hath testified against me, and the Almighty hath afflicted me?" (Ruth 1:20–21).

Even if we have never lost a loved one, I think we can all relate to how Naomi felt. Have you ever moved from a ward or a neighborhood where you felt close to people, and then come back years (or even months) later and realized that things have changed? We see, often with shock, that people and relationships are no longer the same and that we are no longer who we were before. I think we can feel this even more dramatically when we experience tragedies. Trials and deep sorrow refine and change our souls, sometimes even turning us into completely new people. Naomi had been through a lot of hard living since she had left, and instead of coming back prosperous and happy she'd returned empty and devastated. She was so sad that she didn't even try to mask her feelings.

I think that how Naomi handled her grief, in a very public way, is much better than the private way we often handle our grief today. I sometimes wish that we still practiced the tradition of wearing black, or even sackcloth and ashes, when we are grieving. There is nothing worse than feeling like your soul has been torn apart but still feeling like you must keep a happy face on.

The beautiful part about Naomi's story is that at its heart, it is a story about compensation. Naomi's bitterness ran its course, and not long after she arrived in Bethlehem, she found that her life was happier and fuller than she had ever hoped for. When Ruth gave birth to Naomi's first grandchild, a little boy named Obed (who would later become the grandfather of King David), the women gathered and gave her a blessing. The women promised Naomi, speaking of Obed, that "he shall be unto thee a restorer of thy life, and a nourisher of thine old age: for thy daughter in law, which loveth thee, which is better to thee than seven sons, hath born him" (Ruth 4:15).

Then Naomi did a very curious thing. She "took the child, and laid it in her bosom, and became nurse unto it" (Ruth 4:16).[3] Often when the word *nurse* is used in the scriptures it is the Hebrew word *yanaq*, which means "to suckle or to suck" and refers to a woman who breastfeeds a child. However, word used to describe Naomi as a nurse is the Hebrew word *aman*, which is a verb meaning "to support, uphold, and nourish." This word is never used in the scriptures to refer to the literal act of breastfeeding a child. Instead, *aman* is

most often translated as the word *believe* and is used to indicate when a person, or a people, allow themselves to be nourished by the word of God.[4] For example, the famous verse from Isaiah 49:23 uses both the word *aman* and the word *yanaq*: "And kings shall be thy *nursing [aman] fathers, and their queens thy nursing [yanaq] mothers*: they shall bow down to thee with their face toward the earth, and lick up the dust of thy feet; and thou shalt know that I am the Lord: for they shall not be ashamed that wait for me" (emphasis added).

The phrase that is translated "nursing fathers" is the Hebrew word *aman* which means "support," while the phrase "nursing mothers" is the Hebrew word *yanaq*, which means to physically "suckle or suck." Both the word *aman* and *yanaq* can rightly be translated as "nurse," but they refer to two very different ways of nurturing. A "nursing mother" uses her physical body to nourish and support another person physically, while a "nursing father" nourishes and suckles spiritually, preparing a person to believe and accept the word of God.[5] Both types of nurturing are important in a person's life. It is easy to see how an infant would suffer if she didn't have access to her mother's milk. In a similar way, we each require aman, or spiritual nurturing, just as much as we do physical nurturing.

My own life is filled with women who have taken me to their bosoms and been an *aman* to me. One of my aunts with no children of her own became a mother to me during a difficult time in my life. Her love and help sustained me through rough times and helped me until I was strong enough to stand on my own. At other times, I've felt similar nurturing and support come from Relief Society presidents, friends, relatives, and a wonderful mother-in-law who have all fed me with their time, teaching, wisdom, and love. The word *aman*, as used to describe Naomi's relationship with Obed, is a reminder that even though not all women will have the opportunity to *yanaq* or "suckle" a child, all women have opportunities to *aman* or "spiritually nourish" the children around them. Both types of nurturing are equally important.

As I said before, Naomi's story is about compensation. Elder Joseph B. Wirthlin, a former Apostle, taught about what he called "the law of compensation" when he said, "The Lord compensates the faithful for every loss. That which is taken away from those who love the Lord will be added unto them in His own way. While it may not come at the time we desire, the faithful will know that every tear today will eventually be returned a hundredfold with tears of rejoicing and gratitude."[6] The Savior also taught this when He told Joseph Smith, "Search diligently, pray always, and be believing, and all things shall work together for your good" (D&C 90:24).

Sometimes it is hard, especially when we are amid difficulties in our life, to see how *all* things will work together for our good. Yet this is where I think God shines. He can take anything we face—death, loneliness, war, abuse, infertility, bankruptcy, disease, divorce, famine—and somehow make good things come from it. It's almost like magic, but God can use all our experiences for good—absolutely *all* of them. Naomi is a testament to that. Life may not always go as we plan, but it will always turn out just like it should. God makes sure of that.

• Orpah •

Orpah sometimes gets painted in a poor light. Unlike her sister-in-law Ruth, Orpah chose to return home to her family and "to her gods" (Ruth 1:15) instead of going with her mother-in-law, Naomi, to Bethlehem. I have sat in Sunday School lessons where Orpah's character was dragged through the mud as people speculated that she must not have been as converted to the true and living God as Ruth, that she wasn't as dedicated to her mother-in-law, or that she lacked the faith to leave her homeland. Any of those things could possibly be true, but I don't think that reading of her story is completely fair.

Remember that it was *both* Ruth and Orpah who initially resisted Naomi's suggestion that they return home. It also seems apparent from the way in which Orpah and Naomi departed, with much "lifting up" of their voices and crying, that leaving was not an easy choice for Orpah. In fact, in dismissing her daughters-in-law, Naomi told them, "Go, return each to her mother's house: the Lord deal kindly with you, as ye have dealt with the dead, and with me" (Ruth 1:8). The word *kindly* used here is the Hebrew word *hesed*. *Hesed* can be a difficult word to translate, but it is often translated as "lovingkindness," "mercy," "steadfast love," or "compassion." It refers to an all-encompassing love, the type of love that is used to describe God and his son Jesus Christ. The use of the word *hesed* to describe Orpah tells us that she had treated Naomi with Christlike love.

I'd like to think that Orpah's choice to return home was just as inspired as Ruth's choice to stay. Perhaps it was God's plan for Orpah to return to her family, to find a husband, and raise her children among her own people, just as much as it was for Ruth to go with Naomi and find her husband and raise her children among a foreign people. I think it is only fair to Orpah that we leave room for the possibility that, just like Ruth, Orpah was *also* following the instructions the Lord had given her. She just walked a different path.

Ruth

And Ruth said, Entreat me not to leave thee, or to return from following after thee: for whither thou goest, I will go; and where thou lodgest, I will lodge: thy people shall be my people, and thy God my God:

Where thou diest, will I die, and there will I be buried: the Lord do so to me, and more also, if ought but death part thee and me.

When she saw that she was steadfastly minded to go with her, then she left speaking unto her.

Ruth 1:16–18

The Old Testament contains few examples of converts. Ruth is perhaps the most famous of all those converts,[1] not only because she has a powerful conversion story but because she also demonstrates what it takes to *remain* converted and how one person's conversion can affect generations. John S. Tanner, the president of BYU–Hawaii, wrote in his missionary journal, "Conversion is the greatest miracle. It is even more wonderful than healing the sick or raising the dead. For while a person who is healed will eventually fall sick again and ultimately die, the miracle of conversion can last forever and affect the eternities for the convert as well as for his or her posterity. Whole generations are healed and redeemed from death through the miracle of conversion."[2]

Like all converts, Ruth's process of conversion began with a choice. When her husband died, Ruth opted not to return to her family. Going back home would have been the traditional, and logical, thing for Ruth to do, yet instead she was bold—and impressively independent—and insisted on staying with Naomi.

Ruth's decision was undoubtedly based on a profound love and concern for Naomi. Yet, as she displayed in her famous pledge, her choice was also based on her conversion to Jehovah, the God of Abraham, Isaac, and Jacob. When pressed by Naomi to return to her family so that she would have a chance at marriage and a family, Ruth responded, "Entreat me not to leave thee, or to return from following after thee: for whither thou goest, I will go; and where thou lodgest, I will lodge: thy people shall be my people, and thy God my God: Where thou diest, will I die, and there will I be buried" (Ruth 1:16–17). Ruth was even so bold as to make a covenant with God, saying that if she was ever unfaithful to her mother-in-law (and presumably to her faith) that death should be her consequence, "and more also, if ought but death part thee and me" (verse 17).

Ruth's conversion to the God of Israel, and her choice to dwell among the people of Israel for the rest of her life, was doubly impressive because Ruth was a Moabite. The Moabites were distantly related to the Israelites, but throughout the Bible there was constant warfare between the two kingdoms.[3] The kingdoms were not far apart (about fifty to seventy-five miles), but they spoke different languages and the Moabites worshiped different gods. Even though there was peace between Judah and Moab during Ruth's time, it is easy to imagine that she would have faced prejudice.

Despite her minority status, Ruth worked hard to be faithful to her promises and to become a part of the community. Naomi and Ruth arrived in Bethlehem at the beginning of the barley harvest, which happened in early spring.[4] Knowing that it would be her responsibility to provide for herself and Naomi, Ruth immediately went to glean in the field of Boaz, one of Naomi's rich kinsmen.[5] Ruth was now both poor *and* a stranger, so she was more than entitled to glean in Boaz's field. We can imagine that Ruth, who had not been accustomed to poverty, may have found it hard to assume that role.

Not long after, when the barley harvest was underway, Boaz came to inspect how it was going and noticed Ruth in the field. After asking his servant about who she was, he took her aside and gave her a generous invitation, telling her that she should "go not to glean in another field" but that for the remainder of the harvest she should "abide here fast by my maidens . . . and go thou after them" (Ruth 2:8–9). He told her she was free to drink from the water he provided for his workers and to eat with them. He also let her know that he had specifically told the young men who were working in the field to not harass or hurt her.

Ruth was understandably grateful and "fell on her face, and bowed herself to the ground" (Ruth 2:10). She asked Boaz why he, the master of the whole property, was taking notice of her. Boaz responded that he had heard all that she had done for her mother-in-law and about her conversion and that he was impressed by her. He even gave her his blessing, telling her, "The Lord recompense thy work and a full reward be given thee of the Lord God of Israel, under whose wings thou art come to trust" (verse 12).

In one magnanimous gesture, Boaz transformed Ruth from an outsider to a fully invited participant in the barley harvest. He reached out to her and included her at a time when she most desperately needed to be included. I think sometimes we forget what an important influence one person can have, especially when it comes to making other people feel welcome and included. A sincere invitation, like Boaz's to Ruth, can go a long way in helping someone who feels like an outsider feel like they belong.

I have a good friend who is a recent convert to the Church. Many times I have seen how joining the Church has been a culture shock for her. She has had to learn how to dress, speak, eat, and live her life differently because of the covenants she has made to follow Jesus Christ. It isn't always easy for her, especially in a congregation where many of the members have been doing those things their whole lives. When I think about her and so many others like her, I think about how wonderful it would be if every convert in this church had a "Boaz," someone who reached out and found ways to make them feel included in the work.

After Boaz's invitation, Ruth stayed with his servants throughout the barley harvest, as well as the wheat harvest, which finished at the end of July. At the end of the harvest, Naomi realized that Boaz was one of their "next kinsmen," and that under the practice of Levirate marriage (see Tamar on page 197), it was his duty to marry Ruth and have a child with her so that Ruth's dead husband's patriarchal line would not die out. Naomi instructed Ruth to dress and anoint herself in a special way and go to the threshing floor on the night when the men would be threshing the barley. It was common for the master of the field and some of his men to sleep on the threshing floor to protect the crop. Naomi told Ruth that she should wait until the men were asleep and then find Boaz and "go in, and uncover his feet, and lay thee down; and he will tell thee what thou shalt do" (Ruth 3:4).

Ruth followed her mother-in-law's instructions. When Boaz lay down, she "came softly and uncovered his feet" (Ruth 3:7). The phrase "uncovered his feet" is strange. Because the phrase in not used elsewhere in the Bible, it is hard to know exactly what it means. Some people have speculated that because the word *feet* can sometimes be used in the scriptures as a euphemism for genitalia, that Ruth was making sexual advances toward Boaz.[6] I am skeptical of that interpretation because that type of behavior does not fit with what we know about Ruth or what was appropriate in that culture.

I think it is more likely that Ruth did exactly what the text suggests and simply removed his shoes or the blanket that was covering his feet. Deuteronomy 25:9 says that if a man was unwilling to perform his Levirate marriage duty, then the widow was entitled to "come unto him in the presence of the elders, and loose his shoe from off his foot, and spit in his face" and publicly humiliate him for his selfishness. It is interesting to think that perhaps Ruth's "uncovering" of Boaz's feet was her way of privately, and gently, reminding him of his obligation to her.

This interpretation might work because after she uncovered his feet, Boaz awoke. The first thing Ruth told him was to "spread therefore thy skirt over thine handmaiden; for thou art a near kinsman" (Ruth 3:9). Ruth's language here was clearly sexual. The phrase "spread thy skirt" means just what it sounds like and is used elsewhere in the Bible to refer to the act of marriage.[7] Ruth was asking quite boldly that Boaz marry her and supply her with a child, as was her right under the practice of Levirate marriage.

Despite the sexual overtones of their conversation, the text does not suggest that Ruth and Boaz had any sexual interaction that night on the threshing floor. In fact, it appears that Boaz went to great lengths to ensure that Ruth's (and his) reputation was protected, having her leave early in the morning before anyone could know that she had been there. Boaz also told Ruth, that "all the city . . . doth know that thou art a virtuous woman" and that he had noticed that she "followedest not young men, whether poor or rich" (Ruth 3:10–11). Having illicit sex on the floor of the threshing room does not fit well with what the biblical text tells us about Ruth or Boaz's character. Ruth's proposal of marriage to Boaz may have been nontraditional, but I do not think it was immoral.

Boaz was more than happy to accept Ruth's proposal, but he had to admit to her that he was not her nearest kinsman, that there was someone more closely related than he. But, Boaz told her, "If he will not do the part of a kinsman to thee, then will I do the part of a kinsman to thee" (Ruth 3:13). The next morning Boaz went to the city gate and waited until this kinsman passed by on his way out of the city to his field. Boaz stopped him and gathered a group of elders to witness their conversation.

Boaz presented his case carefully. The Israelites believed that all their land belonged to God and that each family had been given a stewardship over it. If, for some reason, land was lost or sold, it was considered the duty of the family to buy it back or "redeem" it. Boaz told his kinsman about Naomi and how, since her husband and sons had died, the family's land was available to be redeemed. Boaz made it clear that if the kinsman did not redeem it then he would. The kinsman was clearly eager to increase his land. Then Boaz dropped the deal breaker and told the kinsman about Ruth and that "what day thou buyest the field of the hand of Naomi, thou must buy it also of Ruth the Moabitess, the wife of the dead, to raise up the name of the dead upon his inheritance" (Ruth 4:5).

This kinsman was not interested in buying encumbered land that, if Ruth produced an heir, would be inherited by the son of another man. The kinsman told Boaz that the land, along with Ruth, were his to redeem. According to the custom of the time, Boaz took off his shoe and gave it to the kinsman as a witness that they had made a deal. Boaz announced that he had "bought all that was Elimelech's, and all that was Chilion's and Mahlon's. . . . Moreover Ruth the Moabitess, the wife of Mahlon, have I purchased to be my wife" (Ruth 4:9–10).

After the agreement was final, the elders blessed Boaz and gave him this beautiful promise that, "the Lord make the woman that is come into thine house like Rachel and like Leah, which two did build the house of Israel. . . . And let they house be like the house of Pharez, whom Tamar bare unto Judah, of the seed which the Lord shall give thee of this young woman" (Ruth 4:11–12). This promise proved prophetic because not long after their marriage, Ruth gave birth to a son whom they named Obed. This was miraculous when we remember that Ruth had been childless in her previous marriage. On top of that, though, Obed would later become the father of Jesse, who was the father of King David, whose lineage Jesus Christ would be born through. In fact, Ruth is one of five women—along with Mary, Rahab, Bathsheba, and Tamar—who is mentioned in Christ's genealogy (see Matthew 1). She was a builder of the line Judah, the matriarchal line of the Savior.

The Bible Dictionary explains that conversion "denotes changing one's views, in a conscious acceptance of the will of God. . . . Complete conversion comes after many trials and much testing" (Bible Dictionary, "Conversion"). Ruth is a model for such a conversion.

She left a different culture and religion and faced heartbreak, poverty, alienation, and uncertainty to embrace her testimony of the gospel. I think it helped that she had a "Boaz" and a "Naomi" in her life who included and nurtured her, but I also think that it was because her heart was deeply loyal to God. She jumped onto the path of conversion with her whole soul and was committed to seeing it to the end. A single choice sent her life and the lives of her posterity on a completely new trajectory—one that eventually included the birth of the Savior.

> "Whole generations are healed and redeemed from death through the miracle of conversion."

Peninnah

And he had two wives; the name of the one was Hannah, and the name of the other Peninnah: and Peninnah had children, but Hannah had no children. . . .

And when the time was that Elkanah offered, he gave to Peninnah his wife, and to all her sons and her daughters, portions:

But unto Hannah he gave a worthy portion; for he loved Hannah: but the Lord had shut up her womb.

And her adversary also provoked her sore, for to make her fret, because the Lord had shut up her womb.

1 Samuel 1:2, 4–6

It is no secret that women can be hard on each other when it comes to childbearing. We have even coined the phrase "mommy wars" to describe the judgment and hostility that can arise between women who make different mothering choices. This proclivity to judge is not unique to modern women. The Bible has several examples of women caught up in feminine conflicts, one of which is the story of Peninnah and Hannah.

Hannah and Peninnah were the wives of Elkanah, who was from the tribe of Ephraim. While Peninnah had been blessed with many children, both sons and daughters, Hannah remained childless. This was a sore spot between the two women. Like most family problems, hard feelings flared up around holidays. In the case of Hannah and Peninnah, it was the annual trip that Elkanah made with his family to the tabernacle in Shiloh so that the family could offer sacrifices to the Lord. In preparation for the trip, Elkanah gave each of his children "portions," and even though Hannah had no children, he made sure to give her a "worthy portion" because "he loved Hannah but the Lord had shut up her womb" (1 Samuel 1:5).

During this time, Peninnah seems to have made Hannah's grief over being unable to have children almost unbearable. 1 Samuel 1:6–7 states, "Her adversary also provoked her sore, for to make her fret, because the Lord had shut up her womb. . . . Year by year, when she went up to the house of the Lord, so she provoked her; therefore she wept, and did not eat." The word *adversary* is the Hebrew word *tsarah* and connotes a female enemy, especially a rival wife.[1] In the Septuagint, the Greek translation of the New Testament, we learn that Elkenah loved Hannah more than Peninnah, which may have been one of the reasons Peninnah tried to make Hannah feel worthless. The Bible account tells us that Hannah "was in bitterness of soul" (1 Samuel 1:10). The Hebrew word that is used to describe Hannah's weeping is *bakah*, which implies lamenting and wailing as though for the dead. Hannah must have been desperate for a child, not only to fulfill her maternal longings but to assure herself that God didn't hate her and had not forgotten her.

On the other hand, it is easy to see how Peninnah, with her many children, might have allowed herself to feel proud and assume that her children were evidence of God's approval. I'd even wager that much of Peninnah's self-worth was tied to her children and that she felt superior to Hannah because of them. Pride can often make

us blind. Instead of being kind and understanding to Hannah's situation, Peninnah tried to bolster her own feelings of self-worth by pulling someone else down. Her behavior reminds me of the famous quote by C.S. Lewis: "Pride gets no pleasure out of having something, only out of having more of it than the next man."[2]

Even though it is easy to view Peninnah in a condemning light, I bet that most of us have behaved, at some point in our lives, just like her. Have we ever judged women who don't have children, women who have too many children, women whose children are spaced too close together, or too far apart? Have we intentionally or unintentionally made judgments about another person? Have we ever said something (even behind their backs) that might make another person "fret" or weep "in bitterness of soul"? How often do we make judgments before we understand what someone is going through? If we are honest with ourselves, I think we will all admit that there have been times that pride has kept us from seeing things clearly. That is the first lesson from Peninnah and Hannah's story—don't judge, just love.

The second lesson is just as important but can be equally as hard to implement. It is interesting to note that the Septuagint doesn't mention anything about Peninnah "provoking [Hannah] sore" (1 Samuel 1:6). So, on one hand, Peninnah may have taunted Hannah and made her feel inadequate because she didn't have children. On the other hand, Peninnah may not have provoked Hannah at all. Perhaps Hannah's feelings of inadequacy as a mother and a woman were her own perceptions of the situation. In her mind, she may have decided that Peninnah was judging her and looking down on her because she didn't have children when, in fact, Peninnah wasn't doing anything of the sort.

How many of us have behaved like Hannah at some point in our lives? Have we ever allowed our insecurities to cloud our perceptions? Have we made ourselves miserable worrying about what other people think when they don't care as much as we think they do? When we are unsure of ourselves, it is easy to project our insecurities. Where we are at personally in our lives, and what we are struggling with, can often shape our perceptions. Here is the second lesson from Peninnah's story—don't assume other people are judging you.

I find it appropriate that later in the Bible when Samuel, the son that Hannah would eventually give birth to, was looking for a man to be king of Israel, God told him, "The Lord seeth not as man seeth; for man looketh on the outward appearance, but the Lord looketh on the heart" (1 Samuel 16:7). God was reminding Samuel that despite how hard we try to be fair, our perceptions of people will always be clouded by our own perspective. We may try to put on another lens and step into other people's shoes, but we will never be able to truly understand them like the Lord can. He alone can see their hearts. Peninnah and Hannah remind us all we can do—whether we have a dozen children or no children—is to love each other, encourage each other, and let God be the judge.

> *"For man looketh on the outward appearance, but the Lord looketh on the heart."*

Hannah

Hannah, why weepest thou? And why eatest thou not? And why is thy heart grieved? Am not I better to thee than ten sons?

1 Samuel 1:8

Hannah is one of the most well-known women in the Bible. When we talk about her we usually remember her trial with barrenness, her miraculous pregnancy, and her faith-filled promise to dedicate her son to the Lord. Yet we seldom consider the equally inspiring story of her relationship with her husband, Elkanah.

During Hannah's trial with barrenness, Elkanah became concerned about her because she was apparently losing her will to live. He confronted her and asked, "Hannah, why weepest thou? and why eatest thou not? and why is thy heart grieved? am not I better to thee than ten sons?" (1 Samuel 1:8). Taken at face value, this comment can sound like Elkanah was being insensitive to Hannah's pain, wondering why she would be sad when she had him, an amazing specimen of a man (comparable to ten men, nonetheless) who would make any woman happy.

However, if we dig a little deeper, we see that his comment was not self-centered at all. Elkanah, in his role as a righteous husband, was mirroring back to Hannah the type of love and acceptance that her Heavenly Father had for her. He was reminding Hannah that even though she felt great pressure from herself and from her culture to become a mother that it wasn't all there was to live for. He was really asking his wife, "Why are you so sad that you want to die? Your worth in my eyes is not dependent upon how many children you have or don't have. You have my love. Doesn't that count for something?"

Perhaps buoyed up by her husband's support, Hannah decided to approach God in prayer during her annual trip to the tabernacle. At this time, worship was formal and ritualistic. If someone wanted to approach God to give thanks, repent, or ask a blessing, they had to present a sacrifice and assist as the priest took it before the Lord. The idea of going to the tabernacle and praying personally to God was unheard of. Author Vanessa Ochs wrote the following about Hannah's plea:

> Hannah's direct and intimate speech to God was such an unusual form of religious devotion for its time that Eli the priest, observing her, had no idea what she was doing. Who had ever stood in the temple, moving her lips and crying? Such odd behavior! It didn't conform to any way of worship that Eli recognized. Not imagining it could be a legitimate style of worship he didn't know about, Eli concluded Hannah had to be drunk! It is not surprising that a religious leader witnessing an unfamiliar expression of women's spirituality would decide that it was transgressive.[1]

Not only did Hannah break the mold in her style of prayer, but she also made a vow to God, promising that if He would give her the deepest desire of her heart—a child—she would return His gift to Him with a grateful heart.

Hannah's vow to dedicate her child to the Lord would have been meaningless if it hadn't been for the support of her husband. In Numbers 30, it outlines the Mosaic laws pertaining to vows, or personal covenants. Both men and women could make vows, but the terms were a little different for women than for men. For men the law stated that if he made a vow to God he was bound by covenant to keep it, no matter what.

For women, the law was similar but gave several exceptions. For example, if a woman was in her youth and still in her father's house, she could swear a vow but would only be held to it if her father allowed her to keep her vow. If a woman was married, the law was similar. She could make a vow, but the Lord would only hold her to it if her husband supported her in her vow. Women's situations were often much more complicated because of their dependence upon their fathers and their husbands. Ideally, every woman would have had a righteous father or a husband who would have supported her in her promises to the Lord, but as we know, that wasn't always the case.

In view of women's complicated situation, the Lord qualified that if a husband "holds his peace" when he heard his wife make a covenant and allowed her to keep it, but then somehow prevented her from fulfilling the promise she had made to God, "then *he* shall bear her iniquity" (Numbers 30:15; emphasis added). A woman was only held accountable for her vow if the men in her life allowed her to keep it. If they hindered her, then the man would then be held accountable to God for the broken covenant

Even though many women in today's world have much more personal autonomy than women did in Old Testament times, I can still think of plenty of situations when a husband or father might hinder a woman from keeping her vow to the Lord. For example, a father who won't allow his daughter to be baptized, a husband who won't let his wife pay her tithing, a man who refuses to marry, a husband who won't support his wife in her callings, a father who won't let his daughter participate in Church activities, or even a husband who refuses to consider having a baby are all examples of unrighteous dominion that might keep a woman from fulfilling her covenants to the Lord.

Elkanah's support of Hannah's vow shows that he understood, and respected, his wife's spiritual relationship with God. Dedicating your only son to the temple would not have been easy. Elkanah's willingness to uphold Hannah's vow, even when it was difficult, shows the type of faith and trust he had in her ability to receive revelation and to act with spiritual power. Hannah and Elkanah's relationship is a wonderful example of a righteous marriage and partnership, one in which both husband and wife support the covenants the other has made, even if it requires sacrifice.

> *"You have my love. Doesn't that count for something?"*

Phinehas's Wife

And his daughter in law, Phinehas' wife, was with child, near to be delivered: and when she heard the tidings that the ark of God was taken, and that her father in law and her husband were dead, she bowed herself and travailed; for her pains came upon her.

And about the time of her death the women that stood by her said unto her, Fear not; for thou hast born a son. But she answered not, neither did she regard it.

And she named the child I-chabod, saying, The glory is departed from Israel: because the ark of God was taken, and because of her father in law and her husband.

And she said, The glory is departed from Israel: for the ark of God is taken.

1 Samuel 4:19–22

The story of Phinehas's wife is a story of suffering, in both body and spirit. Her name is unknown to us, but we know that she was married to Phinehas, the son of Eli, the high priest of the tabernacle. Phinehas, along with his brother Hophni, served as priests in the tabernacle, but their wicked behavior vexed their father and God. They had abused their power as priests by engaging in illicit behavior, such as taking the best portion of sacrifices for themselves and having sexual relations with the sanctuary's serving women (see 1 Samuel 3–4).

We don't know if Phineas's wife knew of her husband's sins, but her story does give us reason to suspect that she was deeply troubled mentally and spiritually. Not long after Hannah took her son, Samuel, to serve in the tabernacle, the Israelites engaged in battle with the Philistines. Because of their wickedness, God was not with the Israelites and they suffered great casualties, including the deaths of Phinehas and Hophini. Perhaps even more disheartening to the Israelites was that that during the conflict, the Philistines captured the ark of the covenant and carried it out of Israel, a sign that God had literally departed from them (see Samuel 4:10–11).

When Eli, who was then very old and nearly blind, was told the news of his sons and the loss of the ark of the covenant, he "fell from off the seat backward by the side of the gate, and his neck brake, and he died: for he was an old man, and heavy" (1 Samuel 4:18). He was not the only one to take the news badly. His daughter-in-law, Phinehas's wife, was pregnant, and when she heard that the ark had been taken, that her husband had been killed, and that her father-in-law had died of grief, "she bowed herself and travailed; for her pains came upon her" (1 Samuel 4:19).

Imagine this poor woman bowed down under her sorrow, grief, and heartache, trying bravely to cope with the added pain of childbirth! It appears that her labor was difficult and that it left her weakened and just as despondent as before. The woman who attended her in childbirth tried to buoy her up by saying, "Fear not; for thou hast born a son" (1 Samuel 4:20). They were trying to remind her that even though things looked bleak, she was needed and had a reason to live. Still, she refused to hold or take care of her newborn son. Her soul and mind were troubled, and all she could see was darkness. She had no desire to live. She even named her son I-chabod, which in Hebrew means "Where is the glory?" (in 1 Samuel 4:21,

footnote *a*). She told the women attending her, "The glory is departed from Israel: for the ark of God is taken" (verse 21). Afterward she died.

It is true that her future and the future of the children of Israel looked bleak. Wicked priests had corrupted the tabernacle. The ark—the symbol of God's covenant with Israel—had been captured and defiled, and it looked like the end of the nation and people she loved. Yet she couldn't see that just down the road was the age of Samuel, David, and Solomon, a time in which Israel would rise to its true greatness as a people, a time in which a real house of God, not just a tent—more magnificent than anything she could have possibly imagined—would be built. All of this was not far in the future, but at the time all she could see was the darkness.

I like how writer Jim Lafoon explained her story:

> Even as the news of her husband's death began this young woman's labor pains, so many times God "births" new things out of the most painful moments of our lives. . . .
>
> The young wife of Phinehas was so overwhelmed by her pain, she lost sight of the hope promised by the birth of a new child. This well may be the most dangerous part of the whole process.
>
> When God is birthing something new—in you—out of some crisis or tragedy, your life will either be defined by your pain or your promises. Therefore, it is critical that you hold on to God's promises in these painful moments. . . .
>
> . . . Many times when you are in crisis, you feel as if all your hopes and dreams are gone.

Like the wife of Phinehas, everything in you simply wants to quit. Some of you have even been tempted to curse the precious new thing God is doing in your life. If this is where you are today, this is no time for you to give into despair.

The great pain you are experiencing is a sign of the even greater promise that will follow it. . . . Time after time, I have watched God bring "life" out of "death"[1]

Feelings of darkness, despair, and suffering come to all of us, and it is all too tempting when we feel this "travail" begin in our lives to find a way to escape it, when the only thing to be done is to simply endure it. Like childbirth, once God has started "birthing" something in our lives, it is impossible to stop it. The only way out of it is to keep going until it is over and the birth is completed.

A dear friend of mine suffered for several years with extreme depression and darkness. She contemplated taking her own life. With help (and lots of prayer and fasting), she eventually emerged from the darkness and regained a desire to live. She wrote:

> I keep seeing an image in my mind. I wish I could draw it in a way that would do it justice. It's a woman crawling through a narrow tunnel, clawing her way forward through the rocks and dirt, not knowing that she only has a few more feet before she will emerge into a breathtaking valley full of light and color. That's why we can't give up. . . . Sometimes I weep when I imagine if I had given up before emerging into my breathtaking valley full of light and color. A valley more full of light and color than any emotional landscape I had known before. . . . I'm so glad to be alive.[2]

We can trust that when the Lord begins a "birthing" in our life, when we feel the pangs of travail in our minds, our souls, and our bodies, that there will also one day be a deliverance—a day when our pain will cease, our souls will rejoice, and we will hold new life in our arms. The Lord explained this to Isaiah when He said, "Before she travailed, she brought forth; before her pain came, she was delivered of a man child. Who hath heard such a thing? Who hath seen such things? . . . Shall I bring to the birth, and not cause to bring forth? Saith the Lord: shall I cause to bring forth, and shut the womb?" (Isaiah 66:7–9).

Pain and suffering, while not anyone's first-choice experiences, are often the catalyst for growth and new life. President Spencer W. Kimball taught, "*Being human, we would expel from our lives physical pain and mental anguish and assure ourselves of continual ease and comfort, but if we were to close the doors upon sorrow and distress, we might be excluding our greatest friends and benefactors.*"[3] Just like childbirth, growth and change are often a painful process in which we are stretched to the outer limits of our souls. When we think we can't handle it anymore, we become reborn—a new creature, stronger, different, and better.

I hate to hold Phinehas's wife up as a bad example of someone who failed because she could not bear the darkness any longer. We don't know all the circumstances of her life, and we should give her the benefit of the doubt, trusting that she did the best she could or knew how to do. However, I think that her story is also a powerful reminder to us that we should not give up when we are faced with travail and darkness. All night ends in day, and all winter ends in spring. If we can just hold on and have faith that there is meaning and purpose to what we are experiencing, we will live to see a day much brighter and more magnificent than any we could ever imagine. The ark may have been captured, but don't lose hope; it will return and the days of Samuel, David and the splendor of a palatial temple are ahead.

Michal

Saul also sent messengers unto David's house, to watch him, and to slay him in the morning: and Michal David's wife told him, saying, If thou save not thy life to night, to morrow thou shalt be slain.

So Michal let David down through a window: and he went, and fled, and escaped.

And Michal took an image, and laid it in the bed, and put a pillow of goats' hair for his bolster, and covered it with a cloth. . . .

And Saul said unto Michal, Why hast thou deceived me so, and sent away mine enemy, that he is escaped? And Michal answered Saul, He said unto me, Let me go; why should I kill thee?

So David fled, and escaped, and came to Samuel to Ramah, and told him all that Saul had done to him.

1 Samuel 19:11–13, 17–18

Michal was the youngest daughter of King Saul. Her older sister, Merab, had been promised to David, but Saul—ever fearful of David—changed his mind and married Merab to someone else. However, Michal had fallen in love with David, and as Josephus tells us, "her affection so prevailed over her, that it could not be concealed."[1] David, who had become famous for his victory of Goliath, was about as big a celebrity as you could get in ancient Israel. It is easy to imagine Michal, most likely a young teenage girl, fawning in adoration over David.

When Saul heard that Michal was in love with David, it pleased him because he saw it as an opportunity to get rid of David. Saul told David that he desired to have him as a son-in-law but because he was a poor and had no money to offer for the daughter of a king, he would accept a bride-price of "an hundred foreskins of the Philistines" (1 Samuel 18:25). This meant that David would earn his wife by killing a hundred Philistines and cutting off their foreskins (Josephus says it was their heads) to be brought back to Saul. Saul hoped that David would be killed in battle.

Instead of dying, David victoriously brought back two hundred foreskins. Saul was compelled to honor his promise and Michal was married to David. Instead of this marriage warming Saul's attitude toward David, it only increased his fear of him. Not long after the marriage, Saul made a public attempt at David's life, trying to pin him to the wall with his javelin (see 1 Samuel 19:10). David narrowly escaped. That night Saul dispatched messengers to David's house with instructions to watch it and kill him in the morning.

Michal, realizing the danger David was in, told him, "If thou save not thy life to night, to morrow thou shalt be slain" (1 Samuel 19:11). With no thoughts of loyalty to her father, Michal helped David escape through a window and then took "an image" (in Hebrew, a *teraphim*, or household god) and put it on his bed. She covered it with a blanket, hoping to make it look like David was still in bed. Josephus says she used a still pulsing "goat's liver" under the covers so that "David looked like one that was asthmatic."[2] She could have escaped with David, and perhaps her father assumed she would, but by remaining behind she gave David the precious time he needed to get safely away.

When the messengers came to kill David in the morning, Michal bravely put them off by telling them David was sick. It seems silly to think that men, who'd been ordered to kill him, would be put off by the news that he was sick. Michal must have been a convincing woman! When the messengers reported back to Saul, he ordered them to bring David, bed and all, back to him so that *he* could kill him. When they went back, they discovered Michal's deception and took her to Saul instead. Saul asked Michal, "Why hast thou deceived me so, and sent away mine enemy, that he is escaped?" (1 Samuel 19:17). Michal lied and told her father that David had threatened to kill her if she didn't help him. Josephus records that she told Saul, "I do not suppose that thou wast so zealous to kill thy enemy, as thou wast that I should be saved."[3] Way to use a little guilt!

After this event, Michal didn't see David again for many years. He was now an enemy to her father and lived as an outlaw with his followers in the desert. We can only imagine how her heart must have broken at the loss of her husband, a man whom she had loved so completely. At first she may have hoped that he would come back for her (it seems surprising that he didn't), but as time went by, her hope must have faded. Eventually, Saul, perhaps using David's abandonment of Michal as justification, married Michal to another man, Phalti, the son of Laish (see 1 Samuel 25:44).

Michal's marriage to Phalti seems to have been a happy one. Perhaps she got over her infatuation with David and found joy in her new life. David was a fugitive for fourteen years, during which time we have no record that he ever saw Michal. It must have been a shock for her when David, finally crowned king, asked her brothers to return her to him. It was part of David's condition to ending the conflict with Saul's family and to unify Judah and Israel. Ish-bosheth, Michal's brother, agreed to this and took her from her husband and sent her to Jerusalem to again be David's wife.

In a very touching detail, we learn that her husband "went with her along weeping behind her" (2 Samuel 3:16) until he was forced to leave her. The account doesn't tell us how Michal felt about being forcibly taken from her husband and home. She may have been angry and hurt at having to leave her husband, who obviously cared for her. Or perhaps she still harbored affection for David and was excited to return to him. Maybe her feelings were somewhere in between. It would have been an emotionally complicated situation.

We also might wonder why David, who had many other wives by this point, wanted Michal back. Was it just a power trip? Did he just want her back because she had once "belonged" to him? Did he think that having her again, the daughter of Saul, would strengthen his claim to the throne? Maybe. Or perhaps David wished to honor Michal. She was still his first wife, a position that would grant her high status in the kingdom and within David's household. When Michal returned to David, she would become the queen of all of Judah and Israel. It is possible that David's motivation was to restore Michal to her rightful place as queen and as ruler of her people.

In the next story about Michal, we get the feeling she was not very happy in her new home. David, who had been trying unsuccessfully to move the ark of the covenant back to Jerusalem from where it had been stored during Saul's reign, finally managed to do it the right way. He organized the Levites into their priesthood roles, which had long been neglected, and arranged for them to carry the ark into Jerusalem the way it had been carried anciently. David and all the house of Israel took the ark into Jerusalem with great fanfare and music. David, clothed simply in a linen ephod, "danced before the Lord with all his might" (2 Samuel 6:14). An ephod was a priestly garment, a "shoulder cape" or "mantel" worn over one shoulder and tied around the waist with a belt. The Levites wore it while they served in the tabernacle.

Michal watched from a palace window as David marched into Jerusalem with the ark of the covenant and 30,000 men. When she saw David "leaping and dancing before the Lord," clothed, it appears *only* in a linen ephod, she "despised him in her heart" (2 Samuel 6:16). Josephus's account is much less hostile, saying that when Michal saw David joining in the music and playing on his harp she "laughed at him."[4] Whatever emotion she was feeling; it is clear it was not admiration or love for David. She seemed to view him with a haughty pride, making fun of his enthusiasm for God.

When David returned to the palace, after having made a burnt offering to God and feasting with the people of the city, he was met with Michal's disapproval. She reproached him for his behavior in the street, sarcastically saying, "How glorious was the king of Israel to day, who uncovered himself to day in the eyes of the handmaids of his servants, as one of the vain fellows shamelessly uncovereth himself!" (2 Samuel 6:20). She felt that David, in his unbridled worship for God, had behaved in a way unbecoming of a king. She accused him of acting vain—or common—like an ordinary peasant or slave instead of like a king.

David, who had been born a poor shepherd himself, related to the "common" or "vulgar" people that Michal seemed to view distastefully. Again, Josephus's account is much gentler, explaining that before Michal reproached David for his behavior she "wished him all other happiness: and entreated that whatsoever he should further desire, to the utmost possibility, might be given him by God, and that he might be favorable to him."[5]

Michal was also upset by what David had worn, "uncovering" himself before the common women of his kingdom. The word *uncovered* used by Michal can mean "to be naked" in the literal sense and could just refer to the fact that he may have been scantily clad. Yet it is also the word used to described Noah when his son's "uncovered" his nakedness, or when the God "uncovered" himself to Jacob in Beth-el (see Genesis 35:7). It is possible that Michal was upset by the way in which David had approached priestly or sacred things, making them accessible and open to not just a privileged few but to all of Israel.

David's response to Michal was strong but unsympathetic. He reminded her that God had chosen him to rule over Israel. "Therefore," David said, "will I play before the Lord. And I will yet be more vile [common] than thus, and will be base in mine own sight" (2 Samuel 6:21–22). He told Michal that these common people she held in low esteem, these maidservants, would honor him for how he had behaved. Josephus states that David replied he would "do what was acceptable to God . . . that he would play frequently and dance, without regard to what the handmaidens and herself thought of it."[6]

There was a disconnect between how David and Michal viewed life and religion. Michal was a princess, while David was a poor shepherd who had been raised up by God to be a king. Michal seemed to be of an elitist mindset, while David related to the common people. There must also have been years of hurt, abandonment, anger, and frustration between them. These issues did not necessarily need to divide them, except that it seems that they were unable to reconcile them. However, we cannot blame Michal completely. David was as much at fault for not taking her concerns seriously, acknowledging his mistakes, or being willing to work it out.

After this conversation, the next line in Michal's story is, "Therefore Michal the daughter of Saul had no child unto the day of her death" (2 Samuel 6:23). The "therefore" suggests that was a result of this animosity between Michal and David that she never bore a child. Perhaps this means that, though Michal would have remained in the palace, she lived apart from David and never again shared his bed. That was about as close to divorce as Israelite kings got.

Michal's story certainly lacks a "happily ever after," which is what makes her story so relatable. When we are young, all of us hope for the fairytale ending. But let's be honest; it doesn't always work out. The people we love deceive us, take advantage of us, and abandon us. Peace and contentment are taken away at a moment's notice. Ideals are shattered, dreams irretrievably lost. We get hurt, confused, and angry. People change, not always for the better. These are all things I think Michal would have understood.

Throughout her story, we see Michal change from an idealistic, passionate, and loving young woman to a proud, angry, and bitter older woman. She may have begun her life full of hope and dreams, but she seems to have let her trials turn her whole life "barren." While others danced, she watched. While others sang, she remained quiet. While others feasted, she sat alone. While others worshiped, she despised. While others rejoiced, she criticized. Perhaps the lesson to be learned from Michal is to not let life's disappointments and tragedies make us bitter, to not let our heartache turn to anger, our insecurity to pride, and our love to hate.

How do we do that? How do we face injustice, pain, and disappointment without losing our youthful hope, passion, and optimism? It is possible when we focus on Jesus Christ and remember that He already drank the "bitter cup" (3 Nephi 11:11) for each of us. I once had a Relief Society lesson that explained this well. The teacher brought in a cup of lemon juice, a pitcher of water, and a cup of sugar. She explained that going through life without relying on the Atonement of Jesus Christ is like drinking the lemon juice plain, in all its bitterness. On the other hand, adding sugar and water to the mix is like adding the Atonement to our lives. It doesn't take the bitterness away, but Christ's grace and mercy sweeten it and give us a hope.

• Did Michal Have Children? •

Even though 2 Samuel 6:23 states that Michal had no children, in 2 Samuel 21:8 we read about the "five sons of Michal, the daughter of Saul, whom she brought up for Adriel the son of Barzillai the Meholathite." One explanation for this incongruity is that the biblical author made a mistake and recorded Michal's name instead of Merab's, Michal's sister who was married to Adriel the Meholathie. It is also possible that the biblical author put the wrong husband's name in, when it should have been Michal's husband Phalti, the son of Laish. Josephus tells us in his history that when Michal lived with Phalti she had born him five children.[7]

Another possibility is that the biblical author made no mistake and that when Merab died Michal took custody of her nephews and raised them. The only problem with this scenario is that the Hebrew word translated as "brought up" means "to give birth to," though it can also refer to a woman who assists in a birth as a midwife. Regardless of her relationship to them, these children were yet another source of tragedy in Michal's life because during a conflict with the Gibeonites, all five of them were hanged (see 2 Samuel 21: 8–11).

We don't know if Michal had children or not, though I think the Hebrew text gives us clues that she probably did. If that is true, then there are no—absolutely none—"barren" women in the scriptures who do not eventually give birth. All of them—Sarah, Rebekah, Rachel, the mother of Samson, the Shunamite woman, Hannah, Elisabeth, and Michal—all eventually bear children of their own.

Abigail

And when Abigail saw David, she hasted, and lighted off the ass, and fell before David on her face, and bowed herself to the ground,

And fell at his feet, and said, Upon me, my lord, upon me let this iniquity be.

1 Samuel 25:23–24

Abigail is introduced to us as "a woman of good understanding, and of a beautiful countenance" (1 Samuel 25:3). Like many of the beautiful woman of the Bible, Abigail's wisdom and beauty was the result of a Christlike soul. Yet this was not because her life was easy. Abigail was married to a man named Nabal. In Hebrew, the name *Nabal* literally means "insensitive," "vulgar," or "rude," which is exactly how he is described in the biblical account: "churlish and evil in his doings" (1 Samuel 25:3).[1] As the wife of Nabal, Abigail's life was hard, which makes what she did for her husband even more incredible.

Abigail lived when King Saul was spending much of his time pursing his nemesis, David. Though pursued by Saul, David repeatedly showed mercy to him. Perhaps the most famous of these stories was when David, finding Saul asleep in a cave, refused to kill him. Instead David cut off a piece of Saul's skirt and then waking him, declared that he would spare Saul's life and that "I have not sinned against thee; yet thou huntest my soul to take it. The Lord judge between me and thee" (1 Samuel 24:11–12). Saul, realizing how close he had come to death, repented and told David, "Thou art more righteous than I: for thou hast rewarded me good, whereas I have rewarded thee evil" (1 Samuel 24:17). After parting peacefully, David and his men returned to the wilderness of Paran.

At this point, David had a group of four hundred men in his care, and they were in desperate need of provisions. When David heard that Nabal was shearing his sheep, he sent ten men up to request a portion of Nabal's harvest. In the past, David and his men had protected Nabal's shepherds while they were watching their sheep. David had every right to expect that Nabal would generously repay such a service. Yet when Nabal heard the request, he denied any obligation and insulted David by characterizing him as a common thief.

When David heard this insult, he was irate and began to march with his men toward Carmel with the intent to kill "any that pisseth against the wall" (1 Samuel 25:22), a crude way of saying that he intended to seek revenge. David's decision was a little rash because it was a long journey from Paran, where David and his men were, to Carmel, where Nabal lived. It is surprising the foolish things anger can motivate you to do.

One of Nabal's servants who had heard what was said to David's men perceived that they were in trouble. The servant went to Abigail and explained how good David's men had been to them while they were the fields, how they had been "a wall unto us both by night and day, all the while we were with them keeping the sheep" (1 Samuel 25:16). He told Abigail he feared that "evil is determined against our master" but that he could not speak to him because he was "such a son of Belial" and would not listen (1 Samuel 25:17).

Abigail wasted no time in quickly preparing for David and his men a peace offering of "two hundred loaves, and two bottles of wine, and five sheep ready dressed, and five measures of parched corn, and an hundred clusters of raisins, and two hundred cakes of figs" (1 Samuel 25:18). Remember, she didn't have a Costco to run to and pick up enough food for four hundred famished men. Preparing this gift would have required days of work. Seeing that her husband was unaware of these preparations shows she apparently had great freedom and power over the domestic tasks within her household.

Then, like Jacob meeting Esau, Abigail sent her servants with the food to meet David and his men while she rode behind. Perhaps she hoped that seeing the gift would calm David down enough that he would listen to what she had to say. It seems to have worked because she and David met in a valley where "David and his men came down against her" (1 Samuel 25:20). David was a dangerous and feared man in his time. I doubt many men would have had the courage to ride out and meet David and his four hundred men as they "came down against" them. Yet Abigail "met them" (verse 20) with impressive audacity.

When Abigail saw David, she got off her donkey and bowed at his feet. The first thing she told David was that she would take responsibility for the mistake, and told him, "Upon me let this iniquity be" (1 Samuel 25:24). Even though she was a wealthy lady, she called herself his handmaiden and begged him to listen to her. This display of great humility must have disarmed David more than anything else.

I took a mediation course in college, and one of the first things I was taught was the power of using "I statements" when you are working through an argument or a problem. There is nothing that puts people on the defensive more than saying things like, "*you* did this" or "*you* made me feel this." On the other hand, when someone takes responsibility for part of the disagreement and uses phrases such as "*I* feel like this" or "*I* recognize this," it breaks down walls and opens hearts. Abigail seems to have understood this because throughout her conversation with David she uses "I statements" liberally and avoided placing blame. She was a master peacemaker!

Once she had David's attention, she told him to not give much credence to Nabal because he was just like his name suggested—insensitive and churlish. She implored David to not shed blood and gave him a blessing promising him that if he would be merciful to Nabal, even though he had been wronged, the Lord would deal mercifully with him. She promised David, "The Lord will certainly make my lord a sure house; because my lord fighteth the battles of the Lord, and evil hath not been found in thee all thy days" (1 Samuel 25:28).

She reminded David that he had just spared the life of Saul, a man who had done him much more harm but now was now ready to kill a whole household simply because his pride had been offended. She reminded him that God was preparing him to be a king and that if he did this wicked deed he might have reason to regret it later because he had "shed blood causeless" (verse 31). She admonished him to leave the matter in God's hands.

No one knew better than Abigail that Nabal deserved to be punished. He was a mean man who had acted cruelly and dishonestly.

By all accounts, David was perfectly justified in seeking revenge. The most powerful part of Abigail's story is that despite her own mistreatment by Nabal, she was willing to take his sin as her own. When she approached David she didn't ask him to forgive Nabal; she asked him to forgive *her*. By doing this Abigail became a Christlike figure, offering to David the type of mercy and forgiveness that Christ offers each of us. Author James L. Ferrell wrote:

> Abigail's message was that forgiveness was for the one who was forgiving, not the one who was being forgiven. David needed to forgive so that, in the words of Abigail, he would continue to be found without evil, so that the Lord could make him a sure house. David might have felt justified in withholding his forgiveness from Nabal, however sinful such withholding may have been, but from Abigail? No, her offering on behalf of another obliterated every justification David might otherwise have had. She freed him from the blind comfort of his grudges. Through this merciful act, she created for David the most forgiveness-friendly environment that could possibly be created. David was never more able to do what he needed most to do—forgive, or more precisely, repent of his failing to forgive—than when the request for forgiveness was made by one who had atoned in full for the sin David was raging against.

> The Lord, by taking the sins of our Nabals upon his head, extends us the same mercy. "Upon me let this iniquity be," he pleads. "Let me deal with it if there is any dealing to be done. But you, my dear son or dear daughter, let it go. Let me take it, as I already have done. Forgive."[2]

It is easy when we are mistreated to respond like David did, buckling on our armor and strapping our sword to our side. We jump into the situation with hot heads, justifying our actions by the intensity of our feelings. We deal out justice, forgetting that our version of justice is most often cruelty. Think how it would be if each of us were a little bit more like Abigail—free with our mercy and our forgiveness—and a little less like David—revengeful and proud. We need to learn to trust that the Lord can, and will, deal justly and mercifully. If we don't trust the Lord, then like David we face great danger. Again, I think James Ferrell explained this well:

> Abigail invites us to look at the atonement from a different angle—not the perspective of how Christ has atoned for our *own* sins, but rather from the perspective of how Christ has atoned for the sins of *others* against us. Part of that atonement, Abigail suggests, is the idea that the Lord offers to those who have been harmed or potentially harmed by the sins of others the help and substance they need to be made whole. Those deprived of love can receive *his* love. The companionless can find a companion in *him*. Those with a cross to bear can find another who carries and makes it light. With their burdens lifted in this way, the sinned-against are saved from the provocation to sin and are therefore redeemed from their *own* sins.[3]

Abigail's words to David were powerful because she was not merely giving good advice, but she was speaking from experience. If she had been a vindictive woman, she might have seen David's impending attack as her husband's comeuppance. Maybe she would have even welcomed David's actions, feeling that it was her husband's long-deserved punishment. Instead, Abigail sought to protect her husband's life, standing between him and impending disaster, by taking full responsibility for his mistakes. She was living what she was trying to teach David—that only safe path when one has been hurt is to forgive and trust that the Lord will make it okay.

As may be expected, Abigail's words had a profound effect upon David. Instead of being angry, he became teachable and humble. He told her, "Blessed be the Lord God of Israel, which sent thee this day to meet me: And blessed be thy advice, and blessed be thou, which hast kept me this day from coming to shed blood, and from avenging myself with mine own hand" (1 Samuel 25:32–33). Once David's anger was diffused, he saw things clearly. He told Abigail that if it had not been for her, he and his men would have killed everyone in Nabal's house, including her.

David then accepted the food that Abigail took him and told her, "Go up in peace to thine house; see, I have hearkened to thy voice, and have accepted thy person" (1 Samuel 25:35). The use of the word *hearken* is reminiscent of Adam's language when he "hearkened" to Eve's counsel in the Garden of Eden. *Hearken* is a powerful word when used between men and women because it denotes cooperation and implies understanding and respect. When we hearken to someone, we acknowledge that their counsel comes from God. Like Adam, David was submissive to Abigail and respected her counsel.

After David's departure, Abigail returned to her home to find Nabal having a feast and very drunk. She decided not to tell him what had happened that night but waited till he was sobered up the next morning. When she told him of their narrow escape, Nabal's "heart died within him, and he became as a stone" (1 Samuel 25:37). Ten days later he was dead. When David heard of Nabal's death, he expressed gratitude. He now realized that what Abigail had told him was true; that if he put his grievances in the Lord's hands, justice would be done. David said, "The Lord hath returned the wickedness of Nabal upon his own head" (1 Samuel 25:39).

David then "sent and communed" (1 Samuel 25:39) with Abigail, which seems to indicate that he was in correspondence with her. She must have impressed him greatly because he eventually sent messengers to her asking if she would be his wife. She responded with great humility, bowing herself down to the earth, and again calling herself David's "handmaid" (verse 41). Her next words give us great insight into the depth of this great woman's heart. She stated that she would be "a servant to wash the feet of the servants of my lord" (verse 41).

Here was a woman, with servants of her own, offering to wash the feet of David's servants. Either she was totally head over heels crazy for David (he *was* rumored to be very handsome), simply elated at being freed from Nabal's house, or understood completely what Christ would later tell His disciples: "He that is greatest among you shall be your servant" (Matthew 23:11). Abigail's previous behavior indicates that the latter is probably true. In many ways, Abigail was a "type" or "shadow" of Jesus Christ. In fact, I think you'd be hard pressed to find a more Christlike person than Abigail anywhere in the Old Testament.

After their marriage, Abigail's life with David was anything but calm and must have required every inch of her courage and fortitude. She became his third wife (see David's Family Tree on page 282) and lived with him while he was an outlaw in the desert. She was kidnapped and rescued (see page 185) and went with David up to Hebron when he was anointed and crowned King of Judah (see 2 Samuel 2). She bore David his second son whose name was Daniel but whose name is also given as Chileab.[4] Unlike many of David's other sons, who wreaked havoc in his kingdom, we never hear anything about Abigail's son. Perhaps this means he died young or that, like his mother, he was not a fighter but a peacemaker. As we all know, peacemakers rarely make it into the history books.

Abigail models for us a Christlike approach to conflict and teaches us how to create peace, not only between opposing parties, but also within our own hearts. Too often we find ourselves being like David, armed to the teeth with anger and determined to mete out justice. Yet anger has a way of blinding us to our own faults and leads us to become the greater sinner. How much better if we, like Abigail, take the harder road—the road of humility and forgiveness. If we choose love—especially when it is the much harder choice—Christ promises us peace. Abigail's message is Christ's message, "Peace I leave with you, my peace I give unto you: not as the world giveth, give I unto you. Let not your heart be troubled, neither let it be afraid" (John 14:27).

Ahinoam of Jezreel

Ahinoam married David about the same time that Abigail did. She was David's second wife and the mother of his first son, Amnon, who was killed by his half-brother Absalom, for raping his sister Tamar (see page 197). Some scholars speculate that she may be the same woman as Saul's wife, whose name was also Ahinoam, but we have no way of verifying that.[5] We don't know much about Ahinoam except for one action-packed adventure that she and Abigail had in 1 Samuel 30.

While David and his men were encamped with the Philistine army (see 1 Samuel 29), the Amalekites attacked and burned the Judean city of Ziklag, where the families of David and his men were living. The Amalekites took all the women and children captive, including Abigail and Ahinoam. When David and his men returned, they were devastated by the loss and were so upset that they wanted to stone David. David turned to the Lord to know what to do, and God told him to pursue their families. Despite already being tired, and having a three-day-old trail to follow, David and six hundred of his men immediately set out to pursue the Amalekites. They ran so hard that two hundred of the men were unable to continue and were left behind to watch over the equipment that was slowing them down. Amazingly, David and his men caught up to the Amalekites. They were able to recover everyone and everything that had been stolen.

Jesus Christ is called by many names, but in those times when peaceful lives were ransacked, burned to the ground, and people were carried away into new and scary territory, he was the Deliverer. Like David's miraculous deliverance of Ahinoam and Abigail from captivity, Christ knows just where to find us and how to set us free.

Three Daughters of Heman

All these were the sons of Heman the king's seer in the words of God, to lift up the horn. And God gave to Heman fourteen sons and three daughters.

All these were under the hands of their father for song in the house of the Lord, with cymbals, psalteries, and harps, for the service of the house of God, according to the king's order to Asaph, Jeduthun, and Heman.

1 Chronicles 25:5–6

Did you know there was ancient equivalent to the Mormon Tabernacle Choir? While it probably did not sound similar to our modern-day choir, ancient Israel had its own group of "singing women" and "singing men" who were set apart for the express purpose of worshiping God through song and music.[1] These musicians were professional performers who were often in the employ of the prophet, or the king, and were central to religious worship, just like sacred music is to us today.

Under the reign of King David, who was himself a talented musician, music became an even more important part of Israelite worship. In an attempt to restore the pattern of worship established by Moses, David ordained certain families of Levites to oversee and perform the "service of song in the house of the Lord" (1 Chronicles 6:31). Among these Levites was a man named Heman, a singer, who along with his fourteen sons and three daughters served the Lord through music.

Heman was the grandson of the prophet Samuel. While he did not inherit the role of prophet, he had the gift of prophecy and was renowned for his wisdom. 1 Kings 4:31, which extols the wisdom of Solomon, says that Solomon was "wiser than all men" followed by a list of men famous for their wisdom, among whom is Heman. He was also appointed by David to be the lead musician among the Levites and he was considered "the king's seer in the words of God, to lift up the horn" (1 Chronicles 25:5). When David moved the ark of the covenant out of storage (where it had been for the previous twenty years), it was Heman's responsibility to minster "before the dwelling place of the tabernacle of the congregation with singing, until Solomon had built the house of the Lord in Jerusalem"

(1 Chronicles 6:32).[2] Heman is also thought to be the author of Psalm 88.

Heman's three daughters' lives must have been filled with music. 1 Chronicles 25:6 seems to suggest that these women, along with their brothers, were taught to play musical instruments and then used their skills to play music in the tabernacle. The text, after previously mentioning Heman's fourteen sons and three daughters, states, "All these were under the hand of their father for song in the house of the Lord, with cymbals, psalteries, and harps, for the service of the house of God" (1 Chronicles 25:6). We know that other women may have been formally involved in sacred worship in the tabernacle (see Wise-Hearted Women on page 122), and music seems to be another way in which woman participated in religious practices.

We don't often think of the temple as being a musical place. Instead, it often seems the prevalent sound is silence. If you pay attention, you will notice that music is still an integral part of our temple worship. My mother-in-law told me that one of her favorite times to go to the temple is during the session reserved for Tongan patrons. She loves it because before the session, instead of sitting silently in the chapel like patrons usually do, the Tongan patrons sing together. In beautiful strong voices, they sing hymns, which fills the chapel with the sounds of worship. I have never had that experience, but I have often thought of Heman's daughters and the other "singing women" of the Bible when I have sat quietly in the chapel listening to the organ being played, often by a woman.

1 Chronicles 25:7 also explains that Heman's children were "instructed in the songs of the Lord," indicating that there were special musical numbers in the tabernacle. It is also very clear that the Levites were to use only certain musical instruments, such as the cymbals, psaltery, and harp.[3] It is likely that Heman's daughters would have played all three of these instruments.

Just like today, mastering an instrument took time, practice, and skill. I imagine that music—listening, writing, practicing, performing—was a big part of these women's lives. 1 Chronicles 9:33 tells us that music was taken so seriously that some of the Levite musicians lived in the tabernacle and temple complex because "they were employed in that work day and night." The Levites were unique, because unlike the other tribes who had been given a specific portion of land as an inheritance, they were landless and were supported by what we today would call tithing. This means that one of God's greatest gifts to the Levites was time—time to serve in the tabernacle, time to study, time to write, and time to compose and practice music. Much of the art, literature, and music we have from the Israelites come from the Levites because out of all the tribes, they had time.

2 Chronicles 29 tells us that the Levites sang and played their sacred music while the burnt offering—which was offered every morning and night as a sign of Israel's relationship with God—was burning on the altar and didn't cease their music until the entire offering was consumed. This sacrifice, with its smoke and music ascending to heaven, was in essence a prayer, offered morning and evening. Heman's three daughters and the other religious "singing women" in the Bible remind us what Doctrine and Covenants 25:12 says, that the "song of the righteous is a prayer" unto God. Our worship, no matter how devoted, is never complete without music.

• The Book of Psalms •

The book of Psalms is the ancient hymn book. Most Jews would have been familiar with these songs and their content, even if they could not read themselves. In fact, Jesus quoted from the book of Psalms more than he did any other book of scripture. These sacred songs were an important part of religious life. It is likely that ancient women such as the daughters of Heman sang these songs.

I have to admit that until recently, the book of Psalms was my least favorite book in the Old Testament. That changed when I started treating the psalms like songs and not just ancient poetry. I am not very musical, so I found musicians on YouTube who had already put them to music and listened while I followed along in my scriptures. It was amazing how much more sense they made. It was the difference between picking up our modern-day hymnbook and reading it cover to cover, or singing those same songs out loud. There was a big difference! I'd encourage you, if you haven't already, to revisit the book of Psalms but from a musical standpoint. Don't worry; no one knows the tunes or musical system the psalms follow, so you can't mess them up.

Bathsheba

Then king David answered and said, Call me Bath-sheba. And she came into the king's presence, and stood before the king.

And the king sware, and said, As the Lord liveth, that hath redeemed my soul out of all distress,

Even as I sware unto thee by the Lord God of Israel, saying, Assuredly Solomon thy son shall reign after me, and he shall sit upon my throne in my stead; even so will I certainly do this day.

Then Bath-sheba bowed with her face to the earth, and did reverence to the king, and said, Let my lord king David live for ever.

1 Kings 1:28–31

When I asked a friend about what lesson could be learned from Bathsheba, she said, "Don't bathe on the roof." I smiled at her answer because I think that is usually our first thought about Bathsheba. However, I hope that as you learn more about her story, you will see her in a new light and discover that there is much more to her than just a story about adultery and murder. She arose from a difficult situation to become one of Israel's most important queens, and Solomon's kingdom owed much of its prosperity to her wisdom and righteousness.

Bathsheba's story began when David, who chose to stay behind in Jerusalem while his army was away fighting, was walking on the roof of his palace and saw her bathing. Josephus specifies that she was "washing in her own house"[1] when David saw her and not shamelessly bathing out in the open where anyone could see her. The Hebrew word used for "bathe" is used most often to refer to the washing of the hands, feet, and ritual ceremonial washing. 2 Samuel 11:4 also tells us that when David slept with Bathsheba she had recently been "purified from her uncleanness," meaning she had undergone the ceremonial bath required after menstruation. Bathsheba had not been doing anything wrong or provocative. On the contrary, David had been peeping in windows where he should not have.

David, who up till now had been a pillar of righteousness, gave into his temptation rather than fighting against it. He "sent messengers" to Bathsheba's house and "took her" (2 Samuel 11:4). Author Edith Deen wrote, "According to the laws, Bath-sheba could not have resisted had she desired, for a woman in these ancient times was completely subject to a king's will. If he desired her, he could have

her. Consequently her part in the story is neither praiseworthy or blameworthy. Even Sarah, some centuries before, because of her beauty had been taken into the harems of two kings, Abimelech and Pharaoh."[2]

After David lay with Bathsheba (which appears to have happened only once), Bathsheba became pregnant and sent a message to let David know. We don't know what her intent was, but we can assume she felt some measure of desperation. Her being with child, while her husband was away at war, was clear proof that she had been unchaste. If David didn't step in and claim the child as his, she could expect to receive the traditional punishment for adultery—stoning. Through the gratification of his lust, David had put her in a very difficult situation. She was looking to him to somehow make it right.

David's first attempt to correct the situation was to send for Uriah and ask him to report on how the war effort was going. David's hope was that Uriah would take the opportunity to go home and sleep with his wife, thus giving Bathsheba a legitimate explanation for her pregnancy. Uriah, however, was too honorable a solider to leave his men and remained with them in the palace. Next David tried getting Uriah drunk, but again he refused to go home. Finally, feeling angry, David sent a message to his general, Joab, to put Uriah on the front lines of the battle, in a place he was sure to get killed. Joab complied and during the next battle Uriah was killed.[3]

We don't know if Bathsheba knew about any of this, but my suspicion is that she did not. When she learned of her husband's death, she mourned greatly. Josephus tells us she mourned "for many days" until "the tears which she shed for Uriah were dried up."[4] We might suspect that her grief, over everything that had happened to her, was deep. After her mourning period, David "sent and fetched her to his house, and she became his wife" (2 Samuel 11:27). What else could Bathsheba have done? Her husband had been murdered, and she was pregnant with the child of the king. She didn't seem to have much of a choice in the matter.

The scriptures make it clear that it was David that God was displeased with (see 2 Samuel 11:27) and that the blamed rested on David's shoulders. When Nathan, the prophet, learned what David had done, he gave David a parable likening Bathsheba to a "ewe lamb" who had been devoured by a greedy rich man (see 2 Samuel 12). Bathsheba was the innocent one, the lamb, who had been so poorly used.

I think this is important to remember, especially with what happens next., Soon after marrying David, Bathsheba gave birth to his child—a son—who became very sick. Nathan told David when he confronted him about his sin that there would be consequences for what he had done; that "the sword shall never depart from thine house" (2 Samuel 12:10) and that the child who would be born to him would "surely die" (2 Samuel 12:14). David, realizing that if this child died it would be a consequence of his sin, fasted and "lay . . . upon the earth" (verse 16) for seven days. At the end of seven days, the baby died, and David, accepting that there was nothing he could do, washed himself and ate, saying, "Can I bring him back again? I shall go to him, but he shall not return to me" (verse 23)

The book of Psalms is full of David's thoughts and feelings toward God. As we read them, we get a glimpse into his heart and see him suffer and repent for what he had done. Even though in the Doctrine and Covenants we hear God tell Joseph Smith that David, because of his murder of Uriah, "hath fallen from his exaltation" (D&C 132:39), I don't think that means that David did not repent, nor that he could not have been forgiven for what he had done.[5] On the contrary, I think we see a repentant David who, while suffering the consequences of his sin, tried for the rest of his life to undo what he had done.

However, as with most sin, David's mistake did not just impact him. Bathsheba not only lost her child, but she also suffered in the upheaval and violence that soon came to David's house as—the prophet had promised—a result of his sin. What do we do when, like Bathsheba, the result of someone else's sin hurts us and leaves our life in turmoil? Elder James E. Faust, a former Apostle, answered this question:

> The Atonement not only benefits the sinner but also benefits those sinned against—that is, the victims. By forgiving "those who trespass against us" (JST, Matt. 6:13) the Atonement brings a measure of peace and comfort to those who have been innocently victimized by the sins of others. . . .

A sister who had been through a painful divorce wrote of her experience in drawing from the Atonement. She said: "Our divorce . . . did not release me from the obligation to forgive. I truly wanted to do it, but it was as if I had been commanded to do something of which I was simply incapable." Her bishop gave her some sound advice: "Keep a place in your heart for forgiveness, and when it comes, welcome it in." Many months passed as this struggle to forgive continued. She recalled: "During those long, prayerful moments . . . I tapped into a life-giving source of comfort from my loving Heavenly Father. I sense that he was not standing by glaring at me for not having accomplished forgiveness yet; rather he was sorrowing with me as I wept. . . .

"In the final analysis, what happened in my heart is for me an amazing and miraculous evidence of the Atonement of Christ. I had always viewed the Atonement as a means of making repentance work for the sinner. I had not realized that it also makes it possible for the one sinned against to receive into his or her heart the sweet peace of forgiving."[6]

I wonder if Bathsheba's experience was something similar to this woman's story. It would be easy for us to see how after everything that had happened Bathsheba would have never wanted to see David again. He had sexually coerced her, murdered her husband, and was—it appeared—the cause of their child's death. For the rest of her life she would suffer along with David as his life and kingdom were rocked by violence and war, originating from his children. I could easily see her becoming angry, bitter, and vindictive toward David. Yet instead we read that "David comforted Bathsheba his wife" (2 Samuel 12:24) and that she bore him four other sons—Shimea, Shobab, Nathan, and Solomon. Despite all odds, it seems that Bathsheba and David made their marriage work. This could only have happened if David had sincerely repented and if Bathsheba had sincerely forgiven.

Bathsheba's story is even more remarkable because of who she became after her trials. We see her rise in the scriptural account as a true leader and a woman sought after for her wisdom. When David's health began to fail, his son Adonijah maneuvered for the throne. Nathan saw what Adonijah was doing and realized that he, and the priests of the tabernacle, would be excluded from Adonijah's future government. All the work that David had done to prepare for the building of the temple and the restoration of God's covenant would be lost. Nathan, knowing that David was unaware of what was happening, approached Bathsheba with the problem. He told her to urge David to crown Solomon (whom he had already promised would be his heir) as soon as possible.

In true matriarch fashion, Bathsheba approached her husband and advocated for her son. Backed by the support of the prophet, she took control of the destiny of the Jewish kingdom. She bowed and reminded David of his promise, explaining that if he didn't act soon, she and Solomon would soon be "counted offenders" (1 Kings 1:21) in the government being set up by Adonijah. David saw the wisdom of her counsel and, perhaps seeing a way to repair things, told her that he would honor his promise and make Solomon king, which he did that very day.

Writer Edith Deen wrote, "Only an intelligent, respected woman, in whom the aged king had great confidence, could have won so great a victory. Only a righteous woman, it would seem, could have been sought out by the prophet Nathan. And only a much loved mother could have been so warmly greeted as was Bath-sheba when she went to see her son after he became king. When she came before him, he accorded her the place of honor as queen mother on his right side, a place of power and authority."[7]

With Solomon on the throne, the people of Israel and Judah would prosper righteously (at least for a while), and the wealth and wisdom of their king would become legendary. They would build God's temple and worship God again like the prophets of old. They would build a nation and a religious identity that, though scattered, remains today. Even the temple, though it has been destroyed several times, still stands in the same spot where Solomon first built it. Like the ancient matriarchs before her, Bathsheba played an important role in guiding and directing the future of God's covenant and his people. She set the standard for all the queens who would come after her. Though many of these later queens would abuse their power (see Maachah on page 258), Bathsheba was a righteous monarch and matriarch.

Later in the New Testament, we read that Bathsheba, along with several other unconventional Old Testament women, is listed in Christ's genealogy. Matthew states that it was through her son Solomon that Jesus Christ would be born, while Luke states that Christ's lineage was through Bathsheba's other son, Nathan (see Matthew 1 and Luke 3). Despite her difficult beginning, Bathsheba takes a place beside the other great matriarchs of the Old Testament as a woman of wisdom, foresight, and righteousness.

> *"Keep a place in your heart for forgiveness, and when it comes, welcome it in."*

Mother of King Lemuel

The words of king Lemuel, the prophecy that his mother taught him.

Proverbs 31:1

What advice do you hope that people remember from you after you are gone? Is there some phrase you often say, or words of counsel that you have given that you hope will sink deep into someone's heart? I think that most of us, even if we don't consciously realize it, have an innate desire to give advice. There is something deeply satisfying about sharing things that we have learned with others and seeing our words and ideas improve the world. It isn't surprising, then, that the Bible has a whole section—the book of Proverbs—dedicated to documenting good advice.[1]

Perhaps the most famous chapter from the book of Proverbs is Proverbs 31, which describes a "virtuous woman . . . [whose] price is far above rubies" (verse 10). While we know that King Solomon wrote many of the Proverbs, the first verse of Proverbs 31 states that these were the "words of King Lemuel, the prophecy that his mother taught him" (verse 1). No one is sure who King Lemuel was, and many scholars believe that it may have been a pet name or code name for

Solomon.[2] If this was true, then the mother referred to in Proverbs 31 would be Solomon's mother, Bathsheba, whom we know was an adviser to her son and was well respected by him. Yet there is no substantial evidence to suggest that this is true. The identity of King Lemuel and his mother is largely a mystery.

Even though we don't know who she was, we have her words, in the form of advice given to her son. King Lemuel called these words that his mother taught him a "prophecy." The Hebrew word used here is *massa,* which means "a burden, something to be carried; figuratively, an utterance, especially singing; also an oracle, that to which the soul lifts itself up."[3] Lemuel's word choice suggests that these words from his mother were guiding words, perhaps taught to him in a song, that were designed to direct him through his life. Her words are certainly full of sound advice for any young man, especially one preparing to lead a kingdom.

She began by calling him "the son of my womb" and "the son of my vows" (Proverbs 31:2). The type of vow she was referring to here was not a wedding vow but a sacred promise made to God.[4] A more modern version of the Bible translates this phrase as "Listen, my son, the answer to my prayers!" (New International Version, Proverbs 31:2). We don't know what sort of vow she took or how her prayers were answered in relation to her son, but it is apparent that she had prayed long and hard for—and about—her son. He was precious to her.

She then advised her son, "Give not thy strength unto women, nor thy ways to that which destroyeth kings" (Proverbs 31:3). I don't find it surprising that her first counsel to her son was about girls. Much

may have changed over the centuries, but an important part of a mother's job, then and now, is helping her son make good choices when it comes to women—treating them well, using his sexuality correctly, and finding a good woman to marry.

> *"Give not thy strength unto women, nor thy ways to that which destroyeth kings."*

The remainder of her advice advised him to refrain from strong drink. She told him, "Oh Lemuel, it is not for kings to drink wine; nor for princes strong drink: Lest they drink, and forget the law, and pervert the judgment of any of the afflicted" (Proverbs 31:4–5). I wonder if she was speaking from experience. Perhaps she had seen firsthand what happens to men, even good men, when they indulge in their appetites and lusts. She knew that a king who was only interested in gratifying himself would destroy not simply himself but also his nation. She had high hopes for her son and desired to see him become a righteous king, one who would, as she instructed, "judge righteously and plead the cause of the poor needy" (verse 9).

• The Proverbs 31 Woman •

The second part of Proverbs 31 is the most famous part—the description of the ideal woman. If you are anything like me, reading through the (long) list of this woman's virtues and achievements is more discouraging than uplifting. It seems to be an unobtainable ideal, the woman who never complains, makes her own clothes, wakes up early in the morning, never complains, takes care of the poor, plants a vineyard, never complains, only ever speaks wisdom, and whose children call her blessed.

It is unclear if the description given in Proverbs 31 of this ideal woman is a continuation of the advice given to King Lemuel by his mother or if it is his own words. I think either option could possibly be correct. I can imagine King Lemuel, as he reflected upon the wisdom his mother imparted to him, including a tribute the wise woman who raised him. Perhaps the description given in Proverbs 31 was Lemuel's reflection on his own mother, who had worked hard to live a long and Christlike life. When I read the verse with that perspective, it no longer seems like an overwhelming list of

things to do but rather something to strive toward; an inspiring painting of a righteous woman being rightly honored by her son at the end of her life.

The other option is that Lemuel's mother gave him this description of the ideal woman. If that is the case, then we might view these verses as more of a "wish list" of qualities that he should seek for in a woman to marry. Currently, I am the Young Women president in my ward. Several weeks ago during a lesson about marriage, the teacher had the girls make just such a list, one that included all the qualities that they desired in a future husband. Elder Bednar spoke about making these types of wish lists: "The list is not for evaluating someone else. The list is for you . . . and what . . . you need to become. And so if there are three primary characteristics that [you] hope to find in an eternal companion, then those are the things [you] ought to be working to become."[5]

I think viewing the description of the woman given in Proverbs 31 as this type of list changes how we approach it. Instead of it being a checklist for us to feel guilty or inadequate about, it instead becomes something for us to strive toward; someone to *become*.

Tamar, Daughter of David

And Amnon said unto Tamar, Bring the meat into the chamber, that I may eat of thine hand. And Tamar took the cakes which she had made, and brought them into the chamber to Amnon her brother.

And when she had brought them unto him to eat, he took hold of her, and said unto her, Come lie with me, my sister.

And she answered him, Nay, my brother, do not force me; for no such thing ought to be done in Israel: do not thou this folly. . . .

Howbeit he would not hearken unto her voice: but, being stronger than she, forced her, and lay with her.

2 Samuel 13:10–12, 14

Tamar was the daughter of David and his wife Maachah. Her brother was Absalom, who was renowned for his beauty. In 2 Samuel 14:25 we read that "in all Israel there was none to be so much praised as Absalom for his beauty: from the sole of his foot even to the crown of his head there was no blemish in him." He also appeared to have incredible hair, which was so thick and heavy that when he shaved it he sold it for two hundred shekels. We don't have a description of what Tamar looked like, but if she took after her brother we can imagine she was an incredibly beautiful young woman.

We know nothing about her until 2 Samuel 13:1 when David's oldest son and heir, Amnon, fell in love with her and was tormented with impure thoughts about her. He was so vexed with these feelings and the inability to do anything about them that he lost his desire to eat. His cousin, Jonadab, noticed this change in him and Amnon confided to Jonadab that he was in love with Tamar, his half-sister. Instead of pointing Amnon on a wise course of behavior, Jonadab encouraged Amnon's feelings and crafted a plan that would allow him to be intimate with Tamar. "When thy father cometh to see thee," instructed Jonadab, "say unto him . . . let my sister Tamar come, and give me meat . . . in my sight, that I may . . . eat it at her hand" (2 Samuel 13:5).

Amnon followed Jonadab's plan and "made himself sick" (verse 6). I think it is interesting here that it doesn't say that Amnon feigned sickness but that he *made* himself sick through his feelings for Tamar. Our minds are powerful instruments, and they can shape our future much more than we often realize. Like Amnon, Satan will try to tempt all of us, at some point in our lives, with perverted sexual feelings. When that happens, we might do well to remember Amnon and how he lost everything—his kingdom, his spiritual standing, and eventually his life—because he gave in to Satan's temptation and acted upon his feelings.

Jonadab's plan worked, and just like he had predicted, David came to visit Amnon when he heard he was sick. Amnon asked his father if he would send Tamar to his chambers to make "a couple of cakes" (verse 6) for him. He wanted to be able to watch her make them and then have her feed them to him afterward. It seems that Tamar had a special type of cake, maybe similar to a scone or a donut, that she made in a frying pan, and Amnon told David he wanted it.[1] David,

who was probably happy that his ailing son had an appetite, saw no harm in this and told Tamar to go to Amnon's house and make him some cakes. Tamar went to Amnon's house willingly, not suspecting what Amnon had in mind. He was someone she trusted, and she was being a kind sister.

While Amnon laid in bed, Tamar "took flour, and kneaded it, and made cakes in his sight" (2 Samuel 13:8). After baking the cakes, she put them in front of Amnon, but he refused to eat them. Instead he ordered all his servants to leave and asked Tamar to bring the cakes into his bedroom so that he could eat them from her hand. Desiring to make her ailing brother feel better, Tamar brought her cakes into Amnon's bedroom. When she gave them to him he grabbed her and demanded "come lie with me, my sister" (verse 11).

Tamar, finding herself in such an unexpected and precarious situation, showed a surprising amount of self-composure. She responded to his request with a resounding "no" and then began trying to maneuver herself out of the situation by reasoning with Amnon. She first tried appealing to his sense of morality, telling him, "Do not force me; for no such thing ought to be done in Israel: do thou not his folly" (2 Samuel 13:12). When that approach failed, she appealed to him to think about her. "What about me?" she asked. "Where could I get rid of my disgrace?" (New International Version, 2 Samuel 13:13). Perhaps realizing at this point that Amnon cared little about her, she attempted to get him to think about himself, telling him that if he did this he would be "as one of the fools in Israel" (verse 13). Finally, she begged him to "speak unto the king" because "he will not withhold me from thee" (verse 13). Apparently it was not prohibited for half-siblings to marry, and Tamar felt that David would grant such a marriage. We don't know if this suggestion was something Tamar wanted or if, realizing that she wasn't going to escape from Amnon, saw it as her best chance.

Despite Tamar's brave resistance, Amnon "would not hearken to her voice," and he "being stronger than she, forced her, and lay with her" (2 Samuel 13:14). After the rape, all the love Amnon had felt for her turned to hatred. In fact, "the hatred wherewith he hated her was greater than the love wherewith he had loved her" (verse 15). Again, there is a lesson for us to be learned in Amnon's mistakes. Giving in to Satan's temptations and allowing our bodily desires to rule our spirits leads to unhappiness. We cannot do wicked things and expect to be happy.

Feeling the weight of what he had done, but not being willing to repent of it, Amnon tried to get rid of Tamar, telling her to "Arise, be gone" (verse 15). Yet Tamar refused to leave. She told Amnon that there was "no cause" (verse 16) to send her away. Perhaps she hoped that even though Amnon had been terrible to her, he still might do the honorable thing and marry her.

When it became clear that he would not but was going to throw her out like a piece of garbage, Tamar confronted Amnon and told him, "This evil in sending me away is greater than the other that thou didst unto me" (2 Samuel 13:16). Tamar knew that under the law it was Amnon's responsibility to marry her.[2] Yet just as he did when he raped her, Amnon would not "hearken unto her" (verse 16). Finally, seeing as Tamar would not leave, Amnon had to have his servant physically remove her from his house and ordered that the servant "bolt the door after her" (verse 17).

Instead of keeping what had happened to her quiet, Tamar went public with it. She rent her garment and put ashes on her head, a public display of mourning. She then laid her hand on her head and "went on crying" (verse 19). Her brother Absalom saw her distress and suspected right away what had happened to her. "Hath Amnon thy brother been with thee?" he asked her. When she replied in the affirmative, he told her to "hold now thy peace, my sister: he is thy brother, regard not this thing" (verse 20).

By our modern standards this was a poor way for Absalom to respond to his sister's rape. What could be worse than to tell a woman who had just been raped, "Don't worry about it"? We have to remember that at this time it was customary in rape cases for brothers to avenge their sister by killing the perpetrator (remember Dinah on page 81?). Absalom was telling Tamar that because Amnon was her brother—and the heir to the throne—there was nothing that either one of them could do. To Abslom, "fixing" this problem meant killing the man who had hurt his sister.

It does appear, however, that they told Tamar's father because 2 Samuel 13:21 tells us, "When king David heard of these things, he was very wroth." Despite his anger, David took no action against Amnon, and Tamar "remained desolate in her brother Absalom's house" (verse 20). We don't know why David neglected to tackle this huge problem, but we might suspect that it had something to do with his own previous sexual mistakes. In fact, the prophet Nathan, when rebuking David of his behavior with Bathsheba, prophesied that God would "raise up evil against thee out of thine own house" (2 Samuel 12:11). David had already had one son die because of his mistake, and maybe he felt that what had happened to Tamar was also his fault.

David's inaction in the case of Tamar proved to be an enormous mistake. Sometime later, Absalom (whose hate for Amnon had festered) contrived a scheme in which he had his servants murder Amnon while he was drunk. This murder was not done stealthily, and Absalom had to flee. He sought asylum with the King of Geshur, who was his maternal grandfather (see 2 Samuel 13:24–37). Absalom remained in exile for three years, and when he returned, he usurped his father's throne, created a civil war, and nearly destroyed the kingdom. Absalom's revenge, though perhaps nobly done, did nothing to help Tamar, who all the time remained behind in her brother's house.

It has never been easy—now or in Old Testament times—for women to talk about rape and sexual violence. I worked on a rape crisis response team for several years while I was in college and had multiple opportunities to work with women who had been victims of sexual violence. The women I worked with were those who, after the rape had occurred, sought out medical attention so that they could press charges against their rapist. I was astounded at the bravery of these women. It was not easy for them to tell others what had happened to them, and I often had to reassure them that they were doing the right thing. Sister Cheiko Okazaki, former counselor in the General Relief Society Presidency, shared some powerful thoughts about sexual violence:

> I personally believe that the growing awareness of and resistance to sexual abuse is the fulfillment of the scripture which says, "There is nothing covered that shall not be revealed, neither hid that shall not be known. Therefore, whatsoever ye have spoken [and I would add, have done] in darkness shall be heard in the light, and proclaimed upon the housetops." Each survivor who tells her or his story, each

individual who reports abuse, each police officer who arrests a perpetrator, each judge and jury who enforce the law, and each person who teaches children to protect themselves and to report abuse are part of fulfilling this prediction of Jesus Christ about the last days. This evil must be exposed before it can be repented of, and it must be repented of.[3]

Even today, when we are more open about sexual violence than perhaps at any other time in history, our system still can fail women by refusing to believe them, belittling their concerns, protecting and enabling their abuser, and making them feel shame about their experience. I think Tamar would have understood all of this well. She had been brave by making her rape public, but all the men in her life failed her. One scholar wrote the following about Tamar:

> Tamar is . . . characterized as a strong, generous, sexually moral, and shrewd woman. She is presented as intelligent and possessing considerable rhetorical skills. She is good-looking and an obedient daughter and a devoted sister to full and half brothers alike. But her many virtues do not save her from her fate: to be raped without redress, to remain with her shame without being able to complain . . . and to lose all prospects of marriage and bearing progeny. . . .

> In fact, all the male kin who should support Tamar and look after her well-being (her father, David, and Amnon, Absalom, and Jonadab) betray her in one way or another: David by uncritically ordering Tamar to go to Amnon's chambers and by not translating his anger about the rape into action against Amnon; Amnon by raping, then discarding, her; Absalom by plotting revenge that may seem conventionally acceptable but, ultimately, would benefit his own ambition to the throne without affecting Tamar's desolate state; Jonadab by engineering the encounter. Tamar is *not* protected by her male relatives or other male figures in the story, such as servants. She is a pawn in the

power politics between her brothers and between them and their king-father.[4]

After she went to her brother's house, where she presumably would remain for the rest of her life, we know nothing else about Tamar. Yet we know that just because her story of her rape ends on paper, there was much more healing and struggle that went on in Tamar's heart. Healing from abuse is no easy task; it is a wound that heals slowly and is easily reopened. We don't know how Tamar healed (or didn't heal) from her experience. The only clue that the scriptures give us is that she was "desolate," which in Hebrew means "stunned," "stupefied," "devastated."[5] I feel like that is an accurate description of how the women I know have felt after experiencing sexual violence.

Whether we know it or not, we each have women like Tamar in our lives. We may even be Tamar. Yet I am hopeful for Tamar—hopeful that despite what she experienced that she was able to find healing and to find joy again. I am especially struck with the significance of her wearing a *kĕthoneth* (see sidebar) because it tells us that she had made covenants with God and had faith in His power to heal, forgive, and make things whole. Tamar seems to have possessed all the qualities that we hope our daughters will develop—faith, obedience, kindness, intelligence, courage, an understanding of her own self-worth, and beauty of body and spirit. I feel hopeful for her—and all women like her—that she found healing through God's grace and power.

• *Kĕthoneth* •

In 2 Samuel 13:18, we are told that Tamar, as well as all the king's daughters who were virgins, wore a "garment of diverse colors." The Hebrew word used to describe this garment is *kĕthoneth* and refers to a long, shirt-like under garment. The Hebrew word translated as "diverse" refers to a form of measurement, meaning that the length of the garment extended to the wrists. We might re-interpret the Hebrew phrase "garment of diverse colors" as "a long, shirt-like garment that reached to the wrists." Some scholars also suggest that a *kĕthoneth* was embroidered with special markings.

There are two other references to a *kĕthoneth* in the Bible. The first is the "coat of skins" (Genesis 3:21) God made for Adam and Eve, and the other is the "coat of many colours" worn by Joseph of Egypt (see Genesis 37:3, 23, 31–33). The priests of the tabernacle also wore a *kĕthoneth* as part of their sacred clothing (see Exodus 28:4, 39–40 [it is called a "coat" here]). The garment had deep spiritual symbolism, and the fact that Tamar tore her *kĕthoneth* gives us a sense of her deep grief and perhaps indicates that she had feelings of being dirty or unworthy to wear such a garment after what had happened to her.

The fact though that Tamar was wearing a *kĕthoneth* is significant. The garment indicated that the person had made covenants with God. In the case of Joseph of Egypt, it was a sign that he was the birthright son—the heir of the Abrahamic covenant. Besides Eve, Tamar is the only other woman in the Bible who we know wore a *kĕthoneth*, but from her story, we learn that it was a common practice for women (at least those of nobility) to wear one. Understanding this opens our minds to the degree to which women would have participated in spiritual practices in ancient Israel. It wasn't just the male priests who wore the sacred clothing of the priesthood, but women wore it as well.

Wise Woman of Tekoah

Now Joab the son of Zeruiah perceived that the king's heart was toward Absalom.

And Joab sent to Tekoah, and fetched thence a wise woman, and said unto her, I pray thee, feign thyself to be a mourner, and put on now mourning apparel, and anoint not thyself with oil, but be as a woman that had a long time mourned for the dead:

And come to the king, and speak on this manner unto him. So Joab put the words in her mouth.

2 Samuel 14:1–3

This wise woman's story is told in 2 Samuel 14. David's second son, Absalom, had recently fled after murdering his half-brother Amnon for the rape of his sister Tamar. David loved Absalom immensely, and he "mourned for his son every day" (2 Samuel 13:37). Seeing David's distress, Joab, David's right hand man, devised a plan. Knowing that David was quick to see the injustice in the actions of others, but slow to see those same flaws in himself, Joab asked a "wise woman" from Tekoah to approach David in the guise of someone who had been in mourning for a long time.

When this wise woman approached David, she fell on her face and asked him for help. She told him that she was a widow and that her two sons had "strove together in the field" (2 Samuel 14:6) when the younger son killed the oldest son. Her whole family, she told David, demanded that she deliver her younger son to them so that they could kill him and revenge the death of his brother. She didn't want to do this, she explained, because if her other son was killed it would mean her husband's name would be completely erased and he would be left with no heir.

Seeing her plight, the noble and just part of David stirred. "As the Lord liveth," he promised her, "there shall not one hair of thy son fall to the earth" (2 Samuel 14:11). At this point, the wise woman began to abandon her disguise and called David out, asking him why, if he would have compassion on her son, he could not also have compassion on his own son. She showed her wisdom by reminding David, "For we must needs die, and are as water spilt on the ground, which cannot be gathered up again; neither doth God respect any person: yet doth he devise means, that his banished be not expelled from him" (2 Samuel 14:14). Life was short, and even God, as David knew very well, provided ways for those who had sinned against him to return.

David was moved by her words and perceived that Joab had sent her. She told him that he was correct and that she had been sent by Joab to help David see the folly of his anger. Joab's plan worked, and David told him to bring Absalom home. Although he allowed Absalom to return, David specified that Absalom was not allowed to be in his presence. For two whole years, Absalom dwelt in the palace but "saw not the king's face" (2 Samuel 14:28). Joab, whom Absalom knew might be able to soften his father, would not speak to him. So Absalom sent his servants to burn Joab's field to get his attention. It worked, and Absalom asked Joab to let him speak with his father. "And if there be any iniquity in me," Absalom vowed, "let him kill me" (2 Samuel 14:32). After this, Absalom was finally granted permission to see David, during which meeting David's love for his son, despite all that had happened, was evident as he met his son with a kiss.

The wisdom of the wise woman of Tekoah's counsel might be questioned, considering what happened next. Instead of being a humble and repentant son, Absalom slowly began to take power away from his father. The climax occurred when Absalom instigated a coup, ousted David from power, and took over his kingdom (see 2 Samuel 15). Eventually, Joab killed Absalom, and David regained his kingdom, but David wept for his son saying, "O my son Absalom, my son, my son Absalom! Would God I had died for thee, O Absalom, my son, my son!" (2 Samuel 18:33).

We might question David's forgiveness and acceptance of Absalom, seeing that the result was anything but happy. It could be that this wise woman of Tekoah had been misled by Joab's good intentions and that her advice was ill given. However, I think, despite how Absalom turned out, she was right in counseling David to forgive him and give him a second chance. We can never, ever go wrong in extending forgiveness and love to someone. Elder David E. Sorensen of the Quorum of the Seventy, taught that forgiveness brings peace:

> When someone has hurt us or those we care about, that pain can almost be overwhelming. It can feel as if the pain or the injustice is the most important thing in the world and that we have no choice but to seek vengeance. But Christ, the Prince of Peace, teaches us a better way. It can be very difficult to forgive someone the harm they've done us, but when we do, we open ourselves up to a better future. No longer does someone else's wrongdoing control our course. When we forgive others, it frees us to choose how we will live our own lives. Forgiveness means that problems of the past no longer dictate our destinies, and we can focus on the future with God's love in our hearts.[1]

Forgiveness and love are Christlike attributes, and they are always the right choice. However, forgiving someone doesn't mean that we aren't allowed to set boundaries in our lives for those people. Elder Sorenson continued:

> I would like to make it clear that forgiveness of sins should not be confused with tolerating evil. In fact, in the Joseph Smith Translation, the Lord said, "Judge righteous judgment." The Savior asks us to forsake and combat evil in all its forms, and although we must forgive a neighbor who injures us, we should still work constructively to prevent that injury from being repeated. A woman who is abused should not seek revenge, but neither should she feel that she cannot take steps to prevent further abuse. A businessperson treated unfairly in a transaction should not hate the person who was dishonest but could take appropriate steps to remedy the wrong. Forgiveness does not require us to accept or tolerate evil. It does not require us to ignore the wrong that we see in the world around us or in our own lives. But as we fight against sin, we must not allow hatred or anger to control our thoughts or actions.[2]

A Newbery Honor children's book called *Doctor De Soto* illustrates this well. The story is about a mouse who is a dentist and has compassion on a fox with a toothache. Dr. De Soto agrees to fix his tooth, but to do so he must crawl up into the fox's mouth, a precarious situation for a mouse. While the fox is in pain he has no desire to eat Dr. De Soto, but once he starts feeling better the temptation becomes too much for him. He decides that as soon as his dental work is over he will eat Dr. De Soto and his wife. Dr. De Soto, though, is one step ahead. When he puts in the fox's new tooth, he also glues his mouth shut so that the fox is unable to hurt him.[3]

I wonder if David's mistake was not that he showed compassion and love to his son by allowing him to come home, but that he did not maintain the boundary he had set. David allowed Absalom to see him and become close to him again, after having told him that he would not. It was after this renewed intimacy with his father that the temptation of power became too much for Absalom and he began to slowly sabotage David.

> *"There shall not one hair of thy son fall to the earth."*

I am sure we can each think of ways in which we have been like David, either too harsh and unforgiving or too quick to allow people to cross boundaries, which we have put in place for a reason. As we think about our own unique situations, I think we would be wise to remember the counsel that the wise woman of Tekoah gave and the example of David and Absalom. Life is short and we are never wrong to forgive. We just need to remember that it okay, and even necessary, to create strong boundaries with those who have wronged us. It is entirely possible to forgive someone, and even love them, but not allow them back into your life. Like Dr. De Soto did with the fox, we should take smart precautions so that we don't allow ourselves to get hurt again.

• David's Ten Concubines •

When David had to flee from his son Absalom, he took with him most of his household, but left behind ten of his concubines, "to keep the house" (2 Samuel 15:16). The word *keep* here means "to guard or protect."[1] It seems unusual to leave women behind to protect a palace, but I think that David's hope was that by leaving his wives behind it would let Absalom know that he intended to return. David trusted in Absalom's honorable nature to safeguard his concubines, which turned out to be a mistake.

After David fled, Absalom, who by this time had a large following, came into Jerusalem and claimed his father's throne. His advisor, a man named Ahithophel, told Absalom that to validate his right to throne he needed to "go in unto" his father's concubines who had been left behind. The motive behind these rapes would be first, to deeped the divide between David and his son so, as Ahithophel said, "All Israel shall hear that thou art abhorred of thy father: then shall the hands of all that are with thee be strong" (2 Samuel 16:21). Also, by having sex with these concubines, Absalom was making a political statement that he, as the new king, was entitled to all the king's property, including his wives and concubines.

Absalom followed his advisor's advice, and "they spread Absalom a tent upon the top of the house; and Absalom went in unto his father's concubines in the sight of all Israel" (verse 22). This terrible event fulfilled the prophesy the prophet Nathan had given to David after his actions with Uriah and Bathsheba. "Thus saith the Lord," Nathan told David, "I will raise up evil against thee out of thine own house, and I will take thy wives before thine eyes, and give them unto thy neighbour, and he shall lie with thy wives in the sight of this sun. For thou didst it secretly: but I will do this thing before all Israel, and before the sun" (2 Samuel 12:11–12).

Absalom's reign did not last long, and he was soon killed by Joab, David's general (2 Samuel 18). When David returned to Jerusalem he took the ten concubines who had been left behind and made them comfortable in the harem, but from that time he never slept with them again. They were, "shut up unto the day of their death, living in widowhood" (2 Sam. 20:3). This doesn't mean he locked them up, but that they were divorced or "dead" to him. At first this seems harsh, but we need to remember that under the mosaic law, once his son had slept with them, David was forbidden to. By keeping them in his house and providing for them for the rest of their lives, David was being compassionate.

Abishag

Now king David was old and stricken in years; and they covered him with clothes, but he gat no heat.

Therefore his servants said unto him, Let there be sought for my lord the king a young virgin: and let her stand before the king, and let her cherish him, and let her lie in thy bosom, that my lord the king may get heat.

So they sought for a fair damsel throughout all the coasts of Israel, and found Abishag a Shunammite, and brought her to the king.

And the damsel was very fair, and cherished the king, and ministered to him: but the king knew her not.

1 Kings 1:1–4

Late in his life, after having reclaimed his kingdom from his son Absalom, David's health began to fail. As is common in old age when people's metabolisms slow down, David was cold all the time. Today, if our grandparents get cold, they just crank up the thermostat in their houses, but in David's time they had no such luxury. In an attempt to keep him warm, his servants "covered him with clothes" (1 Kings 1:1) but even then "he gat not heat" (1 Kings 1:1). David's servants suggested that they find a young woman who would "stand before the king" and "lie in [David's] bosom, that my lord the king may get heat" (1 Kings 1:2).

This suggestion that she would give the king "heat" possibly has two meanings. The Hebrew word has two meanings, to "become warm" as in an increase in temperature but it can also mean "to become aroused, inflame oneself with."[1] It seems that in addition to just keeping him physically warm, the servants hoped that this young woman would also sexually arouse the King as well. This was time of great political upheaval (David's sons were fighting over who would inherit the kingdom), and it was important that David appear to be a robust and virile king who could hold his kingdom together.

A search was made throughout "all the coasts of Israel" (1 Kings 1:3) for a beautiful young woman to fulfill this role, and Abishag was found. Abishag was a Shunammite and was "very fair" (1 Kings 1:4). Abishag's status in David's family is unclear. We don't know if she was his actual wife or a concubine. Either way, I think it would have taken a very unique young woman to become the companion of an aging king. She seems to have relished her role. 1 Kings 1:4 tells us that she "cherished the king, and ministered to him," meaning that she took care of his physical needs. She was sort of like a live-in nurse to David who seemed to love him, perhaps like she would a father or a grandfather. For, despite his servants' hopes that Abishag would "heat" David sexually, their relationship was platonic and David "knew her not" (1 Kings 1:4).

David's impotence seems to have been political as well as physical. Directly after the verses about Abishag, we read that David's son Adonijah "exalted himself" (1 Kings 1:5) and began a coup to take over the kingdom. Adonijah succeeded for a time, but was outmaneuvered by Bathsheba who convinced David to name her son Solomon as his heir (see Bathsheba on page 189). Fearing that Solomon would kill him, Adonijah "caught hold on the horns of the altar," (1 Kings 1:50), a way of claiming sanctuary. Solomon was gracious toward his half-brother and declared, "If he will shew himself a worthy man, there shall not an hair of him fall to the earth: but if wickedness shall be found in him, he shall die" (1 Kings 1:52).

Adonijah did not give up easily on his ambition to become king. After David's death, Adonijah approached Bathsheba and asked her to speak to Solomon on his behalf, asking if he might have Abishag as his wife. Adonijah was hoping to stake a claim to the throne by marrying one of his father's concubines. In 2 Samuel 16, we see how Abasalom had tried to validate his position as king by raping David's concubines (see page 206). It seems that Adonijah had a similar idea in mind by marrying Abishag.

Bathsheba, either being blind to Adonijah's true purpose or hoping to expose him to Solomon, took his request to her son. When Solomon heard the proposition he became very upset, seeing at once that Adonijah was trying overthrow him as king. "God do so to me, and more also, if Adonijah have not spoken this word against his own life," Solomon declared, "Now therefore, as the Lord liveth, which hath established me, and set me on the throne of David my father, and who hath made me an house, as he promised, Adonijah shall be put to death this day" (1 Kings 2:23–24). Which he was.

We have no other information about Abishag after this story, though there is some speculation that Solomon may have married her and that she is the "Shulamite" spoken of in the Song of Solomon (see Song of Solomon 6:13). She is a young woman with a very interesting story. Yet I can't help but feel a little sorry for her. Her life must have been a hard and lonely one.

> She "cherished the king, and ministered to him."

Wise Woman of Abel

And they came and besieged him in Abel of Beth-maachah, and they cast up a bank against the city, and it stood in the trench: and all the people that were with Joab battered the wall, to throw it down.

Then cried a wise woman out of the city, Hear, hear; say, I pray you, unto Joab, Come near hither, that I may speak with thee.

And when he was come near unto her, the woman said, Art thou Joab? And he answered, I am he. Then she said unto him, Hear the words of thine handmaid. And he answered, I do hear.

Then she spake, saying, They were wont to speak in old time, saying, They shall surely ask counsel at Abel: and so they ended the matter.

I am one of them that are peaceable and faithful in Israel: thou seekest to destroy a city and a mother in Israel: why wilt thou swallow up the inheritance of the Lord?

2 Samuel 20:15–19

After Absalom's death, David reclaimed his kingdom but still faced resistance in reunifying his people. David especially feared that the northern kingdom of Israel, led by a man named Sheba, the son of Bichri, was a threat and sent Joab out to stop him. Joab pursued Sheba until he took refuge in the city of Abel. Joab and his men began to besiege the city and "cast up a bank against the city" and "battered the wall" (2 Samuel 20:15), meaning they built a siege engine and a battering ram.

When their siege efforts were well underway, a "wise woman" yelled over the wall to Joab, requesting that he come and speak with her. We know little about who this woman was. Josephus described her as "a woman of small account, and yet both wise and intelligent"[1] who took it upon herself to scale the wall and, with the assistance of an armed guard, called for Joab. She may have just been a daring woman, concerned for her city, but her actions suggest that she held a position of leadership or responsibility within the city. One scholar wrote:

> She is not called a "judge," although it is clearly in her power to make decisions in the face of a military threat; nor is she a "prophetess," imbued with the power of the spirit to deal with an overwhelming situation. *Charisma* she may or may not have had; but, as the narrator so explicitly relates, it is "in her wisdom" that she advises "all the people" of the town. Sagacity, faithfulness, a commanding presence, and a readily acknowledged influence with her peers—these are the attributes that clearly mark this woman. . . . In the early years of Israel, with its egalitarian principles and desperate need for able minds as well as bodies, such qualities might have placed women not uncommonly in positions of authority in the village-tribal setting.[2]

Her positon of authority is seen when she engaged Joab boldly. She called herself his "handmaiden," a title indicating humility and a desire to serve, but demanded that Joab listen to *her*. Joab was quick to acknowledge her status. When she had Joab's attention, she told him of the important nature of her city. She said, "They were wont to speak in old time, saying, They shall surely ask counsel at Abel: and so they ended the matter" (2 Samuel 20:18). It seems she was alluding to a historical tradition in which Abel, or perhaps a prophet or oracle *in* Abel, was commonly sought out by those needing advice or justice.

After telling Joab this about her city, she gave a rather remarkable introduction of herself. She told Joab, "I am one of them that are peaceable and faithful in Israel" (2 Samuel 20:19). In Hebrew, the entire phrase "I am one of them that are peaceable" is said with one word: *shalam*, which has two related meanings, "to be in a covenant of peace" and "to be completed, finished." The Hebrew word translated as "faithful" is *aman*, which means " to support, uphold and nourish." It is the same word used for Naomi when she became a "nurse" to her grandson Obed (see Naomi on page 157). If we were to rewrite her introduction, we might phrase it this way: "I am one who has made a covenant of peace—one who is complete and whole—and am a nurturer of Israel."

She continued her introduction to Joab by telling him, "Thou seekest to destroy a city and a mother in Israel" (2 Samuel 20:19). It is unclear whether she intended the phrase "mother in Israel" to apply to herself or if she was saying that the city was a "mother in Israel." If we choose to read it to mean that the city was a "mother in Israel," then it makes her next words, "Why wilt thou swallow up the inheritance of the Lord?" (2 Samuel 20:19) easier to understand. She was warning Joab that her city had a rich history and had spiritual importance; he might want to think twice about destroying it.

On the other hand, if we read the scripture to mean that she was calling *herself* a "mother in Israel," then we might see her as a

Deborah-like character, a woman who had been called by God to lead, guide, and protect her people. In fact, some scholars speculate that there was a tradition in Israel, beginning before Deborah and continuing down to the time of Solomon, of females in leadership roles not only in the family but on a community and tribal level as well. This becomes easier to understand when we remember that in ancient times, cities and communities were often just large extended families, with many of their citizens being related either by birth or marriage. In such a family-oriented environment, it would be natural for there to be strong, commanding matriarchs just as there were patriarchs. The title of a "mother in Israel" certainly suggests the idea of a matriarch, one who has special responsibility for the well-being of her people.

The title a "mother in Israel," especially as it could be applied to this wise woman of Abel, helps us expand our idea of what it means to be a mother. Spiritually, the word *mother* means more than one who has given birth to a child. Sister Sheri Dew explained,

> President Gordon B. Hinckley stated that "God planted within women something divine." That something is the gift and the gifts of motherhood. . . .
>
> . . . Just as worthy men were foreordained to hold the priesthood in mortality, righteous women were endowed premortally with the privilege of motherhood. Motherhood is more than bearing children, though it is certainly that. It is the essence of who we are as women. It defines our very identity, our divine stature and nature, and the unique traits our Father gave us.[3]

This wise woman of Abel embodies Sister Dew's description. This woman, though she may have had children of her own, was acting as a "mother" by intervening on behalf of her children—the people of her city—and saving them from destruction. There was no giving birth or changing diapers involved here! Her choices, made out of love for others, made her a mother.

I don't think it is a small thing that the motto of the Relief Society is "Charity Never Faileth." Charity, the highest form of love, is perhaps the most incredible power on earth. It can create, shape, and transform everything and everyone it touches. For me, motherhood has been like "bootcamp" for training in charity. I have literally given parts of myself that I can never get back to create bodies for my children. I have sacrificed my time, ambitions, and sleep to care for them. I have loved them with the most selfless, all-consuming type of love I have ever experienced. I have learned how to put others before myself, how to be humble and ask for forgiveness, how to repent, how not to give up, and how to love someone else unconditionally. The physical act of mothering often forces women to become masters of charity. Yet it is not the only way to be schooled as a mother.

I have watched women whose unfulfilled desire for children has refined and purified their souls, opening up their hearts with love for all of God's children that I can barely comprehend; women whose work and careers have given them incredible opportunities to lead others to do good and make good choices; who advocate for justice and protection for those whose voices are unheard; women whose writing, music, and words nurture and create peace in the hearts of others; women who are unafraid to challenge and to correct misbehavior and whose teaching directs hearts and minds to God; women who are unafraid to climb mountains and scale walls to protect their people. These women are mothers—creators and nurtures of the human race.

I love Sister Patricia Holland's words about motherhood:

> I believe *mother* is one of those very carefully chosen words, one of those words rich with meaning after meaning after meaning. We must not, at all costs, let that word divide us. I believe with all my heart that it is first and foremost a statement about our nature, not a head count of our children. . . . Some women give birth and never "mother" them. Others, whom I love with all my heart, "mother" all their lives but have never given birth. Therefore, we must understand that however we accomplish it, parenthood is the highest of callings, the holiest of arrangements. And all of us are Eve's daughters, married or single, maternal or barren, every one of us. We are created in the image of the Gods to become gods and goddesses. And we can provide something of that divine pattern, that maternal prototype, for each other and for those who come after us.[4]

Motherhood is an eternal prototype, *the* great archetype for all womankind. Many worldly voices try to dismiss motherhood as an unimportant choice or relegate it to a select portion of women. If we are ever going to fully understand our power as women, we have to embrace our motherhood—not just our biological role but our societal and spiritual ones as well.

All of this, I feel, is conveyed in the phrase used by the wise woman of Abel, a "mother in Israel." In fact, this wise woman uses the phrase like she might a title, making it clear to Joab that who she was and what she represented were a force to be reckoned with.

Joab seemed to be humbled and alarmed by her remarks and quickly began to back pedal, telling her, "Far be it, far be it from me, that I should swallow up or destroy" (2 Samuel 20:20). He explained to her that all he wanted was Sheba, the son of Bichri, and that he was willing to leave the city alone if she would deliver him into their hands. She quickly agreed to this arrangement and took it one step further. She wouldn't just turn Sheba over to Joab, but his head would be "thrown to thee [Joab] over the wall" (2 Samuel 20:21). The fact that she made this decision independently and confidently shows us, again, that she was a woman of some importance in the city. She "went unto all the people in her wisdom" and they did as she had promised and "cut off the head of Sheba the son of Bichri, and cast it out to Joab" (2 Samuel 20:22). This satisfied Joab, who blew his trumpet and removed his forces from the city and returned to Jerusalem to report what had happened to King David.

Though the story of this woman is not lengthy, I cannot help but be impressed with the enormous amount of influence she wielded, not only in her own city but also over Joab and consequently all of Israel. With her wisdom and her fearlessness, she intervened to end the siege against her own city, and, with the death of Sheba, prevented further conflict between the not-so-united kingdoms of Israel and Judah. I hope if there is one thing that we take away from her story it is the idea that being a mother is something innate in every woman and that these seeds of motherhood inside of us motivate us to serve, to protect, to nurture and to love the human family. Each of us, no matter what our life circumstances, can be a "mother in Israel."

The *Queen* of *Sheba*

And when the queen of Sheba heard of the fame of Solomon concerning the name of the Lord, she came to prove him with hard questions.

And she came to Jerusalem with a very great train, with camels that bare spices, and very much gold, and precious stones: and when she was come to Solomon, she communed with him of all that was in her heart.

And Solomon told her all her questions: there was not any thing hid from the king, which he told her not.

1 Kings 10:1–3

The Queen of Sheba marches into the pages of the Old Testament like a breath of fresh air. Not only is she fascinatingly independent and wealthy, but she is renowned not for her beauty but for her intellect. She and a great caravan of camels, spices, gold, and precious stones went to visit Solomon after hearing of his wisdom. Specifically, she had heard things "concerning the name of the Lord" (1 Kings 10:1) and was curious. She was not content to receive information and ideas second-hand. She made a personal journey to see Solomon and to "prove him with hard questions" (1 Kings 10:1).

Now here is a woman after my own heart! She wasn't there to talk to Solomon about trade or politics. She gave him the "hard questions."

Josephus tells us that she "was inquisitive into philosophy, and one that on other accounts also was to be admired."[1] She obviously had thought and studied long and deep. She was a curious, and she wanted to know the truth of things for *herself*. Right from the start, we find a woman well worth emulating.

Some traditions maintain that the Queen of Sheba presented riddles to Solomon, testing her intellect against his. Yet the biblical account presents their meeting not so much as battle of the wits but rather as a meeting of two equally great minds. 1 Kings 10:2 tells us that when the Queen of Sheba came to Solomon with her great caravan train of wealth and "communed with him all that was in her heart." He in return "told her all her questions: there was not any thing . . . which he told her not" (verse 3). Don't you wish you could have been a fly on the wall for that conversation? It would be fascinating to know what it was that was in this great woman's heart, and how Solomon was able to answer her questions.

As a woman who also has pondered on "hard questions," I can only imagine what joy this conversation must have been for the Queen of Sheba. Here at last was someone who had answers to her questions. Solomon must have been equally excited to have someone so ready and willing to listen to him explain his God and his faith. The Queen of Sheba was the investigator that every missionary hopes for. It seems that when she first met Solomon, she had a degree of skepticism about him and his God. Perhaps she expected to be able to "prove" him wrong. Yet she did what we hope all our investigators will do—*investigate* the gospel. Isn't that the challenge that Alma sets forth in the Book of Mormon? That we are to "experiment" upon the word of God (Alma 32:27), testing it and trying to see if

it is true? God doesn't expect us to take our faith on the second-hand accounts of others. Like the Queen of Sheba, He expects us to discover it for ourselves.

After their conversation, Solomon took her to see his home and the temple. When she saw the perfect organization of Solomon's home and the worship in the temple, "there was no more spirit in her" (1 Kings 10:5). The phrase "no more spirit in her" can be translated two possible ways: that there was no more "anger or temper" in her, or that there was no more "sorrow or trouble" in her. On one hand, perhaps after hearing Solomon's answers to her questions and the beauty of his home and temple, her desire to be antagonistic and to prove him wrong was gone. Or, perhaps it meant that his answers to her questions had taken away the sorrow and trouble that had been in her heart. Either way, I think that it indicates that the Queen of Sheba had been converted.

The Ethiopian Orthodox Church maintains claims that the Queen of Sheba was from Egypt and Ethiopia, where there is archeological evidence of a strong, independent queen and that she did indeed become converted to Jehovah. They claim that she even married Solomon and, when she returned to her own country, gave birth to a son named Menelik. When Menelik was twenty-two, he went to Jerusalem to meet Solomon, who was delighted with his long-lost firstborn son. Solomon tried to convince him to stay, but Menelik returned to Sheba, taking with him Levite priests and the ark of the covenant.[2] Though we don't know the truth of this story, we can imagine that when the Queen of Sheba went back to her country, she took with her a rich testimony that must have strengthened and uplifted her people.

Before she left Solomon, the Queen of Sheba gave him a great gift of gold, spices, stones, and "almug trees" that Solomon used to build a terrace on the temple (1 Kings 10:10–12). In return, Solomon gave her "all her desire, whatsoever she asked" (1 Kings 10:13). I wonder what she asked for. With great wealth of her own and the hard questions of her heart now appeased, what did she lack?

I am sure that, as all great thinkers, the Queen of Sheba was never completely free from doubts or "hard questions." However, now it seemed she knew where to get answers. In fact, hundreds of years later, Christ himself would extol the virtues of the Queen of Sheba when he told the Jews, "The queen of the south shall rise up in judgment with this generation, and shall condemn it: for she came from the uttermost parts of the earth to hear the wisdom of Solomon; and behold, a greater than Solomon is here" (Matthew 12:42).

"You don't know how good you have it," Jesus was telling the Jews. "Some, like the Queen of Sheba, have made greater sacrifices than you'll ever have to make to gain even just a portion of the knowledge I have to give you. You don't appreciate what you have."

I have often wondered how the Queen of Sheba might feel about us today. Unlike her, we do not have to travel from the "uttermost parts of the earth" to gain incredible wisdom and knowledge. We have the entirety of the restored gospel literally at our fingertips. Joseph Smith said, "Prophets, priests and kings [and may I add in queens] . . . have looked forward with joyful anticipation to the day in which we live; and fired with heavenly and joyful anticipations they have sung and written and prophesied of this our day."[3]

In these latter-days, we have temporal and spiritual knowledge that people of past ages could not even dream of. We have so much, but do we appreciate it? Do we take the light and truth we have for granted, simply because it has been so easily earned or become commonplace to us? President Dieter F. Uchtdorf of the First Presidency taught,

> In the Church of Jesus Christ, we have been given so much. We are surrounded by such an astonishing wealth of light and truth that I wonder if we truly appreciate what we have. . . .
>
> . . . Life-changing truths are before our eyes and at our fingertips, but sometimes we sleepwalk on the path of discipleship. Too often we let ourselves be distracted by the imperfections of our fellow members instead of following the example of our Master. We tread a path covered with diamonds, but we can scarcely distinguish them from ordinary pebbles.[4]

I think the challenge of our day, when so much is available to us, is to learn to appreciate what we have. We need to make sure that we, like the Nephites of old, are not getting "to be less and less astonished at a sign or a wonder from heaven" (3 Nephi 2:1) with hearts that are hard and minds that are blind to the incredible truths of the gospel. How do we do that?

I have a favorite story from the book *Sophie's World* by Jostein Gaarder. Sophie's teacher is trying to explain to her the art of learning. He says that if, one day at breakfast, a baby sees his father begin to fly around the kitchen, he will laugh and giggle. The baby is still learning how the world works and doesn't yet know that people don't always fly. He is delighted to learn something new. On the other hand, his mother screams and faints. She does know that people can't fly, and seeing her husband do it is not delightful to her; it is terrifying. What, the teacher asks Sophie, makes their reactions so different? He says it is because the mother has lost her sense of "wonder," her sense of curiosity in the world. The teacher further explains:

> For various reasons most people get so caught up in everyday affairs that their astonishment at the world gets pushed into the background. (They crawl deep into the rabbit's fur, snuggle down comfortably, and stay there for the rest of their lives.)
>
> To children, the world and everything in it is *new*, something that gives rise to astonishment. It is not like that for adults. Most adults accept the world as a matter of course.
>
> This is precisely where philosophers are a notable exception. A philosopher never gets quite used to the world. To him or her, the world continues to seem a bit unreasonable—bewildering, even enigmatic. Philosophers and small children thus have an important faculty in common. You might say that throughout his life a philosopher remains as thin-skinned as a child.
>
> So now you must choose, Sophie. Are you a child who has not yet become world-weary? Or are you a philosopher who will vow never to become so?[5]

Perhaps this is what Christ meant when he told us that we are to "become as little children" (Matthew 18:3), always meek, humble, and curious. When we are childlike in our approach to learning, when we keep our minds and our hearts open to new wonders and ideas, we begin to find wisdom. When we stop taking things for granted and realize that everyday holds something new to learn and discover, we begin to find deeper truth and meaning in the world around us. We find truth in a variety of circumstances and gain answers to our hard questions by being humble and teachable. The Queen of Sheba illustrates beautifully the type of learner I think God wants each of us to become—one who is tenacious, eager, bold, and above all, curious.

> *"They have sung and written and prophesied of this our day."*

Asherah and Goddess

Worship in Ancient Israel

Most of us are more familiar with the Greek and Roman gods and goddesses than we are with the ancient Canaanite, Mesopotamian, or Phoenician ones. Yet these deities play a huge part in the drama of the Old Testament. According to Canaanite belief, Asherah was married to El, the high God and father of all other gods. He was the "creator" and was said to dwell at the foot of a mountain. His symbol was a bull, and he was associated with rocks and high places. Asherah was known as the "great mother" and the "lady of the sea." She was the mother of a pantheon of Gods, and her symbols were lions representing power, serpents representing immortality and healing, sacred trees representing fertility, and doves representing wisdom. She was the source of deep, mysterious knowledge and the power of creating life. Asherah's son Baal, who some stories say was born through a virgin conception, was called the "lord of the heavens." He was associated with the weather, and it was to him that the ancient people's would pray for rain.

It is evident from the Old Testament that Asherah worship played a key role in much of the Israelite history. For example, we know that Solomon's foreign wives introduced widespread worship of Asherah and other goddess worship among the Israelites (see Maachah on page 258). By the time of the Assyrian and Babylonian invasions, her worship was very common in both the Northern and the Southern kingdoms. In fact, much of the book of Jeremiah is spent repeatedly warning the Israelites that if they did not stop their worship of goddesses, it would destroy them—which, as we see, eventually happens.

For Latter-day Saints, the discovery of the Bible speaking about an ancient mother goddess, married to the father god, whose divine son is called "the Lord" might get us excited. Latter-day Saints, like people in Old Testament times, believe in a divine family—a Heavenly Father, a Heavenly Mother and Their son, Jesus Christ. We might be tempted, in our hunger to know more about Her, to latch on to Asherah as our long-sought-after Mother. Yet doing so would be like accepting Zeus as our Heavenly Father and Hera, Diana, or Aphrodite as a correct depiction of our Heavenly Mother. They are not correct depictions, simply shadows and corruptions of the real thing. Satan is a master at corrupting sacred symbols and practices to bring misery and destruction.

Yet Asherah—as well as many ancient goddesses—embodies many of the archetypes of our Divine Mother (see the list on page 4). In fact, I think that it is possible that the Israelites and other ancient people had knowledge of our Heavenly Mother—perhaps even possessing a better understanding of Her than we have today. There were probably even appropriate representations and symbols of Her in their religious practices and within the temple.

Some scholars have suggested that prophets like Jeremiah and Ezekiel and kings like Josiah and Hezekiah, who took measures to combat goddess worship among the Israelites, were androcentric and intent on destroying evidence of a female deity to promote their patriarchal agenda. I refuse to believe that is entirely true. While it is possible that kings like Josiah (see 2 Kings 23) may have gone a bit too far in their reforms, I think it is apparent that sacred knowledge and practices had been corrupted and perverted over time, so that instead of bringing people closer to God, they began to result in wickedness.

The following are some of the most common references to Asherah worship in the Bible:

• Groves •

Usually when you see the word *grove* in the Old Testament, it is the Hebrew word *asherah* or *asherim*. *Asherim* are mentioned over forty times in the Old Testament and were symbols of Asherah. According to scholar Susan Ackerman, "These cult objects are generally described as being in the shape of a pole or stylized tree. Like a pole or tree, they can be said to be planted, stood up, or erected. Conversely, when destroyed, these cult symbols can be described as being cut down, hewn down, or uprooted; they can also be said to be burned, overturned, or broken. Both the Greek and the Latin translations of the Bible, moreover, render the words *asherah* and *asherim* as 'grove' or 'wood.'"[1]

Asherim could be living trees, planted by altars or in "groves" where worship was conducted. Just what exactly they did in these groves, we have no idea, but the Old Testament prophets seem to hint that worship in groves was sexually promiscuous. We don't know what type of tree asherim usually were, but when the prophets admonished Israel for idolatrous worship, they referred to worship that happened under "every green tree" (Isaiah 57:5). The word "every green" in Hebrew means a "fresh" tree, which might suggest evergreens. Trees like pines and palms that never lost their leaves might have been the preferred type of tree. Even today, we use evergreen trees at Christmas time to remind us of eternal life and Christ's triumph over death. It could be possible that asherim originally had similar symbolism. Yet as one writer suggested, the corrupt asherah poles condemned by the Bible would probably have had more in common with stripper poles than they would with our modern-day Christmas trees.

• High Places •

Associated with groves, the "high places" were open-air shrines constructed in cities, though they may also have been hilltop shrines. They appear to be some sort of tower or platform on which one "went up" to conduct a ritual, like burning incense or making a sacrifice. Smaller ones were also constructed at the gates of cities (see 2 Kings 23:8). Some of the righteous kings offered sacrifices on them (see 1 Kings 3:15), but it seems they were often used for worshiping false deities. These "high places" may have been perversions of temples or the "mountains" where prophets like Moses and Abraham went to receive direction from God.

Some of the most famous "high places" in the Bible were places where child sacrifice to the Canaanite fire god Molech took place. The Bible has numerous references to those who allowed "their sons and their daughters to pass through the fire unto Molech" (Jeremiah 32:35; see also 2 Kings 23:10). Archeologists think that the statue of Molech was like a large stove. A fire was lit inside of him, and children, perhaps those who were deformed or sick, were placed in his arms and rolled down into the fire inside.

• Standing Stones •

Called *massebot* in Hebrew, these were stones erected to commemorate the appearance of a deity. As William G. Dever explained, "The term *massebah* does not denote 'idol' (there are other Hebrew terms for that), but rather a stone "stand-in" for deity . . . any sort of deliberately erected stone—large or small, occurring singly or in multiples—that symbolizes the *presence of a deity*, thought to be particularly visible and efficacious in this particular place."[2]

Jacob, after his dream about the ladder to heaven, erected such a stone monument to God (see Genesis 31:45) as did Joshua when he made a covenant (see Joshua 24: 26). It does not seem that such things were forbidden except that perhaps such stone monuments had been begun to be worshiped and prayed to. The people began to worship the object as divine, and to forget what it represented—God's power and love.

• Incense Burned on Altars •

Burning incense was part of the worship in the tabernacle (see Exodus 30), as outlined to Moses. It was burned morning and night on the altar in front of the Holy of Holies and represented prayers ascending to God, a reminder of the need for constant communication with Him. God warned the Israelites that "Ye shall offer no strange incense thereon" (Exodus 30:9). It seems that what became a problem was people, on their own personal altars or in public "high places," burning incense to Baal and other deities instead of to God.

• Women Who "Wove Hangings for the Grove" •

This practice is described in 2 Kings 23:7 when Josiah broke down "the house of the sodomites, that were by the house of the Lord, where the women wove hangings for the grove." Scholars don't know what this means, but there was an association between public places of (male and female) prostitution and whatever the women were making for Asherah. Dever explains that the word, *hangings* (in Hebrew *battim*) usually means "houses" or "temples." He writes, "It is clear that later editors, translators, and commentators were already puzzled by this reference. The Septuagint . . . renders the term *battim* as 'garments, tunics.'" This suggests that perhaps the women made clothing for the asherah statues. Dever also suggests another possibility, "The term *battim* should be understood *periphrastically*, not as 'houses' but as something like 'tent-shrines.'"[3] It could have been that women wove these "tent-shrines" as a place in which cult prostitution (in which sex between men and women representing the gods would result in fertility and prosperity) was to take place.

• Nehushtan •

When Hezekiah made attempts to get rid of idolatrous practices, "he removed the high places, and brake the images, and cut down the groves, and broke in pieces the brasen serpent that Moses had made: for unto those days the children of Israel did burn incense to it: and he called it Nehushtan" (2 Kings 18:4). It seems that Moses's staff that he had used to heal the Israelites from the fiery serpents (see Numbers 21) had been preserved and, perhaps because

Asherah was associated with snakes, had become to source of idolatrous worship.

Some of these practices might seem bizarre to us, but it is important to remember that in the ancient world, religion was how everyone, Israelite or not, related to the world. Religion was the way in which ancient people explained the world, and they trusted it, much like we trust modern science to explain and giving meaning to our world today. As scholar William Dever so succinctly put it, "Living in antiquity was *being* 'religious,'"[4] while today we might say "Living in modern times is being 'scientific.'"

Just because we explain the world in different terms than our ancient counterparts doesn't mean that we are not in danger of falling into the same practices and mindsets. In fact, in the Book of Mormon, Jesus warned the Nephites that in the Latter-days the Gentiles would be destroyed unless they repented (see 3 Nephi 21:14–19). Jesus then listed all the practices that if they would not stop would destroy them. While He mentioned objects of war, such as "chariots" and "strongholds," Jesus also specified things like "witchcrafts," "soothsayers," "graven images," "standing images," and "groves." His use of these words, which refer to idolatrous worship, are significant. Though we don't think about ourselves as having such practices today, they are still with us, just packaged and practiced differently. I think the challenge we face is to discern, with the help of the Holy Ghost, which parts of these symbols and practices about our Divine Mother are remnants of truth, passed down through the ages, and which are corrupted and false. Sorting this out is a vital task for our generation, because as we can see from history, getting it wrong is a sure recipe for disaster.

Jezebel

And when Jehu was come to Jezreel, Jezebel heard of it; and she painted her face, and tired her head, and looked out at a window.

And as Jehu entered in at the gate, she said, Had Zimri peace, who slew his master?

And he lifted up his face to the window, and said, Who is on my side? Who? And there looked out to him two or three eunuchs.

And he said, Throw her down. So they threw her down: and some of her blood was sprinkled on the wall, and on the horses: and he trode her under foot.

2 Kings 9:30–33

If you are looking for an embodiment of wickedness in the Old Testament, Jezebel is your woman. Her name has become synonymous with evil and licentiousness. Yet among her wicked deeds there is also evidence of an incredibly intelligent and charismatic woman. Author Herbert Lockyer described Jezebel as follows:

> Jezebel was no ordinary woman. . . . We cannot fail to see her as a woman of prodigious force of intellect and will. The sacred narrative does not record that she possessed any of the finer, nobler feminine qualities. She knew nothing of the restraint of higher principles. Savage and relentless, this proud and strong-minded woman carried out her foul schemes. A gifted woman, she prostituted all her gifts for the furtherance of evil, and her misdirected talents became a curse. Persuasive, her influence was wrongly directed. Resolute above other women, she used

her strength of character to destroy a king and her own offspring, as well as pollute the life of a nation.[1]

Jezebel was the daughter of Ethbaal, the king of the Zidonians, another name for the Phoenicians (see 1 Kings 16:31). The Phoenicians were a mighty ship-building people, and it is likely that Ahab, the king of the northern kingdom of Israel, married Jezebel as a political alliance. Such a marriage was clearly against God's covenant, but Ahab did not seem to care. The scriptures say that Ahab, and we may add in, Jezebel, "did more to provoke the Lord God of Israel to anger than all the kings of Israel that were before him" (1 Kings 16:33).

Jezebel was devout. This would have been a desirable characteristic if her dedication had not been to the worship of the false gods, Baal and Asherah. Her influence in Israel was felt immediately after her marriage when Ahab, no doubt encouraged by his new wife, built a temple and an altar for Baal and "made a grove" (1 Kings 16:33), also called an *asherah* (see page 218). It was not long after this that God sealed the heavens and a great famine, lasting several years, afflicted the land.

Jezebel also took measures to "cut off the prophets of the Lord" (1 Kings 18:4) and slaughtered as many "prophets" as she was able to find. Obadiah, whose book is included in the Bible, was one of these prophets persecuted by Jezebel. He hid himself, as well as a hundred other prophets, in a cave and fed them with bread and water where they were safe from Jezebel. The presence of so many prophets may seem surprising, but the word in Hebrew can also mean "an inspired man" or "one who speaks with prophecy." It

seems Elijah was recognized as being "*the* prophet," or spokesman for God, while there were many other men who prophesied in the Lord's work. Perhaps they were not all that different from the Quorums of the Seventy we have today, which are filled with many such "prophets."

In lieu of God's prophets, Jezebel instituted huge groups of false prophets, four hundred each, for Baal and Asherah. These prophets did "eat at Jezebel's table" (1 Kings 18:19), indicating that she personally oversaw to their well-being and support. If Baal and Asherah had a "high priestess," it would have been Jezebel. Author Lockyer wrote, "Baal had no more dedicated devotee than Jezebel. None could match her zeal for the worship of Ashtaroth. . . . In a most relentless fashion Jezebel tried to drive out the true prophets of Jehovah from the land, and thus became the first female persecutor in history. From her idolatrous father, a high priest of Ashtaroth, she inherited her fanatical religious enthusiasm which inspired her to exterminate the worship of the true and living God, and almost succeeded in the attempt."[2]

After returning from Zarephath, Elijah saw how the people's hearts had been turned away from God by Jezebel's idolatry. He asked the people of Israel, "How long halt ye between two opinions? If the Lord be God, follow him: but if Baal, then follow him" (1 Kings 18:21). To this, the people who seem to have been confused over who to believe said nothing. Elijah, knowing that his people needed a reason to believe that he was a prophet of God, challenged Jezebel's priests to a duel. First, Elijah challenged them to kill a bull as a sacrifice but to light no fire underneath it. "Call ye on the name of your gods," Elijah challenged the priests of Baal, "and I will call on the name of the Lord: and the God that answereth by fire, let him be God" (1 Kings 18:24). All day, the priests of Baal called on the name of their God and "leaped upon the altar" and "cut themselves after their manner . . . till the blood gushed out upon them" (1 Kings 18:28). But no fire came.

Seeing the hopeless efforts of the priests, Elijah called the people to watch as he prepared his sacrifice. He took twelve stones, representing the tribes of Israel, and built an altar. He had people pour water on and around the sacrifice so that they would know there was not trickery going on. Then, with all this in place, at the time that the evening sacrifice would usually have been offered to God in the tabernacle, Elijah prayed and asked God to "hear me, that this people may know that thou are the Lord God, and that thou hast turned their heart back again" (1 Kings 18:37). After that fire "fell" and consumed the sacrifice, the stones, and even evaporated the water out of the trench Elijah had dug around it.

When the people saw that, they were astonished and fell on the ground, acknowledging that "the Lord, he is the God" (1 Kings 18:39). Elijah then encouraged the people to kill the priests of Baal, which they did by the banks of the river. Afterward, it miraculously began to rain for the first time in several years.

Ahab, who witnessed all of this, got in his chariot and rode rapidly home. He told Jezebel (who clearly called the shots) everything that Elijah had done. When Jezebel heard, she was furious and made an oath to her gods that she would kill Elijah. She sent a messenger to Elijah, telling him, "So let the gods do to me, and more also if I make not thy life as the life of one of them [the prophets of Baal]

by to morrow about this time" (1 Kings 19:2). Elijah, knowing that she would be true to her oath, fled for his life into the wilderness. Jezebel was not someone to mess with.

Inherent in this story of conflict between Elijah and Jezebel is the greater archetypal conflict of the patriarchy versus the matriarchy. With her goddess worship and unrestrained power, Jezebel is the epitome of the corrupted matriarchy. Elijah, (though he is ironically very nomadic in this story) represents the righteous patriarchy, attempting to restore the true worship of Jehovah and His covenant. I don't see the story of Elijah and Jezebel as an attempt by Elijah to crush or destroy the matriarchy, but rather to bring it back to its true and sacred place—not above or below the patriarchy but at its side.

While Elijah hid in the wilderness, Jezebel continued her reign of wickedness. Her husband, Ahab, wanted to buy a vineyard, but the owner, Naboth, did not wish to sell it because it was part of his tribe's sacred inheritance. Jezebel stepped in. It is clear from the way in which she domineers Ahab in this story and in the way in which her commands are so readily obeyed that Jezebel was a co-ruler (if not the ruler) of Israel. She told Ahab not to worry about the vineyard because "I will give thee the vineyard of Naboth" (1 Kings 21:7). She then ordered men to set Naboth up in a situation where he could be stoned for blaspheme so that, once he was dead, she was able to take his land.

When Elijah heard about what Jezebel had done, he confronted Ahab as he was riding down to his new vineyard and told him that God was not pleased with what he had done. Elijah promised that

God would bring evil to his house and destroy his posterity. Elijah promised that "the dogs shall eat Jezebel" (1 Kings 21:23). Ahab was upset by Elijah's words and humbled himself before God. The Lord told Elijah that because Ahab had been penitent, he would not bring the violence upon him, but "in his son's days will I bring the evil upon his house" (1 Kings 21:29).

Eventually, Jezebel met her end when the prophet Elisha, who had taken up the mantle of Elijah, anointed Jehu, the son of the king of Judah, to be the new king of Israel. A civil conflict erupted in which Jehu eventually overthrew and killed Jezebel's son Jehoram (see 2 Kings 9). Jehu's real design, though, was to kill Jezebel whom he perceived, and rightly so, to be the source of all the "whoredoms" and "witchcrafts" in the land (see 2 Kings 9:22). After getting rid of the opposition, Jehu and his army went to Jezreel, where Jezebel's palace was.

When Jezebel heard of Jehu's approach, she "painted her face, and tired her head" (2 Kings 9:30), which means she put makeup on and did her hair fancy, perhaps putting on a crown or some other adornment. I think this detail tells us a lot about Jezebel. We can't fault her for wanting to look nice when someone was coming. Most women can relate to that. Yet Jezebel was facing an opposing army, one she knew wanted to kill her. To prepare for this battle, she didn't pray or perform a sacrifice to any god. She spent the time making herself beautiful. When it came right down to it, Jezebel trusted in *herself*. When faced with a crisis, she turned to what she felt was the source of her power—her body and her appearance.

Jezebel reminds me of the "daughters of Zion" Isaiah chides. These women put their faith in the "bravery of their tinkling ornaments" and in their "changeable suits of apparel" (Isaiah 3:18, 22). I wonder how often we aren't a little like Jezebel and these "daughters of Zion" who find bravery and self-worth in the way we dress or do our hair and makeup. I'm not saying anything against being well-dressed or self-confident. Yet I think it might be helpful to reexamine ourselves occasionally to see where we are putting our confidence. If we are running late in the morning, do we spend what little time we have making sure we say our prayers or that we have mascara on? Do we spend more time thinking about what we are going to wear to Church or preparing ourselves to take the sacrament? Do we spend more time reading our scriptures or our social media feeds? If we want to feel good about ourselves, do we go to the temple or do we post a selfie and check it obsessively for comments? I bet that most of us could do a little better about putting our trust in God rather than trusting in ourselves.

When Jezebel had gotten herself ready, she looked out her window and called haughtily down to Jehu, who was below. Jehu saw her in the window, and knowing he had no way to reach her, called out, "Who is on my side? Who?" (2 Kings 9:32). These were similar to the words that Moses used when he came down from the mountain to find the children of Israel worshiping a golden calf. To discern who still worshiped the Lord, and had not turned their hearts to idolatry, Moses called out "Who is on the Lord's side? Let him come unto me" (Exodus 32:26). All those who still believed in God gathered to Moses and then went and slew all the men who were worshiping the idol.

Jehu must have realized that these words would have been familiar to any in Jezebel's palace who still believed in God, and he was right. Several eunuchs inside of Jezebel's palace heard Jehu's call and responded. They made their allegiance to God known by grabbing Jezebel and throwing her out of the castle window. Her blood was "sprinkled on the wall, and on the horses" (2 Kings 33) where she was trampled to death. Now in sacrament meeting when you sing "Who's on the Lord Side? Who? Now is the time to show,"[3] you can imagine eunuchs throwing Jezebel out a window. It gives the song a whole new meaning!

After Jehu had gone into the city and had rested, he sent men out to find Jezebel's body and bury it. He conceded that even if she was a "cursed woman" (2 Kings 9:34), she was still the daughter of a king and deserved a proper burial. Yet when the men went out to find her, they "found no more of her than the skull, and the feet, and the palms of her hands" (2 Kings 9:35). The rest had been eaten by dogs—a fulfillment of Elijah's prophesy.

I can't help but feel Jezebel's story is a tragedy. What if, instead of investing all her incredible talent and charisma in to the worship of false ideals, she had spent that energy in the service of God? How, then, might the story—even the whole course of the Old Testament—have been changed! As I think about the story of Jezebel, I am reminded of Jehu's question, "Who is on the Lord's side? Who?" I think each of us, no matter what our talents or strengths, needs to ask ourselves that question. We don't want to find ourselves fighting on the matriarchy's side or the patriarchy's side. We want to be found on *God's* side. The side where there is a beautiful blend, a perfect harmonizing of both the matriarchy and the patriarchy; where men and women truly become one.

> ——— ✦ ———
>
> *"Who's on the Lord's side? Who? Now is the time to show."*
>
> ——— ✦ ———

Widow of Zarephath

And she said, As the Lord thy God liveth, I have not a cake, but an handful of meal in a barrel, and a little oil in a cruse: and, behold, I am gathering two sticks, that I may go in and dress it for me and my son, that we may eat it, and die.

And Elijah said unto her, Fear not; go and do as thou hast said: but make me thereof a little cake first, and bring it unto me, and after make for thee and for thy son.

For thus saith the Lord God of Israel, The barrel of meal shall not waste, neither shall the cruse of oil fail, until the day that the Lord sendeth rain upon the earth.

And she went and did according to the saying of Elijah: and she, and he, and her house, did eat many days.

1 Kings 17:12–15

When I began my blog on women in the scriptures more than eight years ago, the first woman I chose to write about was the widow of Zarephath. Her story has resonated with me many times in my life and has given me courage to face the unknown. I feel like her story is the story of every person who sets forth on the path of faith—a story of walking to the outer limits of your understanding and trusting that God will catch you.

This widow's story is set during the reign of Ahab and Jezebel, when the prophet Elijah "seal[ed] the heavens" (1 Kings 17, chapter heading) because of the idolatry and wickedness of the Israelites and a great drought swept through land. The widow of Zarephath, however, was not an Israelite. Zarephath was part of Zidon, also known as Phoenicia (if you look at map 1, "Physical Map of the Holy Land," in the Bible Maps section, you will see Sidon at the top left side of the map). Even though she was outside the boundaries of Israel, she and her people also suffered the effects of the famine that lasted three and half years.

During the famine, Elijah hid from Ahab and Jezebel near a brook called Cherith, which was one of the small tributaries that fed into the Jordan River. If you look at your Bible map again, you will notice that the Jordan River runs between the Sea of Galilee and the Dead Sea, meaning that Elijah was a far distance from Zarephath, where this widow lived. Understanding the geography makes the instructions that Elijah received from God even more significant.

The famine became so severe the brook dried up. Like everyone else, Elijah was suffering from the effects of the famine. The Lord commanded him to travel to Zarephath because "I have commanded a widow woman there to sustain thee" (1 Kings 17:9). We naturally want to ask why. Why did God command Elijah to travel such a long distance to find someone who would feed him?

Jesus himself answered this question for us when he taught the people in his hometown of Nazareth that "no prophet is accepted in his own country" (Luke 4:24). Jesus went on to explain, "Many widows were in Israel in the days of Elias, when the heaven was shut up three years and six months, when great famine was throughout all the land; But unto none of them was Elias sent, save unto Sarepta, a city of Sidon, unto a woman that was a widow" (Luke 4:25–26). Jesus's message was that just like Him, Elijah was not accepted by his own people. Instead, the Lord sent him to someone who would listen, an obscure widow in the faraway town of Zarephath.

When Elijah arrived in Zarephath, he found a widow woman gathering sticks near the gate of the city. Seeing her, Elijah asked her to bring him "a little water in a vessel" (1 Kings 17:10). The famine was well underway, and it is likely that water was scarce. It is impressive that she seems to have made no objection to sharing her water with him. Yet when Elijah asked her for "a morsel of bread in thine hand" (1 Kings 17:11), she replied that she had none. All she had was "an handful of meal in a barrel, and a little oil in a cruse" (1 Kings 17:12). It was the last of her food, and she was gathering sticks so that she could return home and "dress it for me and my son, that we may eat it, and die" (1 Kings 17:12).

This widow was at the end of her rope. She and her son were starving, and she was resigned to her fate. All things considered, she seems to have been approaching death with a remarkable degree of fortitude. Then Elijah gave her the kicker. He told her, "Fear not; go and do as thou hast said: but make me thereof a little cake first, and bring it unto me" (1 Kings 17:13). I can just imagine what this woman's face must have looked when she heard this: astonishment, perhaps tinged with a little anger that Elijah would ask this of her. What sort of man would take away food from a dying widow and a child?

Elijah's request was accompanied by a powerful promise: "For thus saith the Lord God of Israel," Elijah told her, "The barrel of meal shall not waste, neither shall the cruse of oil fail, until the day that the Lord sendeth rain upon the earth" (1 Kings 17:14). Even just reading those words, hundreds of years after they were said, I can feel the spiritual power in them. The widow must have felt the power in them too because she obeyed and "went and did according to the saying of Elijah" (1 Kings 17:15).

I wonder if Elijah had shown up several months, or even days before, when she still had more food to eat if she would have been so willing to turn it all over to him. It seems like Elijah's timing was right on, coming at exactly the time when she was at rock bottom and was prepared to be humble. Her suffering had brought her to a place where she was willing to take a flying leap into the dark— to give all that she had—because the only alternative was to die. Her faith paid off because things happened just as Elijah said they would. "The barrel of meal wasted not, neither did the cruse of oil fail," and "she and he, and her house, did eat many days" (1 Kings 17:15–16).

I've always wondered just how this happened. In all the video depictions I've seen of this story, the oil is instantly replenished each time she uses it, and after she scoops meal out of the barrel it magically reappears. I have no doubt that God could work a miracle like that, but it has been my experience that such miracles usually happen through much more ordinary ways. I love a particular story about a pioneer woman named Hannah Cornaby, who, like the widow of Zarephath, also found herself without enough to feed her children. She wrote:

One morning having, as usual, attended to family prayer, in which, with greater significance than is often used, we asked, "give us this day our daily bread;" and having eaten a rather scanty breakfast— every morsel we had in the house—Edith was wondering what we should have for dinner and why 'Pa did not send us some fish. I, too, was anxious. . . . So telling my darlings I would go and see if Sister Ellen Jackson . . . had heard any news, I started off. Sister Jackson had not heard from the fishery; but was quite cheerful, and telling me how well her garden was growing, adding that the radishes were fit for use, and insisted that I must have some. . . . Passing, on my way, the house of brother Charles Gray, sister Gray asked me where I had got such fine radishes. I told her, and offered to divide them with her, to which she agreed, providing I would take in exchange some lettuce and cress, of which she had plenty. She filled a pan with these; and I hurried away thinking how pleased my children would be, if only we had some bread to eat with them. As I was passing brother Simons Baker's house, sister Baker saw me and invited me in. . . . She then asked me where I had got such nice green stuff, and when I told her, and offered her some . . . she then gave me a piece of nice fresh butter . . . and also a large slice of cheese. If I only had bread, I thought, how good these would be! Just then my eyes rested upon a large vessel full of broken bread. Sister Baker, seeing I had noticed it, told me its history. It had been sent the day before, in a sack, to the canyon, where her husband had a number of men working. On the way it had fallen from the wagon, and been crushed under the wheel. She did not know what to do with it, remarking that she would offer me some of it but feared

I would feel insulted, although she assured me it was perfectly clean. I accepted her offer, when, filling a large pan, she sent her daughter home with me to carry it.

The children were watching for my return; and when they saw the bread, they clapped their hands with delight. Bread, butter, cheese, radishes, lettuce and cress! What a dinner we had that day! Elijah never enjoyed the dinner the ravens brought him, more than I did that meal; nor did he more fully understood that a kind Providence had furnished it.[1]

The thing that impresses me the most about Hannah Cornaby's story is that she, knowing she had nothing to feed her children at home, offered to split the radishes with her neighbor. From that one generous action, she was blessed to be able to gather a large meal for her family. Had she not been generous, it is likely all she would have had to give her children at the end of her walk was radishes. Her miracle was facilitated by her willingness to consecrate, to share all that she had.

I wonder if the widow's miracle of the oil and meal happened in a similar way, that perhaps it wasn't that her barrel and cruse became magical, with unexplained food appearing in them, but that somehow she found that she always had enough. I often feel that way with tithing and my bank account. When my husband and I pay our tithing, no matter what our debts or financial obligations, there is always "magically" enough in our account to cover our needs and expenses. Like the widow watching her oil and meal never fail, I, too, witness a miracle.

The widow's story doesn't end here. Sometime later, her son became so sick "that there was no breath left in him" (1 Kings 17:17), which sounds like he was dead. Elijah, who had been living with her, went to comfort her, but his presence distressed her. She was unkind to Elijah and told him, "What have I to do with thee, O thou man of God" (1 Kings 17:18), not intending the title as a sign of respect but rather as sarcasm. She asked Elijah if he had come to "call my sin to remembrance" and to "slay my son" (1 Kings 17:18). We don't know what sin she was talking about her, but it is evident that she felt that God was punishing her from some previous mistake.

Elijah was undisturbed by her criticism and asked for her son. He carried the boy up to his own room where he laid him upon his bed and prayed that God would not bring evil upon the widow by slaying her son. He then "stretched himself upon the child three times, and cried unto the Lord, and said, O Lord my God, I pray thee, let this child's soul come into him again" (1 Kings 17:21). After this prayer, "the soul of the child came into him again, and he revived" (1 Kings 17:22).

When Elijah brought her son back down, the woman was humbled. She repented and told Elijah, "I know that thou art a man of God, and that the word of the Lord in thy mouth is truth" (1 Kings 17:24). This time there was no sarcasm in her voice. She saw clearly this time who Elijah was and realized how good God had been to her and her son.

When I was at BYU, I took a class on women in the scriptures by Camille Fronk Olsen. She said something about the widow of Zarephath that I have never forgotten: "If we allow Him, God will take us to that place where there is no one else to help us but Him."¹ I have mulled over her comment for years, and it has come to have great personal meaning for me. As I have learned to let go and to trust the Lord, I have discovered that He has taken me to places where I know that I am sustained by His hand, and His hand alone.

It is a scary place to get to because it requires sacrifice, but I think, as the widow of Zarephath teaches us, if we want to thrive and not just merely survive on our mortal journey—it is our only choice. We must be willing to let go of our fears and trust that God is a God of abundance. We must be willing to let go of the worldly things we put our security in and put our trust in Him. We must be willing to walk to the edge of our faith—the very bottom of our barrel—and trust that He will be there.

• Woman Who Borrowed Pots •

In 2 Kings 4, we read of a widow who approached Elisha the prophet in desperation. Her husband had died and had left her with debts that she could not pay. "The creditor," she told Elisha, "is come to take unto him my two sons to be bondmen" (2 Kings 4:1). In response to her plea, Elisha asked her what she had in her house, to which she replied, "Thine handmaid hath not any thing in the house, save a pot of oil" (2 Kings 4:2). This reply suggests that she had already sold everything she owned but that it was still not enough to pay the debt.

Elisha told her to go and borrow vessels (pots) from all of her neighbors, even if they were empty. Once she had collected a great many of them she was to "shut the door upon thee and upon thy sons" (2 Kings 4:4). Then she should pour what she had into all those vessels, setting aside the ones that were filled. The widow did just as Elisha told her to do and began pouring the contents of the vessels into one another until they were full. She was astonished when, sometime into this process, she asked her son to bring her another vessel only to discover that all the vessels she had borrowed were now all filled with oil. When she told Elisha what had happened, he told her, "Go, sell the oil, and pay thy debt, and live thou and thy children of the rest" (2 Kings 4:7). She now had more than enough to save her sons and to live on—a true miracle.

The important lesson to be learned from this story is being willing to ask for help. It seems that at the times when we most desperately need help, we are the least inclined to ask for it. We clam up and shut ourselves off from others and the help they can offer. I don't think Elisha made oil "magically" appear in this woman's pot, but rather the true miracle was that he got her to open up to her neighbors and ask for help. I bet this woman's neighbors were thrilled when she came to them for help. I wouldn't be surprised if some of them intentionally let her borrow pots that had extra oil in them, knowing that she would receive it humbly from them. Sometimes, like this widow's story teaches us, it takes a real miracle for us to move past our fear—and pride—and ask others for help.

Great Woman of Shunem

And it fell on a day, that Elisha passed to Shunem, where was a great woman; and she constrained him to eat bread. And so it was, that as oft as he passed by, he turned in thither to eat bread.

And she said unto her husband, Behold now, I perceive that this is an holy man of God, which passeth by us continually.

Let us make a little chamber, I pray thee, on the wall; and let us set for him there a bed, and a table, and a stool, and a candlestick: and it shall be, when he cometh to us, that he shall turn in thither.

2 *Kings* 4:8–10

This woman lived in the town of Shunem, which is very close to where the city of Nazareth would be built in New Testament times. The account calls her a "great woman" (2 Kings 4:8). In Hebrew the word *great* indicates wealth, importance, and seniority. It is interesting that, even though we know she had a husband, this Shunemite woman unequivocally ran the show, with references to "her house," "her lands," and "her people" sprinkled throughout her story. She might even be compared to the "ideal woman" outlined in Proverbs 31, a virtuous, industrious, compassionate, and commanding woman.

When Elisha, who had recently received the mantle of the prophet from Elijah, passed through Shunem, this great woman "constrained him to eat bread" (2 Kings 4:8) in her house. After that, Elisha stopped at her house every time he passed through Shunem. After a while, the Shunemite woman told her husband, "Behold now, I perceive that this is an holy man of God, which passeth by us continually" (2 Kings 4:9). She was perceptive to the Spirit and had felt a confirmation of Elisha's calling from God. Feeling this, she wanted to keep him close. She told her husband to make "a little chamber" (2 Kings 4:10) for him. The words *little chamber* mean "roof-room" or "loft" in Hebrew. It was customary for a guest to be lodged in the upper rooms of the house.

This room, however, was unique because it was to be specifically set aside for Elisha's use. It was furnished with a bed, a table, a stool, and candlestick. The Shunemite woman wanted Elisha to know that he was always welcome, that he had a place in her home.

I once attended a stake conference in which a visiting General Authority shared practical advice about how to teach our family the gospel. His easy-to-follow advice was to hang pictures of the temple and other gospel related things on our walls, to put inspirational quotes on the fridge (where he said teenage boys were most likely to see them), and to have gospel reading materials in places where people tended to sit, such as by the kitchen counter or table. Just as the Shunemite woman made room in her home for Elisha, doing

these things is literally making space in our homes for the prophet and his teachings.

Besides making physical space in our home for the prophet, we also must make spiritual space in our hearts. When I was pregnant with my first child, my midwife asked me a very interesting question. I was days away from delivery, and instead of asking me if I had everything all ready for the birth, she asked, "Do you have room for this child?"

"Oh, yes," I told her. "We have the crib set up and the spare room decorated for him."

"Good," she said, "that is an important step, but that only answers part of my question. Do you have room for this baby, this new person, in your heart?"

I have asked myself this question with every baby since. "Do I have room?" I have discovered that sometimes the room is first made in my heart, which prompts me to rearrange my life and house to make physical space for a new person. Other times, when my heart has been less willing, the act of physically making room—moving things around and finding a physical place for a baby in my life—has opened the room in my heart. I think something similar happens to us with the gospel was well.

Sometimes, like the Shunemite woman, we are perceptive to things of the Spirit and our hearts open first. At these times, we have plenty of room for prophetic and scriptural counsel and embrace them wholeheartedly. Other times we must go through the physical process of clearing out our spiritual and emotional "house" to make room for things of the Spirit. At these times, we may feel like we don't have room for prophetic counsel in our lives. We may even feel constrained and quashed by it. Yet as Alma taught, "if ye *give place*, that a seed may be planted in your heart, behold, . . . if ye do not cast it out by your unbelief . . . it will begin to swell within your breasts" (Alma 32:28; emphasis added). If we want to know the truth of what the prophet teaches, we must first make room—no matter how slight—for it in our hearts and in our lives.

Making a room for the prophet in her house turned out to be a good thing for the Shunemite woman. Moved by her kindness, Elisha desired to give her a blessing in return. During one of his visits, he asked her what he could do for her. Would she like him to speak to the king on her behalf, or maybe put in a good word for her with the captain of the guard? To both requests she replied in the negative, stating simply, "I dwell among mine own people" (2 Kings 4:13). In other words, she was secure and content just as she was. There was nothing that Elisha could offer that she needed.

This contentment and sense of well-being is surprising considering what we learn about her. Elisha, knowing there must be something he could do for her, asked his servant Gehazi what he thought. Gehazi pointed out that the Shunemite woman "hath no child, and her husband is old" (2 Kings 4:14). Despite not having children, and perhaps not even having hope of a child, the Shunemite woman was content. This is so different from the majority of barren women in the scriptures, whose grief over their loss and struggle for children is the main subject of their story.

Instead, the Shunemite woman seems to have accepted her situation and learned to be happy just as she was. I don't think this means she didn't want children or that she had not grieved and hoped for them. I'm sure she had. Yet it also seems that she had reconciled herself to her current situation. Her desire for a child was still there, but it didn't consume her life. She had accepted it.

When Elisha called her back and told her, "About this season, according to the time of life, thou shalt embrace a son" (2 Kings 4:16), instead of responding with joy, she chastised Elisha. She told him, "Nay, my lord, thou man of God, do not lie unto thine handmaid" (2 Kings 4:16). She didn't want him giving her false hope and opening old wounds.

Despite her apparent lack of faith, things happened just as Elisha prophesied. Within a year, she had a son. I have often wondered if it is an unwritten law of the universe that as soon as we learn to accept and appreciate our current circumstances, then, and only then, will God change them. I have experienced this several times with Church callings. Whenever I have a Church calling that I dislike, it seems like I am stuck in it until I genuinely learn to love it, which is just about the time I get released. I think that often God puts us in certain situations to help us learn and grow, and when we do, He brings our problems to a close and moves us on to a new challenge.

Several years later, when the Shunemite woman's son was older, he was out with his father in the field when he began to complain that his head hurt. The field workers carried the boy back to his mother, where he "sat on her knees till noon, and then died" (2 Kings 4:20).

What a tragic thing to happen! The child she had waited for so long, her gift from God, was quickly and unexpectedly taken away from her.

Surprisingly, her response to this tragedy was not one of despair. When she saw that her son was dead, she took him up to the room she had prepared for Elisha and laid him on the prophet's bed and shut the door. Then, astonishing her husband, she told him to get one of the donkeys saddled up because she was going to see Elisha. "Wilt thou go to him to day?" asked her husband, "It is neither new moon, nor sabbath" (2 Kings 4:23). Those were the traditional days of worship. She reassured him, "It shall be well," (2 Kings 4:23). These are remarkable words for someone whose only son had just died in her arms.

She rode hard, and when she arrived at Elisha's house, Gehazi met her and asked how her husband and son were doing. Instead of telling him that her son was dead, she said, "It is well" (2 Kings 4:26). Either this was a blatant lie, designed to avoid talking about a painful subject, or it was a remarkable statement of faith. Based on what we know of this woman's character, I'm inclined to think it was the latter.

In fact, the word she actually used in Hebrew is *shalom* which means "peace, quiet, tranquility, contentment."[1] Her use of this word helps us see that, despite the difficulty of her situation, she was still at peace. Her words are reminiscent of the pioneer hymn "Come, Come Ye Saints" in which the refrain of "All is well, all is well" is the commanding message of the song.[2] President Uchtdorf taught,

I am very much aware that all was not well with these Saints. They were plagued by sickness, heat, fatigue, cold, fear, hunger, pain, doubt, and even death.

But despite having every reason to shout, "All is not well," they cultivated an attitude we cannot help but admire today. They looked beyond their troubles to eternal blessings. They were grateful in their circumstances. Despite evidence to the contrary, they sang with all the conviction of their souls, "All is well!" . . .

. . . They understood that happiness doesn't come as a result of luck or accident. It most certainly doesn't come from having all of our wishes come true. Happiness doesn't come from external circumstances. It comes from the inside—regardless of what is happening around us.

The pioneers knew that, and with that spirit they found happiness in every circumstance and in every trial—even in those trials that reached down and troubled the deep waters of their very souls.[3]

Just like the early pioneers, whose faith sustained them through hardships, this Shunemite woman seems to have had faith that whether her son lived again or not, that everything would be all right. She was faithfully optimistic.

Yet, when she was taken in to meet Elisha, she could not restrain her grief. She fell at his feet and cried. Gehazi tried to pry her away, but Elisha said, "Let her alone; for her soul is vexed within her: and the Lord hath hid it from me, and hath not told me" (2 Kings 4:27). The woman then told Elisha what had happened. "Did I desire a son of my lord? did I not say, Do not deceive me?" (2 Kings 4:28). She wasn't asking Elisha to heal her son. She seemed to be looking for comfort and asking him to help her understand what had happened. Why would God give her a son, only to take him away so soon?

Instead of answering her question, Elisha prepared to leave. He had faith that he could heal this woman's son, and he gave Gehazi his staff and told him to leave immediately, not stopping for any reason, and to go lay it on the child's face. Despite just having had a long trip herself, the Shunemite woman told Gehazi that she would accompany him, showing complete faith in Elisha's instructions. When they arrived at her home, Gehazi laid Elisha's staff on the child's face but nothing happened.

When Elisha finally arrived at the house, he locked himself in his room with the child and prayed to the Lord. Elisha seems to have received instructions during his prayer as to how to revive the child because he "lay upon the child, and put his mouth upon his mouth, and his eyes upon his eyes, and his hands upon his hands: and he stretched himself upon the child; and the flesh of the child waxed warm" (2 Kings 4:34). Even though the child showed signs of reviving, he knew his work was not finished. He "returned, and walked in the house to and fro; and went up, and stretched himself upon him: and the child sneezed seven times, and the child opened his eyes" (2 Kings 4:35).

After this miraculous revival, Elisha called the Shunemite woman to come and told her, "Take up thy son" (2 Kings 4:36). She went into the room and, seeing her son alive, fell at Elisha's feet in gratitude and then "took up her son, and went out" (2 Kings 4:37). Her optimistic faith had seen her through. Her words had proved to be prophetic. All was well.

We have one last story about this great woman from Shunem. In 2 Kings 8, we read how Elisha, knowing that there would be great famine in the land for seven years, warned her to take her family and leave. She followed his advice, and she and her household fled to the land of the Philistines, where they lived for seven years.

After seven years, the famine ended and the Shunemite woman and her family returned to their homeland. Upon her return, she discovered that her home and her lands had been seized during her long absence. Hoping to get her house and land back, she "went forth to cry unto the king" (2 Kings 8:3). Though we don't hear her say it, we might assume that her attitude again in the face of this trial was her optimistic, "It shall be well."

It just happened that as she was making this trip, the king was speaking with Gehazi, asking to hear "all the great things that Elisha hath done" (2 Kings 8:4). Gehazi was in the middle of telling the king how Elisha had brought the Shunemite woman's son back to life when the Shunemite woman arrived! "My lord, O king," Gehazi cried. "This is the woman, and this her son, whom Elisha restored to life" (2 Kings 8:5). Talk about good timing.

The king asked her to tell her story, which she did. He must've been impressed by it because he called one of his officers over and told him, "Restore all that was hers, and all the fruits of the field since the day that she left the land, even until now" (2 Kings 8:5). She hadn't even needed to ask for her lands back; they were freely given. Once again, God took care of her.

We can learn a great lesson from the Shunemite woman. When we have faith in God's prophets and make room in our lives for their instructions, He blesses us and protects us. We can be faithfully optimistic that everything will work out just like it should. If the Shunemite woman were here today, I'm sure that her words of advice, no matter what magnitude of trial you are facing, would be the same. It shall be well.

• New Moon •

The Hebrew calendar is lunar based, so each new moon was the beginning of a new month. The Hebrew word for *month* is *hodesh*, which means "new moon." Because it was the basis of their calendar, it was extremely important to the Jews to know the exact time in which the moon appeared. Some people's job was to watch the moon. When the first sliver of the new moon appeared, these watchers would blow trumpets and light fires on the hills to signal the beginning of the new month (see Psalm 81:3).

The new moon was also a mandated day of celebration and rest, like that of the Sabbath and other holy days. It was observed with the offering of a burnt sacrifice (see Numbers 28:11), the cessation of work and commerce, and family meals (see 1 Samuel 20:18–24). Like the Sabbath, it was a time of new beginning and renewal, a time to reflect on one's relationship with God.

Throughout the Old Testament, the Israelites observed the new moon with varying degrees of faithfulness. During times of righteousness, they honored it, but during times of wickedness, it became an empty practice, entangled with idol worship (see Hosea 2:11 and Isaiah 1:13–14). We no longer celebrate the new moon as a holy day,[4] but I have a friend who makes it a point to set "new moon" intentions each month, using it as a time to check in with God. I think that is a neat way to honor our ancient Jewish roots while at the same time working on our own spiritual growth.

The *Little Maid*

And the Syrians had gone out by companies, and had brought away captive out of the land of Israel a little maid; and she waited on Naaman's wife.

And she said unto her mistress, Would God my lord were with the prophet that is in Samaria! For he would recover him of his leprosy.

And one went in, and told his lord, saying, Thus and thus said the maid that is of the land of Israel.

2 Kings 5:2–4

The Bible is amazing in its ability to tell meaningful stories and paint dynamic characters in few words. One example is the story of the little maid, told in 2 Kings 5. We only have four sentences about her, but they tell us a remarkable amount about this little girl and the part she played in one of the most miraculous healings in the Old Testament.

This girl lived in the household of Naaman, the captain of the guard for the Syrian king. Naaman was a "great" and "honourable" man, who was "a mighty man in valour" (2 Kings 5:1). Through Naaman, the Lord had brought victories to the Syrian army. One of these victories was against the northern kingdom of Israel. It was customary for the victorious Syrians to carry off anything valuable, including slaves. Among these slaves seized after the victory over Israel was a little girl—the scriptural account simply calls her "a little maid"—who became the servant of Naaman's wife.

Naaman had one significant problem that neither his money nor valor could fix: he was a leper. He had tried everything he could think of to cure himself, without success. His situation distressed many people, including the King of Syria and, I'm sure, his wife. One day while waiting upon Naaman's wife, the little maid told her mistress, "Would God my lord [Naaman] were with the prophet that is in Samaria! For he would recover him of his leprosy" (2 Kings 5:3).

I always envision Naaman's wife crying while the little maid is doing some sort of task for her, putting on her shoes or brushing her hair. Then, moved by the distress of her mistress, the little maid found herself unable hold back her expression of faith. I think the warmth of the little maid's exclamation gives us insight into her feelings. Despite her status as a slave and the fact that she had been forcibly taken from her home by Namaan's military campaigns, she evidently had great love for her mistress and her master.

Her expression of love and faith was overheard by another servant who told Naaman about the prophet in Samaria whom the little maid said could cure his leprosy. The fact that this other servant gave credence to the little maid's words tells us that she was honest and had integrity. It is evident that, before she was taken captive, she had been taught to have faith in God and in His prophet. Perhaps she had come from a religious home and had parents who also believed in the miracles and teachings of God's prophet. We have no idea how old this little maid was, but we can assume by the Hebrew word used for her that she was under twelve—a Primary child! I can only imagine that her mother, wherever she happened to be, would have been proud to know that what she had taught her daughter had stuck with her.

The result of the little maid's faith was that her expression of confidence made it all the way up to the king of Syria, who, desiring to see his captain of the guard healed, sent a letter to the king of Israel telling him that he was sending Naaman to him, "that thou mayest recover him of his leprosy" (2 Kings 5:6). When the king of Israel got the letter, he rent his clothes with worry, thinking that the king of Syria was looking for a reason to provoke him. He cried, "Am I God, to kill and to make alive, that this man doth send unto me to recover a man of his leprosy?" (2 Kings 5:7).

When Elisha, the prophet, heard of the king's distress, he sent him a message telling him that when Naaman arrived, he should send him to Elisha and "he shall know that there is a prophet in Israel" (2 Kings 5:8). Naaman, with great pomp and importance, came to Elisha only to be met by his servant who told Naaman to go and wash himself seven times in the Jordan River. Naaman was incredibly angry at being denied an audience with Elisha and with the simplicity of the solution. "Are not . . . [the] rivers of Damascus, better than all the waters of Israel?" he exclaimed. "May I not wash in them, and be clean?" (2 Kings 5:12). He was just about to return home in anger when several of his servants came forward and reiterated the faith-filled sentiments of the little maid. They asked him, "But father, if the prophet had bid thee do some great thing, wouldest thou have not done it?" Why then, they inquired, would he not do a simple thing and "wash, and be clean" (2 Kings 5:13).

I sometimes feel like Naaman, especially when I watch general conference. I'll admit that every time I approach conference with eager anticipation of some great announcement or news of some great revelation, I have been guilty of feeling disappointed or discouraged, wishing for something big—something important—to do. Instead, I am told to read my scriptures, to pray, to not get angry, to forgive others, to attend the temple, to serve humbly in my calling, and to love others. These are the seemingly "small" things that, like Naaman, we may want to push aside or ignore because of their simplicity. It is much harder to be consistently obedient to the small things than it is to be spontaneously enthusiastic about the big ones. Yet just like Naaman, it is the small and simple things we do each day that clean and purify our souls.

Humbling himself, Naaman followed his servants' advice and went and washed in the Jordan River. "His flesh came gain like unto the flesh of a little child, and he was clean" (2 Kings 5:14). Naaman had already demonstrated faith in God and in his prophet by traveling all the way to Israel. Yet it wasn't until he followed the prophet's advice and acted on it himself that he gained a sure testimony. "Now I know," Naaman told his company, "that there is no God in all the earth, but in Israel" (2 Kings 5:15).

The little maid is an awesome example of a missionary. She shared her faith enthusiastically with the people she cared about, and the result was not just a miraculous healing but also the conversion of Naaman and presumably his family. Her example gives me strength because I often feel discouraged with missionary work. No one I've shared the gospel with has yet joined the Church. Not long ago, when I was feeling discouraged with my attempts at missionary work, a friend reminded me that my job is not to change people or convert them to the gospel—the Holy Ghost is the only one who can do that. My job is simply to open my mouth and invite people to "come and see."

Several years ago in Utah, the Church put up billboards along the freeway with a picture of Temple Square and the caption "Come and See." A sister in my Relief Society remarked that she had thought these advertisements gimmicky until she realized that Jesus had used the phrase "come and see." In John chapter 1 when several people asked Jesus where he lived, he responded, "Come and see," (John 1:39) and invited them to his home to listen to his words. Among those who came and saw was Andrew, the brother of Simon Peter. He was impressed by the way Jesus lived and spoke and went back and told his brother that he had found the Messiah. After that, Andrew and his brother Simon Peter followed Jesus for the rest of their lives.

As Jesus demonstrated, much of our missionary work is simply inviting people to "come and see" the way we live and sharing with them our simple testimonies. Like the little maid, we need to open our mouths and not be afraid to share the words that the Holy Ghost puts into our minds and hearts. The Lord promises us in Doctrine and Covenants 33:10 that if you "open your mouths," then "they shall be filled." When it comes to missionary work, I think we could all learn a lesson from the little maid and enthusiastically live and share our faith without fear. We never know what miracles may happen because of simple, childlike faith.

Athaliah

But when Athaliah the mother of Ahaziah saw that her son was dead,
she arose and destroyed all the seed royal of the house of Judah.

2 Chronicles 22:10

An idolatrous, sinful, and violent woman, Athaliah was the daughter of King Ahab and Queen Jezebel of the kingdom of Israel.[1] King Jehosaphat of Judah, who spent his life forging peace and "doing that which was right in the sight of the Lord" (2 Chronicles 20:32), arranged for her to marry his son Jehoram as a political alliance between the two kingdoms. But just as her mother had done, Athaliah brought the worship of Baal to Judah, and as one scholar put it, "transferred the poison of idolatry into Jerusalem's veins."[2]

Jehoram only ruled for eight years before dying. His oldest son, Ahaziah, took the throne with Athaliah as his chief counselor. She influenced her son to do "evil in the sight of the Lord . . . to his destruction" (2 Chronicles 22:3–4). After only one year as king, Ahaziah was killed in battle. Athaliah recognized an opportunity to seize the throne. But Ahaziah's sons—her grandsons—were the rightful heirs to the throne, so she "arose and destroyed all the seed royal of the house of Judah" (2 Chronicles 22:10).

What type of woman murders her own grandsons? A despotic and cruel woman, she came close to stamping out the line of Judah, the promised lineage from which the Messiah would be born. She was stopped only by the intervention of a righteous woman, Jehosheba, who rescued her nephew, Athaliah's grandson Joash, and hid him in the temple (see Jehosheba on page 244).

After her bloody murders, Athaliah reigned for six years as the sole ruler—one of only two women who ever sat on the throne of Judah.[3] During her reign, she suppressed worship of Jehovah and forced worship of Baal and Asherah. She even had parts of Solomon's temple pulled down and used to build a temple for Baal (see 2 Chronicles 24:7). After six years, Jehoiada, the high priest of the temple, led the people in a revolt against her. He brought eight-year-old Joash out of hiding and crowned him as king.

When Athaliah "heard the noise of the people running and praising the king" (2 Chronicles 23:12), she went to the temple where she saw Josah standing "at his pillar" with all the princes and the people praising his coronation (2 Chronicles 23:13). She rent her clothes and yelled treason. Jehoiada ordered the soldiers to kill her, but outside of the temple so she would not defile it. The soldiers pursued her until "she was come to the entering of the horse gate by the king's house, they slew her there" (2 Chronicles 23:15). Like her mother, Jezebel, who was killed by dogs, she too died an ignoble death among animals.

The people tore down all worship of Baal, and "the people of the land rejoiced: and the city was quiet, after that they had slain Athaliah with the sword" (2 Chronicles 23:21). Apparently, no one—not even her family—was sad to see her go. She lived by violence and she died by violence. Or, as Christ would later teach, "All they that take the sword shall perish with the sword" (Matthew 26:52).

Jehosheba

But Jehosheba, the daughter of king Joram, sister of Ahaziah, took Joash the son of Ahaziah, and stole him from among the king's sons which were slain; and they hid him, even him and his nurse, in the bedchamber from Athaliah, so that he was not slain.

2 Kings 11:2

Jehosheba (who is also called Jehoshabeath) was the daughter of Athaliah and the granddaughter of Jezebel, two of the most wicked women in the entire Bible.[1] Jezebel is notorious for her persecution of the prophet Elijah and promoting goddess and idol worship throughout the kingdom of Israel (see page 223). Jezebel's daughter was Athaliah, who when her son Ahaziah took the throne of Judah, became her son's primary advisor and "was his counsellor to do wickedly" (2 Chronicles 22:3). When Ahahziah died, Athaliah claimed the throne, and to make sure her reign was uncontested, she murdered the remaining royal family of Judah, including all her grandsons. Athaliah was not the best role model to have for a mother.

Despite her unfortunate family, Jehosheba chose to become a righteous woman. 2 Chronicles 22:11 tells us that she was married to Jehoiada, who was the high priest of Solomon's temple and an incredibly good man.[2] In a time when many in Israel, including her own family, were engaged in worshiping false deities, Jehosheba chose to worship Jehovah, the one true God.

Jehosheba witnessed her mother's bloody rise to power and did not sit idly by and watch. By some miraculous intervention, Joash, one of Ahaziah's sons, was not killed. Jehosheba found the baby and was able to steal him "from among the king's sons which were slain" (2 Chronicles 22:11). She took little Joash, and his wet nurse, and hid them in a bedchamber in the palace so that Athaliah would not find them. When it was safe, she moved Joash and his nurse to the temple, where she and her husband hid them for six years. When Joash was about seven years old, Jehoiada brought him out of hiding and placed him on the throne. The people of Judah rallied around him, and Athaliah was killed by her soldiers.

Jehosheba's rescue of Joash was heroic, but she is also an incredible figure because she was a "chain breaker." Most of us are familiar with God's commandment that says, "Thou shalt not make unto thee any graven image. . . . Thou shalt not bow down thyself to them, nor serve them" (Exodus 20:4–5), but we may not have paid much attention to what God tells us the consequences is of breaking that law. He states, "For the Lord thy God am a jealous God, visiting the iniquity of the fathers upon the children unto the third and fourth generation" (Exodus 20:5). God's promise is that if we worship—place our trust and faith—in something other than Him, it will result in wickedness and injustice not just for us but for generations of our posterity.

That might seem like a harsh punishment, but it is the natural one. All of the choices we make in life affect the lives of others, including the lives of those who will come after us. Our posterity not only inherits things such as eye color or heart disease from us but also cultural, emotional, and spiritual patterns. For example, an ancestor's choice to leave the Church does not just affect them but means that their children, grandchildren, and maybe even their great-great-grandchildren will be raised without a testimony of Jesus Christ. From our ancestors, we might also have inherited patterns of gossiping, judging, speaking unkindly, breaking the Sabbath, holding grudges, and becoming easily angered or offended. Or even more serious, we may have inherited patterns of sexual or verbal abuse, abandonment, or addiction.

Jehosheba's story gives us hope that with the guidance of the Holy Ghost, we don't have to repeat the mistakes our parents, grandparents, or great-grandparents made. Jehosheba had inherited a very wicked and messed-up family situation. Her parents and grandparents were both entrenched deeply in the practice of goddess worship, building groves and high places in which sins such as sexual perversions and child sacrifice were practiced. Jehosheba, by her good choices, broke that chain of behavior. She broke out of the pattern of idolatry, sin, and dysfunction she had inherited and forged a new path for herself. Because of her faith in God (and I think marrying a good, faithful man), her life was much better than that of her grandmother and her mother.

We all have chain-breakers like Jehosheba somewhere in our family tree. One of them in my family was Margaret Jones. Margaret was born in Wales in the 1870s. At the age of ten, she lost her mother and was abandoned by her father, who went to Australia. She and her younger sister had to fend for themselves. By the age of sixteen, she had given birth to two illegitimate children in a workhouse. Eventually she married and had five children, one of whom was my great-grandmother, but her husband soon proved to be a drunk who abused her and the children. After divorcing him, she was baptized, along with some of her children, into the LDS Church. Her life was on the upswing, but she later became pregnant with twins, out of wedlock, and was excommunicated.

Her story could have ended there, without any chains being broken, but it didn't. Despite all odds, Margaret's daughter, my great-grand-mother, came to the United States, married a Mormon boy, and settled down in Idaho. Eventually she and her husband sent for the rest of her family, including Margaret, who had married the father of her twins and been rebaptized into the Church. Now, more than a hundred years later, many people in Margaret's posterity are righteous and prosperous members of the Church. Her choice to join the Church and her even harder choice to *rejoin* the Church after excommunication had a direct impact on my life. I am grateful for her courage.

Being a chain-breaker is not easy, but it is possible when we rely upon the power of Jesus Christ and embrace truth with our whole souls. Good choices have the power to work miracles, not just for us but for generations. Dawn Armstrong, the missionary mom from the movie *Meet the Mormons*—who has her own incredible chain-breaking story—said, "One choice can change everything. And then that one choice turns into another amazing choice and just, like, one bad choice can spiral into just despair and hopelessness, good choices can turn into miracles and potential unrealized."[3]

Jehosheba's story is a testament to the powerful impact that good choices can have. She teaches us that we don't have to allow our families' choices to shape the type of person we become. All it takes is one person to make a good choice and follow the Lord to change the future for generations upon generations. Unfortunately, the opposite is also true, that it only takes one person who chooses to turn *away* from the gospel and from the Lord for generations to wander in darkness until another "Jehosheba" emerges and chooses to embrace the light again.

"One choice can change everything."

Gomer

And the Lord said to Hosea, Go, take unto thee a wife of whoredoms and children of whoredoms: for the land hath committed great whoredom, departing from the Lord. So he went and took Gomer the daughter of Diblaim.

Hosea 1:2–3

The story of Hosea and Gomer is one of the best loved stories in the whole standard works. Not only is their story a powerful allegory of God's infinite capacity to forgive, but it also teaches us important lessons about the undying nature of God's love for each of us.[1]

Hosea was a prophet at the time of King Jeroboam II, in the northern tribes of Israel, and peached during a time when the people were in a state of great wickedness and decline. He was the only prophet from the northern kingdom to leave written records behind. Not long after his ministry, Israel fell to the Assyrians and the people were taken captive. Hosea's mission was to warn the people to turn back to God. His writings greatly influenced the prophets who followed, including Isaiah, Jeremiah, and Ezekiel (see Isaiah 40–66; Jeremiah 2, 3; Ezekiel 16, 33). Hosea was called to prophesy and warn the people in a unique way. Hosea 1:2 tells us that God commanded him to "take unto thee a wife of whoredoms." This doesn't necessarily mean that he was supposed to marry a harlot, but that he was to marry a woman from among the people who had "committed great whoredom, departing from the Lord" (Hosea 1:2). Hosea did as God commanded him and married a woman named Gomer, the daughter of Diblaim (Hosea 1:3).

It seems unusual that God would command a man as good and righteous as Hosea—a prophet—to marry a woman who had been brought up in idolatry and who, as she later proved, had adultery in her heart. Yet Hosea's marriage to Gomer was, from the start, intended to be a deeply symbolic lesson about the extent of God's love for his covenant people.

Not long after they were married, Gomer began to be unfaithful to Hosea, chasing after other men. Before Hosea became aware of his wife's infidelity, Gomer bore a son whom the Lord told them to name Jezreel, a symbolic name meaning "God sowed" and prophetic of the future when the Lord would destroy the kingdom of Israel in the valley of Jezreel (see Hosea 1:4–5).[2] Sometime after Jezreel's birth, Hosea realized that Gomer was being unfaithful to him. During this time, Gomer bore two more children, a girl named Lo-ruhamah and a boy named Lo-ammi. Both names were also symbolic.[3] The word *lo* means "not" in Hebrew, and so Lo-ruhamah's name is translated as "she will not be shown compassion," and Lo-ammi's name means "not my people." These names indicate that perhaps Hosea knew that Lo-ruhuamah and Lo-ammi were not his biological children. He wrote in Hosea 2:4–5 that "they be the children of whoredoms. For their mother hath played the harlot: she that conceived them hath done shamefully."

Yet the beautiful part is that despite his wife's unfaithfulness and his knowledge that the children were not his, Hosea reached out to them with love. In chapter 2 verse 1, Hosea called his children "Ammi" and "Ruhamah," taking away the "lo" part of their name. This changes his son's name from "not my people" to "my people" and his daughter's name from "not having obtained mercy" to "having obtained mercy." If we remember that Hosea's family is symbolic of God's relationship with Israel, His covenant people, then this simple change is powerful.

It appears that after giving birth to Lo-ammi, Gomer left Hosea completely, living a life of idolatry. Hosea 2 gives a long list of things that Gomer did during her time of unfaithfulness to Hosea; she slept with other men, conceived children out of wedlock, used her beauty to attract men who could provide her with clothes and rich food, spoke lewdly, made offerings and burned incense to idols, and participated in the sexually charged worship of goddesses. Her actions grieved Hosea, and he begged her to "put away her whoredoms and out of her sight and her adulteries from between her breasts" (Hosea 2:5) and warned her that there would be consequences of her choices.

Yet despite all the promises she had broken and the hurt she had caused him, Hosea still loved her. He wrote to Gomer, and symbolically to all of Israel, that despite her transgressions against him he would, "take away the names of Baalim [idols] out of her mouth, and they shall no more be remembered by their name. And in that day I will make a covenant. . . . And I will betroth thee unto me for ever; yea, I will betroth thee unto me in righteousness, and in judgment, and in lovingkindness, and in mercies" (Hosea 2:17–19).

Hosea's response to Gomer's betrayal of him is exceptional. I think that if most of us were in the same situation as Hosea, having been betrayed by an unremorseful spouse, we would find it difficult to act with love. Hosea exhibited true godlike love toward someone who had hurt him deeply. Through his unchanging love for Gomer, Hosea demonstrated how completely and passionately God loves each one of us, no matter what we have done. It is no wonder the prophets who came after were inspired by him.

Unlike the children of Israel, who eventually get carried away captive by the Assyrians, Gomer's story does have a happy ending. After running around for years in her whorish manner, Gomer finally hit rock bottom. At the beginning of Hosea 3 God told Hosea to go to the slave market where he would find Gomer bound and being sold as a slave. In her completely humbled and degraded state, Hosea was able to buy her back, paying for her "fifteen pieces of silver, and for an homer of barley, and an half homer of barley" (Hosea 3:2).[4] His redemption of her had one condition, that she would "abide with me many days; thou shalt not play the harlot, and thou shalt not be for another man," (Hosea 3:3). Then, adding this beautiful Christlike promise, he told her, "So will I also be for thee" (Hosea 3:3).

So many beautiful lessons can be gleaned from Gomer and Hosea's story. We can see it as an example of how to forgive those who have hurt us, especially our spouses. We can see it as a story, similar to that of the prodigal son, of repentance and returning. We can also see it as a manifestation of God's love for His children. As I've thought about Gomer's story, there is one word that keeps coming to my mind—*faithful*.

The word *faithful* is used several ways in our modern vernacular. We often use it to describe the ideal type of relationship between husband and wife, that they are *faithful* to one another. We also commonly use the word faithful to describe our ideal relationship with God, such as "remaining faithful" or "being faithful to our covenants." Before studying Gomer's story, I would have told you that these were different types of faithfulness, that the type of faithfulness we have for God is different from the type of faithfulness we have for our spouse. I no longer think that is true.

Ideally in marriage, a husband and wife are striving to be unified in all things, or as God told Adam and Eve, to become "one flesh" (Genesis 2:24). Being faithful means that you are sharing the most precious parts of your body, your mind, and your heart with your spouse, and only your spouse. It is impossible to be 95 percent faithful to your marriage partner. You either are faithful or you aren't.

We can look at our relationship with the Lord the same way. When we make covenants with Him, He expects us to be 100 percent faithful to Him. Like a bridegroom, He asks for everything we have—body, mind, and spirit. He desires for us to be one with Him in every way. A covenant with God is no ordinary contract; it is a marriage covenant full of deep, abiding love. President Henry B. Eyring addressed this when he spoke about his experience teaching Hosea to a group of seminary students:

> All my life I had heard explanations of covenants as being like a contract, an agreement where one person agrees to do something and the other agrees to do something else in return.

For more reasons than I can explain, during those days teaching Hosea, I felt something new, something more powerful. This was not a story about a business deal between partners, nor about business law. This was not a story of business. This was a love story. This was a story of a marriage covenant bound by love, by steadfast love. What I felt then, and it has increased over the years, was that the Lord, with whom I am blessed to have made covenants, loves me, and you . . . with a steadfastness about which I continually marvel and which I want with all my heart to emulate.[5]

The reason God makes covenants with us is that He loves us. Like a groom loves his bride, God wants us to be with Him always and never, ever leave him. Yet I think that most of us are a lot like Gomer, falling short of perfect faithfulness to the Lord. We stray, we flounder, we doubt, we sin, we betray, and we leave. Yet just like Hosea, God's love for us never changes—no matter what we do. The real challenge, then, is for us to learn to love God like He loves us. In fact, even though Gomer and Hosea's love story is beautiful, I think the *greatest* love story of the Bible is the one between God and His children; the story that reminds us that *we* are His beloved.

The Prophetess, Wife of Isaiah

And I went unto the prophetess; and she conceived, and bare a son. Then said the Lord to me, Call his name Maher-shalal-hash-baz.

For before the child shall have knowledge to cry, My father, and my mother, the riches of Damascus and the spoil of Samaria shall be taken away before the king of Assyria.

Isaiah 8:3–4

Out of all the words Isaiah could have used to describe his wife, he chose to call her "the prophetess." This may have been simply a way as referring to her status as the wife of a prophet, like saying "Mrs. Prophet" or "Mrs. Isaiah." Yet the Hebrew word Isaiah used for her is the word *nebiy'ah* and is the same word used to describe the other prophetesses of the Bible—Miriam, Deborah, and Huldah. The use of this word seems to indicate that Isaiah's wife was a woman of similar prophetic qualities and had the ability to prophesy by the Spirit and testify of truth.

We have no direct example in the scriptures of Isaiah's wife using her prophetic gift. All we know about her is that Isaiah "went in unto her" (Isaiah 8:3) and she conceived a son, whom the Lord commanded Isaiah to name Maher-shalal-hash-baz. At first, this lack of information about Isaiah's wife, who apparently was quite a spiritual figure, is disappointing. As is, her story is kind of boring.

Yet as I have pondered her story, I've begun to see her in a different light. It is true her story is very quiet—there is no leading people across an ocean, destroying a foreign army, or interpreting ancient scripture—she is just a woman, taking care of her family. In that respect, she is very much like each of us. It is unlikely that most of us will do something huge that will get our names in the history books, but we each can be "prophetesses" within our own sphere of influence and within our own families. As righteous women, we may live our life simply and quietly, but we do it with great power.

Let's just imagine for a minute what life must have been like for Isaiah's wife. She was married to a man who spent most of his time composing and delivering poetic sermons to the people of Judah, most of whom did not like him or listen to him. She would have understood the isolation and the exhaustion that can come from having a husband in an important and time-demanding calling. She also would have understood the sacrifices made to be supportive and faithful to your faith when it is unpopular. In fact, when I imagine Isaiah's wife, I imagine the wives of our modern-day prophets and the sacrifices they have made to support their husband's prophetic call. I wonder if Isaiah's wife would agree with something something written about Marjorie Pay Hinckley, that "[it was] her

own belief—that when you know the Church is true there is no such thing as working too hard."[1]

In addition to her being married to a prophet, both of her sons were given very strange and prophetic names. Her oldest son was named Shear-Jashub, whose name means "the remnant shall return" (Isaiah 10:21) and was prophetic of the future gathering of Israel. The Lord also commanded Isaiah to name of their second son Maher-shalal-hash-baz, which means "destruction is imminent" (2 Nephi 20:6)—a name which was prophetic of the destruction that would soon come upon the Jewish nation. She literally, by giving birth to her sons, "brought forth" prophecy. Her sons were living testaments to what she believed and what she knew would soon befall her people.

Also, I bet her son's names were strange even back then and that every time someone asked her children's names, she had opportunities to explain what they meant; daily opportunities to prophesy! I have sometimes felt like Isaiah's wife in this respect because several of my children have somewhat unusual Bible names—Asher, Abraham, and Tabitha. I often have opportunities to tell people the Bible stories behind my children's names and explain why my husband and I chose those names for them. Instead of being annoyed by those experiences, I have relished them as opportunities to share my faith and my testimony with others.

Isaiah, and perhaps his wife as well, understood the important role his children played in his ministry. In Isaiah 8:18, he wrote, "I and the children whom the Lord hath given me are for signs and for wonders in Israel." The Lord even commanded Isaiah to take

Shear-Jashub with him when he met with King Ahaz to warn him of the upcoming war. In this meeting, Isaiah warned Ahaz of the impending doom and destruction that was coming to his people because of their wickedness, but he also bore testimony to Ahaz of the coming of Jesus Christ, prophesying, "Behold, a virgin shall conceive, and bear a son, and shall call his name Immanuel. Butter and honey shall he eat, that he may know to refuse the evil, and choose the good." (Isaiah 7:14–15). The presence of Shear-Jashub, whose name meant "a remnant shall return," was a small, but powerful prophetic reminder of the hope that lay in the future.

I think that perhaps we often underestimate the importance of the small, but daily ways, in which we contribute to God's kingdom. Sometimes it may seem that our contributions to God's kingdom are small—bearing your testimony, supporting your husband in his calling, being a good visiting teacher, accepting callings, paying your tithing, teaching others, attending the temple, raising children. These small things can seem insignificant, especially compared to the big earth-shaking stories we see on the news or read about in history.

I want to challenge you to look at things differently. Look closely at the situation and the circumstances in which God has placed you. They may not be your "ideal" circumstances, but withhold judgment on them for a moment and try to see your situation for what it is. In what ways has the Lord blessed you? Why has God put you where you are? Is there someone here who needs you? What are you passionate and interested in? How might you use that passion to be an instrument in God's hands? What do you have an abundance of? How can you share that with someone who needs it? How can you, like Isaiah's wife, be a "prophetess" in your current situation? What ways can you share your love for Jesus Christ?

Do you get any ideas? If so, I hope you will act on them because as our civilization grows increasingly wicked, like that of the Jews in the days of Isaiah, it will become even more important to find small, everyday ways to stand for our faith and to share our testimony. We may not be called to lead an army or guide people across the desert, but we can all be "prophetesses" by listening to the Spirit and being willing to "stand as witnesses of God at all times and in all things, and in all places that ye may be in" (Mosiah 18:9). Do not underestimate your potential.

Huldah

And Hilkiah, and they that the king had appointed, went to Huldah the prophetess, the wife of Shallum the son of Tikvath, the son of Hasrah, keeper of the wardrobe; (now she dwelt in Jerusalem in the college:) and they spake to her to that effect.

And she answered them, Thus saith the Lord God of Israel, Tell ye the man that sent you to me.

2 Chronicles 34:22–23

When Lehi dwelt in Jerusalem, it is likely that he rubbed shoulders with, and even prophesied with, many of the great Old Testament prophets such as Jeremiah, Habakkuk, Zephaniah, and Ezekiel. It is also likely that Lehi also knew one of the Old Testament's greatest female prophets—the prophetess Huldah.

Huldah lived in Jerusalem during the reign of King Josiah, who took the throne in 640 BC. Like Deborah (see page 137), she was described as a "prophetess," meaning she possessed the spiritual gift of prophecy. Huldah was married to a man named Shallum, who was the "keeper of the wardrobe" (2 Chronicles 34:22). We don't know what that meant, but it could be that he oversaw the king's royal clothing or oversaw the priestly clothing in the temple.

We also know that Huldah dwelt in the "college" (2 Chronicles 34:22). The word *college* in Hebrew is *mishneh*, which means "second, or repetition." Some scholars have taken this to mean that she lived in a place where the oral tradition was preserved and taught, and Jewish tradition maintains that she had a school in Jerusalem. Another thought is that the college (*mishneh*) was a "second" or newer part of Jerusalem. Camille Fronk Olsen explained, "Believed to be the newly developed area in the western quarter of the city bordered by Hezekiah's twenty-three foot wall, the Mishneh became home to the city's more recent inhabitants. Refugees who fled the northern kingdom with the Assyrian invasion made up some of the original occupants of the Mishneh. Because Lehi and Sariah were descendants of the tribe of Manasseh, which was assigned land in the territories of what became the northern kingdom, they may have lived in this quarter along with other descendants of Israelites refugees—and in 622 BC, at the same time as Huldah."[1]

It had been about one hundred years since the Assyrians had destroyed and scattered the ten tribes of the northern kingdom of Israel. It is interesting to think about Huldah and Lehi and Sariah being connected and perhaps even knowing and interacting with each other in Jerusalem. It connects the Bible and the Book of Mormon in an intriguing way.

This was not a peaceful time to live, but it helped that King Josiah was a righteous king. At sixteen, he had a conversion moment and "began to seek after the God of David his father" (2 Chronicles 34:3). At twenty, he began a widespread purge throughout all of Judah to get rid of idolatrous worship. At twenty-six, he turned his attention to repairing Solomon's temple, which had been used by previous kings for the worship of Baal and Asherah.

While the temple was being repaired, Hilkiah, the high priest, found "a book of the law of the Lord given by Moses" (2 Chronicles 34:14). We don't know what document this was, but some scholars speculate that it was the book of Deuteronomy (which deals extensively with the Mosaic law) or even the complete five books of Moses. When Josiah's scribe read him the book, he rent his clothes because he realized that "our fathers have not kept the word of the Lord, to do after all that is written in this book" (2 Chronicles 34:21). His words suggest that the scriptures, or at least the words of Moses, had been lost (or disregarded) and that the people had been following traditions that were not correct. Josiah understood that the calamities that had come upon Israel happened because they had not been following God's law.

Josiah commanded Hilkiah the priest and some of his trusted servants and scribes to "go, enquire of the Lord for me, and for them that are left in Israel and in Judah, concerning the words of the book that is found" (2 Chronicles 34:21). In response to his request, Hilkiah and "they that the king had appointed" (2 Chronicles 34:22) took the book to Huldah to have her verify the authenticity of its words, and to know what King Josiah should do.

Again, just as with the story of Deborah, one of the most surprising things about Huldah's story is the casual way in which the biblical author refers to her story; unsurprised that a king and a priest would ask a woman for prophetic counsel even when other male prophets like Jeremiah and Lehi were plentiful in Jerusalem. Scholar Claudia V. Camp wrote, "Modern readers, unaccustomed to thinking of ancient women in positions of authority, may find Huldah's story remarkable. The biblical evidence, however, makes clear that prophecy was a role open to women on an equal basis with men."[2]

This is an important point for modern women, especially Latter-day Saint women, to remember—that prophecy is a gift available equally to men and women. Yet it is also important to differentiate between the position of "the prophet" and the gift of prophecy, which is a spiritual gift. Elder Dallin H. Oaks explained,

> When we hear the word *prophet* in our day, we are accustomed to thinking of *the* prophet. These words signify him who holds the prophetic *office* and is sustained as *the* prophet, seer, and revelator. The priesthood offices and powers exercised by the President of the Church are unique. As we learn in the Doctrine and Covenants, it is given to him to have "all the gifts of God which he bestows upon the head of the church."
>
> The spiritual gift of prophecy is quite different. As we read in the Book of Revelation, "The testimony of Jesus is the spirit of prophecy" (Rev. 19:10). The Prophet Joseph Smith relied on this scripture in teaching that "every other man who has the testimony of Jesus" is a prophet. . . .
>
> The scriptures often use the word *prophet* and its derivatives in the broad sense of one who teaches and testifies of God. . . . In our day, Elder Joseph Fielding Smith declared that "all members of the Church should seek for the gift of prophecy, for their own guidance, which is the spirit by which the word of the Lord is understood and his purpose made known."

It is important for us to understand the distinction between a prophet, who has the *spiritual gift of prophecy*, and *the* prophet, who has the *prophetic office*.[3]

I have often wondered if when we teach our children the song "Follow the Prophet"[4] we aren't (unintentionally) teaching false doctrine. We put prophets like Jonah and Daniel—men with the spiritual gift of prophecy but who held no priesthood keys—on par with Adam, Enoch, Noah, Abraham, Moses, and Samuel, who had priesthood keys and held the prophetic office. Maybe I am getting too hung up on details here, but I think, like Elder Oaks said, it is important for us to differentiate. Huldah, Deborah, and Miriam could easily be included in the song "Follow the Prophet" if the way in which we are using the term *prophet* refers to the spiritual gift of prophecy. But if we mean it to refer to the prophetic office, then they wouldn't fit in (and neither would Daniel and Jonah).

Either way, Huldah is a testament that God is no respecter of persons when it comes to bestowing spiritual gifts. Elder James E. Talmage said, "No special ordination in the Priesthood is essential to man's receiving the gift of prophecy. . . . This gift may be possessed by women also."[5]

Even more remarkable than the fact that the king and his priests turned to a woman for prophetic guidance is the actual message Huldah gave them. She told Hilkiah to go back to king Josiah and tell him that the Lord "will bring evil upon this place . . . even all the curses that are written in the book" (2 Chronicles 34:24). This, she explained, was because the people had forsaken God and "burned incense unto other gods," and for that, God's "wrath shall be poured out . . . and shall not be quenched" (2 Chronicles 34:25).

Huldah told them that because King Josiah had humbled himself before God that he would be "gathered to thy grave in peace" (2 Chronicles 34:28) and that he would not see the destruction that God would bring upon his people. One may doubt the credibility of Huldah's prophecy when you know that Josiah was slain in battle by the Egyptians—not what you might call a peaceful death. Yet when one considers the incredible destruction and intense suffering (like people starving and eating their children) that befell Jerusalem when it was besieged by the Babylonians—only thirty-seven years after Huldah's prophecy—it makes Josiah's death look pretty nice.

Hilkiah and the other servants took Huldah's message back to King Josiah. Instead of giving up on his people as hopelessly lost, Josiah immediately went to work trying to teach them. He had the book of the law read throughout his entire kingdom and "made all that were present in Israel to serve, even to serve the Lord their God" (2 Chronicles 34:33). As we know, Josiah's efforts didn't save his people. It is their destruction at the hands of the Babylonians—and the complete scattering of the Jewish people—that brings an end to the Old Testament.

Huldah's role in this drama is significant and perhaps overlooked. She delivered a prophetic message of warning to Jerusalem like those of other contemporary prophets. She even used the phrase "thus saith the Lord" in her address four times, showing that she felt confident in receiving revelation from the Lord. She also gives an important female perspective, showing us that not all women (as some scholars would like us to believe) participated in the idol and goddess worship common at this time (see page 218). Huldah makes it clear that she knows that those practices were not correct and that they provoked God to anger.

Most important, though, Huldah plays an important role in the formation of our modern-day scripture. She was the first person in the Bible to declare a written document to be the word of God. Claudia V. Camp wrote, "[Huldah] authorizes what will become the core of Scripture for Judaism and Christianity. Her validation of the text thus stands as the first recognizable act in the long process of canon formation. Huldah authenticates a document as being God's word, thereby affording it the sanctity required for establishing a text as authoritative, or canonical."[6]

Huldah was truly a remarkable woman for her time and for ours. We probably owe much of our modern Bible to her subtle influence. Huldah's example has encouraged me and reminded me that women can be master scriptorians, receiving revelation from God and interpreting and speaking about the scriptures with confidence—including for, and in front of, men. Our world—full of idolatry and ripening for destruction—is not all that different that on the one in which Huldah lived. Perhaps as He did then, God needs a woman—or many women—to declare boldly and fearlessly the words written in the scriptures.

Maachah and the Queen Mothers of Judah

King Mosiah in the Book of Mormon warned his people, "If it were possible that you could have just men to be your kings, who would establish the laws of God . . . then it would be expedient that ye should always have kings to rule over you" (Mosiah 29:13). Yet King Mosiah lamented, "Because all men are not just it is not expedient that ye should have a king or kings to rule over you. For behold, how much iniquity doth one wicked king cause to be committed, yea, and what great destruction!" (Mosiah 29:16–17). This pattern certainly holds true in the Old Testament where you can trace the path to the Israelites' destruction by the wickedness of their kings. Perhaps even more interesting, though, you can directly trace the wickedness of the Israelites to the kings' *mothers*.

When each king of Judah is introduced, the scriptures record his name, age, how long he reigned, and the name of his mother, followed by either of these statements: "He did that which was right in the sight of the Lord" or "he did that which was evil in the sight of the Lord." The righteous kings were those who made efforts to tear down and stop the worship of false gods, specifically the cults of Baal and Asherah, and promote worship of Jehovah.

Righteous kings like Joash, Amaziah, Hezekiah, and Josiah all put forth varying degrees of effort to repair the temple and encourage correct worship in it.[1] In contrast, the wicked kings did just the opposite. They incorporated their worship of Baal and Asherah into the temple and other sacred rituals. This was the type of worship that prophets like Jeremiah, Ezekiel, and the prophetess Huldah warned the Israelites would lead to their destruction—which it eventually did.

The inclusion of mothers' names in these kings' histories is important because in the Judean kingdom the king's mother occupied a special place in the government. The Hebrew word that is used for her is *gebira*, which means "great lady." The *gebira* was the "great lady" or the queen mother of Judah, and some scholars think that she may have reigned as coregent with her son.[2] What is certain is that the *gebira* had significant political and spiritual influence over her son and over the kingdom.

We first see a queen mother exercising political power in the story of Solomon and his mother, Bathsheba. In 1 Kings 2, she we read how she was approached by Adonijah, David's son who had lost the throne to Solomon. Adonijah asked Bathsheba if she would approach her son and ask a favor for him because, as he said, "he will not say thee nay" (1 Kings 2:17). When Bathsheba approached her son while he sat in court, he "rose up to meet her, and bowed himself unto her . . . and caused a seat to be set for the king's mother; and she sat on his right hand" (1 Kings 2:19). While it seems that Bathsheba did not sit beside her son regularly enough for a throne to always be ready for her, it is apparent by Solomon's conduct that his mother occupied an important place in his life and in his government. Sitting on the right hand was a symbolic gesture of preference and respect. It seems to suggest that he viewed his mother as an equal, someone to take counsel *from* rather than give counsel *to*.

While Bathsheba appears to have been a righteous queen, many of the other *gebiras* after her were deeply involved in the worship of Asherah and spread their idolatrous practices throughout the kingdom. One mother, Maachah, was even removed from her place as *gebira* by her son, Asa, because she had "made an idol in a grove" (1 Kings 15:13). The word *idol* here is the Hebrew word *miphletseth*, and it means "horrid thing; a terror."[3] It is only used once in the Bible, and it comes from a rare Hebrew verb that means "to shudder" or "to be horrified."[4] Many of the idolatrous practices were tinged with sodomy and child sacrifice, but it seems that whatever Maachah did in her role of *gebira* was especially horrifying.

It is also interesting that in writing about this final destruction of the Jewish people, the prophet Ezekiel specifically blamed two queen mothers, Nehushta and Hamutal, for Judah's demise. Though he did not mention names, Ezekiel used figurative language to describe two of Judah's last kings—Jehohaz and Jehoiachin—who led the people to sin and who were both taken captive by invading armies. Ezekiel lamented for them, saying that it was because of the lioness (their mothers) who had lain "down among lions" (Ezekiel 19:2) and taken one "of her whelps, and made him a young lion" (Ezekiel 19:5) that such wickedness had come to Judah. The princes, the young lions, had been taught by their mothers to "catch the prey" and devour men and made the land desolate by "the noise of [their] roaring" (Ezekiel 19:6–7).

It may not have been fair for Ezekiel to place the whole demise of a nation upon the shoulders of two queens, but it lets us know that these women wielded a lot of influence—for good and bad—over their sons and over their people. Studying their stories can help us examine our own hearts. Are we firmly planted next to the Lord's altar, or have we planted ourselves, perhaps more deeply than we realize, near the altar of a false god (or goddess)? These queen mothers—these *gebiras*—remind us that the choices we make can determine the course of entire civilizations.

• The Kings of Judah and Their Queen Mothers •

Name of Ruler	Mother's Name	Righteous or Bad	Length of Reign	Relation	End of Reign	Other Facts	Prophet(s)
Rehoboam	Naamah the Ammonitess (1 Kings 14:21, 31; 2 Chronicles 12:13)	Bad	17 years	Son of Solomon	Died	Had 18 wives and 60 concubines who built "high places, and images, and groves, on every high hill, and under every green tree" (1 Kings 14:23)	Ahijah the Shilomite (1 Kings 14:18) Shemaiah (1 Kings 12:22; 2 Chronicles 12:15)
Abijam	Maachah, the daughter of Abishalom (1 Kings 15:2–3; 2 Chronicles 11:20–22; 13:2)	Bad	3 years	Son of Rehoboam	Died	It appears that since his son has the same mother, he married his own mother!	
Asa	Maachah, the daughter of Abishalom (1 Kings 15:10–14)	Righteous	41 years	Son of Abijam	Died	Removed his mother from her place as gebira because of her involvement in goddess worship	Hanani
Jehoshaphat	Azubah, the daughter of Shilhi (1 Kings 22:42; 2 Chronicles 20:31)	Righteous	25 years	Son of Asa	Died		
Jehoram	Unknown	Bad	8 years	Son of Jehoshaphat	Stricken by God (bowels fell out)	Married Athaliah (daughter of Jezebel) from Israel as alliance	Elijah Micaiah Elisha
Ahaziah	Athaliah (see page 242)	Bad	1 year	Son of Jehoram	Murdered by Jehu		
Athaliah	Jezebel (see page 223)	Bad	6 years	Mother of Ahaziah	Murdered by her army	Took the throne by force after she murdered her grandchildren	
Joash (Jehu Jehoash)	Zibiah of Beersheba (2 Kings 12:1; 2 Chronicles 24:1)	Righteous	40 years	Son of Ahaziah	Murdered by servants	Began to be less righteous toward the end of his life	Joel (possibly)
Amaziah	Jehoaddan of Jerusalem	Righteous	29 years	Son of Joash	Murdered by court members		Jonah

• The Kings of Judah and Their Queen Mothers (continued) •

Name of Ruler	Mother's Name	Righteous or Bad	Length of Reign	Relation	End of Reign	Other Facts	Prophet(s)
Azariah (Uzziah)	Jecholiah of Jerusalem (2 Kings 15:2–4)	Righteous	52 years	Son of Amaziah	Stricken by God (leprosy)	Isaiah makes specific prophecies about this time period.	Amos
Jotham	Jerusha, daughter of Zadok (2 Kings 15:33–34)	Righteous	18 years	Son of Amaziah	Died		Isaiah
Ahaz	Unknown	Bad	19 years	Son of Jotham	Died		Micah
Hezekiah	Abi/Abijah, the daughter of Zachariah (2 Kings 18:2–4; 2 Chronicles 29:1)	Righteous	29 years	Son of Ahaz	Died		
Manasseh	Hephzibah (2 Kings 21:1–3)	Bad	55 years	Son of Hezekiah	Died		
Amon	Meshullemeth, the daughter of Haruz of Jotbah (2 Kings 21:19–20)	Bad	2 years	Son of Manasseh	Murdered by servants		
Josiah	Jedidah, the daughter of Adaiah of Boscath (2 Kings 22:1–2)	Righteous	31 years	Son of Amon	Wounded in battle against Pharaoh of Egypt	Rebuilt the temple and found the Book of the Law that was interpreted by Huldah the prophetess	Huldah
Jehoahaz	Hamutal, the daughter of Jeremiah of Libnah (2 Kings 23:31–32)	Bad	3 month	Son of Josiah	Died in Egypt	Captured by Egyptians and taken to Egypt	Habakkuk Jeremiah Lamentations (written by Jeremiah) Ezekiel Zephaniah

• The Kings of Judah and Their Queen Mothers (continued) •

Name of Ruler	Mother's Name	Righteous or Bad	Length of Reign	Relation	End of Reign	Other Facts	Prophet(s)
Jehoiakim	Zebudah, the daughter of Pedaiah of Rumah (2 Kings 23:36–37)	Bad	11 years	Brother of Johoahaz	Died in Babylonian Siege	People forced to pay tribute to Egyptians until Egyptians overthrown by Babylonians	Huldah Habakkuk Jeremiah Lamentations (written by Jeremiah) Ezekiel Zephaniah
Jehoiachin	Nehushta, the daughter of Elnathan of Jerusalem (2 Kings 24:8–9, 12, 15)	Bad	3 months	Son of Jehoiakim	Taken captive to Babylon	He and his mother were taken captive by the Babylonians when Jerusalem was besieged	
Zedekiah	Hamutal, the daughter of Jeremiah of Libnah (2 Kings 24:18–19)	Bad	11 years	Uncle of Jehoiachin and brother of Jehoahaz	Jerusalem destroyed and taken captive to Babylon. He was the last of the Jewish kings.	Was put in as "puppet" leader by Nebuchadnezzar. In the first year of his reign, Lehi and his family left Jerusalem (see 1 Nephi 1:4)	

Women who Baked Bread for the Queen of Heaven

Then all the men which knew that their wives had burned incense unto other gods, and all the women . . . answered Jeremiah, saying,

As for the word that thou hast spoken unto us in the name of the Lord, we will not hearken unto thee.

But we will certainly do whatsoever thing goeth forth out of our own mouth, to burn incense unto the queen of heaven, and to pour out drink offerings unto her, as we have done, we, and our fathers, our kings, and our princes, in the cities of Judah, and in the streets of Jerusalem: for then had we plenty of victuals, and were well, and saw no evil.

Jeremiah 44:15–17

After the Babylonians destroyed Jerusalem, the Jews who remained in the land were afraid. They didn't know whether to stay and struggle under the Babylonians or to leave and go to Egypt where it was peaceful. Jeremiah received direction from God that the people should stay in the land. "If ye will still abide in this land," God told Jeremiah on behalf his people, "then I will build you, and not pull you down, and I will plant you, and not pluck you up. . . . I am with you to save you, and to deliver you from his hand" (Jeremiah 42:10–11).

As usual, the people didn't listen. "We will not dwell in this land," they told Jeremiah, "but we will go into the land of Egypt, where we shall see no war, nor hear the sound of the trumpet, nor have hunger of bread, and there will we dwell" (Jeremiah 42:13–14). When the people left for Egypt, Jeremiah went with them. His assignment from God was to preach unto his people, no matter where they went.

When they got to Egypt, it didn't take the people long to "burn incense, and to serve other gods, whom they knew not" (Jeremiah 44:3). It appears that it was especially the women who were burning incense to these strange gods and goddesses. God warned Jeremiah that if the people—the women—didn't stop their wickedness that He would "punish them that dwell in the land of Egypt, as I have punished Jerusalem, by the sword, by the famine, and by the pestilence: So that none of the remnant of Judah, which are gone into the land of Egypt to sojourn there, shall escape or remain" (Jeremiah 44:13–14).

Jeremiah called the women and "the men which knew that their wives had burned incense unto other gods" (Jeremiah 44:15), which was a large group, and warned them. The women responded haughtily, telling Jeremiah that they would not listen to him, "but we will certainly do whatsoever thing goeth forth out of our own mouth"

(Jeremiah 44:17). They told Jeremiah that they had a long tradition of practicing such rituals, and they were not about to give them up. They explained that in times past "we, our fathers, our kings, and our princes" burned incense to the "queen of heaven," poured out drink offerings to her, and made cakes to worship her (Jeremiah 44:17). When they had done this, they told Jeremiah, "Then had we plenty of victuals, and were well, and saw no evil" (Jeremiah 44:17). It was only when they stopped worshiping the queen of heaven that they "wanted all things" and had "been consumed by the sword and by the famine" (Jeremiah 44:18).

This logic was faulty and Jeremiah tried to explain to them that they had it backwards. It was not because they had *stopped* worshiping the "queen of heaven" but because they *had* been worshiping her that such destruction had come upon them. "The Lord could no longer bear, because of your evil doings," Jeremiah explained to them, "therefore this evil is happened unto you" (Jeremiah 44:22–23).

These Israelite women had turned to the "queen of heaven" because they felt like worshiping Jehovah had not gotten them what they wanted. The nice thing about the ancient world was that if you didn't like your assigned god, there was a plethora of ones to choose from. If praying to or worshiping one god wasn't working out for you, no problem; try someone else! We see this mentality in the story of Jonah when the sailors, who were all praying to their gods during the storm, woke Jonah up, and told him to "arise, call upon thy God, if so be that God will think upon us, that we perish not" (Jonah 1:6). *One of these gods has got to work out,* they were thinking, *so let's just pray to them all.*

That mindset might seem silly to us, who have been taught to believe in and worship one God, but we aren't all that different from the ancient sailors on Jonah's boat, or the women baking bread for the queen of heaven. How often, when our prayers and devotion do not seem to be getting us what we want, do we turn to other avenues? Do we ever find ourselves searching for things other than God to fill the voids in our life? Instead of *losing* our faith, do we just *shift* our faith and place it in another "god," someone or something we think will get us what we want?

Even though these women who baked bread to the queen of heaven were misguided in their devotion, I think that they can teach us much. First, they teach us how powerful female expressions of faith and rituals can be and how they can be powerful motivators in our life. Vanessa Ochs wrote:

> Learning about our women ancestors who worshipped a goddess doesn't mean we plan to replicate what they did. Studying their ways, however, does help us make our own rituals more women-centered. . . .
>
> The women who bake cakes for the Queen of Heaven bid us to honor their memory as we recall their practices and other women's sacred practices throughout history that have been criticized, forgotten, or suppressed.
>
> They bid us, as well, to note those aspects of our own lives and our own yearning that are not well-represented in the kinds of worship that are now available to us. Do our rituals connect us to nature, helping us to observe the cyclical changes in seasons and celebrate the particular blessings each season brings? Do they connect us to the earth, helping us to tend it and be grateful for its yield? Do they remind us

that each of us can, in our own kitchen, create a humble and lovely cake?

> The women who bake cakes for the Queen of Heaven challenge us to be sure that the rituals of our lives reflect us. They encourage us to hold on to rituals that express our agency, power, and distinctive connections to the sacred. Where such rituals are lacking, we must with wisdom and with loving ties to the traditions we have inherited, create them.[1]

On the flip side, I wonder how often we try to offer sacrifices to the Lord that are as fruitless as these cakes. It seems like today when we want to find favor with God, when we want Him to bless us with something, we step up our game. We pray harder, fast longer, go the temple more, and try to pull down blessings from heaven. Are we, like these women with their cake offerings, ever guilty of trying to "buy" God's blessings with our good works or with our piousness? The truth is that today the *only* offering that God asks of us—or will accept from us—is one of a "broken heart and a contrite spirit" (D&C 59:8).

For a long time, I thought that word *broken* meant I had to be heartbroken. Then I realized that a horse is "broken," not when its spirit has been crushed but when it has become obedient. The word *contrite* is a harder one. The Webster 1828 dictionary says that *contrite* means, "Literally, worn or bruised"[2] and seems to connote the same ideas as *heartbroken*. Yet as I thought about it, the idea of an old shoe came to mind and how when it has been "worn" and "bruised" it takes on a new shape, conforming more to that of its owner's foot. I realized that if I want to give God an acceptable offering, one that is "broken" and "contrite," it would require a transformation of who I was on the inside. My good works and pious efforts might help me in that transformation, but they themselves were not an acceptable offering. The only offering God would accept was me—broken, worn, contrite, and obedient.

After hearing the women's assertions that they would not give up their worship of the queen of heaven, Jeremiah tells them, rather sadly, that because they will not give up their traditions that they will lose the protection of God. "Behold, I will watch over them for evil, and not for good," the Lord told Jeremiah, "and all the men of Judah that are in the land of Egypt shall be consumed by the sword and by the famine, until there be an end of them" (Jeremiah 44:27).

The lesson to be learned here is twofold. First, there is beauty and power in creating our own unique rituals and expressions of faith. They can be powerful ways for us to deepen our connection to God and to connect us to our past and our future. Second, in creating such traditions we must be careful that we do not lose track of who we are worshipping—the one true God. Like these women in the book of Jeremiah, we are all in danger of idolatrous worship when we begin to put our faith in ideas, things, and rituals of our own making. God has told us that He is a "jealous God" (Exodus 20:5), not because He fears competition but because He knows that it is in Him—and Him alone—that we find what we need.

• Who Was the Queen of Heaven? •

Though we don't know for certain, we might guess that the "queen of heaven" these women were worshiping was the Canaanite goddess Astarte or the Mesopotamian Ishtar who were both linked with fertility and prosperity. The women told Jeremiah that they had made cakes for her "to worship her" (Jeremiah 44:19). That phrase can also be translated as "impressed with her image" (Jeremiah 44:19, NIV), meaning that the cakes were shaped in or marked with her image. Archeologists have found evidence of molds, shaped like goddesses, that they believe might have been used to make such breads.[3] We don't know what the women did with these cakes—if they ate them, burnt them, or just left them in front of the statue—but it is clear that they felt doing this was important for them, their families, and their nation.

Daughters of Shallum

And next unto him repaired Shallum the son of Halohesh, the ruler of the half part of Jerusalem, he and his daughters.

Nehemiah 3:12

The daughters of Shallum are in the book of Nehemiah, which even though it is placed before the book of Esther in the Bible, happened chronologically after the story of Esther. Nehemiah was the cupbearer to the Persian king Artaxerxes, who was most likely the son of Xerxes (also called Ahasuerus), the king of Esther's story. As the king's cupbearer, Nehemiah was responsible for guarding the king's cup so that it could not be poisoned. Being the cupbearer was a position of great trust and honor. He, like Esther before him, had been divinely positioned to be able to help the Jewish people in their time of need.

Nearly a hundred years before Nehemiah's time, the Persian king Cyrus had allowed the captive Jews to return to Jerusalem. Some, but not all, of the Jews returned and began to rebuild the temple. Yet because of opposition and violence, it took the Jews nearly twenty-five years to finish it. Even after the temple was rebuilt, the Jews in Jerusalem faced constant persecution and hardship.

In the first chapter of the book of Nehemiah, he wrote that, after learning of the ongoing struggles of the Jews in Jerusalem, his heart was heavy and he "sat down and wept, and mourned certain days, and fasted, and prayed before the God of heaven" (Nehemiah 1:4). Nehemiah must have been a normally upbeat person because when he took wine into King Artaxerxes, the king immediately noticed that something was wrong. Artaxerxes asked Nehemiah, "Why is thy countenance sad, seeing thou art not sick? This is nothing else but sorrow of heart" (Nehemiah 2:2).

Nehemiah told him of the hardships the Jews in Jerusalem were facing. He told the king that he wanted to return to Jerusalem and rebuild the walls. Artaxerxes and the queen,[1] who was sitting beside him, gave Nehemiah permission to return as well as royal letters that allowed him safe passage and permission to cut wood from the king's forests to use to rebuild the walls of Jerusalem.

With the support of the king and the queen, Nehemiah traveled to Jerusalem and for several days told no one what he intended to do. Instead, he and his men went out by night and surveyed the damage that had been done to the walls and to the city. Even though the damage was extensive, Nehemiah began to rally the people to begin rebuilding the wall. It seems they were hesitant until Nehemiah told them that the hand of God was with him and that he had come with the support of the king. Buoyed by Nehemiah's sense of purpose and passion, the Jews agreed to begin rebuilding the wall.

The greatest opponents of the Jews in Jerusalem at this time were the Samaritans. The name *Samaritan* means "guardians/watchers of the law." When the Jews were carried away captive into Babylon,

those who remained behind saw themselves as the guardians of the Israelite religion and holy places. These "left behind" Jews attempted to preserve the Jewish religion but also began intermarrying with nearby pagan peoples and adopting their practices. When the Jews returned to Jerusalem under the reign of Cyrus to rebuild the temple, the Samaritans were eager to help, saying, "Let us build with you: for we seek your God, as ye do; and we do sacrifice unto him" (Ezra 4:2). Yet the Jews did not view the Samaritans as being "true" Jews and didn't recognize their claim. Instead they told them, "Ye have nothing to do with us to build an house unto our God; but we ourselves together will build unto the Lord God of Israel" (Ezra 4:3).

In response, the Samaritans used every sort of guerilla tactic they could think of to oppose the rebuilding of Jerusalem and the temple, even writing the Persian king to slander the Jews and garner political support against them.[2] When Nehemiah announced his intention to rebuild the wall, he incurred the wrath of Sanballat the Horonite, the Samaritan leader, and his allies. In response to their threats, Nehemiah answered them, "The God of heaven, he will prosper us; therefore we his servants will arise and build: but ye have no portion, nor right, nor memorial, in Jerusalem" (Nehemiah 2:20).

As you can imagine, this response only increased the Samaritan violence. Jews rebuilding the wall were under constant threat of attack. Nehemiah 4:14–23 mentions how those who worked on the project carried weapons with them and took turns standing guard while the other half of the workers worked. Nehemiah described "every one with one of his hands wrought in the work, and with the other hand held a weapon" (Nehemiah 4:17).

Among the Jews whom Nehemiah listed as undertaking the work of rebuilding the wall was "Shallum the son of Halohesh, the ruler of the half part of Jerusalem, he and his daughters" (Nehemiah 3:12). We know there must have been many other women living in Jerusalem, but these daughters of Shallum are the only ones mentioned as working on rebuilding the wall. It makes me wonder what special skills they had, or what type of women they were, to have been included (and to want to have been included) in what was obviously a male-dominated endeavor. They clearly made an impression on Nehemiah, who recorded their participation.

The rebuilding was a massive undertaking and was a dangerous job. It is likely that, like the other workers, the daughters of Shallum carried weapons (which they had reason to use) because Nehemiah emphasized, "For the builders, *every one* had his sword girded by his side, and so he builded" (Nehemiah 4:17; emphasis added). Perhaps, because it was so dangerous, the Jews were motivated to rebuild the wall quickly. Nehemiah 6:15 tells us that they completed repairing and rebuilding Jerusalem's wall in just fifty-two days.

I love to imagine what it must have looked like to see these women, with a sword in one hand and a tool in the other, working alongside their father to build the fortifications for their beloved city. I am sure that these women could cook, clean, sew, and rock a baby on their hip, but they also could fight, build, and work shoulder-to-shoulder alongside the men. It is an awesome example of men and women working together. The daughters of Shallum remind us that we can't let gender roles or traditions hold us back from using our talents or passions to bless our families, our nation, and our God. When there is work to be done, it doesn't matter if you are a man or a woman; every contribution and every talent in needed.

> *"Let us build with you: for we seek your God, as ye do."*

Vashti

[King Ahasuerus] made a feast unto all his princes and his servants. . . .

On the seventh day, when the heart of the king was merry with wine, he commanded [that the chamberlains] bring Vashti the queen before the king with the crown royal, to shew the people and the princes her beauty: for she was fair to look on.

But the queen Vashti refused to come at the king's commandment by his chamberlains: therefore was the king very wroth, and his anger burned in him.

Esther 1:3, 10–12

Vashti's story is told in the first chapter of Esther. Her husband was Ahasuerus, the king of Persia. Persia was the largest kingdom in the world, and so Ahasuerus was arguably the most powerful man in the world. To celebrate his kingdom, he threw a large feast to show off his power to the neighboring kingdoms. At the same time, Vashti held her own feast for the women. It was seven days long, and on the last day, when "the heart of the king was merry with wine" (Esther 1:10), he commanded his counselors to bring Vashti, with her royal crown, so that he could show off her beauty to all the men.

Vashti flatly refused to come. She knew that what the king was asking of her was degrading to her as a woman and beneath her position as queen. I am sure that she was horrified at the thought of being paraded before a drunken crowd of men. Jewish tradition even goes so far as to speculate that when the king asked her to wear her royal crown, it might have been *all* he meant for her to wear. The king's request was a total misuse of his power and showed disregard for Vashti's feelings and dignity. No one can blame Vashti for not going.

Her firm stance against the king was impressive. She refused to be degraded or to allow a man, even her husband, to cross her personal boundaries. She set limits and bravely stood by them. I love how Vanessa Ochs portrayed her story in her fictionalized account of Vashti:

> The women saw Vashti taking care of herself by saying "no." They knew she was taking care of them too, by modeling what they often imagined doing themselves, but too rarely did. She showed that the boundaries of a woman's dignity may not be violated. She demonstrated that any woman, not just a queen, could say: "Not now, not unless it's on my terms as well, not unless I'm fully comfortable, not unless I am treated with dignity." Only a woman who is respected can be expected to show respect.
>
> "I will not go." Her words stayed in the women's heads in the days after they had left the banquet, as they brushed their daughters' hair. They could say it too, and they could teach it to their daughters. They practiced the words in their heads: "I will not go."[1]

Vashti did what we all wish we could do when people use us to gratify themselves or when they treat us with disrespect. She was bold and strong, and didn't allow herself to be forced into doing something she knew was degrading and went against her standards. She stood up against a corrupt patriarchy.

Vashti's public refusal of the king required bravery and was necessary, but it only made things worse for her and for all the women in the kingdom. Her disobedience made the king angry. More than that, though, as one of the king's counselors pointed out, "Vashti the queen hath not done wrong to the king only, but also to all the princes. . . . For this deed of the queen shall come abroad unto all women, so that they shall despise their husbands in their eyes. . . . Thus shall there arise too much contempt and wrath" (Esther 1:16–18).

Basically, this counselor was afraid that Vashti had opened a can of worms, and that if the king didn't do something, then Persia would have a regular feminist movement on its hands. This scared the king, and so he commanded that Vashti be removed as queen. He sent a proclamation throughout the land stating that "every man should bear rule in his own house" (Esther 1:22) and that "all the wives shall give to their husbands honour, both to great and small" (Esther 1:20). Feminist movement squashed, right? Wrong.

Enter Esther.

After Vashti's demotion, the king's servants brought all the fair virgins of the land to the palace to be dressed, washed, and pampered for six months. Afterward, each was given a chance to win the king's affection and become the new queen. The king chose a simple Jewish girl named Esther. Esther's heritage caused a problem when later the king's advisor, Haman, convinced the king that he should exterminate the Jews in his kingdom.

The king's decree put Esther in a hard place. Fearing political assassination, King Ahaserus had a rule that no one, absolutely no one, could come into his presence without his permission. The penalty for breaking the rule was death, plain and simple. Esther needed to talk to the king about the extermination order facing her people, but the king had not called her to be with him for more than thirty days. Perhaps this was an indication that she had fallen out of favor with him or that his affection was focused on another of his many wives.

It is ironic that Esther was facing almost the exact same problem that Vashti encountered, except that this time instead of disobeying by *not coming* before the king, Esther was disobeying by *coming* before the king. It is likely that Esther, as she considered her choices, remembered what had happened to Vashti. Yet I also think that it was very possible that Vashti influenced Esther and gave her courage. Vashti had demonstrated that you didn't have to sit idly by and let things happen to you. I wonder if Esther remembered that as she made her choice, that she didn't have to let herself, or her people, be treated unjustly without putting up a fight.

After fasting and praying, Esther dressed in her royal apparel and stood in the inner court of the king's house. Eventually the king noticed Esther, and instead of being angry, he was pleased to see her and held out his golden scepter as an indication that she could approach. Esther had blatantly disobeyed him, but instead of getting angry, he did exactly the opposite—he offered her anything she wanted, even unto half of his kingdom. This was a perfect time to ask for the king to not kill your people, right?

But Esther didn't ask for that. Instead, she invited the king and Haman to a private banquet that she had prepared for them. That night the king asked her what she wanted, but all she did was invite them to another banquet. By the second night, the king was begging Ester to tell him what she wanted and promised that he would give her anything. When he finally found out what Haman was up to and saw that he had been deceived, his attitude did a one-eighty. In fact, his heart was so changed that he sent a decree throughout all the kingdom, proclaiming that the Jews were to be honored and protected instead of killed. This change was so enormous that even thousands of years later, the Jews still celebrate the story of Esther and what she did for her people.[2]

I think that the key difference in why Esther was successful in making a long-lasting change in the lives of her people was the way that she took a one-on-one approach motivated by love and not anger or indignation. It is important to note that Vashti and Esther were in much different circumstances. Esther wasn't facing a drunken king and all his buddies, and she had more time to plan and prepare. Yet there are some key differences in how Esther approached the king versus how Vashti did, which made Esther more successful. Her pattern is a good one to follow.

First, when Esther wanted to approach the king about a mistake he was making, she didn't do it publicly. She could have said everything right there in the throne room in front of everyone, but she didn't. She waited to discuss what was bothering her until the king was in a setting where he felt safe and at ease. Second, she gave him time to think. Not only did she not mention anything about his mistake while they were in a public space, but she didn't even lay out her grievances during her first meeting. She held on to her message until the timing was right. Third, Esther's actions were completely devoid of any confrontation. She didn't confront the king about his stupid decision to kill the Jews; she simply told him how she felt: "If I have found favor in thy sight . . . let my life be given me at my petition, and my people at my request: For we are sold, I and my people, to be destroyed" (Esther 7:3–4). Her tone completely disarmed the king and softened his heart. Esther acted as a matriarch, intervening to save her people.

Both Vashti and Esther should be praised and used as wonderful examples of strong women who knew their hearts and made hard choices. I think that if we examine the basis for change we see that both Vashtis and Esthers are needed. We need the Vashtis to bring the issues to the forefront, to be strong and bold and not let things get swept under the rug. Yet we also need the Esthers, those who work privately and quietly, changing hearts and minds one-on-one. Both types of women have important roles to play to make the world a better place for all of God's children.

For example, suffragists exerted a lot of Vashti-like effort to secure the vote for women in the United States in 1920. They rallied, debated, and did all they could to convince men, especially state senators, to support the Nineteenth Amendment, which would grant women the right to vote. Yet you could also argue that we owe the passage of the Nineteenth Amendment to the mother of a young twenty-four-year-old senator from Tennessee, Harry Burn. In the Senate, the ratification of the Nineteenth Amendment was deadlocked, and suffrage activists feared it wasn't going to pass. Burns was staunchly antisuffrage until he received a note from his mother encouraging him to vote in favor of women's suffrage. He shocked everyone when he changed his vote at the last moment. When asked about why he changed his vote, he simply said, "I know that a mother's advice is always safest for her boy to follow, and my mother wanted me to vote for ratification."[3]

In a very Esther-like move, this mother, whose name was Phoebe Ensminger Burn, used her influence in her son's life to create a lasting change for all the women in the United States. She didn't need to campaign or lobby in front of the senate building; she simply sent her son a note telling him how she felt. It is apparent that because of the relationship she had with him, one of love and trust, her son listened to her and granted her request. In a similar way, I think this is how Esther's conversion of King Ahasuerus worked. She approached him from a place of love. Because he felt safe and respected, he listened to her.

The more I study history, the more I see that what Alma taught in the Book of Mormon, that it is by "small and simple means" (Alma 37:6) that the Lord brings about great things, is so true. We often feel that making things better or changing the world requires colossal efforts—rallies, publicity, parades, social media campaigns, the works. Yet I think that what Vashti and Esther teach us is that seemingly small, individual efforts can make an impact. Sometimes all it takes is saying "no," standing your ground, hosting a dinner, writing a note, having a heart-to-heart conversation, and choosing to be kind to make an enormous change that blesses you and your posterity.

Esther

Now when the turn of Esther, the daughter of Abihail the uncle of Mordecai, who had taken her for his daughter, was come to go in unto the king, she required nothing but what Hegai the king's chamberlain, the keeper of the women, appointed. And Esther obtained favour in the sight of all them that looked upon her. . . .

And the king loved Esther above all the women, and she obtained grace and favour in his sight more than all the virgins; so that he set the royal crown upon her head, and made her queen instead of Vashti.

Esther 2:15, 17

When I was a teenager, I remember feeling discouraged by the fact that many of the important women in the scriptures were beautiful. For example, Sarah was so beautiful that even when she was ninety years old kings fell in love with her (see Genesis 20). Mary, the mother of Christ, was "exceedingly fair" (1 Nephi 11:13). Rachel was "beautiful and well favored" (Genesis 29:17). Abigail was "of a beautiful countenance" (1 Samuel 25:3), and there were "no women found so fair" as the daughters of Job (Job 42:15). The cream of the crop was Esther, whose beauty allowed her to save her people.

To my teenage heart, it felt like God only used beautiful girls to do His work. I remember wondering, because I wasn't "exceedingly" beautiful, if I would ever be of any importance in God's work. Almost two decades later, it is easy for me to look back at my teenage worry and smile. I've learned there are many ways to be beautiful and that *true* beauty usually has very little to do with what a person looks like and everything to do with who she is.

Esther, along with other of the most beautiful young women in Persia, was selected to build a harem for the king from which he could select a new queen. Persia was the largest empire in the world and stretched from India to Greece, so the young women gathered would have been very diverse. Esther herself was Jewish. She lived with her cousin Mordecai, who had been taken captive to Persia when Nebuchadnezzar had taken over Jerusalem. Her parents were dead (presumably having died during the exile), and Mordecai had taken her for his own daughter.

Her Jewish name was Hadassah, but when she was selected, Mordecai instructed her not to tell others that she was Jewish. The conquered Jews, though scattered and without a temple, still managed to preserve a strong sense of identity and many of their spiritual practices. Yet it is evident, from the events that later transpire in Esther's story, that there was strong anti-Jewish sentiment in the empire. Perhaps Mordecai was concerned for her safety, or for Hadassah's chances with the king if her heritage was widely known. We can also speculate that this is probably the time when she began to go by the Persian name of Esther.

The chosen women were taken to the palace, Shushan, and put under the care of Hegai, the "keeper of the women" (Esther 2:15). Hegai had been ordered to oversee the purification of all the young virgins before they would be allowed to sleep with the king. This purification lasted a whole year; the first six months they were purified with myrrh oil, after which would follow six months with "sweet odours" and "other things for the purifying of women" (Esther 2:12). It is not clear what the purpose of the purification was, but the Hebrew word used means "a scraping, rubbing, or a remedy for an injury."[1] We might guess that the purification process was not to just to improve the skin and beauty of each woman but to also make sure that she was free from disease or other maladies that might infect the king and thus the entire harem.

I imagine that when Esther arrived in the palace her heart was hurting. Being carried away to become a concubine in the king's harem had probably not been in her life plan. I imagine that the bitterness she felt about being torn from her family and her way of life matched the bitterness of the myrrh oil she bathed in. In a symbolic way, that year of purification was a time of transformation for Esther, a time when her old self and life died and she was washed and anointed to become the woman God needed her to be. Though God is never expressly mentioned in the book of Esther, His hand is apparent through her whole story, quietly manifesting in a hundred small ways and bearing testimony to what Mordecai would later ask Esther as she prepared to ask the king to save her people: "Who knoweth whether thou art come to the kingdom for such a time as this?" (Esther 4:14).

In fact, it is during Esther's time in the house of the women that we first get a glimpse of what made her so special and so beautiful. The biblical text tells us that she quickly made friends with Hegai. He made sure that she had everything she needed, as well as seven maidens to wait on her. He even moved her and her maidens to the best place in the house of the women. It's evident that Esther possessed the ability to make others feel valued and good about themselves. In fact, the Hebrew word for *beautiful* that is used to describe Esther can also be translated as "good," as in "agreeable," "pleasant," or morally right.[2] Beyond just being physically beautiful, Esther was also spiritually beautiful, possessing the ability to make others feel beautiful when they were around her. Author Vanessa Ochs gives this insight about Esther's beauty:

> Beauty is an asset to use well, a gift like intelligence, faith, physical strength, creative talents, wealth, or having the right connections. Beauty opens doors, and such access can be used for the good. We all know that the initial allure of beauty fades unless it is augmented by substance. Esther reminds us that the substance behind her beauty was her capacity to be intrigued by others, to pull out the best in them, and to reflect it back for them to see. . . .
>
> . . . She knew that being thought beautiful was a blessing. It made her feel good about herself, and it drew people to her, making her feel success and accomplishment for having done nothing at all. She was also aware that people found her beautiful for reasons that had little to do with her appearance. She could access the beauty of the other and radiate it back. It was this conviction—that beauty was a two-way matter—that gave Esther the courage to find her way into the palace of Shushan and the heart of the king.[3]

This is also the type of beauty that President Elaine Dalton called "deep beauty." In one of her general conference messages, she shared how once, when she was in college, she was given the unique opportunity to meet the prophet David O. Mckay and his wife, Emma Ray:

> We were seated in the prophet's living room, surrounding him. President McKay had on a white suit, and seated next to him was his wife. He asked for each of us to come forward and tell him about ourselves. As I went forward, he held out his hand and held mine, and as I told him about my life and my family, he looked deeply into my eyes.
>
> After we had finished, he leaned back in his chair and reached for his wife's hand and said, "Now, young women, I would like you to meet *my queen.*" There seated next to him was his wife, Emma Ray McKay. Although she did not wear a crown of sparkling diamonds, nor was she seated on a throne, I *knew* she was a true queen. Her white hair was her crown, and her pure eyes sparkled like jewels. . . . Hers was a beauty that cannot be purchased. It came from years of seeking the best gifts, becoming well educated, seeking knowledge by study and also by faith. It came from years of hard work, of faithfully enduring trials with optimism, trust, strength, and courage. It came from her unwavering devotion and fidelity to her husband, her family, and the Lord.[4]

Sister Dalton then shared how this experience reminded of her divine identity. She understood that real beauty, or "deep beauty," was something that shines from the inside out. She said:

> It is the kind of beauty that cannot be painted on, surgically created, or purchased. It is the kind of beauty that doesn't wash off. It is *spiritual* attractiveness. . . .
>
> . . . When you are virtuous, chaste, and morally clean, your inner beauty glows in your eyes and in your face. . . .
>
> We have been taught that "the gift of the Holy Ghost . . . quickens all the intellectual faculties, increases, enlarges, expands and purifies all

the natural passions and affections. . . . It inspires virtue, kindness, goodness, tenderness, gentleness and charity. *It develops beauty of person, form and features.*" Now, that is a great beauty secret! That is the beauty . . . that really matters and the only kind of beauty that lasts.[5]

Esther had "deep beauty." Not only was she kind to Hegai, the keeper of the women, but when her time came to finally spend her night with the king, she didn't ask for any special type of adornment or clothing. She simply "required nothing but what Hegai the king's chamberlain, the keeper of the women, appointed" (Esther 2:15). Apparently, the way in which she conducted herself impressed others so that she "obtained favour in the sight of all them that looked upon her" (Esther 2:15), including the king who selected her, out of all the young maidens, to be his queen.

I think this is one reason that we love Esther's story so much. She reminds us that we don't need fancy clothes, beautiful hair, makeup, perfect skin, the right body size, or naturally attractive features to be beautiful. Real beauty, the type that makes us stand out in a crowd, comes from treating others—including ourselves—with Christlike love. We don't need anything else.

The last idea I want to share about Esther's story has to do with power. So often in today's world women are taught that beauty—or "sex appeal"—is a way to gain power, to get what you want—especially from men. Even some of the most "empowered" women in our society still buy into false promises of power from things such as bikinis, plastic surgery, and designer clothing. Esther gives us a refreshing example of a woman who, while beautiful, demonstrated authentic feminine power.

Esther's power over the king and the power she used to save her people didn't come from her physical beauty. That power came through fasting, prayer, kindness, patience, service, and a desire to do God's will. She was even willing to sacrifice her life for others, saying, "So will I go in unto the king, which is not according to the law: and if I perish, I perish" (Esther 4:16). It wasn't being beautiful that made her so affective; it was God's power flowing through her that made her truly and deeply beautiful—and remarkably powerful.

• Myrrh •

Myrrh, which Esther was treated with for the six months of her preparation, is derived from the resin "tears" of a desert tree and is especially fragrant and bitter. Anciently it was often associated with the worship of female deities and fertility. As such, it was often used in perfumes and beauty treatments.[6] For example, the Song of Solomon talks about the practice of putting a bundle of myrrh on your chest during the night.[7] Due to the preservative nature of myrrh, it was also commonly used in embalming and burials. In the New Testament, Nicodemus brought "a mixture of myrrh and aloes, about an hundred pound weight" (John 19:39) to prepare Jesus's body for the grave. Esther, during her six months of myrrh treatments, was being symbolically reborn.

• Zeresh •

Zeresh was the wife of Haman, and it appears that she was her husband's advisor and confidant. When Haman complained about Mordecai, the Jew who would not bow to him, Zeresh suggested he build a gallows 50 cubits high and seek permission from the king to hang Mordecai on it. Haman, pleased by his wife's suggestion, acted on it that very night.

Yet, in a cruel twist, at the exact moment Haman arrived to present his request, the king was thinking about how Mordecai had recently saved him from an assassination plot. The king asked Haman how he should honor a man to whom he was indebted. Haman assumed the person to be honored was himself, so he told the king to dress him in the royal attire and parade him through the street. The king thought this was a great idea and horrified Haman when he instructed him to bestow this honor on Mordecai.

The next day, after having personally paraded Mordecai through the city, Haman came home in "mourning, having his head covered" and told Zeresh what had happened. She took this turn of events as a bad omen and told Haman, "If Mordecai be of the seed of the Jews, before whom thou hast begun to fall, thou shalt not prevail against him, but shalt surely fall before him" (Esther 6:11). Despite her evil intentions, Zeresh was perceptive enough to realize that God was no longer smiling upon them and their fortune was about to change. It did, and quickly.

That night, Esther revealed her Jewish heritage to the king. Haman's plot to destroy the Jews was quashed. Furthermore, in an attempt to beg his life, Haman fell down on the bed where Esther was lying. The king accused Haman of trying to rape Esther and had him forcibly removed from the palace. Haman and all his ten sons were hanged on the very gallows that had been built for Mordecai.

We don't know what happened to Zeresh after her husband's death, but we do know that Esther later gave Mordecai possession of Haman's household. Like many of the wicked women of the Bible, Zeresh's actions backfired and she lost everything. I can think of several different sayings that embody the lesson of Zeresh's story, such as, "what goes around comes around" or "do unto others and you would have them do unto you." But I think Alma said it best: "Wickedness never was happiness" (Alma 41:10).

Conclusion

This is the end of the book, but it is certainly not the end of the women in the Old Testament. Some perceptive readers will have realized that I did not include the stories of all the Old Testament women. The stories of some important women are missing, like Bilhah and Zilpah, the servants of Leah and Rachel who gave birth to four of the tribes of Israel. Many minor and obscure women are also missing, like Rizpah the concubine of King Saul, whose vigil over her dead sons changed the heart of her nation (see 2 Samuel 21), and Sherah (see 1 Chronicles 7:24), who is credited as being the builder of three important cities—with one of them, Uzzen-sherah (which means "listen to Sherah"), being named after her! The only excuse I can give for excluding these women's stories is space. The Old Testament has more the three hundred women in it, and though their stories are just as interesting and important, this book would have been far too hefty if I had included all their stories; so I had to choose.

Yet I hope that this taste into the women of the Old Testament has inspired you and made you curious. Curious, like the Queen of Sheba was, to know things for yourself. To not just take my word or opinion about these women's stories, but to search them out and study them for yourself. To form your own ideas and create your own relationship with these scriptural women, and discover the hundreds of other women waiting within the pages of the Old Testament. These ancient stories are full of powerful archetypes and symbolism that can teach us fundamental truths about who we are and what we are capable of. Studying them is worth the work.

I want to end this book with a final thought from one of my favorite sets of books, C. S. Lewis's The Chronicles of Narnia. One of the characters, Prince Caspian, after assuming the throne of Narnia, feels inadequate in his high position because of his family's history of violence, corruption, and greed. He expresses to Aslan (a Christ-figure in the story) that he wishes he "came of a more honorable lineage." I think that many of us can relate to Caspian's sentiment, especially as we read the Old Testament.

Some of the stories I have shared in this book are ones that make us proud of our spiritual history, stories like Sarah and Abraham, Deborah and Barak, or Hannah and Elkenah. Yet there are other stories, like those of the concubine in Judges 19, Jephthah's Daughter, and Jezebel and Athaliah that hurt our hearts, the stories in which women are abused or disregarded or which they become the vile oppressors, corrupted by power and greed. These are the stories we avoid telling to our children, the ones we skip over in Sunday School and try to forget ever happened. We, like Prince Caspian, find ourselves wishing that our lineage—our spiritual lineage—was more "honorable." Aslan's response to Caspian is incredibly insightful. "You come of the Lord Adam and the Lady Eve," said Aslan. "And that is both honor enough to erect the head of the poorest beggar, and shame enough to bow the shoulders of the greatest emperor on earth. Be content."[1]

Inherent in Aslan's words is a reminder of the dual nature of our life in mortality. The good and the bad of humanity are our inheritance from our First Parents. Yet this isn't necessarily a bad thing. As Mother Eve explained herself, it is in the knowing of good and evil that we learn "the joy of our redemption, and the eternal life which God giveth unto all the obedient" (Moses 5:11). As children of Eve, we will inevitably see the good and bad in ourselves and in others. As Aslan said, I hope we can learn to "be content." Content to experience all that life—and history—has to offer. Content to walk in both the light and the darkness. Content to taste the bitter with the sweet. Content to learn from mistakes and from triumphs. Content to be the children of Lady Eve and Lord Adam—because that is truly a great honor.

> "You come of . . . Lady Eve. . . .
> And that is both honor enough to erect
> the head of the poorest beggar, and
> shame enough to bow the shoulders of
> the greatest emperor on earth.
> Be content."

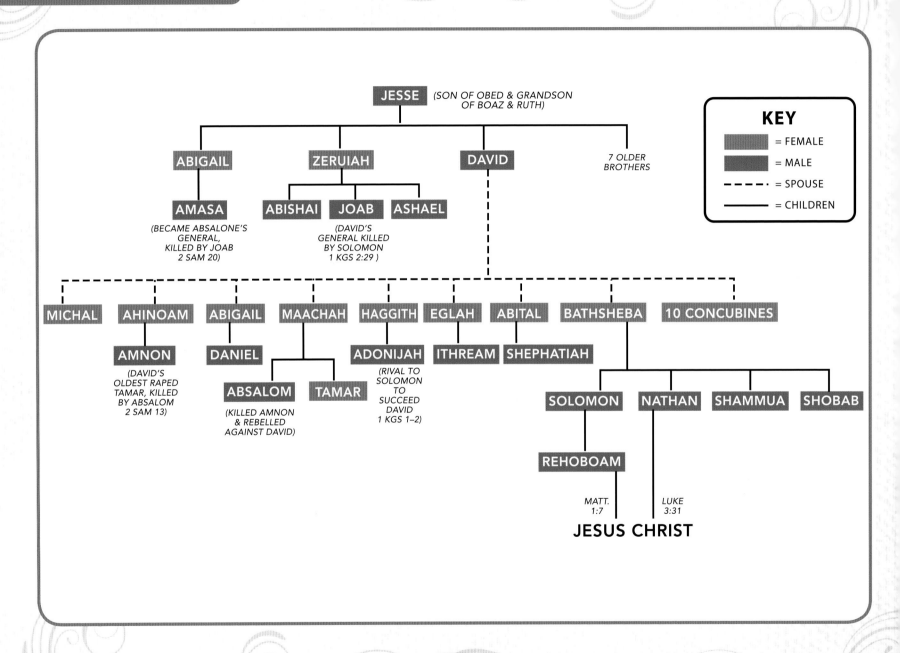

KEY

= FEMALE

= MALE

--- = SPOUSE

— = CHILDREN

JESSE *(SON OF OBED & GRANDSON OF BOAZ & RUTH)*

ABIGAIL

ZERUIAH

DAVID

7 OLDER BROTHERS

AMASA *(BECAME ABSALONE'S GENERAL, KILLED BY JOAB 2 SAM 20)*

ABISHAI

JOAB

ASHAEL *(DAVID'S GENERAL KILLED BY SOLOMON 1 KGS 2:29)*

MICHAL

AHINOAM

ABIGAIL

MAACHAH

HAGGITH

EGLAH

ABITAL

BATHSHEBA

10 CONCUBINES

AMNON *(DAVID'S OLDEST RAPED TAMAR, KILLED BY ABSALOM 2 SAM 13)*

DANIEL

ADONIJAH *(RIVAL TO SOLOMON TO SUCCEED DAVID 1 KGS 1–2)*

ITHREAM

SHEPHATIAH

ABSALOM *(KILLED AMNON & REBELLED AGAINST DAVID)*

TAMAR

SOLOMON

NATHAN

SHAMMUA

SHOBAB

REHOBOAM

MATT. 1:7

LUKE 3:31

JESUS CHRIST

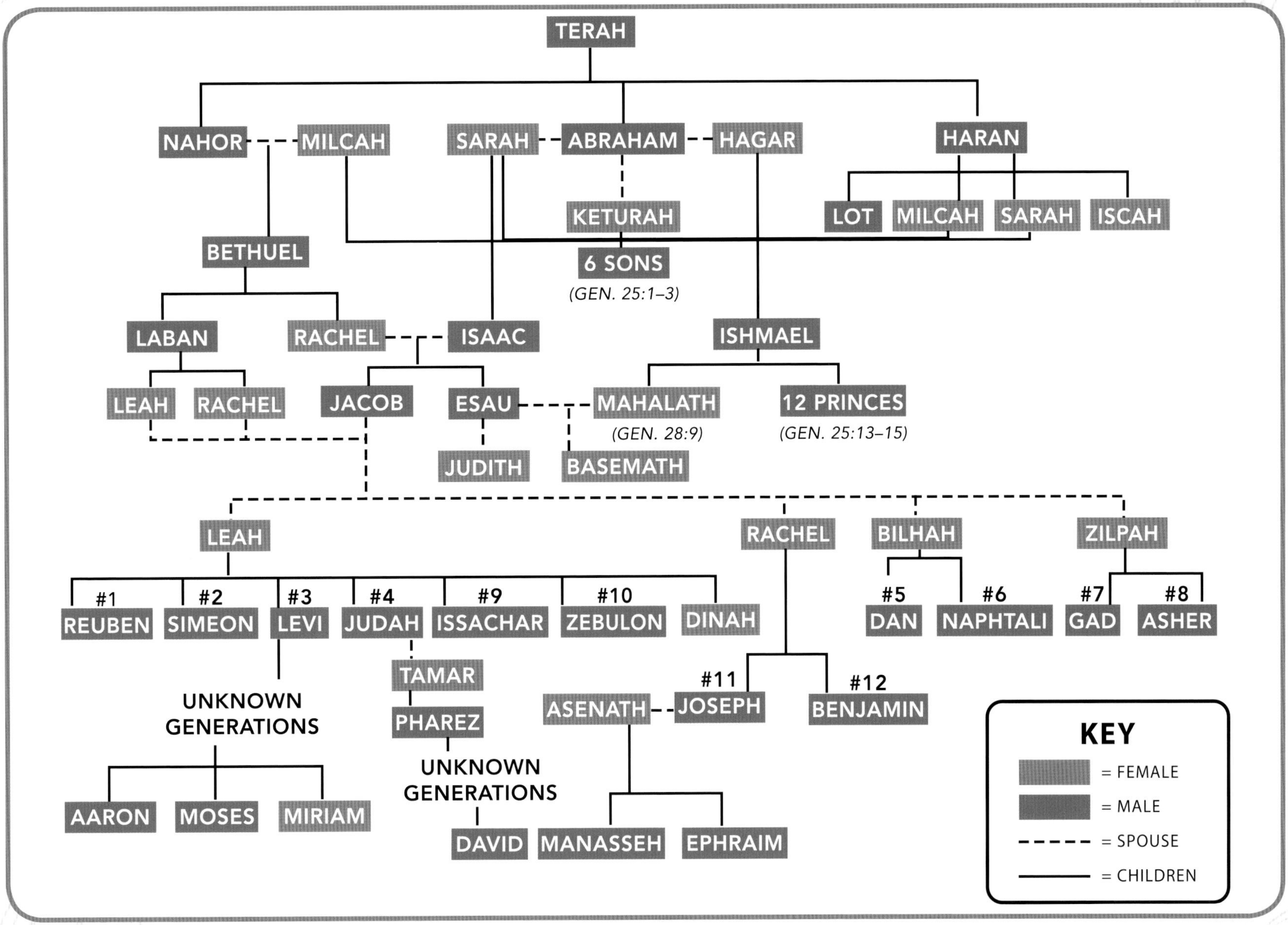
TERAH
NAHOR
MILCAH
SARAH
ABRAHAM
HAGAR
HARAN
KETURAH
LOT
MILCAH
SARAH
ISCAH
BETHUEL
6 SONS
(GEN. 25:1–3)
LABAN
RACHEL
ISAAC
ISHMAEL
LEAH
RACHEL
JACOB
ESAU
MAHALATH
(GEN. 28:9)
12 PRINCES
(GEN. 25:13–15)
JUDITH
BASEMATH
LEAH
RACHEL
BILHAH
ZILPAH
#1 REUBEN
#2 SIMEON
#3 LEVI
#4 JUDAH
#9 ISSACHAR
#10 ZEBULON
DINAH
#5 DAN
#6 NAPHTALI
#7 GAD
#8 ASHER
TAMAR
PHAREZ
UNKNOWN GENERATIONS
ASENATH
#11 JOSEPH
#12 BENJAMIN
UNKNOWN GENERATIONS
AARON
MOSES
MIRIAM
DAVID
MANASSEH
EPHRAIM
KEY
= FEMALE
= MALE
= SPOUSE
= CHILDREN

INTRODUCTION

1. *Old Testament Student Manual: Genesis–2 Samuel* (Church Educational System manual, 1980), 115.

2. Vanessa L. Ochs, *Sarah Laughed: Modern Lessons from the Wisdom and Stories of Biblical Women* (Philadelphia, PA: Jewish Publication Society, 2011), xviii, xxi.

LEARNING TO SEE THE DIVINE FEMININE

1. Patricia T. Holland, *A Quiet Heart* (Salt Lake City: Bookcraft, 2000), 54–55.

2. Lately I have also been keeping a list of masculine symbols in the scriptures. I am sure that there are many more than this, but this is just what I have found so far. Many of these are symbols of our Heavenly Father and Jesus Christ: rock, cornerstone, nails, shepherd, lion, potter, sword, bull, eagle, bear, mountain, husband, father, son, brother, king, master, gardener, lord, servant, seeds, sowing/planting, battle/war, squares, builder, and frankincense.

3. I am indebted to my friend Erika DeCaster for much of this list.

4. When God spoke to Abraham in Genesis 17:1, He called himself *El Shaddai* (also spelled *El Shadday*). The King James Version translates this name as "God Almighty." According to William Dever, "'Shadday' means 'mountain' . . . possibly in the dual, so the divine name is really, 'El, the One of the mountains.' . . . The Hebrew term *shad*, 'mountain,' derives from earlier West Semitic *thad*, 'breast.'" Dever points out that this name for God, while clearly male, is associated with female imagery, the mountains being breasts sticking up out of the earth. He says the name could be similar to the name of the mountain range in Idaho, the Grand Tetons, which in French means "large teat." (William G. Dever, *Did God Have a Wife?: Archeology and Folk Religion in Ancient Israel* [Grand Rapids, MI: William B. Eerdmans Publishing, 2005], 257.)

> Some have even suggested that this name could be translated as "the many-breasted One," but author John J. Parsons wrote against this, saying, "Such language suggests the abominable practices and idols common in various ancient fertility cults—customs that were later subject to the most severe judgment of God upon the seven Canaanite nations. It should be clear, in light of the overall context of the revelation given in the Torah, that the name of El Shaddai is directly connected with the sanctity of the promise given to Abraham regarding the future growth of his family, and ultimately of the coming of the promised Seed, the Messiah." (John. J. Parsons, "Parashat Lekha—God as 'El Shaddai,'" Hebrew for Christians, accessed July 12, 2017, http://www.hebrew4christians.com/Scripture/Parashah/Summaries/Lekh_Lekha/El_Shaddai/el_shaddai.html.)

5. Kathryn H. Shirt, "Women in the Image of the Son: Being Female and Being Like Christ" in *LDS Women's Treasury: Insights and Inspiration for Today's Woman* (Salt Lake City: Deseret Book, 1997), 53.

6. Parley P. Pratt, *Key to the Science of Theology* (Liverpool: F. D. Richards, 1855), 98.

> The original quote reads: "An intelligent being, in the image of God, possesses every organ, attribute, sense, sympathy, affection, of will, wisdom, love, power and gift, which is possessed by God Himself.
>
> "But these are possessed by man, in his rudimental state, in a subordinate sense of the word. Or, in other words, these attributes are in embryo; and are to be gradually developed. They resemble a bud—a germ, which gradually develops into bloom, and then, by progress, produces the mature fruit, after its own kind."

7. Ibid.

8. Carol Lynn Pearson, "Motherless House," in "Healing the Motherless House," chap. 10 in *Women and Authority*, ed. Maxine Hanks (Salt Lake City: Signature Books, 1992), 232.

EVE

1. Carolyn Custis James, *Lost Women of the Bible: The Women We Thought We Knew* (Grand Rapids, MI: Zondervan, 2005), 29–30.

2. Bruce R. McConkie, "Eve and the Fall," in *Woman* (Salt Lake City: Deseret Book, 1979), 67–68.

3. Ibid., 58.

4. Ibid., 59.

5. Erastus Snow, in *Journal of Discourses* 19:269–70.

6. Diana Webb, *Biblical Lionesses: Protectors of the Covenant* (printed by author, 2014), 153.

7. In the Abraham account of the Creation, Adam doesn't name the animals until after Eve is created. Regardless of when Adam named the animals, I think that the experience of naming them, even with Eve at his side, would still have been a learning experience. He would have seen that Eve was uniquely designed to be his help meet. Among all of God's creations, there would be no other that he could turn to or rely on. He needed to learn to appreciate Eve and realize what a treasure he had.

8. Beverly Campbell, *Eve and the Choice Made in Eden* (Salt Lake City: Bookcraft, 2002), 24.

9. Diana Webb, *Forgotten Women of God* (Springville, UT: Bonneville Books, 2010), 4.

10. Ibid., 3.

11. Ibid., 4.

12. Campbell, *Eve and the Choice Made in Eden*, 25.

13. The only clue the scriptures give us about how Adam and Eve were really created is in the book of Moses when God tells Adam that he was "born into the world by water, and blood, and the spirit, which I have made, and so became of dust a living soul" (Moses 6:59). This scripture seems to suggest that Adam, and presumably also Eve, were born in the world in the same manner that all humans have been born. How that exactly happened, we have no idea. In view of this, we should take the creation of Adam and Eve from the dust of the earth and from Adam's rib to be rich in symbolism.

14. *Strong's Exhaustive Concordance of the Bible*, s.v. "H1129 banah," accessed July 12, 2017, https://www.blueletterbible.org/lang/lexicon/lexicon.cfm?Strongs=H1129&t=KJV.

15. It is also interesting to think about which meaning came first. Were the sides and walls of the tabernacle and the ark of the covenant described as *teslas* because they were symbolic of Eve, or was Eve described as being created out of a *tesla* because she was being compared to the tabernacle or the ark of the covenant? Either way, I think the symbolism is interesting and powerful. Like the tabernacle and the ark of the covenant where only a man authorized by the Lord has permission to enter, a woman's body is also a sacred space. Eve's body (and the bodies of all women) housed sacred power of creation, which is only to be accessed by a man who had been authorized by the Lord (and permitted by the woman) to enter.

16. Hugh Nibley, "Patriarchy and Matriarchy," (annual women's conference address, Brigham Young University, February 1, 1980), https://publications.mi.byu.edu/transcript/patriarchy-and-matriarchy.

17. Russell M. Nelson, "Lessons from Eve," *Ensign*, November 1987, 86.

18. *Gospel Principles* (2011), 219.

19. John A. Widtsoe, *Evidences and Reconciliations*, arr. G. Homer Durham, 3 vols. in 1 (Salt Lake City: Bookcraft, 1960).

20. *Discourses of Brigham Young*, sel. John A. Widtsoe (Salt Lake City: Deseret Book, 1941), 103.

21. Beverly Campbell, "Mother Eve Mentor for Today's Woman: A Heritage of Honor" (address, 11th annual Collegium Aesculapium, Salt Lake City, Utah, April 2, 1993).

22. Nehama Aschkenasy, as quoted in Campbell, *Eve and the Choice Made in Eden*, 71.

23. *Strong's Exhaustive Concordance of the Bible*, s.v. "H8378 ta'avah," accessed July 12, 2017, https://www.blueletterbible.org/lang/lexicon/lexicon.cfm?t=kjv&strongs=h8378.

24. Nibley, "Patriarchy and Matriarchy."

25. Campbell, "Mother Eve Mentor for Today's Woman."

26. Nibley, "Patriarchy and Matriarchy."

27. Jeffrey R. Holland, "Of Souls, Symbols, and Sacraments" (Brigham Young University devotional, January 12, 1988).

28. Nibley, "Patriarchy and Matriarchy."

29. *Teachings of Presidents of the Church: Joseph Smith*, (2011), 104.

30. Ibid.

31. Kathleen Slaugh Bahr and Chari A. Loveless, "Family Work," *BYU Magazine*, Spring 2000, https://magazine.byu.edu/article/family-work; italics in original.

32. If each generation only doubled itself, then by the eighth generation, a person would have 256 descendants (it would go 2, 4, 8, 16, 32, 64, 128, 256). We know that Adam and Eve had more than two children, so it is easy to see how in just a few generations there could have been quite a lot of people on the earth!

33. "Statement of Zebedee Coltrin," Minutes, October 3, 1883, Salt Lake School of Prophets, LDS Church Archives, Salt Lake City, Utah, 66–67.

Note: In his account of this same vision Abraham Cannon, who was not present during it, said that it was not Adam and Eve whom Joseph and the other men saw but rather the Father and the Mother plus the Savior. He wrote: "One day the Prophet Joseph Smith asked him (Zebedee Coltrin) and Sidney Rigdon to accompany him into the woods to pray. When they had reached a secluded spot Joseph laid down on his back and stretched out his arms. He told the brethren to lie one on each arm and then shut their eyes.

"After they had prayed he told them to open their eyes. They did so and they saw a brilliant light surrounding a pedestal which seemed to rest on the ground. They closed their eyes and again prayed. They then saw, on opening them, the Father seated upon a throne; they prayed again and on looking saw the Mother also; after praying and looking the fourth time they saw the Savior added to the group. He had auburn brown, rather long, wavy hair and appeared quite young" (Journal of Abraham H. Cannon, August 25, 1880, LDS Church Archives).

34. The matriarchal power, that of creating human life, is the most obvious "godlike" power granted to us on earth. In his talk "Of Souls, Symbols, and Sacraments," Jeffrey R. Holland said:

"I know of nothing so earth-shatteringly powerful and yet so universally and unstintingly given to us as the God-given power available in every one of us from our early teen years on to create a human body, that wonder of all wonders, a genetically and spiritually unique being never seen before in the history of the world and never to be duplicated again in all the ages of eternity—a child, your child—with eyes and ears and fingers and toes and a future of unspeakable grandeur. . . .

"Human life—that is the greatest of God's powers, the most mysterious and magnificent chemistry of it all—and you and I have been given it, but under the most serious and sacred of restrictions. You and I who can make neither mountain nor moonlight, not one raindrop nor a single rose—yet we have this greater gift in an absolutely unlimited way. Surely God's trust in us to respect this future-forming gift is awesomely staggering. We who may not be able to repair a bicycle nor assemble an average jigsaw puzzle—yet with all our weaknesses and imperfections, we carry this procreative power that makes us very much like God in at least one grand and majestic way." (Holland, "Of Souls, Symbols, and Sacraments.")

35. Bryan Sykes, *The Seven Daughters of Eve: The Science That Reveals Our Genetic Ancestry* (New York: W. W. Norton, 2002), 289.

36. Campbell, *Eve and the Choice Made in Eden*, 48.

ADAH AND ZILLAH

1. Carol Meyers, "Naamah 1," in *Women in Scripture: A Dictionary of Named and Unnamed Women in the Hebrew Bible, the Apocryphal/Deuterocanonical Books, and the New Testament*, ed. Carol Meyers, Toni Craven, and Ross S. Kraemer (Grand Rapids, MI: William B. Eerdmans Publishing, 2001), 129.

2. Hugh Nibley, "A Strange Thing in the Land: The Return of the Book of Enoch, Part 8," *Ensign*, December 1976.

3. Beverly Campbell, "Mother Eve Mentor for Today's Woman: A Heritage of Honor" (address, 11th annual Collegium Aesculapium, Salt Lake City, Utah, April 2, 1993).

4. Hugh Nibley, "Patriarchy and Matriarchy," (annual women's conference address, Brigham Young University, February 1, 1980), https://publications.mi.byu.edu/transcript/patriarchy-and-matriarchy.

5. Ibid.

6. Ibid.

7. Ibid.

8. Elijah demonstrates the righteous patriarchy through his charitable actions toward women in need (see the Great Woman of Shunem on page 233, and the Widow of Zarephath on page 228).

NOAH'S WIFE

1. In Jewish tradition and in the book of Jasher, she is called "Naamah." The Greeks called her "Doris" the wife of Nereus (Noah), the "wet one." In the Book of Jubilees, she is named as "Emzara." Islamic tradition calls her "Amzurah."

2. Hugh Nibley, "A Strange Thing in the Land: The Return of the Book of Enoch, Part 8," *Ensign*, December 1976.

JOB'S WIFE

1. Herbert Lockyer, *All the Women of the Bible* (Grand Rapids, MI: Zondervan, 1967), 214.

2. The corrections are found in both Job 1:6 and 2:1 in the Joseph Smith Translation. I've noticed that in both the Old and New Testaments, the Joseph Smith Translation offers changes in wording that makes the verses more gender inclusive. I feel like this is just another one of the blessings of the Restoration—a Bible in which women are much more included.

3. It is also interesting to note that the book of Job is widely thought to be the oldest book in the Bible. Genesis covers content that is older than Job's time period (which would have been around the time of the patriarchs), but it is apparent by the literary style of Hebrew used that the book of Job was written much earlier than any of the five books of Moses. Some scholars think it may even be the oldest book in the world.

4. *Anne of Green Gables*, directed by Kevin Sullivan (1985; Toronto, Canada: Sullivan Entertainment), VHS.

5. Testament of Job 23:11, as translated in Diana Webb, *Forgotten Women of God* (Springville, UT: Bonneville Books, 2010), 51.

6. Testament of Job 24:1–6, as translated in Webb, *Forgotten Women of God*, 52.

7. Testament of Job 25:9–10, as translated in Webb, *Forgotten Women of God*, 53.

8. Daniel Darling, "The Most Misunderstood Woman in the Bible: Why Job's Wife May Have Gotten a Bad Rap," *Christianity Today*, May 2011, accessed July 14, 2017, http://www.todayschristianwoman.com/articles/2011/may/mostmisunderstood.html; italics in original.

9. Richard G. Scott, "Trust in the Lord," *Ensign*, November 1995, 17.

10. Job 1:5 expresses Job's concern about his children: "And it was so, when the days of their feasting were gone about, that Job sent and sanctified them, and rose up early in the morning, and offered burnt offerings according to the number of them all: for Job said, It may be that my sons have sinned, and cursed God in their hearts. Thus did Job continually."

11. James R. Baker, *Women's Rights in Old Testament Times* (Salt Lake City: Signature Books, 1992), 163–64.

12. Take, for example, the family of Abraham whose passage of the "birthright," or family inheritance, wasn't just about money but about which son was best entrusted with the responsibilities of the Abrahamic covenant (see Rebekah on page 63).

13. President Joseph Fielding Smith stated, "It is within the privilege of the sisters of this Church to . . . receive authority and power as queens and priestesses" ("Relief Society—An Aid to the Priesthood," *Relief Society Magazine*, January 1959, 5–6).

SARAH

1. Angelo S. Rappoport, *Myth and Legend of Ancient Israel*, vol. 1 (London: Gresham, 1928), 276–77.

2. The Genesis Apocryphon, column 19.

3. Geza Vermes, *The Complete Dead Sea Scrolls in English* (London: Penguin Books, 1987), 255–256.

4. Ibid.

5. Ibid.

6. Vanessa L. Ochs, *Sarah Laughed: Modern Lessons from the Wisdom and Stories of Biblical Women* (Philadelphia, PA: Jewish Publication Society, 2011), 112.

7. Ibid., 113.

8. Ibid., 119.

HAGAR

1. This is the same type of situation that Leah and Rachel participated in with their handmaidens Bilhah and Zilpah (see Genesis 30). The children that these handmaidens bore were named by their mistresses, an indication that Leah and Rachel had claim on the children just as much as their birth mothers did.

2. The Book of Jasher 16:25

3. The Book of Jasher 16:29–30

4. *Strong's Exhaustive Concordance of the Bible*, s.v. "H6031 anah," accessed July 17, 2017, https://www.blueletterbible.org/lang/lexicon/lexicon.cfm?Strongs=H6031.

5. Diana Webb, *Forgotten Women of God* (Springville, UT: Bonneville Books, 2010), 141–42.

6. Interestingly, Isaac (Sarah's son) would later dwell by this well, called "Lahai-roi" before and after his marriage to Rebekah (see Genesis 24:62 and 25:11).

7. Ishmael's son's names were Nebajoth, Kedar, Adbeel, Mibsam, Mishma, Dumah, Massa, Hadar, Tema, Jetur, Naphish, and Kedemah (see Genesis 25:13–15).

8. We know that Ishmael was circumcised when he was thirteen years old (see Genesis 17:25) and that Isaac was born one year after that.

9. We know that these events happened at Isaac's weaning party. Since children weren't weaned till three to four years old in ancient times, this

would make Ishmael, who was about fourteen when Isaac was born, about seventeen or eighteen years old.

10. In Galatians 4:29, Paul wrote about how Hagar and Sarah are symbolic of God's covenant with his children. In his sermon, Paul wrote about Ishmael and Isaac, saying, "He that was born after the flesh persecuted him that was born after the Spirit." Paul's choice of the word *persecute* seems to indicate that there was animosity between Ishmael and Isaac (or possible Hagar and Sarah) that resulted in Hagar and Ishmael's departure.

11. For example, the word *tsachaq* is used in Genesis 26:8 as the word *sporting* when it says, "And it came to pass, when he had been there a long time, that Abimelech king of the Philistines looked out at a window, and saw, and, behold, Isaac was sporting with Rebekah his wife." *Tsachaq*, translated as "mock," is also used by Potiphar's wife when she tells her husband, "And she spake unto him according to these words, saying, The Hebrew servant, which thou hast brought unto us, came in unto me to mock me" (Genesis 39:17).

12. We see this pattern again with Esau and Jacob and then again with Joseph and his brethren. Even Adam and Eve's children demonstrate this pattern with Abel, the youngest brother who inherited from his father instead of Cain, the older brother.

13. Muslims also believe that when Hagar ran out of water and Ishmael (an infant in their story) began to die, she ran back and forth seven times between two hills in search of water. On the seventh time Ishmael hit the ground with his heel and water sprung out of the ground. Today Muslims believe that the Zamzam Well (not far from Mecca) is the place where this occurred, and stopping at it and running seven times back and forth between the hills is a part of the pilgrimage that all Muslims make at Mecca.

14. Doctrine and Covenants 132:39 makes it clear that all of David's wives were given to him by God through the prophet Nathan, except for Bathsheba, whom he took without permission (and later killed her husband).

LOT'S WIFE

1. Between the time Abraham and Lot parted ways until Genesis 19, there is more to Lot's story. In Genesis 14, Sodom was being ransacked by foreign enemies, Lot and his family were taken captive by the fleeing Sodomites and taken to a nearby mountain (see Genesis 14). When Abraham heard what had happened to his nephew, he "armed his trained servants, born in his own house, three hundred and eighteen" (Genesis 14:14) and went and rescued Lot and his family. The king of Sodom was impressed by Abraham and tried to get Lot back by offering Abraham money. Yet Abraham would not take a "shoelatchet" from the king of Sodom "lest thou shouldest say, I have made Abram rich" (Genesis 14:23). Somehow, after this exchange, Lot and his family went to "sojourn" in Sodom, making it, and not the land Abraham had given them, their home.

2. *International Standard Bible Encyclopedia Online*, s.v. "Slime; Slime pits," accessed July 17, 2017, http://www.internationalstandardbible.com/S/slime-slime-pits.html.

3. Jeffrey R. Holland, "'Remember Lot's Wife': Faith Is for the Future" (Brigham Young University devotional, January 13, 2009), 2–3, speeches.byu.edu; italics in original.

4. Michelle Stone, "Claiming our Heroines—The Untold Story of Lot's Wife," *Feminist Mormon Housewives*, posted May 1, 2014, http://www.feministmormonhousewives.org/2014/05/claiming-our-heroines-the-untold-story-of-lots-wife.

5. Amy, "'Relief' Society vs. 'Fix-it' Society," *Women in the Scriptures*, posted March 24, 2016, http://www.womeninthescriptures.com/2016/03/relief-society-vs-fit-it-society-by-amy.html; italics in original.

6. Stone, "Claiming our Heroines."

Endnotes ❖

REBEKAH

1. Julie B. Beck, "Choose Ye This Day to Serve the Lord" (Brigham Young University Women's Conference address, April 29, 2010), 2, womensconference.byu.edu.

2. Ibid.

3. In the Joseph Smith Translation, it changes the servant's prayer to ask God that this woman, the one who would water the camels, would be "the one" who God has chosen for Isaac.

4. Bonnie D. Parkin, "Personal Ministry: Sacred and Precious" (Brigham Young University devotional, February 13, 2007), 1, speeches.byu.edu.

5. We don't know what the nature of this gift was, if it was in fact a betrothal gift in which Rebekah (independently) had already accepted the servant's proposal of marriage to Isaac, or if it was just a thank you gift for watering his camels.

6. Josephus records that Bethuel was dead by this point in the story, which is why Rebekah's brother Laban plays such a large role in her marriage and why Genesis 24:28 calls it "her mother's house" instead of her "father's house."

7. "Nephi's Courage," *Children's Songbook*, 120.

8. Josephus, Antiquities of the Jews 1.18.1

9. Julie B. Beck, "'And upon the Handmaids in Those Days Will I Pour Out My Spirit," *Ensign*, May 2010, 11.

10. Diana Webb, *Rebekah and Other Lionesses* (unpublished manuscript).

11. Diana Webb, *Biblical Lionesses: Protectors of the Covenant* (printed by author, 2014), 101–102.

12. Beck, "Choose Ye This Day to Serve the Lord," 2.

LEAH AND RACHEL

1. David had this job in his family as well (see 1 Samuel 16:19).

2. Diana Webb, *Rebekah and Other Lionesses* (unpublished manuscript).

3. The New International Version and the English Standard Version of the Bible both render the phrase this way. Some other translations, however, seem to take the phrase to mean that she had plain-looking eyes.

4. Diana Webb, *Biblical Lionesses: Protectors of the Covenant* (printed by author, 2014), 147.

5. Patricia T. Holland, *A Quiet Heart* (Salt Lake City: Bookcraft, 2000), 58.

6. Sara, "On Being a Woman," *The Faith Friends*, posted February 14, 2017, http://www.thefaithfriends.com/blog/on-being-a-woman.

7. Tikva Frymer-Kensky, "Leah: Bible," *Jewish Women's Archive*, accessed July 19, 2017, https://jwa.org/encyclopedia/article/leah-bible.

8. William G. Dever, *Did God Have a Wife?: Archeology and Folk Religion in Ancient Israel* (Grand Rapids, MI: William B. Eerdmans Publishing, 2005), 183–84.

9. Josephus, Antiquities of the Jews 1.19.10

10. Ibid.

DINAH

1. Josephus, Antiquities of the Jews 1.21.1

2. *Old Testament Student Manual: Genesis–2 Samuel* (Church Educational System manual, 1980), 89.

3. Leslie G. Nelson, *Touching His Robe: Reaching Past the Shame and Anger of Abuse* (Covington, WA: West Lotus Press, 2014), 64–66; italics in original.

4. Vanessa L. Ochs, *Sarah Laughed: Modern Lessons from the Wisdom and Stories of Biblical Women* (Philadelphia, PA: Jewish Publication Society, 2011), 76–77.

5. Diana Webb, *Forgotten Women of God* (Springville, UT: Bonneville Books, 2010), 153.

6. It should be pointed out that the word is Levirate, not Levitical. It is derived from the Latin word *levir*, which means "husband's brother." It isn't related to the Levites, who were the priestly tribe of Israel.

7. James R. Baker, *Women's Rights in Old Testament Times* (Salt Lake City: Signature Books, 1992), 149–150.

POTIPHAR'S WIFE

1. The lyrics to the song go:

She was beautiful but evil,
Saw a lot of men against his [Potiphar's] will . . . Joseph's looks and handsome figure,
Had attracted her attention,
Every morning she would beckon,
Come and lie with me love,
Joseph wanted to resist her,
Till one day she proved too eager,
Joseph cried in vain, Please stop,
I don't believe in free love!

(Tim Rice and Andrew Lloyd Webber, "Potiphar," from *Joseph and the Amazing Technicolor Dreamcoat* [London Palladium Cast Recording, 1991].)

2. It has been speculated that Potiphar may have been a eunuch (a castrated man) because the Hebrew word *cariyc*, which is translated in this story as "officer" of Pharaoh, can also be translated as "eunuch." Traditionally eunuchs were used (or made) in order to protect the sexual purity of a king's harem or family. Yet scholars have agreed that the use of this word does not necessarily indicate that the man was castrated. That could be used in a general way to describe someone who was a high official in the king's court. In the Bible the word *cariyc* is translated as "officer" or "chamberlain" thirteen times and translated as "eunuch" seventeen times. Seeing that Potiphar was married, it is likely that he was not a "real" eunuch but that this word was used to describe his high rank. However, it is always possible that he was.

3. Kenneth W. Matheson, "Fidelity in Marriage: It's More Than You Think," *Ensign*, September 2009, 14.

ASENATH

1. Another Jewish tradition claims that Asenath was the daughter of Jacob's daughter Dinah, conceived during her rape by Shechem. Jacob's sons wanted to kill the baby, but Jacob stopped them. Instead, he put a gold plate around her neck with the story of her birth and sent her away. An angel orchestrated it so that she was found by Poti-pherah, the priest of the Egyptian city of On, who took her as his daughter. In this way, Jewish tradition claims, God provided Joseph with a bride of his own lineage even though he was living among pagans in Egypt.

2. The tribe of Ephraim was given the blessing of carrying the birthright. In the latter days, the children from the tribe of Ephraim have the privilege to first carry the message of the Restoration of the gospel to the world and to lead the gathering of the ten scattered tribes.

THE WOMEN WHO DELIVERED MOSES: JOCHEBED, PUAH, SHIPHRAH, AND PHARAOH'S DAUGHTER

1. According to Jewish Midrash, Jochebed was conceived as Jacob and his sons traveled to Egypt. This is how they explain why the Bible mentions seventy people from Jacob's household went to Egypt but why sixty-nine people are listed in the account given in Genesis 46. Jewish tradition

claims it is because Jochebed was counted in her mother's womb. However, it is also important to note that there was a gap of about three hundred or more years between the time that Jacob and his family settled in Egypt and the time that Moses was delivered them from bondage. It may still have been possible, though, for Jochebed to be the actual daughter of Levi if she was born to one of his (perhaps younger) wives toward the end of his life, and if she was older when she bore Moses.

2. The Book of Jasher 68:1–2

3. Jospehus, Antiquities of the Jews 2.9.2

4. In Hebrew, Shiphrah means "beautiful one," and Puah means "splendid one." It easy to me to see how these could have been honorific names given them by grateful Hebrews for their courageous stance toward life.

5. The Book of Jasher 68:9–11

6. Diana Webb, *Forgotten Women of God* (Springville, UT: Bonneville Books, 2010), 91.

7. Vanessa L. Ochs, *Sarah Laughed: Modern Lessons from the Wisdom and Stories of Biblical Women* (Philadelphia, PA: Jewish Publication Society, 2011), 134.

8. Webb, *Forgotten Women of God*, 93.

9. The Book of Jasher 68:15–21

10. Webb, *Forgotten Women of God*, 94.

11. E. T. Sullivan in Gordon B. Hinckley, "Behold Your Little Ones," *Ensign*, October 1978.

WHAT DOES IT MEAN FOR A WOMAN TO BE "UNCLEAN"?

1. Kressel Housan, "The Jewish Facts of Life," Kressel's Korner, accessed August 30, 2017, http://www.beingjewish.com/kresel/facts.html.

2. Ibid.

ZIPPORAH

1. He is also called Reuel (see Exodus 2:18).

2. James R. Baker, *Women's Rights in Old Testament Times* (Salt Lake City: Signature Books, 1992), 67.

3. Ibid., 174–75.

4. We do not know which son was circumcised. If I had to guess, I'd say it was their second son, whom they named Eliezer. The name Eliezer means "God is my help" or "God is my savior." A boy's name was often given at the time he was circumcised, and I can see how Eliezer might be a meaningful name for someone who was named during Moses and Zipporah's circumcision experience.

5. "Plural Marriage in Kirtland and Nauvoo," LDS.org, accessed July 21, 2017, https://www.lds.org/topics/plural-marriage-in-kirtland-and-nauvoo.

6. It is interesting that when the children of Israel finally entered the land of Canaan after forty years in the wilderness, one of the first things Joshua did was to command that all the men be circumcised (see Joshua 5). This was because, while all the men who had left Egypt had been circumcised, none of the children who had been born in the wilderness had been circumcised. We don't know why they hadn't circumcised them "by the way" (Joshua 5:7), but perhaps it could have had something to do with Moses's repulsion to the idea of circumcision.

7. Rochel Holzkenner, "Why Women Don't Need Circumcision," *The Jewish Woman*, accessed July 21, 2017, http://www.chabad.org/theJewishWoman/article_cdo/aid/2287938/jewish/Why-Women-Dont-Need-Circumcision.htm.

8. Doctrine and Covenants 74:6–4 also says something similar: "Children might remain without circumcision; and that the tradition might be done away, which saith that little children are unholy; for it was had among the Jews; But little children are holy, being sanctified through the atonement of Jesus Christ; and this is what the scriptures mean."

MIRIAM

1. "Spiritual Ego," *Wisdom of Spirit*, accessed July 21, 2017, http://www
.wisdom-of-spirit.com/spiritual-ego.html.

2. *Teachings of Presidents of the Church: Brigham Young*, (1997), 78–84

3. Ibid.

4. The Prophet Joseph Smith said, "I will organize the women under
the priesthood after the pattern of the priesthood" (From Eliza R. Snow's
Relief Society Minute Book). President Eliza R. Snow, the second president of the Relief Society, taught this about Relief Society: "Although the
name may be of modern date, the institution is of ancient origin. We were
told by our martyred prophet that the same organization existed in the
church anciently" (in *Daughters in My Kingdom: The History and Work of
Relief Society*, 1).

5. Lorenzo Snow, in *Daughters in My Kingdom: The History and Work of
Relief Society*, 7; emphasis added.

ELISHEBA AND THE DAUGHTERS OF AARON

1. In fact, one of Elisheba's descendants would also be named "Elisabeth" and would be the mother of John the Baptist, the steward of the
Aaronic Priesthood. It is also interesting to note that the Old Testament
Elisheba had a sister-in-law named Miriam, who was of the tribe of Levi.
The name Miriam is translated in Greek as "Mary." It is interesting that in
the New Testament we again find an Elisabeth and a Mary who are from
the tribes of Judah (Mary) and Levi (Elisabeth) and that through them
both of the priesthoods would come—the Aaronic through John the Baptist and the Melchizedek through Jesus Christ.

2. The high priest of the tabernacle wore slightly different sacred clothing than did the priests. Exodus 28:4 explains that Aaron wore "a breast-
plate, and an ephod, and robe, and a broidered coat, a mitre, and a girdle."

3. Though we are accustomed to thinking of the priest as being the ones
who killed the animals the original tabernacle ceremony called for the
person sacrificing the animal to slaughter it. The LDS Bible Dictionary
explains that "the sacrificer himself slew his sacrifice (at the north side of
the altar), and thus carried out actually the dedication to God that he had
ceremonially expressed by the laying on of hands. A later custom was for
the Levites or priests to slaughter the victims."

4. The story of Hannah told in 1 Samuel 1 gives us some additional insight into how a family, men and women, would have worshiped at that
tabernacle. In 1 Samuel 1:4–5, we read about how Hannah's husband, Elkanah, was the one who "offered" the sacrifice and then ensured that each
of his wives and children were given a "portion," and Hannah was given
a "worthy portion." It is likely that Elkanah was offering a peace offering
and that his family was joining with him in the sacrificial meal that followed. This meal appears to have been eaten near the tabernacle (see 1
Samuel 1:9), and it appears that on one occasion, Hannah was so sad about
her barren condition that she couldn't eat. Yet after her conversation with
the priest, where she was promised her prayer would be answered, she
"did eat, and her countenance was sad no more" (1 Samuel 1:18). From this
part of the story, it is clear that Elkanah offered a sacrifice on behalf of the
whole family, in which the women and the children then partook. Yet in
1 Samuel 1:24–25, after Hannah had borne Samuel and weaned him, we
read that, "*she* took him up with her, with three bullocks, and one ephah
of flour, and a bottle of wine, and brought him unto the house of the Lord
in Shiloh. . . . And *they* slew a bullock, and brought the child to Eli" (emphasis added). This account seems to suggest that this offering was being
made by Hannah, not her husband, and that they slew it together. We can
also deduce that she was offering a burnt offering because she brought
bullocks as well as flour and wine for the Minchah, which was required
for burnt and peace offerings but not for sin or trespass. This type of offering seems appropriate as the animal was completely consumed in a burnt
offering, symbolizing consecration to the Lord. Hannah, in dedicating

her son to service in the temple, was consecrating herself and her child to God.

5. In Latin, the word for "salt" is *sal*, and in Rome soldiers were paid with *salarium argentum*, which was basically the amount of money they would need to buy salt. It is the root of our English word *salary*.

6. "Salt preserves food by stopping the growth of bacteria and destructive enzymes. When salt comes in contact with the surface of food, the salt molecules try to achieve a balance between the number of salt molecules inside and outside the food. It does this by drawing water molecules out of the food and inserting salt molecules into the food through osmosis across semipermeable cell membranes. As a result, the number of free water molecules is reduced to a point where most bacteria cannot survive and most enzymes cannot operate because, basically, they get dehydrated." ("The Salt of the Earth," *Ensign*, January 2015, 66.)

7. David A. Bednar, "The Atonement and the Journey of Mortality," *Ensign*, April 2012, 42–43.

8. Exodus 36 speaks of how men worked on creating the linen curtains of the temple and even embroidered them. Men are also spoken of as weavers in 1 Chronicles 4:21. Weaving and embroidery were a fine skill, and it appears that both men and women were capable of it. In fact, it almost seems as if our modern-day society is more restrictive about what is "women's work" and what is "men's work" than they were in Bible times. Throughout the Bible, we have evidence of women doing big building projects (such as the daughters of Shallum who built the walls of Jerusalem and Sherah who oversaw the construction of cities) and men doing work such as weaving, embroidery, and baking bread. It seems that if there was a job to be done it didn't necessarily matter who did it but that it got done in order to keep the community moving and flourishing.

9. Dallin H. Oaks, "Desire," *Ensign*, April 2011.

10. There may also be a reference to them in Numbers 25:6 when it speaks of those "who were weeping before the door of the tabernacle of the congregation."

11. It appears that there was a special seat near the gate of the tabernacle where the high priest would sit. In 1 Samuel 4:18, Eli fell off this seat and died when he was told that the ark of the covenant had been lost.

12. In Herod's temple, women were allowed into the outer courtyard, known as the "courtyard of the women" and were allowed to approach the door of the inner courtyard to present their offerings. In New Testament times, though, it was clear that women were not allowed to enter into the inner court, the "court of the Israelites," where the men and priests killed the sacrifices and placed them on the altar.

13. *Strong's Exhaustive Concordance of the Bible*, s.v. "H6633 tsaba'," accessed July 25, 2017, https://www.blueletterbible.org/lang/lexicon /lexicon.cfm?t=KJV&strongs=H6633.

14. None of the drawings I have seen of the tabernacle, which are usually based off the description in the Bible, depict an area where women would have gathered. The temple in Jerusalem had a special outer court where women were allowed to enter, and the story of the women in the Old Testament seems to suggest to me that something like that existed for them as well. Hannah's story in 1 Samuel makes it clear that she was praying by the door of the tabernacle, where Eli the priest was seated on special seat, but that she was still praying at the tabernacle. It seems to suggest to me that there must have been some outer tent or courtyard before the door, where only men and priests could enter, where women were allowed to go. I haven't yet though seen any drawings that incorporate this idea into them. It would be neat if there was one!

DAUGHTERS OF ZELOPHEHAD: MAHLAH, NOAH, HOGLAH, MILCAH, TIRZAH

1. We don't know who Zelophehad's wife was, but we do know a little about his family history. His father was Hepher, who was the son of Gilead, who was the son of Machir and a woman named Maacah, who was of the tribe of Benjamin and the sister of Huppim and Shuppim. Machir was the son of Manasseh and his "concubine the Aramitess" (1 Chronicles 7:14).

RAHAB

1. James R. Baker, *Women's Rights in Old Testament Times* (Salt Lake City: Signature Books, 1992), 73.

2. Ibid., 74.

3. Ibid., 75.

ACHSAH

1. *Strong's Exhaustive Concordance of the Bible*, s.v. "H5496 cuwth," accessed July 25, 2017, https://www.blueletterbible.org/lang/lexicon/lexicon.cfm?Strongs=H5496&t=KJV.

2. *Strong's Exhaustive Concordance of the Bible*, s.v. "H7704 sadeh," accessed July 25, 2017, https://www.blueletterbible.org/lang/lexicon/lexicon.cfm?Strongs=H7704&t=KJV.

3. David M. Gunn and Danna Nolan Fewell, *Narrative in the Hebrew Bible*, Oxford Bible Series (New York: Oxford University Press, 1993), 161.

4. Heidi M. Szpek, "Achsah's Story: A Metaphor for Societal Transition," *Andrews University Seminary Studies* 40, no. 2 (2002): 251.

DEBORAH

1. Herbert Lockyer, *All Women of the Bible* (Grand Rapids, MI: Zondervan, 1967), 41.

2. Deborah is called "the wife of Lapidoth." Some scholars argue that since the word translated as "wife" can also be translated as "woman," she may not have been married but rather may have been "the woman of Lapidoth." Because the name *Lapidoth* means "torches," these scholars argue that this phrase might be read "woman of torches," or in other words "fiery woman." While I think Deborah's feistiness is easily apparent, most Bible translations render this phrase to mean that Deborah was married to a man named Lapidoth, which raises some interesting questions about her husband. Who was he? Did they have children? How did he feel about Deborah's role as a judge? Again, we don't know the answers to these questions, but I think we find in Lapidoth (assuming he was still living) an impressively supportive husband.

3. Josephus, Antiquities of the Jews 5.5.1

4. The Iron Age is commonly thought to have begun in about 1200 BC and gone till 1000 BC. The era of the Judges is thought to be from about 1375 to 1020 BC.

5. Camille Fronk Olsen, *Women of the Old Testament* (Salt Lake City: Deseret Book, 2009), 119.

6. Josephus, Antiquities of the Jews 5.5.3

7. I'm thinking here of the story of Gideon, defeating the Philistines with horns and lamps, the Israelites bringing down the walls of Jericho without any sort of fight, the battles of the Nephites in the Book of Mormon, and even more modern equivalents like the Revolutionary War in which a small group of rebels overthrew the greatest army in the world. God often demonstrates, in the Bible and in history, that His power is complete and that when He stands behind a group, they will prosper.

8. Willard Ropes Trask, trans., *Joan of Arc: Self Portrait* (New York: Collier Books, 1961), 19.

9. Olsen, *Women of the Old Testament*, 123.

JEPHTHAH'S DAUGHTER

1. *Strong's Exhaustive Concordance of the Bible*, s.v. "H7464 re'ah," accessed July 26, 2017, https://www.blueletterbible.org/lang/lexicon/lexicon.cfm?Strongs=H7464&t=KJV.

2. Brook Andreoli, personal correspondence, March 2017.

SAMSON'S MOTHER

1. It is important to note that Jesus was a *Nazarene*, meaning he came from the city of Nazareth. There is no evidence that Jesus made a lifelong *Nazarite* vow, though some scholars wonder if his refusal to drink of the "vine" (see Matthew 26 29; Luke 22:18) indicates that he took a Nazarite vow before completing the Atonement. Still, it is likely that the words *Nazareth* and *Nazarite* come from the same root and symbolize Jesus being a consecrated or holy person.

2. Exceptions I can think of would be Zacharias, who was visited by the angel in the temple to announce the birth of John the Baptist, and Abraham, who was told (while his wife was listening through the tent) by the messengers that Sarah would bear a child. Joseph, the husband of Mary, was also told about the divine nature of his child but only after Mary had been told. That seems to be a more common pattern for women to get the primary revelation and men to get a confirming one.

3. M. Russell Ballard, "The Sacred Responsibilities of Parenthood," *Ensign*, March 2006, 29–30.

4. *Strong's Exhaustive Concordance of the Bible*, s.v. "H6383 pil'iy," accessed July 26, 2017, https://www.blueletterbible.org/lang/lexicon/lexicon.cfm

?Strongs=H6383&t=KJV. The only other place this word is used in the Bible is in Psalm 139:6 where it says, "Such knowledge is too wonderful for me; it is high, I cannot attain unto it."

5. James E. Faust, "The Prophetic Voice," *Ensign*, May 1996, 6.

DELILAH

1. Her son Micah also attempted to "hire" a Levite to be his priest. He seems to have been trying to set up his own type of worship of God, based on the worship that went on in the tabernacle. Eventually, his images were image seized by the tribe of Dan, who felt outrage that a non-Israelite would worship in such a way. Eventually Micah's images would end up at the Tabernacle in Shiloh (see Judges 18:31).

THE CONCUBINE OF JUDGES 19

1. Josephus, Antiquities of the Jews 5.2.8

2. *Strong's Exhaustive Concordance of the Bible*, s.v. "H1100 beliya'al," accessed July 27, 2017, https://www.blueletterbible.org/lang/lexicon/lexicon.cfm?Strongs=H1100&t=KJV.

3. Josephus, Antiquities of the Jews 5.2.8

NAOMI

1. The term "mother's house" is used in Genesis 24:28 in the story of Rebekah and then twice in the Song of Solomon (3:4; 8:2).

2. Carol Meyers, "Ruth," in *Women in Scripture: A Dictionary of Named and Unnamed Women in the Hebrew Bible, the Apocryphal/Deuterocanonical Books, and the New Testament*, ed. Carol Meyers, Toni Craven, and Ross S. Kraemer (Grand Rapids, MI: William B. Eerdmans Publishing, 2001), 252.

3. It is also interesting to note that Ruth 4:17 tells us that it was "the women her neighbors" who named the baby Obed. It wasn't Ruth, Naomi, or Boaz who named him but rather the women of the neighborhood. It makes me wonder about what type of influence or power these women had over their families and communities.

4. For example, Exodus 4:1 says, "And Moses answered and said, But, behold, they will not believe [*aman*] me, nor hearken unto my voice: for they will say, The Lord hath not appeared unto thee." 2 Kings 17:14 also uses the word *aman*, saying, "Notwithstanding they would not hear, but hardened their necks, like to the neck of their fathers, that did not believe [*aman*] in the Lord their God."

5. Too often, like Moses laments, the children do not "*aman*"—they won't believe, they won't suckle—but instead harden their hearts to the milk of the gospel of Christ.

6. Joseph B. Wirthlin, "Come What May, and Love It," *Ensign*, November 2008, 28.

RUTH

1. Other conversion stories include those of Abram, Rahab, and Naaman. More conversion stories are told in the New Testament. They are surprisingly scarce in the Old Testament.

2. John S. Tanner in Susan W. Tanner, "Helping New Converts Stay Strong," *Ensign*, February 2009, 23.

3. The Moabites were the descendants of Lot's oldest daughter, who had conceived her son Moab with her father after the fall of Sodom and Gomorrah (See Genesis 19:37). Examples of contention between Moab and Israel can be seen in Numbers 22–25; Judges 3:12–30; 11:17; 2 Samuel 8:2; 2 Kings 3:6–27; 13:20; 24:2; 1 Chronicles 18:2; 2 Chronicles 20:1–25.

4. Barley harvest started in the Hebrew month of Avi, which is equivalent to about mid-March to mid-April. The beginning of the harvest was the start of the new calendar year, with Avi being the first month of the year. So Naomi and Ruth would have arrived in Bethlehem at the start of the year, a proper time for new beginnings and fresh starts.

5. Gleaning is the process of collecting the crops that were left over in the field after the fields had been harvested. In the book of Leviticus, God instructed the Israelites to use gleaning as way of providing for the poor: "And when ye reap the harvest of your land, thou shalt not make clean riddance of the corners of thy field when thou reapest, neither shalt thou gather any gleaning of thy harvest: thou shalt leave them unto the poor, and to the stranger: I am the Lord your God" (Leviticus 23:22).

6. For example Isaiah 7:20 speaks of the Lord shaving the "hair of the feet," which refers to pubic hair. Also there are examples of women giving birth "between their feet" (Deuteronomy 28:57). Some argue the seraphim in Isaiah 6 who use their three pairs of wings to fly, cover their face, and cover "their feet" is a euphuism for covering their genitals in order to stay modest. Another example that is highly debated is when David instructed Uriah to go home and "wash his feet." He may have been telling Uriah to go home and have sex with his wife. This is construed mainly because in response to David's instruction Uriah remains with his men, telling David that it was not fair that he, as a commander, should go back and sleep with his wife while his men remained in the field. This reading of the word *feet* is debated because it is just as likely that David was simply telling Uriah to go home and wash up—with the hope and expectation that a solider returning to his wife after a long time would naturally sleep with her. It is important to note that the use of the word *feet* does not always—or even very often I think—connote genitalia in the Bible. Most times feet are simply just that—feet.

7. The phrase "spread forth thy skirt" is used in Ezekiel 16:8 and Deuteronomy 22:30 to refer to marriage.

PENINNAH

1. *Strong's Exhaustive Concordance of the Bible*, s.v. "H6869 tsarah," accessed July 27, 2017, https://www.blueletterbible.org/lang/lexicon/lexicon.cfm?Strongs=H6869&t=KJV.

2. C. S. Lewis, *Mere Christianity*, rev. ed. (1952; repr., New York: HarperOne, 2001), 122.

HANNAH

1. Vanessa L. Ochs, *Sarah Laughed: Modern Lessons from the Wisdom and Stories of Biblical Women* (Philadelphia, PA: Jewish Publication Society, 2011), 194.

PHINEHAS'S WIFE

1. Jim Laffoon, "Lessons from the Book of 1 Samuel: Ichabod's Birth," *Our Daily Blog*, posted May 24, 2010, https://jimlaffoon.wordpress.com/2010/05/24/lessons-from-the-book-of-1-samuel-ichabod's-birth-3.

2. Lani Axman, "Something to Hold On To," *Magdala Rising*, posted on October 1, 2016, http://www.magdalarising.com/heroes/something-to-hold-on-to.

3. Spencer W. Kimball, *Faith Precedes the Miracle* (Salt Lake City: Deseret Book, 1972), 98.

MICHAL

1. Josephus, Antiquities of the Jews 6.10.2

2. Ibid., 6.11.4

3. Ibid.

4. Ibid., 7.4.2

5. Ibid., 7.4.3

6. Ibid.

7. Ibid.

ABIGAIL

1. Seeing as this is quite a harsh name, it was most likely a nickname or what people called him behind his back (or maybe to his face). It may also have just been one of the many word plays that the Bible authors used to get the point of their story across.

2. James L. Ferrell, *The Peacegiver: How Christ Offers to Heal Our Hearts and Homes* (Salt Lake City: Deseret Book, 2004), 65.

3. Ibid., 52.

4. Samuel 3:3 has him as Chileab, and 1 Chronicles. 3:1 has his name as Daniel.

5. In 2 Samuel 12:8, the prophet Nathan, when chiding David for his behavior with Bathsheba, told him, "I have you your master's [meaning Saul's] household and your master's wives into your arms." This may mean that Saul's wife Ahinoam was given to David as his wife. However, it states that David had Ahinoam as a wife even before Saul died, which makes the situation a little less likely, though still possible.

THREE DAUGHTERS OF HEMAN

1. Singing women (and singing men) are mentioned in 2 Samuel 19:35, 2 Chronicles 35:25, Ezra 2:65, and Nehemiah 7:67. They are often listed along with the servants, so it is a good guess that these women and men were of a lower social class than other Israelites, perhaps even slaves. It is also interesting to notice that whenever singers are mentioned they are listed as either "singing men" and "singing women," suggesting that perhaps men

and women did not sing together and that there were separate ensembles or groups, especially for men and for women.

2. One of the first things David did when he became king of United Israel was to move the ark of the covenant out of storage, where it had been for the last twenty years. His first attempt to move it was unsuccessful (it almost fell off the cart and several people were killed), and he realized that it could only be moved properly when it was carried by the Levites, like it had been anciently. David called the families of the Levites together and re-assigned them the tasks that Mosen had been given them. Among the Levites were two groups: priests and non-priests. The non-priests were not ordained to the priesthood, but they were given specific responsibilities pertaining to the maintenance, transport, and construction of the tabernacle. For example, the sons of Kohath were responsible for carrying the sacred articles, such as the altar, candlesticks, and so on after the priests packed them up. The sons of Gershon were responsible for all the fabrics, coverings, and partitions of the tabernacle, and the sons of Merari were in charge of taking apart and re-assembling the physical structure of the tabernacle.

3. A psaltery was a long stringed instrument that was played with a bow and greatly resembled our modern violin. The type of harp (also called a lyre) used in biblical times would have been much smaller than our modern-day versions. It was triangular-shaped and depending on its size had eight to ten strings. Smaller versions were held in the hand and plucked with the fingers, while larger versions were played with a plectrum, a thin piece of slightly flexible material (like tortoiseshell) that was used to strum the strings. It was similar to our modern-day guitar. King David was famous for his skill on the harp.

The other type of instrument these women would have played was the cymbals. To most of us, a cymbal conjures up images of marching bands and drum sets, but ancient cymbals were much thicker and smaller. Archeologists have found evidence of bronze cymbals ranging in size from about one to two inches to four to five inches in diameter. The smaller ones would have been worn on the fingers or hands, while the larger ones would have been used to make defined musical tones. The scriptures use the phrase "melodic cymbals" for this type of instrument, making it more like our modern-day hand bells.

BATHSHEBA

1. Josephus, Antiquities of the Jews 7.7.1

2. Edith Deen, *All of the Women of the Bible* (New York: Harper and Row, 1983), 114.

3. Josephus mentions that Joab even ordered some of Uriah's men to abandon him when the saw the enemy advancing so that Uriah would be left by himself (Josephus, Antiquities of the Jews 7.7.1).

4. Josephus, Antiquities of the Jews 7.7.2

5. It is important to note that the context in which God is speaking in Doctrine and Covenants 132 is that of plural marriage. David was being given as an example of one who failed to live the law of plural marriage correctly, and because he broke this law, he would "not inherit them [his wives] out of the world, for I gave them unto another" (D&C 132:39). I don't think this indicates that David was not repentant or that he could not be forgiven under the Atonement, but that because he had broken the laws concerning plural marriage would no longer be allowed to practice it.

6. James E. Faust, "The Atonement: Our Greatest Hope," *Ensign*, November 2001.

7. Deen, *All of the Women of the Bible*, 116.

MOTHER OF KING LEMUEL

1. The LDS Bible Dictionary entry dealing with the book of Proverbs says, "The Hebrew word rendered *proverb* is *mashal*, a similitude or

parable, but the book contains many maxims and sayings not properly so called, and also connected poems of considerable length. There is much in it that does not rise above the plane of worldly wisdom, but throughout it is taken for granted that 'the fear of the Lord is the beginning of wisdom.'"

2. In Hebrew, the name *Lemuel* means "devoted to God," which Solomon (at times in his life) certainly was.

3. *Strong's Exhaustive Concordance of the Bible*, s.v. "H4853 massa'," accessed July 28, 2017, https://www.blueletterbible.org/lang/lexicon /lexicon.cfm?Strongs=H4853&t=KJV.

4. This tells us that she had made some sort of promise with God concerning her son. The Hebrew word is *neder*, and it refers to a promise, or a vow, made to God.

5. David A. Bednar, in "Elder and Sister Bednar—Episode 1," *Mormon Channel*, aired April 7, 2009, https://www.mormonchannel.org/listen /series/conversations-audio/elder-and-sister-bednar-episode-1.

TAMAR, DAUGHTER OF DAVID

1. The Hebrew word is *labiybah*. It is used only once in the Bible, in reference to the cakes that Tamar made. It seems to refer to a type of cake that was fried. (*Strong's Exhaustive Concordance of the Bible*, s.v. "H3834 labiybah," accessed July 28, 2017, https://www.blueletterbible.org/lang /lexicon/lexicon.cfm?Strongs=H3834&t=KJV.)

2. See James R. Baker, *Women's Rights in Old Testament Times* (Salt Lake City: Signature Books, 1992), 131.

3. Chieko Okazaki, "Healing from Sexual Abuse," Brigham Young University presentation, October 23, 2002, https://www.youtube.com /watch?v=Rs4XJURtSug or text on http://www.the-exponent.com /chieko-okazakis-healing-from-sexual-abuse.

4. Athalya Brenner, "Tamar," in *Women in Scripture: A Dictionary of Named and Unnamed Women in the Hebrew Bible, the Apocryphal/Deuterocanonical Books, and the New Testament*, ed. Carol Meyers, Toni Craven, and Ross S. Kraemer (Grand Rapids, MI: William B. Eerdmans Publishing, 2001), 164.

5. *Strong's Exhaustive Concordance of the Bible*, s.v. "H8074 shamem," accessed July 28, 2017, https://www.blueletterbible.org/lang/lexicon /lexicon.cfm?Strongs=H8074&t=KJV.

WISE WOMAN OF TEKOAH

1. David E. Sorenson, "Forgiveness Will Change Bitterness to Love," *Ensign*, May 2003.

2. Ibid.

3. William Steig, *Doctor De Soto* (New York: Farrar, Straus and Giroux, 1982).

DAVID'S TEN CONCUBINES

1. *Strong's Exhaustive Concordance of the Bible*, s.v. "H8104 shamar," accessed August 28, 2017, https://www.blueletterbible.org/lang/lexicon /lexicon.cfm?Strongs=H8104&t=KJV.

ABISHAG

1. *Strong's Exhaustive Concordance of the Bible*, s.v. "H2552 chamam," accessed August 28, 2017, https://www.blueletterbible.org/lang/lexicon /lexicon.cfm?Strongs=H2552&t=KJV.

WISE WOMAN OF ABEL

1. Josephus, Antiquities of the Jews 7.11.8

2. Claudia V. Camp, "The Wise Women of 2 Samuel: A Role Model for Women in Early Israel?" in Alice Bach, ed., *Women in the Hebrew Bible: A Reader* (New York: Routledge, 2013), 202.

3. Sheri L. Dew, "Are We Not All Mothers?" *Ensign*, November 2001.

4. Patricia T. Holland, *A Quiet Heart* (Salt Lake City: Bookcraft, 2000), 58–59.

ABISHAG

1. *Strong's Exhaustive Concordance of the Bible*, s.v. "H2552 chamam," accessed August 28, 2017, https://www.blueletterbible.org/lang/lexicon /lexicon.cfm?Strongs=H2552&t=KJV.

THE QUEEN OF SHEBA

1. Josephus, Antiquities of the Jews 8.6.5

2. This story is told in the *Kebra Nagast* (The Glory of Kings) dated somewhere between the sixth and fourteenth centuries AD.

3. Joseph Smith in Jeffrey R. Holland, "This, the Greatest of All Dispensations," *Ensign*, July 2007, 55.

4. Dieter F. Uchtdorf, "O How Great the Plan of Our God!" *Ensign*, November 2016, 20.

5. Jostein Gaarder, *Sophie's World: A Novel About the History of Philosophy*, trans. Paulette Moller (New York: Farrar, Straus and Giroux, 2007), 19–20.

ASHERAH AND GODDESS WORSHIP IN ANCIENT ISRAEL

1. Susan Ackerman, "Asherah/Asherim: Bible," *Jewish Women's Archive*, accessed July 31, 2017, https://jwa.org/encyclopedia/article /asherahasherim-bible.

2. William G. Dever, *Did God Have a Wife?: Archeology and Folk Religion in Ancient Israel* (Grand Rapids, MI: William B. Eerdmans Publishing, 2005), 99.

3. Ibid., 213.

4. Ibid., 3.

JEZEBEL

1. Herbert Lockyer, *All the Women of the Bible* (Grand Rapids, MI: Zondervan, 1967), 73–74.

2. Ibid., 74.

3. "Who's on the Lord's Side?" *Hymns*, no. 260.

WIDOW OF ZAREPHATH

1. Hannah Cornaby, *Autobiography and Poems* (Salt Lake City: J. C. Graham & Co., 1881), 41–42.

2. Camille Fronk Olsen, "Women in the Scriptures" (lecture, Brigham Young University, Provo, UT, 2005).

GREAT WOMAN OF SHUNEM

1. *Strong's Exhaustive Concordance of the Bible*, s.v. "H7965 shalowm," accessed July 31, 2017, https://www.blueletterbible.org/lang/lexicon /lexicon.cfm?Strongs=H7965&t=KJV.

2. "Come, Come, Ye Saints," *Hymns*, no. 30.

3. Dieter F. Uchtdorf, "All Is Well," *Ensign*, July 2015, 4–5.

4. Paul explained to the Colossians, "Let no man therefore judge you in meat, or in drink, or in respect of an holyday, or of the new moon, or of the sabbath days: Which are a shadow of things to come; but the body [the reality] is of Christ" (Colossians 2:16–17).

ATHALIAH

1. The Bible account is not clear about who Athaliah's mother was, but it is assumed that since her father was Ahab, her mother was probably Jezebel.

2. Herbert Lockyer, *All the Women of the Bible* (Grand Rapids, MI: Zondervan, 1967), 32.

3. The other is a woman named Salome Alexandra, who ruled Judah from 76 to 67 BC. She was the last ruler of the independent Judean nation before it was conquered by the Romans. Unlike Athaliah, she was kind and well liked.

JEHOSHEBA

1. Or possibly the step-daughter of Athaliah. The account tells us that Jehosheba was Ahaziah's sister, but it is possible she could have been a half-sister, sharing the same father but not having Athaliah as her mother.

2. In 2 Chronicles 24:16, we learn that when Jehoiada died, the people buried him "in the city of David among the kings." This is a remarkable honor for a man who was only the high priest in the temple and not the king. It gives us insight into what sort of couple he and Jehosheba must have been and how respected they were by the people. Since wives were often buried next to their husbands, it is possible that Jehosheba may also have been buried in a place of honor.

3. Dawn Armstrong, in *Meet the Mormons*, directed by Blair Treu (Salt Lake City: Intellectual Reserve, 2014), DVD.

GOMER

1. It is important to note that some scholars think that the story of Gomer and Hosea was purely a symbolic story, fabricated by Hosea for the purpose of teaching the people of Israel about God's love for them. The description of Gomer, especially her sexual sin and worship of goddesses, was indicative of Israelite society at the time and could have represented any number of women (and men) in Israel's society.

2. The Jezreel Valley is a large fertile plain by the sea of Galilee in Israel.

3. It is interesting to think that Isaiah, who came after Hosea, may have been influenced by this pattern of giving his children symbolic and prophetic names (see the Wife of Isaiah on page 251).

4. A *homer* was a unit of grain measurement. Up until modern times, many farmers would measure land not by acres or another geometrical figure but rather by how much grain it would take to sow the field. For example, one homer (also called *omer* or *chomer*) was approximately 6.5 bushels of grain and would sow about six acres of land. Leviticus 27:16 says, "And if a man shall sanctify unto the Lord some part of a field of his possession, then thy estimation shall be according to the seed thereof: an homer of barley seed shall be valued at fifty shekels of silver." Fifty shekels of silver was a lot of money, but it wasn't the seed that was worth that much but the land that could be sowed with that amount of seed. Hosea's payment of fifteen shekels of sliver, one homer, and a half a homer of barley was a significant investment.

5. Henry B. Eyring, "Covenants and Sacrifice" (address given at the Church Educational System symposium, August 15, 1995).

THE PROPHETESS, THE WIFE OF ISAIAH

1. In Virginia H. Pearce, *Glimpses into the Life and Heart of Marjorie Pay Hinckley* (Salt Lake City: Deseret Book, 1999), 26.

HULDAH

1. Camille Fronk Olsen, *Women of the Old Testament* (Salt Lake City: Deseret Book, 2009), 154.

2. Claudia V. Camp, "Huldah: Bible," *Jewish Women's Archive*, accessed August 1, 2017, https://jwa.org/encyclopedia/article/huldah-bible.

3. Dallin H. Oaks, "Spiritual Gifts," *Ensign*, September 1986.

4. "Follow the Prophet," *Children's Songbook*, 110.

5. James E. Talmage, *Articles of Faith* (Salt Lake City: Deseret News, 1899), 231–32.

6. Camp, "Huldah: Bible," https://jwa.org/encyclopedia/article/huldah-bible.

MAACHAH AND THE QUEEN MOTHERS OF JUDAH

1. In the case of Hezekiah, he charged the Levites to go into the temple and bring out "all the uncleanness that they found in the temple of the Lord" (2 Chronicles 29:16), which most likely referred to cult artifacts like asherah poles, incense stands, and standing stones.

2. See Zafrira Ben-Barak, "The Status and Right of the Gebira," *Journal of Biblical Literature* 110, no. 1 (Spring 1991): 23–34; Susan Ackerman, "The Queen Mother and the Cult in Ancient Israel," *Journal of Biblical Literature* 112, no. 3 (Autumn 1993): 385–401.

3. *Strong's Exhaustive Concordance of the Bible*, s.v. "H4656 miphletseth," accessed August 1, 2017, https://www.blueletterbible.org/lang/lexicon/lexicon.cfm?Strongs=H4656&t=KJV.

4. William G. Dever, *Did God Have a Wife?: Archeology and Folk Religion in Ancient Israel* (Grand Rapids, MI: William B. Eerdmans Publishing, 2005), 185.

THE WOMEN WHO BAKED BREAD FOR THE QUEEN OF HEAVEN

1. Vanessa L. Ochs, *Sarah Laughed: Modern Lessons from the Wisdom and Stories of Biblical Women* (Philadelphia, PA: Jewish Publication Society, 2011), 205–06.

2. *Webster's Dictionary 1828—Online Edition*, s.v. "contrite," accessed August 1, 2017, http://webstersdictionary1828.com/Dictionary/contrite.

3. William G. Dever, *Did God Have a Wife?: Archeology and Folk Religion in Ancient Israel* (Grand Rapids, MI: William B. Eerdmans Publishing, 2005), 241. Archeologists also think that these types of molds may have been used to mass produce images or figurines of goddesses.

DAUGHTERS OF SHALLUM

1. Some scholars speculate that the queen sitting beside Artaxerxes was Queen Esther. If so, this would explain why the king was so eager and willing to help the Jews. It is also likely, though, that this queen was a different queen who reigned after Esther's time. Either way the important thing to notice about her is that she, like her husband, viewed the Jews in a positive light and was willing to help them.

2. It is interesting to think that perhaps it was this political maneuvering on part of the Samaritans that resulted in the decree given by King Ahasuerus, in the story of Esther, to exterminate the Jews.

VASHTI

1. Vanessa L. Ochs, *Sarah Laughed: Modern Lessons from the Wisdom and Stories of Biblical Women* (Philadelphia, PA: Jewish Publication Society, 2011), 168.

2. The holiday that celebrates Esther is called Purim. It is a fun holiday full of traditional foods and children dressing up in costumes. The story of Esther is read in the synagogue, and when the name Haman is said, everyone boos and makes noise.

3. Harry Burn, in *Senate Journal of the Sixty-First General Assembly of the State of Tennessee* (Nashville, TN: 1920), 95.

ESTHER

1. *Strong's Exhaustive Concordance of the Bible*, s.v. "H8562 tamruwq," accessed August 2, 2017, https://www.blueletterbible.org/lang/lexicon /lexicon.cfm?Strongs=H8562&t=KJV.

2. *Strong's Exhaustive Concordance of the Bible*, s.v. "H2896 towb," accessed August 2, 2017, https://www.blueletterbible.org/lang/lexicon/lexicon .cfm?Strongs=H2896&t=KJV.

3. Vanessa L. Ochs, *Sarah Laughed: Modern Lessons from the Wisdom and Stories of Biblical Women* (Philadelphia, PA: Jewish Publication Society, 2011), 63–64.

4. Elaine S. Dalton, "Remember Who You Are!" *Ensign*, May 2010, 121–22; italics in original.

5. Ibid., 122.

6. In Egypt, Isis and Hathor are associated with myrrh. In Greek mythology there is Myrrha (the mother of Adonis), who was transformed into a myrrh tree. Myrrh comes from a wound or a weeping in the tree, so that is another reason it is associated with sorrow.

7. "A bundle of myrrh is my wellbeloved unto me; he shall lie all night between my breasts" (Song of Solomon 1:13).

CONCLUSION

1. C. S. Lewis, *Prince Caspian* (1951; repr., New York: HarperCollins, 2002), 233.

List of Women in the Old Testament

I was unable to write about all, or even most of the women in the Old Testament. I hope that this list will inspire you to look up their stories for yourself and study them closer. I've listed them in the order they appear in the Bible. Several names are repeated (for example there are five "Maachahs") but each woman listed is a unique individual. Also, I have not listed women that metaphorical of figurative, such as the "daughter of Zion" or "Jerusalem." Happy Scripture Studying!

Eve—Gen. 2:21–25; 3; 4–1–2, 25; 2 Cor. 11:3; 1 Tim. 2:13–15; 1 Ne. 5:11; 2 Ne. 2:18–21; 9:9; Alma 12:21–26; D&C 138:39; Moses 2:27; 3:22–25; 4:6–30; 5:1–27; 6:2–6, 9; Abr. 5:16–19

Cain's Wife—Gen. 4:19–25; Moses 5:28, 42

Adah—Gen. 4:19–25; Moses 5:44–55

Zillah—Gen. 4:19–25; Moses 5:44–55

Naamah—Gen. 4:22; Moses 5:46

Daughters of Adam—Gen. 5:4

Daughters of Seth—Gen. 5:7

Daughters of Enos—Gen. 5:10

Daughters of Cainan—Gen. 5:13

Daughters of Mahalaleel—Gen. 5:16

Daughters of Jared—Gen. 5:19

Daughters of Enoch—Gen. 5:22

Daughters of Methuselah—Gen. 5:26

Daughters of Lamech—Gen. 5:30

Daughters of Men—Gen. 6:1–4

Noah's Wife—Gen. 6:18; 7:7, 13; 18:16, 18; Moses 8:12

Noah's Daughters-in-Law—Gen. 18; 7:7, 13; 8:16, 18

Daughters of Shem—Gen. 11:11

Daughters of Arphaxad—Gen. 11:13

Daughters of Salah—Gen. 11:17

Daughters of Peleg—Gen. 11:19

Daughters of Rev—Gen. 11:21

Daughters of Serug—Gen. 11:23

Daughters of Nahor—Gen. 11:25

Sarai/Sarah—Gen. 11:29–30; 12:5, 11–20; 13:1; 16:1–6; 17:15–21; 18:6–15; 20:2–18; 21; 1–10; 23:1–2, 19; 24:36, 67; 49:31;

Isa. 51:2; Rom. 4:19; 9:9; Gal. 4:23–31; Heb. 11:11; 1 Peter 3:6–7; 2 Ne. 8:2; D&C 132:29, 34–37; 137:5–6; Abr. 2

Iscah—Gen. 11:29

Milcah—Gen. 11:29; 22:20–33; 24:15, 24, 47

Maidservants of Egypt—Gen. 12:16

Women of Lot's Household—Gen. 14:16

Hagar—Gen. 16:1–16; 17:20; 21:9–21; 25:12; Gal. 4:22–31; D&C 132:34, 37, 65

Lot's Daughters—Gen. 19:8, 12, 15–16, 30–38

Lot's Married Daughters—Gen. 19:14

Lot's Wife—Gen. 19:15–16; 26

Abraham's Mother—Gen. 20:12

Abimelech's Wife—Gen. 20:17–18

Abimelech's Maidservants—Gen. 20:17–18

Ishmael's Egyptian Wife—Gen. 21:21

Reumah—Gen. 22:24

Rebekah—Gen. 22:23; Gen. 24–29; 35:8; 49:31; Rom. 9:10–13; D&C 132:37

Daughters of the Canaanites—Gen. 24:3, 37; Gen. 28:1, 6, 8

Daughters come to draw water—Gen. 24:13

Rebekah's Mother—Gen. 24:53–60

Deborah, Rebekah's Nurse—Gen. 24:59; 35:8

Rebekah's Damsels—Gen. 24:61

Keturah—Gen. 25:1–6; 1 Chr. 1:32–33; D&C 132:37

Judith—Gen. 26:34–35

Bashemath—Gen. 26:34–35

Daughter of Heth—Gen. 27:46

Mahalath—Gen. 28:9

Rachel—Gen. 29–35; 46:19,22, 25; 48:7; Ruth 4:11; 1 Sam. 10:2; Jer. 31:15; Matt. 2:18; D&C 132:37

Leah—Gen. 29–35; 46:15, 18; 49:31; Ruth 4:11; D&C 132:37

Bilhah—Gen. 29:29; 30:3–8; 31:33; 32:17; 35:22, 25; 37:2; 46:25; 1 Chr. 7:13; D&C 132:37

Zilpah—Gen. 29:24; 30:9–13; 31:33; 32:22; 35:26; 37:2; 46:18; D&C 132:37

Jacob's Maidservants—Gen. 30:43

Dinah—Gen. 30:21; 34:1–31; 46:15

Daughters of the Land of Shechem—Gen. 34:1

Wives of Shechem—Gen. 34:29

Adah, Wife of Esau—Gen. 36:2, 4, 10, 12, 16

Aholibamah—Gen. 36:2, 5, 14, 18, 25

Anah—Gen. 36:2, 14, 18, 25

Bashemath, Ishmael's Daughter—Gen. 36:3–4, 10, 13, 17

Timna—Gen. 36:12, 22; 1 Chr. 1:39

Mehetabel—Gen. 36:39; 1 Chr. 1:50

Matred—Gen. 36:39; 1 Chr. 1:50

Tamar—Gen. 38; Ruth 4:12; 1 Chr. 2:4; Matt. 1:3

Daughter of Shuah—Gen. 38:2–5, 12; 1 Chr. 2:3

Midwife Who Assisted Tamar—Gen. 38:28–30

Potiphar's Wife—Gen. 39

Asenath—Gen. 41:45–52; 46:20

Wives of the People of Israel—Gen. 45:19; 46:5

Jacob's Daughters and Granddaughters—Gen. 37:35; 46:7, 15

Simeon's Canaanite Wife—Gen. 46:10; Exod. 6:15

Serah, Daughter of Asher—Gen. 46:17; Num. 26:46 (spelled Sara) ; 1 Chr. 7:30

Jacob's Daughters-in-Law—Gen. 46:26

Shiphrah—Exod. 1:15–22

Puah—Exod 1:15–22

Hebrew Women in Egypt—Exod. 1:19; 2:7

Jochebed—Exod. 2:1–10; 6:20; Num. 26:59; Heb. 11:23

Miriam—Exod. 2:4–10; 15:20–21; Num. 12:1–16; 20:1; 26:59; Deut. 24:9; 1 Chr. 6:3; Mic. 6:4

Pharaoh's Daughter—Exod. 2:5–10

Attendants of Pharaoh's Daughter—Exod. 2:5

Seven Daughter of the Priest of Midian—Exod. 2:16–20

Zipporah—Exod. 2:16–22; 4:20, 24–26; 18:2–6

Egyptian Women Borrowed From—Exod. 3:22; 11:2

Elisheba—Exod. 6:23

Daughter of Putiel—Exod. 6:25

Women who Danced with Miriam—Exod. 15:20–21

List of Old Testament Women ✦

Women Who Gave Gold Earrings—Exod. 32:2–3

Wise-Hearted Women—Exod. 35:22–29

Women Assembled at the Door of the Tabernacle—Exod. 38:8

Daughters of Levites—Lev. 10:14

Shelomith—Lev. 24:10–13

Women Baking Bread—Lev. 26:26

Wives/Daughters of Korah, Dathan and Abiram—Num. 16:27

Daughters of Aaron—Num. 18:11–13, 19

Daughters of Moab—Num. 25:1

Cozbi—Num. 25:6–18

Daughters of Zeolphehad (Mahlah, Noah, Hoglah, Milcah, Tirzah)—Num. 26:33; 27:1–11; 36:1–11; Josh. 17:3–6 ; 1 Chr. 7:15

Women of Midian—Num. 31:9, 15–18, 35

Wives/Daughters of the Tribes of Reuben and Gad—Num. 36:16–17, 26

Women of Heshborn—Deut. 2:34; 3:6

Wives of Israelites—Deut. 3:19

Daughters Passed Through Fire—Deut. 12:31; 18:10; 2 Kgs. 17:17; 23:10; Psal. 106:37–38' Jer. 7:31; 32:35; Ezek. 16:20–21

Rahab—Josh. 2:1–21; 6:17–25; Heb. 11:31; Jam. 2:25–26; Matt. 1:5 (possibly)

Women of Jericho—Josh. 6:21

Daughters of Achan—Josh. 7:24–25

Women of Ai—Josh. 8:25

Women of the Congregation—Josh. 8:35

Achsah—Josh. 15:16–19; Judg. 1:12–15; 1 Chr. 2:49

Canaanite Women Married to Israelites—Judg. 3:5–6

Deborah—Judg. 4–5

Jael—Judg. 4:17–22; 5:24–27

Mother of Sisera and Her Wise Ladies—Judg. 5:28–30

Mother of Gideon—Judg. 8:19

Wives of Gideon—Judg. 8:30–31

Concubine of Gideon, mother of Abimelech—Judg. 8:31; 9:1–3, 18

Women of Shechem—Judg. 9:49

Women of Thebez—Judg. 9:51

Certain Woman of Thebez—Judg. 9:53–54; 2 Sam. 11:21

Mother of Jephthah—Judg. 11:1

Gilead's Wife—Judg. 11:2

Daughter of Jephthah—Judg. 11:34–40

Companions of Jephthah's Daughter—Judg. 11:37–38

Daughters of Israel who Lament Jephthah's Daughter—Judg. 11:40

30 Daughters and Daughters-in-law of Ibzan—Judg. 12:9

Samson's Mother—Judg. 13:1–25; 14:3–9; 16:17

Samson's Philistine Wife—Judg. 14:1–20; 15:1–6

Younger Sister of Samson's Philistine Wife—Judg. 15:2

Harlot of Gaza—Judg. 16:1

Delilah—Judg. 16:4–20

Philistine Women Killed by Samson—Judg. 16:27

Mother of Micah—Judg. 17:1–4

Concubine of Bethlehem-Judah—Judg. 19–20

Daughter of Old Man of Gibeah—Judg. 19:24

Daughters of Israel as Potential Brides for Benjaminite's—Judg. 21:1–25

Woe of Jabesh-gilead—Judg. 21:10–14

Daughters of Shiloh—Judg. 21:10–12, 21–25

Orpah—Ruth 1:4–14

Naomi—Ruth 1–4

Ruth—Ruth 1–4; Matt. 1:5

Ruth's Mother—Ruth 1:8; 2:11

Boaz's Maidens—Ruth 2:8, 13, 23; 3:2

Naomi's Neighbor Women—Ruth 4:14–17

Hannah—1 Sam. 1 and 2:1–11, 18–20

Peninnah—1 Sam. 1:1–7

Daughters of Peninnah—1 Sam. 1:4

Daughters of Hannah—1 Sam. 2:21

Women Assembled at the Door of the Congregation—1 Sam. 2:22

Phinehas' Wife—1 Sam. 4:19–22

Women Attending Phinehas' Wife—1 Sam. 4:20

Young Women Who Direct Saul's Servants—1 Sam. 9:11–13

Merab—1 Sam. 14:49; 17:25; 18:17–19; 2 Sam. 21:8 (possibly)

Michal—1 Sam. 14:49; 18:20–28; 19:11–17; 25:44; 2 Sam. 3:13–16; 6:16–23; 21:8; 1 Chr.15:29

Ahinoam, Saul's Wife—1 Sam. 14:49–50; 20:30 (possibly)

Mother of Agag—1 Sam. 15:33

Women Singing and Dancing to Meet Saul—1 Sam. 18:6–7

Jonathan's Mother—1 Sam. 20:30

David's Mother—1 Sam. 22:3–4; 2 Sam. 19:37

Women of Nob—1 Sam. 22:19

Abigail—1 Sam. 25:3–44; 27:3; 30:1–19; 2 Sam. 2:2; 3:3; 1 Chr. 3:1

5 Damsels of Abigail—1 Sam 25:43

Ahinoam of Jezreel—1 Sam. 25:43; 27:3; 30:1–20; 2 Sam. 2:2; 3:2; 1 Chr. 3:1

Woman of Endor—1 Sam. 28:7–25

Wives/Daughters of David's Men—1 Sam. 30:2–22

Women of Ziklag—1 Sam. 30:2–3, 6, 19, 22

Zeruiah—1 Sam. 26:6; 2 Sam. 2 :13, 18; 3:39; 8:16; 14:1; 16:9, 10; 17:25; 18:2; 19:21–22; 21:17; 23:18, 37; 1 Kgs. 1:7; 2:5, 22; 1 Chr. 2:16; 11:6, 39; 18:12, 15; 26:28; 27:24

Maacah—2 Sam. 3:3; 1 Chr. 3:2

Abital—2 Sam. 3:4; 1 Chr. 3:3

Eglah—2 Sam. 3:5; 1 Chr. 3:3

Rizpah—2 Sam. 3:7–8; 21:8–11

Nurse of Mephibosheth—2 Sam. 4:4

David's Concubines/Wives Taken in Jerusalem—2 Sam. 5:13

David's Daughters—2 Sam. 5:15; 13:18; 19:5; 1 Chr. 14:3

Women at Ark Ceremony—2 Sam. 6:19

Bathsheba—2 Sam. 11; 2–27; 12:1–24; 1 Kgs. 1:5–31; 2:12–25; 1 Chr. 3:5; Psa. 51; Matt. 1:6; D&C 132; 39

Tamar, Daughter of David—2 Sam. 13:1–22, 32; 1 Chr. 3:9

Wise Woman of Tekoah—2 Sam. 14:1–20

Tamar, Daughter of Absalom—2 Sam. 14:27

10 Concubines of David—2 Sam. 15:16; 16:21–22; 19:5 20:3:1 Chr. 3:9

Woman of En-rogel—2 Sam. 17:17–20

Abigail, David's Sister—2 Sam. 17:25; 1 Chr. 2:16–17

Singing Women—2 Sam. 19:35; Eccl. 2:8; 12:4

Mother of Barzillai—2 Sam. 19:37

Woman of Abel-Beth-maachah—2 Sam. 20:16–22

Abishag—1 Kgs. 1:1–4, 15; 2:13–25

Haggith—2 Sam. 3:4; 1 Kgs. 1:5–6, 11; 2:13; 1 Chr. 3:2

Pharaoh's Daughter, Wife of Solomon—1 Kgs. 3:1; 7:8; 9:16,24; 11:1; 2 Chr. 8:11

2 Harlots who Approach Solomon with Baby—1 Kgs. 3:16–28

Taphath—1 Kgs. 4:11

Basmath—1 Kgs. 4:15

Mother of Hiram of Tyre—1 Kgs. 7:14; 2 Chr. 2:14

Queen of Sheba—1 Kgs. 10:1–15; 2 Chr. 9:1–9; Matt. 12:42; Luke 11:31

Solomon's Foreign Wives—1 Kgs. 3:1; 7:8; 10:8; 11:1–8; Neh. 13:26

Tahpenes—1 Kgs. 11:18–20

Sister of Tahpenes—1 Kgs. 11:19–20

Zeruah—1 Kgs. 11:26

Jeroboam's Wife—1 Kgs. 14:1–17

Naamah—1 Kgs. 14:21, 31; 2 Chr. 12:13

Maachah—1 Kgs. 15:2, 10, 13; 2 Chr. 11:20–22; 13:2 (called Michaiah); 15:6

Jezebel—1 Kgs. 16:31; 18:4–19; 19:5–25; 2 Kgs. 9

Widow of Zarephath—1 Kgs. 17:9–24

Mother of Elisha—1 Kgs. 19:20

Wives of Ahab—1 Kgs. 20:3, 5, 7

Azubah—1 Kgs. 22:42; 2 Chr. 20:31

Woman who Borrowed Vessels—1 Kgs. 4:1–7

Great Woman of Shunem—2 Kgs. 4:8–37; 8:1–6

Little Maid—2 Kgs. 5:2–4

Famished Woman of Samaria—2 Kgs. 6:26–30

Daughter of Ahab—2 Kgs. 8:18; 2 Chr. 21:6

Athaliah—2 Kgs. 8:26; 11:1–20; 1 Chr. 8:26; 2 Chr. 22:2–12; 23:12–21; 24:7; Ezra 8:7

Jehosheba—2 Kgs. 11:2–3; 2 Chr. 22:11 (Jehoshebeath)

Nurse of Joah—2 Kgs. 11:2–3; 2 Chr. 22;11–12

Zibiah—2 Kgs. 12:1; 2 Chr. 24:1

Shimeath—2 Kgs. 12:21; 2 Chr. 24:26

Jehoaddan—2 Kgs. 14:2; 2 Chr. 25:1

Jecholiah—2 Kgs. 15:2; 2 Chr. 26:3

Women with Child "Ripped" up—2 Kgs. 15:16; Amos 1:13

Jerusha—2 Kgs. 15:33; 2 Chr. 27:1

Abi—2 Kgs. 18:2; 2 Chr. 29:1 (called Abijah)

Hephzibah—2 Kgs. 21:1

Meshullemeth—2 Kgs. 21:19

Jedidah—2 Kgs. 22:1

Huldah—2 Kgs. 22:12–20; 2 Chr. 34:22–28

Women Who Wove Hangings for Grove—2 Kgs. 23:7

Zebudah—2 Kgs. 23:36

Hamutal—2 Kgs. 23:31; 24:18; Jer. 52:1

Zebudah—2 Kgs. 23:26

Nehushta—2 Kgs. 24:8, 12, 15

Wives of Jehoiachin—2 Kgs. 24:15

Azubah—1 Chr. 2:18–19

Jerioth—1 Chr. 2:18

Ephrath—1 Chr. 2:19, 50; 4:4 (called Ephrath—1 Chr. 2:19, 50; 4:4 (called

Daughter of Machir—1 Chr. 2:21–22

Abiah—1 Chr. 2:24

Atarah—1 Chr. 2:26

Abihail—1 Chr. 2:29

Ahlai—1 Chr. 2:31

Daughters of Sheshan—1 Chr. 2:34–35

Ephah—1 Chr. 2:46

Maachah—1 Chr. 2:48–49

Shelomith—1 Chr. 3:19

Hazelelponi—1 Chr. 4:3

Helah—1 Chr. 4:5, 7

Naarah—1 Chr. 4:5–6

Mother of Jabez—1 Chr. 4:9

Miriam—1 Chr. 4:17

Jehudijah—1 Chr. 4:18

Bithiah—1 Chr. 4:18

Hodiah—1 Chr. 4:19

6 Daughters of Shimei—1 Chr. 4:27

Aramitess Concubine of Manasseh—1 Chr. 7:14

Maachah—1 Chr. 7:15–16

Hammoleketh—1 Chr. 7:18

Wife of Ephraim—1 Chr. 7:23

Sherah—1 Chr. 7:24

Shua—1 Chr. 7:32

Hushim—1 Chr. 8:8, 11

Baara—1 Chr. 8:8 (maybe Hodesh in vs. 9)

Hodesh—1 Chr. 8:9

Maachah—1 Chr. 8:29; 9:35

Daughter of Eleazar—1 Chr. 23:22

Daughters of Heman—1 Chr. 25:5–6

Mahalath—2 Chr. 11:18

Abihail—2 Chr. 11:18–20

18 Wives and 60 Concubines of Rehoboam—2 Chr. 11:21

60 Daughters of Rehoboam—2 Chr. 11:21

Michaiah—2 Chr. 13:2

14 Wives of Abijah—2 Chr. 12:21

16 Daughters of Abijah—2 Chr. 13:21

Wives of Judah—2 Chr. 20:13

2 Wives of Jehoiada—2 Chr. 24:3

Shimrith—2 Chr. 24:26; 2 Kgs 12:21 (called Shomer)

Judean Women Taken Captive by Israelites—2 Chr. 28:8, 10–15; 29:9

Singing Women Who Lament—2 Chr. 35:35

Daughter of Barzillai the Gileadite—Ezra 2:61; Neh. 7:63–64

Foreign Wives who were Divorced—Ezra 9:2; 10:1–19, 44; Neh. 10:28, 30; 13:23–27

Queen, Wife of Artaxerxes—Neh. 2:6

Daughters of Shallum—Neh. 3:12

Women in Rebuilt Jerusalem—Neh. 4:14; 5:1–5

Noadiah—Neh. 6:14

Vahsti—Esther 1:9–20; 2:1

Women at Vashti's Banquet—Ether 1:9

Women of Persia and Media—Esther 1:18–20

Young Virgins from Empire—Esther 2:2–3, 8, 12–14, 17, 19

Esther—Book of Esther; Ezra 4:6

Esther's Maids—Esther 2:9; 4:4, 16

Zeresh—Esther 5:10, 14; 6:13–14

3 Daughters of Job—Job. 1:2, 4, 13, 18

Job's Sisters—Job 42:11

Job's Daughters (Jemima, Kezia and Keren-happuch)—Job 42:14–15

Mother of Solomon's Son—Prov. 1:8; 6:20

Mother of King Lemuel—Prov. 31:1–31

Prophetess (Wife of Isaiah)—Isa. 8:3

Women Who Bake Cakes to the Queen of Heaven—Jer. 7:18; 44:15–25

Daughter of my People—Jer. 8:11, 19–22; 9:1; 14:17

Mourning Women—Jer. 9:17, 20

Cunning Women—Jer. 9:17, 20

Women/Daughters consumed by Famine—Jer. 11:22; 14:16; 16:2–4; 19:9

Widows Increased—Jer. 15:8; 18:21

Jeremiah's Mother—Jer. 1:5; 15:10; 20:14, 17–18

Women Left in Zedekiah's House—Jer. 38:22–23; 41:10, 16; 43:6–7

Women Not carried Away Captive by the Babylonians—Jer. 40:7; 41:16–17; 43:5–6

Women Who went to Egypt—Jer. 43:6; 44:7, 15, 24–25

Wicked Queens/wicked Wives—Jer. 44:9

Women Weeping for Tammuz—Jer. 8:14

Women that Sew Pillows for Statues—Ezek. 13:17–22

Aholah (Samaria)—Ezek. 23

Aholibah (Jerusalem)—Ezek. 23

Ezekiel's Wife—Ezek. 24:18

Wives and Concubines of Belshazzar—Dan. 5:2–3, 23

Queen of Babylon—Dan. 5:10–12

Women Cast into the Lion's Den—Dan. 6:24

Gomer—Hosea 1:3–11; 2:1–18, 23; 3:1–3

Lo-ruhamah—Hosea 1:6, 8; 2:1–2

Huzzab (the Queen)—Nah. 2:7

Heather Farrell's love for the scriptures began early in her life when at the age of eleven she hid a flashlight under her pillow so she could read the Old Testament late at night. Her love for the women in scriptures began when her oldest son was born around Christmastime and she felt a kinship with Mary, the mother of Jesus. As she began to research Mary, she realized that there were hundreds of women in the scriptures, but very little had been written about them. Excited by all the women she discovered, she began sharing what she learned on her popular blog, *Women in the Scriptures* (womeninthescriptures.com). Primarily self-taught in the scriptures, Heather is a testament to the truth that becoming a scholar of the gospel is not beyond anyone's reach. It just takes an inquisitive mind and the companionship of the Holy Ghost. Heather lives in Pocatello, Idaho, with her husband and five children.

Mandy Jane Williams grew up in the little town of Darlington, Idaho. She has always had a love for beauty and art, which her parents encouraged. Mandy met her husband, Bryan Williams, in 2005, and they were married in the Idaho Falls Temple. Though Mandy has taken classes in art and photography, becoming a mother has played the biggest role in her finding herself as an artist. Beauty, joy, passion—all are intensified when you open your heart to loving others. Little things stand out to you in daily life, and you are able to notice and be grateful to them with artistic eyes. From the way the rising sun catches the eyelashes of a sleeping baby to the look on a child's face when Daddy comes home—all of these are an inspiration and a blessing. Mandy currently lives in East Idaho with her husband, Bryan, and her five greatest works of art—Kate, Case, Holland, Alice, and Brant.